INTERNATIONAL MARKET ENTRY
AND DEVELOPMENT

INTERNATIONAL MARKET ENTRY AND DEVELOPMENT

Strategies and management

S. Young
J. Hamill
C. Wheeler
J.R. Davies

HARVESTER WHEATSHEAF

PRENTICE HALL

First published 1989 by
Harvester Wheatsheaf,
66 Wood Lane End, Hemel Hempstead,
Hertfordshire, HP2 4RG
A division of
Simon & Schuster International Group

First published in the United States of America by
Prentice Hall
Englewood Cliffs,
NJ 07632

Printed and bound in Great Britain by
BPCC Wheatons Ltd, Exter

Library of Congress Cataloging-in-Publication Data

International market entry and development.
  Includes bibliographical references.
  1. Export marketing—Management.   2. International
trade.   3. Joint ventures.   4. International
business enterprises—Management.   I. Young,
Stephen, 1944-
HF1416.I613   1989   658.8'48   89-23119
ISBN 0-13-471517-9

British Library Cataloguing in Publication Data

International market entry and development.
  1. International business enterprise. Management
I.Young, Stephen, *1944 —*
658'.049

ISBN 0-7450-0379-6

---

4 5 94 93

ISBN 0-13-471517-9

CONTENTS

ABBREVIATIONS

ATP	Aid and Trade Provision (UK)
BC-Net	Business Co-operation Network (EC)
BOTB	British Overseas Trade Board
BRITE	Basic Research in Industrial Technologies for Europe (EC)
CARICOM	Caribbean Community and Common Market
CBI	Confederation of British Industry (UK)
CIB	Counterfeiting Intelligence Bureau (International Chamber of Commerce)
CIF	Cost, insurance and freight
COMECON	(also CMEA) Council for Mutual Economic Assistance
DCs	Developed countries
ECGD	Export Credits Guarantee Department (UK)
EC	European Community
EPC	European Patent Convention
EPZ	Export processing zone
ESPRIT	European Strategic Programme for Research and Development in Information Technology (EC)
FCC	Federal Communications Commission (USA)
FDI	Foreign Direct Investment
FOB	Free on board
FTZ	Free trade zone
GAIFZ	General Authority for Investment and Free Zones (Egypt)
GATT	General Agreement on Tariffs and Trade
GOFI	General Organisation for Industrialisation (Egypt)
ICA	Industrial co-operation agreement
ILO	International Labour Office
IMF	International Monetary Fund
INTI	National Institute of Industrial Technology (Argentina)
LDCs	Less developed countries
LES	Licensing Executives Society
MOFERT	Ministry of Foreign Economic Relations and Trade (China)
MNE	Multinational enterprise
NIC	Newly industrialising country

ODA	Overseas Development Administration (UK)
OECD	Organisation for Economic Co-operation and Development
OPEC	Organisation of Petroleum Exporting Countries
PCT	Patent Co-operation Treaty
PRC	People's Republic of China
R&D	Research and development
ROI	Return on investment
SEZ	Special Economic Zone (China)
SMEs	Small and medium-sized enterprises
SPRINT	Strategic Programme for Innovation and Technology Transfer (EC)
THE	Technical Help for Exporters (UK)
UAE	United Arab Emirates
UNCTAD	United Nations Conference on Trade and Development
UNCTC	United Nations Centre on Transnational Corporations
UNIDO	United Nations Industrial Development Organisation
VAT	Value Added Tax
WIPO	World Intellectual Property Organisation

TABLES

FIGURES

EXHIBITS

PREFACE

The proliferation of research and writings on foreign direct investment and the multinational enterprise has not to date been matched either by comparable studies on the smaller and newly internationalising company or by work on the so-called 'new forms of international investment' (licensing and franchising and other contractual arrangements, joint ventures and the like) despite the rapid growth of the latter in recent years. For the smaller and medium-sized company approaching international markets, thought processes are still myopically focused on exports, when other forms of arrangement may well be more suitable on occasion, if not for international market entry then certainly for international market development. 'Internationalisation' – a concept which concentrates on the ultimate objective, which is the penetration of international markets – is the key. The objective of this book is to facilitate a wider view of the international market entry and development options and processes, with chapters covering the various alternatives, from exporting through to equity joint ventures and wholly owned subsidiaries. The aim is to combine academic and practical orientations, with a comprehensive literature review and guidelines for companies both being incorporated.

This book has had an interesting, not to say lengthy, gestation period. The seeds go back to Spring 1985 when two of the present authors representing Strathclyde Business School participated in a British Council–led mission to Algeria. The purpose of this was to evaluate the possibilities for collaboration in the areas of international trade and finance with the newly formed Institut Superieur de Gestion et de Planification (ISGP). A collaboration programme was eventually set up between the two institutions, financed by the British Council (Overseas Development Administration) and directed by Stephen Young. This involved the preparation of a training manual on International Commerce and Finance and the writing of a number of case studies; the training of ISGP staff; and the running of a series of short courses for managers in state enterprises in Algeria, with the overall aim of gradually improving the export and import performance of these enterprises. This book actually bears rather little resemblance to the training manual prepared for the Algerian project, but its origins stem from this; and the authors are grateful to the British Council's support which undoubtedly had an influence on the emergence of the text – this was not only financial but also personal, and the assistance, encouragement and hospitality of Shirley Wilson and Garth Glentworth in London and of Bill Jefferson and Tom and Jane Cowin in Algiers is especially acknowledged.

The book is being used in courses run by Strathclyde Business School (SBS) both at home and abroad. In respect of the latter, the Department of Marketing at SBS has recently launched its Master of Commerce in Marketing degree in distance-learning format abroad; and this book is used as a core text on one of the elective courses, a series of study guides having been written to accompany the text. The book is also in use on the MBA programme at Strathclyde, as well as on executive programmes. If the end-result is to assist present and aspiring executives to 'think international' and then 'go international' successfully and profitably, we will be satisfied.

Having had its conception in an international environment, it is fitting that its birth (the completion of this preface) should also be in the international arena – in this case the campus of HEC (Hautes Etudes Commerciales), Jouy-en-Josas, France, where Stephen Young was a Visiting Professor in the Spring of 1988. The 'real work' as always was undertaken in Glasgow by Betty and Sally.

Stephen Young

1

ALTERNATIVE METHODS OF INTERNATIONAL MARKET ENTRY AND DEVELOPMENT

SUMMARY

1. Within a much changed global environment, internationalisation is viewed as almost inevitable if corporate expansion goals are to be achieved. But also because of environmental change, increasing importance is attached to the mode of market entry and development employed by firms in overseas markets.

2. There are a wide range of international market entry and development methods, including the following:

   Exporting Transfer of goods and/or services across national boundaries via indirect (export house, confirming house, trading company, piggybacking, etc.) or direct (agents, distributors, company export salesmen, sales subsidiaries) methods.

   Licensing Contracts in which licensor provides licensees abroad with access to one or a set of technologies or know-how in return for financial compensation. Typically, the licensee has rights to produce and market a product within an agreed area in return for royalties.

   Franchising Contracts in which franchisor provides franchisee with a 'package' including not only trade marks and know-how, but also local exclusivity and management and financial assistance and joint advertising. Management fees are payable. Most important in services.

   Management contract An arrangement under which operational control of an enterprise, which would otherwise be exercised by a board of directors or managers elected and appointed by its owners, is vested by contract in a separate enterprise which performs the necessary management functions in return for a fee.

   Turnkey contract A contractor has responsibility for establishing a complete production unit or infrastructure project in a host country – up to the stage of the commissioning of total plant facilities. Payment may be in a variety of forms including countertrading. 'Turnkey plus' contracts include product-in-hand and market-in-hand contracts.

   Contract manufacturing/international subcontracting A company (the principal) in one country places an order, with specifications as to conditions of sale and products required, with a firm in another country. Typically the contract would be limited to production, with marketing being handled by the principal.

   Industrial co-operation agreement Conventionally applied to arrangements between Western companies and government agencies or enterprises in the Eastern Bloc.

Include licensing, technical assistance agreements, turnkey projects and contract manufacturing, as well as contractual joint ventures and tripartite ventures.

Contractual joint venture Formed for a particular project of limited duration or for a longer-term co-operative effort, with the contractual relationship commonly terminating once the project is complete. May relate to *co-production, co-R&D, co-development, co-marketing* plus *co-publishing, consortium ventures* by banks to finance large loans, etc.

Equity joint ventures Involves sharing of assets, risks and profits and participation in the ownership (i.e. equity) of a particular enterprise or investment product by more than one firm. Relative equity stakes will vary, *inter alia*, because of host nation legislation.

Wholly owned subsidiaries 100 per cent owned operations abroad. May be manufacturing or sales/service ventures. May be formed through acquisitions or greenfield operations.

3. The forms of international market entry and development vary according to a number of characteristics:

Locus of control High in wholly or majority-owned manufacturing subsidiaries and in exports supported by direct investment in marketing.

Resource commitment Substantial in direct investment production and turnkey operations.

Resources transferred The wholly owned manufacturing subsidiary involves a complete package of resources.

Motivation Market penetration as opposed to coalition or collaborative motivations.

Other Time limitations, space limitations, payment methods.

4. In analysing international market entry and development modes, a variety of approaches have been taken. Contributions from economics stress the interrelationships between ownership, locational and internalisation variables; the 'stages-of-development' approach suggests an incremental, evolutionary approach to foreign markets; while the business-strategy approach focuses upon the nature of decision-making in organisations and the role of corporate planning. When the various approaches are brought together a balance between risk, control and motivation emerges.

INTRODUCTION

This book is concerned with the subject of the internationalisation of business, where the latter is defined to include the whole range of methods of undertaking business across national frontiers, some of which involve flows of goods and services between countries, some of which do not. The title is *International Market Entry and Development: Strategies and Management*, and, reflecting this, the book aims to provide a comprehensive evaluation of the alternative (and complementary) means of undertaking international business activities, mainly from a management perspective. The global, high-tech economy has brought with it a whole new range of business dynamics, with enterprises, technologies and governments interacting within a global marketing and production arena; more than ever before the issue of how to enter and develop international markets is a crucial dimension in competitive advantage internationally.

The term 'international market entry and development strategy' is used as one way of describing the methods employed by companies to penetrate international markets, but other terms exist too, including 'foreign market-servicing strategies' and 'foreign market entry strategies'. The disadvantage of the latter is that it focuses on entry only, whereas any of the methods employed by firms to supply markets overseas may involve longer-term international business relationships – both entry and subsequent market development. 'Foreign market-servicing strategies' is, however, an equally accurate description of the activities of exporting and international supply and will be used synonomously with the latter in this book.

When reading the literature, particularly that relating to developing countries, all of these forms of international business may be regarded as different methods of 'technology transfer'. Interest and concern over technology transfer relates to the desire by developing nations to acquire technology appropriate to their development needs, and to the costs of the technology. And in selecting among the various forms of international business as mechanisms for technology transfer, consideration will be given to the ease of obtaining the technology component as opposed to other parts of the resource package. For example, the establishment of a subsidiary of a multinational firm involves the collective transfer of resources, involving factor inputs such as capital and entrepreneurship as well as technology; and, what may be equally significant, involves the establishment of a *foreign* enterprise. With other methods of international supply it may be possible to obtain the technology component alone. The association of international business and international market development strategies with technology transfer is thus important in drawing attention to the need to consider the contribution to the host country as well as to the firm itself.

It is the case that under the influence of internal and environmental factors, methods of supplying foreign markets will change over time, and the term 'internationalisation' is commonly used to describe the developmental process of increasing involvement in international business. In this book the term is also applied more generally to firms' international market entry and market development activities. It may be that there is some evolutionary process in companies' international involvement. On the other hand, to achieve fairly wide market penetration overseas, firms will need to be flexible enough and have the capabilities to operate a range of methods of foreign operations. Lack of success will lead to withdrawal and 'de-internationalisation'.

The focus of this book is companies' outward international business activities – exporting abroad, licensing a producer in a foreign market, entering into joint ventures overseas, and so on. It must be recognised, nevertheless, that international business is commonly a two-way process, even for the same firm. Cross-licensing represents one of the commonest interrelationships, as firms in an industry collaborate to strengthen their respective positions in their home markets. Countertrading too involves reciprocal trading activities, and although a wide range of operations are included within the generic term, the essence is some agreement in which the sale of goods and services to a country is linked to an obligation to buy from that country. International subcontracting, which links exports of unfinished or semi-finished products to a subsequent re-import of the finished goods, is a further illustration.

Having noted briefly what the book is about, it is necessary in addition to establish the limits within which the topic of international market entry and development is to be discussed. The multinational enterprise (MNE) is conventionally defined as 'a corporation which owns (in whole or in part), controls and manages income-generating assets in more than one country'.[1] On this wide definition, the MNE is thus formed by direct investment abroad whether in marketing operations (e.g. sales offices, warehousing facilities) or production operations. As such, many of the activities discussed in this book involve MNEs. On the other hand, the emphasis is on the medium-sized and smaller enterprise, or at least non-dominant enterprises, rather than on the large multinational corporation with regionally or globally integrated operations.

There is an extensive literature on the globalisation of business and strategies for global competition, in which international business and methods of supplying international markets are regarded as integrated or linked activities.[2] All of the business forms discussed here may be utilised by such global enterprises, but as part of global corporate actions which may include seeking consortia arrangements with partners in other countries to capitalise on synergies by sharing one or more functions such as manufacturing; entering into joint ventures with companies to take advantage of their strong function by correspondingly supplementing the firm's weak ones; setting up a production base in the competitor's home market to take advantage of a supplier's infrastructure, and so on.[3] Underlying all such moves is the worldwide co-ordination of company resources behind global objectives.

In the case of the medium-sized and non-dominant firms which are the focus of this book, international business operations are less likely to involve integrated business systems that are planned and operated together to achieve established regional or global objectives. Rather the companies will often operate on a market-by-market basis, using market servicing flexibility as one of a variety of means to gain competitive advantage; extensive intra-firm transactions across national frontiers will not be a feature of such firms.

THE CHANGING SHAPE OF INTERNATIONAL BUSINESS

International business in its trade form is nearly as old as mankind or at least as old as sea-based transportation. Multinational enterprises, moreover, have their origins in the international activities of medieval bankers, and in the seventeenth and eighteenth centuries the British, Dutch and French East India Companies and the Hudson Bay Company were forerunners in some respects of present-day MNEs. In recent years, however, the range of forms of international involvement has expanded enormously and, in principle, is limited only by the imagination of entrepreneurs and policymakers.

The term 'new forms of international investment' has been given to the forms of international business operations which lie between simple exports on the one hand and majority- or wholly owned foreign direct investments on the other.[4] These encompass joint international business ventures in which foreign-held equity does not exceed 50 per cent, and contractual arrangements where the initiating firm may not contribute any equity capital but which provide it with some control or returns even after the project is operational.

The explanations for the growth of the new forms are very varied, relating to factors internal to the company itself, to host- or home-country factors or to more general environmental conditions. To give only a few illustrations at this stage, in developing countries the growth of the new forms in part reflects the aim of technology transfer and the development of local technological capacity. For example, the emergence of product-in-hand contracts in Algeria was designed to ensure an indigenous familiarity with plant operations, which was not possible through turnkey contracts (see page 15 for a discussion). In the components sector of the motor industry in Western Europe and elsewhere, the big growth in collaborative agreements between enterprises has been a consequence of the high costs of technological innovation, overcapacity and government barriers to divestment and transnational mergers. A characteristic of many of these new forms is that they involve co-operative ventures or strategic alliances of various kinds. Firms who may be competitors from different countries are joining together in product development, production, marketing or service arrangements. This is quite different from conventional exporting where the only collaborator for the international businessman is the foreign distributor or a trading company. Within the EC, small-firm collaboration is being promoted through the Business Co-operation Network (BC-Net) which links up several hundred business advisers throughout the Community, with all aspects of the innovation process, and particularly exchanges of technology being aided through the Strategic Programme for Information and Technology Transfer (SPRINT). Other programmes which support European research and development include BRITE, ESPRIT, EUREKA, etc.[5]

The conventional forms of international business have themselves been subject to major changes. The expansion of countertrading has been mentioned already. In the modern era, countertrading was used in the 1930s to assist the German economy out of recession, and a variety of international agreements provided for the exchange of goods under bilateral clearing terms in the early post-war years. Aside from trade with the Eastern Bloc, however, it was not until the 1980s that countertrading 'took off'. The initiator was Indonesia which, facing foreign currency shortages as oil revenues dropped sharply, introduced, in December 1981, mandatory 100 per cent counter-trade requirements in respect of all civilian public-sector contracts financed by the state budget and by export credits.[6] In terms of foreign direct investment in production activities, the 1960s and 1970s saw widespread nationalisation and expropriations in developing countries; whereas in the late 1980s the debt crisis in some of these same nations was leading to discussions on innovative solutions, such as debt–equity swaps. In Mexico, for instance, the major bidders for Mexican debt have been foreign MNEs wishing to expand their operations in that country or at least to finance working capital at a favourable cost. For the international banks to whom the debt is owed, some reduction in their Mexican portfolios may be achieved, while the more efficient use of funds by multinationals should raise Mexico's future debt-service capacity.[7]

The international business environment is thus more challenging. Add-itional to the factors noted above are floating exchange rates, exchange controls and multiple rates; protectionism on the one hand, and liberalis-ation on the other, as in the moves to create a unified internal market in the EC by 1992, the Canada–US Free Trade Agreement and the gradual opening up of the Eastern Bloc and the People's Republic of China; and the emergence of the Pacific Rim countries as competitors and markets. Never-theless, the fact remains that companies opt out at their peril. Both manufac-turing and service industries have become increasingly internationalised, meaning stronger competition at the national market level; and firms in countries with small domestic markets, or in historically free-trading coun-tries such as the UK, or in countries with limited agricultural and mineral resources may be especially vulnerable. On the positive side, international business is big (and growing) business.

BUSINESS POLICY, INTERNATIONAL BUSINESS AND ALTERNATIVE METHODS OF INTERNATIONAL SUPPLY

The topic of international market development strategy represents one of a series of decisions to be made by the firm within the framework of its overall business policy. Typically, the strategic management process would begin with the analysis of internal and external environments and the determin-ation of objectives, leading on to analysis and selection of strategies, and thereafter to the implementation of strategies and evaluation and control. In considering strategic alternatives, a clear distinction needs to be made between the development strategies chosen; the directions of development in terms of products, markets, etc.; and the methods of achieving these such as acquisitions, joint ventures, etc. The possibilities are presented in Figure 1.1.[8]

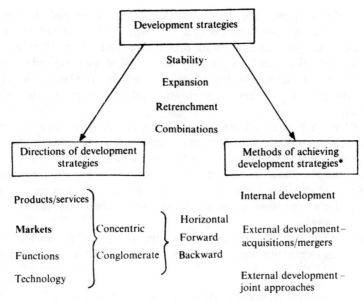

*For retrenchment strategies the development approaches would include liquidation or sell-out and divestment.

Figure 1.1 Development strategies of the firm.

Under the heading of broad development strategies a distinction may be made between the following:

1. Stability: remaining in the same business with a similar level of effort, implying the pursuit of existing objectives and incremental improvement of performance.
2. Expansion: into new business areas, with the aim of increasing sales, profits or market share at a higher rate than competitors.
3. Retrenchment: withdrawing from some parts or all of the business, with the objective of creating a smaller organisation, a leaner management structure and more efficient production and marketing.
4. Combination: some combination of the above, simultaneously or sequentially, mainly relevant to large, divisionalised companies.

Thereafter the firm must decide upon the direction of development associated with these broad strategies. Thus products, markets, functions and technology may be involved. For each of these groupings, furthermore, the approach may be a concentric one (related products, related markets, etc.) or a conglomerate (unrelated) one; and it may involve either horizontal or vertical (backward or forward) developments.

Having determined the direction upon which it is going to embark, the firm must then select the method of achieving its strategy, as between internal development, acquisitions or some joint, collaborative approaches. As with most strategic decisions, trade-offs between cost, speed and risk will ultimately determine the decisions taken. It is recognised that in many ways, internal development offers a company distinct advantages in terms of facilitating planned expansion: production facilities, marketing arrangements, technology and so on may be modified and expanded so as to complement the firm's existing assets and meet future planned needs. However, the process is likely to be slower, and to that extent also, risks are increased.

Within the framework set out in Figure 1.1, market strategies represent only one of a variety of options open to the company; although the arguments presented above indicate that extension of activity into wider geographical areas at home and abroad would soon become inevitable if the objective of expansion was to be achieved. Some of the options open to the firm seeking expansion, leading ultimately to internationalisation, are illustrated in Figure 1.2.

Assuming that the firm does make the choice to 'go international' to achieve its expansion objective, essentially the whole series of decisions on

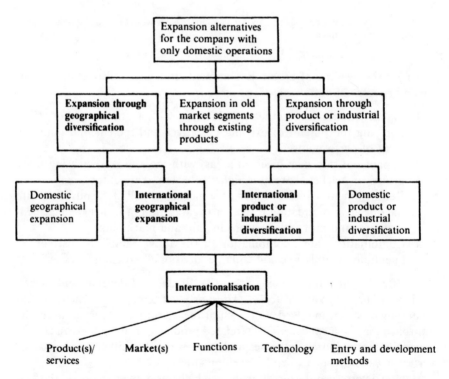

Figure 1.2 Classification of domestic and international expansion alternatives (for the firm with domestic operations only). Source: Luostarinen, R., *The Internationalization of the Firm*, Helsinki School of Economics, 65.

direction of development and methods of achieving development have to be replicated. Issues to be considered include the following:

1. Product(s)/service(s). Within this decision area, the company must determine the nature of the product or service to be offered as well as the range and extent of diversification; and the marketing methods to be employed in approaching the target market(s). Issues of whether and to what extent products/services and marketing methods require adaptation emerge. In fact, the whole 'product concept' may need to be rethought: as the newly industrialising countries (NICs) become increasingly competitive in standardised and mature products, developed-country enterprises may move into software components, e.g. from engineering products into engineering services.
2. Market(s). The choice has to be made on which overseas market or markets to approach, and the number of such markets to be tackled simultaneously. There is evidence of companies, especially in the early stages of internationalisation, directing their efforts to countries which are closest in terms of 'psychic distance' – a concept which takes into account physical distance, but perhaps more important cultural similarities, incorporating language, legal systems, methods of doing business, etc.[9] Again, as the firm becomes more experienced in international business, questions arise on whether to concentrate resources on a few key markets or to engage in market spreading and thereby to spread risks and provide greater flexibility.[10]
3. Functions. Organisational and functional management issues arise at the international business level in relation to communications between headquarters and overseas, and the control of overseas activities. The human resource management function is thus of major importance, as, indeed, is finance – currency of pricing, management of exchange risk, financing of exports, raising investment finance, etc.
4. Technology. The case for a specific technology policy at the present time lies particularly in the ubiquitous nature of the technologies associated with and deriving from microelectronics. The latter impacts upon product and process, components and final goods, consumer and industrial goods, and all functional areas of business. Specifically in an international context the company must decide *inter alia* whether to operate with manual or automatic systems in relation to local factor costs; the extent of technology to be incorporated into the product itself; how far to apply information technology in sales and marketing (e.g. streamlined distribution systems, sales control systems), product design and development, operations (e.g. inventory management and procurement systems), and so forth. Of course, as in the comments on functions above, many of these options are not applicable (or apparent) to the small and newly internationalising firm where the inter-

nationalisation decision itself may be traumatic and all-consuming in terms of time, energy and resources.
5. Entry and development methods. It has been remarked that choice of entry mode is a 'frontier issue' in international marketing.[11] Despite the importance of the other decision areas, therefore, the method the company uses to supply the market will have a major influence upon its success overseas. The market servicing method will impact upon costs – transportation, manufacture, marketing, etc. – as well as upon revenues – through quality, adaptation to local demand conditions, delivery and after-sales performance and the attitudes of governments and other consumers to product source (e.g. nationalistic and chauvinistic attitudes, buy-national policies of governments and public-sector organisations). The common suggestion is that foreign direct investment is the best way to defend a market share. Alternatives, such as exporting and licensing, 'do not allow on-the-spot, controlled reactions to competitors' moves, nor do they allow the firm to gauge precisely the market's needs as an investment does'.[12] While this may be so, there is rather little evidence on the subject, and several surveys of how firms actually make the entry-mode decision reveal that rather few weigh up the options through systematic cost–benefit analysis.[13]

All of these elements would be incorporated within the international business/international marketing plans, setting forward the objectives, goals, resources and policies to direct the company's foreign activities over a three- to five-year time horizon. The discussion has assumed that the firm is pursuing an expansion strategy overall. A generic strategy of retrenchment would, conversely, entail withdrawal of markets and products, divestments and changes in international supply methods – de-internationalisation as opposed to internationalisation.

EXPORTING AND ALTERNATIVE METHODS OF INTERNATIONAL MARKET ENTRY AND DEVELOPMENT: DEFINITIONS AND FORMS

There are a wide variety of methods of classifying international business arrangements. In defining the various forms below, the distinction is made broadly between market-servicing methods in terms of risk and control, progressing from export modes through the range of contractual modes, such as licensing, to direct investment production modes. The descriptions are kept fairly brief since all the various modes are discussed at length in later chapters. Following the definitions and descriptions, an effort is made to distinguish more precisely between the distinctive characteristics of the alternative forms of supply.

Exports

Exporting is generally recognised as being the least-risk method of internationalisation and, as such, normally represents the 'toe in the water' in international business.[14] A firm is an *indirect exporter* when its products are sold in foreign markets without any special activity for this purpose being undertaken within the company. The export operations, including all documentation, physical movement of goods and channels of distribution for sale, are carried on by others, and indeed may take place without the knowledge of the manufacturer himself. Indirect exporting may occur through an export house, or confirming house, say in the City of London, which will buy directly from the firm on behalf of a foreign principal and then arrange for the export of the goods. Another form of indirect exporting is the use of a trading company. The best known trading companies are Japanese (and indeed the Hong Kong and South Korean firms) as well as the firms of European origin; their area of activity tends to vary and so the European firms are strongest in the former colonies, e.g. the United Africa Company in Africa. 'Piggybacking' is a third form of indirect exporting, where the company sells its goods abroad through the overseas distribution facilities of another producer; the two firms would normally have complementary, noncompetitive products. Finally, exporting may take place even more indirectly when foreign buyers (perhaps from foreign department stores or wholesale or retail organisations) approach a company to buy a product which they regard as suitable and desirable for their home markets abroad; or a buyinghouse operating on behalf of clients undertakes the same activity.

Direct exporting represents quite a different mode of supply, since the firm undertakes the export task itself, and therefore has to build up contacts, undertake market research, handle documentation and transportation, establish pricing policies, and so forth. The product is then typically sold overseas by agents or distributors, a major difference between these two being that the distributor actually takes title to the goods and represents the manufacturer in the sale and service of the product which he carries; or through company technical specialist export salesmen; or through a sales subsidiary established by the exporting firm. Generally, the move to direct exporting shows a genuine commitment to exporting, which may be absent when the indirect route is used, and facilitates greater control, information feedback from the foreign market and the development of 'exportise';[15] to be set against this is the fact that it is also a more expensive alternative. But the setting up of a sales subsidiary represents the most significant step in terms of export commitment since it requires direct investment in marketing institutions located in the target country.

Licensing[16]

International licensing is often used as a generic term to cover a wide variety of contractual arrangements between companies located in different countries for effecting transfers of rights and resources. Here, however, the term is used in its more exact sense to mean contracts in which a foreign licensor provides a local licensee with access to one or a set of technologies or know-how, in exchange for financial compensation. Typically the licensee would have the exclusive rights to produce and market a product within an agreed area for a period of time in return for a royalty based on sales volume. A licence agreement may relate to the following:

1. Patents, where a patentor may license others to use his invention, until the period of expiration of the licensed patents.
2. Copyright, which protects expression as in book publishing, films and television and, most recently, computer programs and other information transfer systems.
3. Trade marks, being words or symbols used to distinguish particular goods and services and to indicate their origin. As with patents, duration is likely to vary between countries, although it is fairly easy to renew a trade mark registration once it has expired.
4. Trade secrets and know-how, which are information not generally available and which may be disclosed either by itself or as part of a patent or trade mark licence. This may include product and process specifications, quality-control procedures, factory layout drawings, instruction manuals and the like. Know-how is different from patents and trade marks in the sense that the latter enjoy a measure of additional legal protection.

The licence package may comprise a wide variety of components in addition to the above, including commissioning to achieve a performance guarantee; technical and commercial training; product literature and other sales support material; access to the licensor's design office and development facilities; and direct export sale of associated plant and equipment, and the continuing supply of components. The payment terms in licensing agreements will vary but will involve some combination of the elements listed below:

1. A first down-payment on obtaining the written-up part of the technology.
2. Progress payments leading up to the commissioning of one or more products to the performance specification of the licensor.
3. A minimum royalty, which may be inflation-adjusted; in part the intention is to encourage the licensee to enter the market as quickly as possible.
4. A running royalty, which is usually expressed as a percentage of net

selling price – 3 to 5 per cent is common – or as a fixed amount of money per unit of output.

The actual payment terms arranged will largely depend on market circumstances. High political risk, for instance, is likely to be associated with substantial up-front payments. Conversely, if the market prospects are good, and relatively risk-free, or there are other licensors competing for business, then royalty rates may be fairly low. In essence, then, bargaining power and negotiating strength are important elements, and not only in setting direct 'payment' terms as above, but also in determining equally significant contract components such as markets to be supplied, tie-in clauses, etc.

The period of the licence will vary but typically might run for three to five years. A successful licensing arrangement might in fact be fairly automatically renewable, and examples exist where licences have run for twenty-five years or more. A more problematic situation occurs when a former licensee sets up a rival organisation at the end of an agreement.

Compared with exporting, production under licence takes place in the foreign market with both manufacturing and marketing the responsibility of the licensee. The licensor avoids the capital investment required to establish production and distribution facilities, and licensing permits entry to markets which may be closed to exports or other forms of market servicing; conversely, control is lost and the company's good name rests on the performance of the licensee.

Franchising

A franchise is a particular type of licensing or technical assistance agreement. Normally, the franchisee operates under the name of the franchisor, and the former provides the franchisee with a 'package' including not only trade marks and know-how but local exclusivity and management and financial assistance and joint advertising as well. Fundamentally, the franchisee runs a controlled business using the reputation and techniques of the franchisor. The business operated by the franchisee, moreover, is viewed by the public as part of a country-wide chain rather than a single business enterprise. Payment will comprise an initial fee, royalties, and compliance with certain company regulations. Franchise arrangements are most important in services, but there are a range of different types including the manufacturer – retailer type (car distributorships), manufacturer – wholesaler (soft drinks bottlers), wholesaler – retailer (grocery and hardware stores), trade mark licensor – retailer (fabricated textiles) and retailer – retailer systems (where the franchisor runs directly owned outlets as well as franchise operations). Internationally the sectors in which most rapid growth has been achieved are soft drinks, fast foods and car rentals, although retailing of clothing and other consumer goods and medical services (hospital support services, home nursing franchises) are emerging sectors. To a greater extent than licensing, franchising is very common between domestic firms as well as a form of international business, and there has been a great deal of interest in such agreements for generating small-firm growth. Thus franchising can be used to segment the market spatially, with a full market coverage being achieved without internal competition.

It is suggested that host-country benefits from franchising are high because training and development of management skills are incorporated within the franchising deal. For the franchisor effective market penetration may be achieved for a limited capital outlay.

Management contract[17]

A management contract represents 'an arrangement under which operational control of an enterprise (or one phase of an enterprise) which would otherwise be exercised by a board of directors or managers elected and appointed by its owners is vested by contract in a separate enterprise which performs the necessary management functions in return for a fee'.[18] The management firm's duties are essentially the same as the administrative and technical functions a multinational company undertakes in running a subsidiary it has created by direct investment. These services may include general management, financial administration, personnel administration, production management and marketing, but are generally limited to ongoing operations and do not give the authority to the management contractor to make new capital investments, assume long-term debt or initiate basic management or policy changes. Various formulae are used for the calculation of management fees. Most contracts include a basic fee along with an incentive fee, with special services including marketing, pre-operations assistance, training and recruitment of personnel, etc., being remunerated separately. Regarding the length of contract term, in many cases this will not be defined but rather will be limited to the time necessary to complete a specific undertaking such as the construction of a plant or a foundry. Where contract terms are specified, these are frequently of seven years or less, but durations of twenty years are common in hotel management contracts; hospital management contracts too may be very lengthy.

Management contracts are commonly found in conjunction with other forms of international market development – for example supplementing licensing, joint ventures or turnkey projects, and facilitating management control which may be absent in the latter arrangements *per se*. The disadvantage that may be presumed for management contracts is that they do not allow a firm to build up a permanent market position; on the other hand, no alternative method of market servicing may be possible. Of more concern is that difficulties have been experienced between management contractors and developing countries in recent years, largely because of different objectives but also as a result of poorly specified contract terms, which have led on occasion to termination or renegotiation. As suggested above, management contracts are concentrated in particular industries, with hotels and transportation being especially important; other industries in which contracts are significant include agriculture, public utilities and mining and minerals.

Turnkey contract[19]

Here a contractor has a responsibility for establishing a complete production unit or infrastructure project in the host country. While differing from project to project, the contractor's responsibilities generally include the basic design and engineering of plant, provision of technology and know-how, supply of complete plant and equipment, design and construction of civil engineering works, complete construction of the plant and installation of equipment, and the commissioning of the total plant facilities up to the stage of start-up. Operation and/or maintenance by the contractor have been added in recent years to eliminate problems that have arisen in this area. Turnkey contractors are often engineering firms who have the ability to mobilise personnel, equipment, technology, etc., and to co-ordinate the activities of subcontractors. Payment may be in a variety of forms, including countertrading, where the supplier takes payment wholly or partly in the form of physical output from the completed plant.

A number of oil-producing developing countries have used turnkey contracts to develop refining capacity and thereby increase revenues and maintain market share without breaking OPEC ranks. Indonesia provides a good illustration where six oil refineries had been built by the end of the 1980s, involving companies such as British Petroleum, Foster Wheeler (US), Mitsui and Mitsubishi (Japan).

There are a variety of modified or turnkey-plus contracts. For example, product-in-hand contracts are turnkey operations in which the contractor's responsibilities end only when the installation is completely operational with local personnel. Therefore, such contracts include provisions whereby the contractor has a responsibility for preparing local management and workers to run the installation. Another form of modified turnkey contract is the market-in-hand agreement. Here the project contractor is required to give assistance in or take responsibility for the sale of at least part of the project's output.

Because of the large size of turnkey deals, negotiations are likely to be lengthy and complex and require sophisticated legal assistance. Even with the most carefully specified contract, there is infinite scope for problems.

Contract manufacturing/international subcontracting

Contract manufacturing, otherwise known as international subcontracting or offshore processing/assembly, involves a company (the principal) in one country placing an order, with specifications as to the conditions of sale and the products required, with a firm in another country. Typically the contract would be limited to production, and marketing would be handled by the principal, sales often taking place in the principal's home market. In order to ensure product standards, the provision of design and product specifications and technical know-how and even the provision of physical equipment for the subcontractor may be part of the arrangement. The latter are formalised in separate licensing/technical assistance agreements between the two parties. There may be considerable differences in the nature of orders placed under contract, as between long-term, short-term and single batch orders with no guarantee of renewal.

Closely related to the issue of international subcontracting is that of export processing zones (EPZs), given that much of the subcontracting takes place in such zones in developing countries which provide for the importation of goods and materials to be used in production, with subsequent export on a bonded duty-free basis. The EPZs are thus enclaves within national customs territories, whose purpose is to attract export-oriented industries. This is where definitional problems arise since the subcontractors are not always wholly locally owned enterprises. In the clothing industry, the most important sector apart from electronics for these arrangements, joint ventures, sometimes with multiple foreign partners, exist, as do wholly foreign-owned and wholly locally owned firms.

Other contractual/collaborative arrangements

It will be clear from the above that there are definitional problems when it comes to identifying forms of market servicing and international supply; and, moreover, that different types of arrangements both shade into each other at the margin and may be encompassed within the same agreement package. In addition, new forms of agreement are appearing fairly regularly. These difficulties are especially apparent when it comes to identifying the range of other contractual and collaborative arrangements which exist within the international business arena.

The term *industrial co-operation agreement* (ICA) is conventionally applied to arrangements between Western companies and government agencies or enterprises in the Eastern Bloc. These arrangements may include many of the forms already identified, including licensing, technical assistance arrangements, turnkey projects and contract manufacturing, as well as contractual joint ventures, and tripartite ventures. A common feature of any such deals with Eastern Bloc countries, including conventional exports, is that they will incorporate countertrade requirements of various types. These are often of the 'compensation' form, whereby the sale or licensing of technology, equipment or a plant is linked to a contractual commitment on the part of the seller to purchase a certain quantity of goods that are produced or derived from the original sale. However, 'counterpurchases' are often found, where the goods offered for sale by the Eastern Bloc country may be unrelated to those exported, and parties unrelated to the sales contract may be involved in the agreement. This important issue of counter-trading is discussed fully as a separate topic later in the book.

A *contractual joint venture* has been defined as

a risk-sharing venture in which no joint enterprise with separate personality is formed. It is a partnership in which two or more companies (or a company and a government agency) share the cost of an investment, the risks and the long term profits. The contractual joint venture may be formed for a particular project of limited duration, or for a longer term cooperative effort, and the contractual relationship may terminate once the project is complete.[20]

In relationships between Western companies and the Eastern Bloc, contractual joint ventures frequently relate to co-production. This is the situation which exists where the Western enterprise supplies technology, components and other inputs to an Eastern Bloc partner in return for a share of the resulting output, which the Western firm then markets in the West; long-term contracts of five to ten years would be involved.

Contractual joint ventures are not only found in arrangements with Eastern Bloc countries. Consortium ventures by banks to finance large loans, such as for oil exploration and production, and co-publishing agreements are examples where developed (and sometimes developing) country firms are involved. Contractual joint ventures of various types are common in the aerospace and particularly the automobile industries. In the latter, co-R&D, co-development (for components and/or new models), co-production and co-marketing agreements may all be involved within the spider's web of collaborative agreements linking the automobile producers worldwide.

For the sake of completeness, mention should be made of a special type of contractual joint venture – *tripartite industrial co-operation*.[21] Originally these were conceived as arrangements where at least three firms, one domiciled in the Eastern Bloc, one in the West and one in a developing country, collaborated to undertake common activities in the developing country. The activities could include exploration and production of natural resources,[22] building physical infrastructure, supplying industrial plant, assembly work and marketing. In reality rather few of such ventures exist.

Joint ventures

The contractual joint ventures discussed above are quite different from the more conventional joint equity ventures, which together with wholly owned subsidiaries represent the main means by which multinational enterprises operate internationally. According to the OECD, 'an equity joint venture implies the sharing of assets, risks and profits, and participation in the ownership (i.e. equity) of a particular enterprise or investment project by more than one firm or economic "group". The latter may include private corporations, public corporations, or even states.'[23] While partners' relative equity shareholdings are commonly 50/50 per cent or 51/49 per cent, virtually any distribution of equity shares is possible in what may be termed minority- or majority-owned joint ventures. The distribution of equity may be related to each partner's financial contribution or it may be based on other contributions, including technology, management or access to world markets. Furthermore, the relative equity stakes of the foreign and domestic partners will vary because of host nation legislation, although there is an important difference between joint ventures where there is a single host-country partner and those where there is a wide dispersion of local ownership. Looking at the essential characteristics of joint ventures, one author has suggested that these are four-fold, viz. 'a community of interests involving doing business in common, the sharing of profits, the sharing of business risks and losses and longevity of co-operation'.[24]

In some countries, 'fade-out' agreements (which may be known as 'fade-in' agreements from the viewpoint of the host country) exist, where the initial equity participation of the foreign investor in a joint venture is subsequently transferred in stages to one or more local parties. Once the process has been completed, the foreign investor may retain minority participation or no equity whatsoever, although even in the latter instance the foreign enterprise is likely to continue to be involved by licensing, management or other contractual arrangements. This introduces a further characteristic of many joint ventures, namely that they may be enforced by host-country regulations. However, this is mainly a developing country and Eastern Bloc phenomenon. Various authors have drawn attention to the advantages which may accrue from taking a pro-active approach to international joint ventures.[25] These can be listed as follows:

1. Joint ventures may represent a way into 'closed' markets.
2. In a situation of rapid technological change and large capital requirements, joint ventures may be the best way for smaller and non-dominant firms to improve their positions in global industries.
3. Joint ventures may be used to ensure access to distribution channels, suppliers and technology, in effect as pre-emptive manoeuvres.
4. Joint ventures may prevent potential entrants from teaming up with more dangerous opponents.
5. Joint ventures may be incorporated into global strategies as product lives shorten, cost advantages become more pronounced and larger numbers of firms become international competitors.

Wholly owned subsidiaries

The end of the implicit spectrum of international market development activity abroad is foreign direct investment in wholly owned manufacturing subsidiaries. Much of the early post-war activities by MNEs took the form of investment in wholly owned subsidiaries, and 100 per cent ownership in subsidiaries in developed countries has become even more important in recent years.[26] From a corporate viewpoint, the preference for wholly owned subsidiaries is generally associated with strategies that require tight controls, either for manufacturing or marketing reasons or to protect proprietary technology. In explaining the recent trend, 100 per cent ownership may be regarded as necessary by multinationals to implement the policies required for survival and growth within the more competitive and depressed market conditions prevailing.

In considering foreign direct investment in wholly-owned subsidiaries (and joint ventures) it is worth distinguishing between three basic types:

1. Market-oriented investment – also known as import substituting investment – where the company replaces exports, wholly or partially by manufacture within the country (although the evidence in fact shows substantial complementarities between investment and exports).
2. Cost-oriented investment, usually based on low-cost labour or other input costs, with the subsidiary being used to service third-country markets or world markets in general, or to be linked into the global manufacturing strategy of the MNE. This is sometimes termed export-platform or rationalised manufacturing investment.
3. Resource-oriented investment. This relates primarily to energy and extractive investments, where the activities of the multinational are vertically integrated from extraction through perhaps to retailing, as in the oil industry.

It is necessary to make a further distinction between wholly owned subsidiaries (or joint ventures again) set up as new, greenfield establishments and those acquired through takeover or merger. Not only is the initial market entry decision quite different, but methods of managing the two forms will require different skills.

Corporate coalitions and strategic alliances

Before concluding this discussion of alternative methods of international market entry and development, it is necessary to draw attention to the most recent writing and research which has focused upon corporate linkages (as opposed to corporate entry strategies *per se*) domestically and internationally. The undoubted upsurge of these arrangements – variously called corporate coalitions, strategic alliances, strategic partnerships – is a response to increasing international and global competition. Corporate link-ups are especially relevant to smaller and non-dominant firms, enabling the companies to build competitive defences against larger, possibly global enterprises. The latter are, however, also actively involved, as in corporate venturing, where partnerships are formed between large and small companies aimed at 'sharing the risks associated with innovation; generating new business development opportunities; making best use of the complementary skills and resources available from each of the parties; and achieving the strategic business development objectives of both parties more quickly and effectively'.[27] Strategic alliances may involve virtually any of the international market development modes but especially licensing and contractual and equity joint ventures; the distinction primarily relates to the motivations for the arrangements as discussed on pages 23 to 25.

CHARACTERISTICS OF ALTERNATIVE METHODS OF INTERNATIONAL MARKET ENTRY AND DEVELOPMENT

As suggested above, the descriptions of alternative supply methods assume some implicit spectrum of involvement from exporting through to wholly owned manufacturing subsidiaries. The aim of this section is to establish more precisely the characteristics of the various forms of market servicing; these are important for the international businessman when it comes to the stage of selecting the mode of involvement overseas.

Figure 1.3 illustrates the alternatives on the basis of various criteria, viz. production in the home market v. production overseas; direct investment v. non-direct investment activities; and production v. marketing operations. The distinction between direct and non-direct investment is obviously significant since the former activity produces the MNE, as defined earlier. But there are various other implications which stem from the categorisation. For instance, production overseas is a riskier activity than that at home; conversely, direct investment gives a power of control over decisionmaking in a foreign enterprise. It is these various dimensions of international supply activity which are now reviewed.

Locus of control

There is no question that control has a critical impact upon the success of a firm in foreign markets.[28] Control enables the company to implement and revise its strategies, to co-ordinate actions and resolve the disputes that inevitably arise between partners operating at a distance and pursuing their own interests. It may also be possible to use control as a means of obtaining a higher share of the foreign enterprise's profits. As against this, certain costs and risks are increased: for example, control involves the commitment of resources, including high overheads, which in turn creates switching costs. In consequence, 'control . . . is the focus of the entry mode literature because it is the single most important determinant of both risk and return . . . Firms trade various levels of control for reduction of resource commitment in the

Production in home market

Non-direct investment marketing operations	Direct investment marketing operations
Indirect goods exports	Sales promotion subsidiaries
Direct goods exports	Warehousing units
Service exports	Service units
Know-how exports	Sales subsidiaries
Partial project exports	

Production overseas

Non-direct investment production operations	Direct investment production operations
Licensing	Assembly
Franchising	Manufacture
Contract manufacturing/ international subcontracting[a]	Wholly owned joint ventures
Turnkey operations	Minority holdings
	'Fade-out' agreements

[a]Assuming that international subcontracting takes place between independent companies in home and overseas markets

Figure 1.3 Forms of international market entry and development (excludes industrial co-operation agreements and the range of forms of contractual joint ventures because of their great variety). Source: Luostarinen, R. (1980), *The Internationalization of the Firm*, Helsinki School of Economics.

hope of reducing some forms of risk while increasing their returns. Hence, focusing on control is consistent with the classical risk-adjusted return perspective.'[29]

It should be added that it is not only the firm which weighs up the risks and returns relating to control; the host country will also be evaluating the potential transfers of technology and skills against the necessity of accepting foreign control over the use of resources.

Establishing the circumstances under which control will reside with the foreign enterprise is not straightforward. This is particularly the case in joint ventures, where control over management and technology may be more important than the equity stake held. Moreover, the equity holding of the foreign investor(s) has to be related to the number and equity holdings of other investors; and whether or not the host-country stake is held by a major company or the government, as opposed to being in the form of equity traded on the stock market. Although there are no tested models on how much control each form of supply provides, it is normally assumed that wholly owned manufacturing subsidiaries or majority foreign-owned ventures offer the highest degree of control; conversely, a minority shareholding may provide only limited control if the majority is held by a host-country partner with strong managerial and technological expertise. Direct exports that are supported by direct investment in marketing operations abroad offer a fair degree of control over production and marketing decisions, proprietary know-how, etc; although as the next section will show there are advantages in internalising production activities within the firm through subsidiary manufacturing operations which are not available to the exporter.

The various contractual arrangements are regarded as providing moderate control. These include management contracts, contract manufacturing, contractual joint ventures, franchising (because the typical agreement permits a high degree of involvement in and monitoring of the franchisee's operations) and some forms of licensing. In regard to the latter, multiple unrestricted licences provide little control, whereas restrictiveness or exclusivity gives the foreign licensor moderate control.[30]

Resource commitment

The issue of resource commitment is closely linked to control, as noted above. Substantial financial and management commitment will increase control, while also increasing financial and political risks. Resource commitment is likely to be substantial in direct investment (and especially direct investment production) operations as well as in turnkey operations and some kinds of contractual joint ventures such as co-production deals. Management commitment alone produces fewer risks, as in a management contract where there are no physical assets involved. By contrast, when factory and warehousing facilities, plant and equipment, inventories, etc., are wholly or partly owned by the foreign enterprise, risks increase and flexibility is reduced. This explains the interest of foreign firms in leasing factory space, restricting production activity to assembly, dual sourcing, and so on.

Resources transferred[31]

The comments on resource commitment draw attention to the different combinations of resources and rights which are transferred via the various market-servicing methods. The wholly owned manufacturing subsidiary involves a package of resources – capital, technology and management – as well as a wide range of rights to develop, manufacture and market products. Alternative methods of supply involve only part of this resource package: for example, licensing arrangements relate to the technology component, whether this is physical technology (machines, blueprints, operating procedures, other know-how) or informational/marketing technology (trademark licensing). With franchising, managerial resource transfers are also involved; and the management contract relates exclusively to managerial resources. By contrast, with exporting no resources are transferred directly, factor inputs being incorporated into the product before it leaves the home country. The exception concerns exporting with direct investment marketing operations, where both capital and management resources are transferred into warehousing and distribution operations, sales subsidiaries, etc.

So the issue of resource transfers is closely related to locus of control and resource commitment from the viewpoint of the foreign enterprise. From the perspective of the host government it is bound up with the theme of technology transfer and debates over 'depackaging' and 'repackaging' resources to meet the country's needs.[32]

Motivation

Earlier comments began to draw attention to the fact that the mode of international market entry is only a means to an end. Conventionally the objective is cost-effective penetration of foreign markets; but wider strategic objectives have emerged, reflected in the terms used such as coalitions, collaborations, co-partnerships, and so on. Although there is a lack of precision in the usage, the concepts do draw attention to another important differentiating characteristic in international market entry and development methods, namely, the strategic motivation for the activity. Aside from the conventional motives such as achieving market entry and building profitable market shares, a number of strategic motivations can be identified:[33]

1. Access to the expertise or attributes possessed by partner enterprises. In this instance there may be asymmetries between firms in certain activities, whether technology or innovative ability, distribution channels,

market access, etc. One example would be a link-up between a Western company and a COMECON (Council for Mutual Economic Assistance) enterprise, whereby the former obtains market access into the Eastern Bloc and the latter obtains access to product. Large firm/small firm collaborations, where the latter contributes innovative and entrepreneurial skills and the former provides resources to facilitate commercialisation, is another of a whole range of illustrations which could be cited.

2. Achievement of economies of scale or learning. Examples include pooling of R&D in industries such as computers, telecommunications and aerospace because of rapidly increasing development costs; and collaboration in production to allow partners to exploit economies of scale in the manufacture of, say, car components.

3. Risk reduction. Even if companies have the size and resources to undertake activities singly, coalitions may be formed to spread risk. Examples include the joint exploration and extraction activities in oil and aluminium industries.

4. Shaping competition. This incorporates a whole variety of competitive motivations, including collusion to raise entry barriers, fix prices, etc.; facilitating entry into a new sector, where two partners on their own may be too small to compete; and defensive motivations relating to survival in a hostile and competitive environment.

5. Diversification: 'toe in the water'; 'ear to the ground'. These motivations mainly apply to large companies linking up with smaller enterprises. In the former instance the objective may be to gain experience of a different industry on a small scale, prior to larger-scale diversification activity. In the latter case, even the largest firms are finding it difficult to stay at the leading edge of research on the wide variety of technical fronts, and alliances with smaller companies provide a means of keeping their 'ear to the ground' and accessing latest developments. It is reported that Japanese companies are in the forefront of such developments, and in one year alone were believed to have paid out more than $500 million in overseas investments in mainly small technology-based ventures.[34]

6. Duress. This is included separately to highlight the point that these so-called collaboration or co-operation agreements may be entered into because there is no option. If a country imposes high tariff and quota barriers and prohibits inward foreign direct investment, then the only option is licensing or some other contractual arrangement. Government regulations requiring 'fade-out' agreements is a further example.

These different motivations may lead to agreements between firms or between an enterprise and a host government covering technology, operations and logistics, or marketing, sales and service, or, indeed, all of these activities. Furthermore, the agreements may be horizontal in nature or involve backward or forward integration (as in the first example above which refers to asymmetries between enterprises). It is clear that there are many sources of instability in inter-firm arrangements internationally. Some of these include mistrust, the relative benefits the different partners gain from coalitions, and changes in relative expertise and contributions over time. Enterprises are effectively sacrificing the control which would be achieved through alternative market-servicing methods such as wholly owned subsidiaries, for what may be only short-to-medium term benefits from collaboration.

Other dimensions[35]

To conclude this discussion of the dimensions of international supply activity, a number of other aspects should be noted. For example, supply methods differ in terms of *time limitations*. Licensing and franchising agreements will operate for a specified time period, as will management contracts, although there may be possibilities for renewal of agreements. Turnkey operations, where there is provision for the handover of control to local interests, fall into a similar category, as do contractual joint ventures. These arrangements thus differ from direct investment production operations and export activities which have no time limit on them; the exception concerns fade-out agreements where the foreign enterprise is required to sell a part or all of its investment stake to the host government or local shareholders over a period of time.

Another dimension concerns *space limitations*, that is the geographical area within which any agreement is valid. Providing government regulations permit, licensing and franchising arrangements are space limited, enabling the licensor or franchisor to segment the market nationally and internationally. Many contractual joint ventures will also relate to particular geographical areas, particularly those involving marketing, sales and service. Although supply methods differ in terms of whether or not there are contractual space limitations, MNEs with manufacturing and marketing subsidiaries will usually clearly identify market franchises for each operation to prevent competition, and thus similarly involve space limitations.

Attention should be drawn finally to *payment methods*: while dividends, royalties and cash payments are still normal, exports, licensing and turnkey operations may involve countertrade transactions, meaning extra risks and costs and a requirement for expertise in handling countertrade.

These dimensions clearly differ in terms of their significance. The control/cost/flexibility issues are of paramount importance and the trade-offs between them are illustrated in Figure 1.4. But motivation also assumes major relevance on occasions, and generally all of the variables may have a role in and assist in understanding the choice of internationalisation mode.

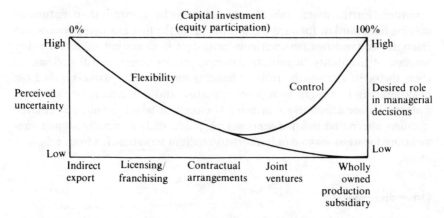

Methods of international supply

Figure 1.4 Some dimensions of international supply activity. Source: Simyar, F. and Argheyd, K. (1987), 'Export Entry and Expansion Strategies', in Rosson, P.J. and Reid, S.D. (eds), *Managing Export Entry and Expansion*, Praeger, New York, 228.

Certainly a simple spectrum running from export modes through contractual modes to direct investment production modes fails to take account of the complexities of the different arrangements and the circumstances under which they are operated.

ANALYSING INTERNATIONAL MARKET ENTRY AND DEVELOPMENT MODE

Contributions from economics

Market entry and market development decisions internationally, with an emphasis on the growth of the multinational enterprise, have been discussed in the economics literature for about thirty years, beginning with the pioneering work of Hymer and Kindleberger.[36] The general proposition originating from the work of these authors was that companies must possess some form of quasi-monopolistic advantage in order to compete in an overseas market against domestic firms possessing local knowledge and the advantages of local nationality. Subsequent authors, including Caves, Aliber, Dunning and others, drew attention to the nature of what are now called the ownership-specific or firm-specific advantages of foreign enterprises, such as technology and marketing skills, organisation and production management, financial variables, size and oligopolistic behaviour, etc.

It was the next stage in the development of theory which is of particular interest here, since it focused on the choice between exporting, licensing and foreign direct investment. Various locational advantages were postulated which could encourage the foreign enterprise to exploit its ownership advantages through production abroad rather than through exporting. And, in 1976, Buckley and Casson, applying the concept of internalisation to international business, showed how the advantages of using an internal market (the firm itself) and the problems with external market transactions (licensing) could lead to foreign production.[37]

Dunning's eclectic theory
These various strands were integrated in Dunning's 'Eclectic theory of international production' which also dates back to 1976.[38] The decision to engage in international business and the choice of mode is seen to depend on the interaction between a set of ownership (O), internalisation (I) and location (L) advantages; the nature of these OLI variables are shown in Table 1.1. For a company to use the foreign direct investment route, three sets of conditions must be fulfilled. First, the firm must possess net ownership advantages over firms of other nationalities. These advantages must be sufficient to offset the additional costs of operating in a foreign environment. Second, it must be more profitable for the company possessing these unique assets to utilise them itself through foreign direct investment rather than to sell the rights to their use to other parties, through licensing agreements, management contracts, etc. That is, it must be more beneficial to use an internal market (taking account of both the costs and returns from internalisation) than to externalise the property rights. Third, assuming the first two conditions are satisfied, it must be advantageous for the firm to exploit its unique assets through production outside its home country rather than through exports. This condition will be met when there are either positive (e.g. lower labour costs) or negative (e.g. trade barriers) factors deterring production at home or encouraging production abroad.

Dunning's eclectic theory revised
In a more recent update of the eclectic paradigm, Dunning places considerable emphasis on structural and transactional market failure.[39] In regard to the *ownership advantages* of MNEs, a distinction is made between the asset and transaction advantages of multinationals. The former arise from the proprietary ownership of specific assets by MNEs compared with those possessed by other firms, and derive from structural market distortions, e.g. product differentiation, monopoly power, cost barriers. Transaction advantages relate to the ability of multinational networks to capture the transactional benefits or reduce the transactional costs from common control of these assets in different countries (as compared with the external market alternative); these are the advantages of common governance in Table 1.1.

Table 1.1 The eclectic theory of international production

1. Ownership-specific advantages (of enterprises of one nationality, or affiliates of same, over those of another)
   (a) Property right and/or intangible asset advantages
   Product innovations, production management, organisational and marketing systems, innovatory capacity; non-codifiable knowledge; 'bank' of human capital experience; marketing, finance, know-how, etc.
   (b) Advantages of common governance
   (i) Which those branch plants of established enterprises may enjoy over de novo firms. Those due mainly to size and established position of enterprise, e.g. economies of scope and specialisation; monopoly power, better resource capacity and usage. Exclusive or favoured access to inputs, e.g. labour, natural resources, finance, information. Ability to obtain inputs on favoured terms (due e.g. to size or monopsonistic influence). Exclusive or favoured access to product markets. Access to resources of parent company at marginal cost. Economies of joint supply (not only in production, but in purchasing, marketing, finance, etc., arrangements).
   (ii) Which specifically arise because of multinationality. Multinationality enhances above advantages by offering wider opportunities. More favoured access to and/or better knowledge about international markets, e.g. for information, finance, labour, etc. Ability to take advantage of geographical differences in factor endowments, markets. Ability to diversify or reduce risks, e.g. in different currency areas, and/or political scenarios.

2. Internalisation incentive advantages (i.e. to protect against or exploit market failure)
   Avoidance of search and negotiating costs.
   To avoid costs of enforcing property rights.
   Buyer uncertainty (about nature and value of inputs, e.g. technology, being sold).
   Where market does not permit price discrimination.
   Need of seller to protect quality of products.
   To capture economies of interdependent activities (see 1(b) above).
   To compensate for absence of future markets.
   To avoid or exploit government intervention (e.g. quotas, tariffs, price controls, tax differences, etc.).
   To control supplies and conditions of sale of inputs (including technology).
   To control market outlets (including those which might be used by competitors).
   To be able to engage in practices, e.g. cross-subsidisation, predatory pricing, etc., as a competitive (or anti-competitive) strategy.

3. Location-specific variables (these may favour home or host countries).
   Spatial distribution of inputs and markets.
   Input prices, quality and productivity, e.g. labour, energy, materials, components, semi-finished goods.
   Transport and communication costs.
   Investment incentives and disincentives (including performance requirements, etc.).
   Artificial barriers to trade in goods.
   Infrastructure provisions (commercial, legal, educational, transportation).
   Psychic distance (language, cultural, business, customs, etc., differences).
   Economies of centralisation of R&D, production and marketing.

Source: Dunning, J.H. (1981), *International Production and the Multinational Enterprise*, Allen & Unwin, London.

In the revised eclectic model, *internalisation advantages* continue to be important: the reasons for the internalisation of markets relate to overcoming risk and uncertainty and exploiting economies of large-scale production, and the desire by firms to integrate different stages of production, engage in product diversification, etc. Dunning notes that: 'The greater the perceived costs of transactional market failure, the more MNEs are likely to exploit their competitive advantages through international production rather than by contractual agreements with foreign firms.'[40] Expressed in this way, the distinction between ownership advantages relating to transactional market failure and internalisation advantages becomes very blurred.

The third strand of Dunning's theory concerns *locational advantages*, where a distinction is again drawn between structural and transaction factors. Structural market distortions arise from government intervention. Transactions' gains derive from common governance of activities in different locations, including reduction of exchange risks, multiple sourcing strategies, the possibility of transfer price manipulation, etc.

Applications and critiques
It is not necessary to accept the eclectic model totally to recognise that it can be helpful in differentiating between different industries in terms of the main forms of international business activity. Considering the textile chain, man-made fibres fit the case of a strongly MNE-oriented sector. Ownership and internalisation advantages are based on advanced technology and heavy expenditures on R&D, backed up by the large optimum scale of production and patent protection. Foreign direct investment has occurred to ensure market access, particularly when imports are prohibited or otherwise controlled. Alternatively, restrictions on foreign direct investment have stimulated licensing arrangements, the now powerful Japanese industry, for example, developing on the basis of the acquisition of a licence for nylon technology by Toray Industries from Du Pont in 1951. By contrast, in a low-technology sector such as clothing, contract manufacturing and international subcontracting have been the predominant modes, as a function of low labour costs and the establishment of export processing zones in developing countries, alongside the ownership-specific advantages of developed-country MNEs in the form of market access and marketing expertise.

Undoubtedly the eclectic theory represents an important step forward, and other recent contributions have been mostly concerned with adaptation and refinement. The internalisation concept, however, has been the subject of active debate involving authors such as Casson, Rugman, Hennart and Teece.[41] The stress has been on attempting to explain why firms engage in collaborative arrangements, joint ventures and the like as opposed to the more clearly defined forms of international market development, namely, wholly owned subsidiaries, licensing and exporting. Internalisation theory has conventionally assumed that joint ventures are a less efficient way of operating internationally than wholly owned subsidiaries. The foreign enterprise may gain knowledge of the local market, customs, business practices, contracts and government; however, it would lose because of the costs of protecting its proprietary know-how from exploitation by the local partner or by a local employee who leaves the joint venture to set up in competition.

In fact, weaknesses of local enterprises and of local technological capacity in many countries will restrict any potential diffusion, and other factors to be taken into consideration include host-government policies towards sourcing inputs, local managerial skills and the nature of the MNE's investment. Where the latter is part of an integrated, rationalised global system, the main linkages of the subsidiary will be with other parts of the MNE, and knowledge of the activity undertaken at any one affiliate may be of little value *per se*.

Alongside these arguments which indicate that technology diffusion through joint ventures and collaborative agreements may not be substantial, are another set of arguments which stress the positive dimensions of inter-firm relationships. Essentially the requirement is to build up trust between the partners through mechanisms for fair distribution of profits, joint decision-making processes and reward and control systems, so that 'the incentives to engage in self-seeking pre-emptive behaviour could be minimized'.[42] Other, and indeed, stronger business strategy arguments in favour of joint ventures were presented earlier: the new forms of international investment may be well suited to the global environmental and competitive conditions of the present time, and to the rapid pace of technological change in many sectors.

The basic criticism of many of the contributions from Economics is their static nature. As Table 1.1 showed, it is possible to establish the circumstances under which one form of international supply will be preferred over another. But the OLI variables change over time, possibly on a sequential basis (as discussed in the following), and there are competitive and strategic factors to be considered which require a dynamic analysis. Some authors have attempted to identify the point at which a switch will take place from one form of market servicing to another. The 1966 work of Vernon on his product cycle model of international trade and investment[43] indicated that the company would:

$$\text{invest abroad when } MPC_x + TC > APC_A$$

where MPC_x is the marginal cost of production for export, TC represents transport costs to the target market, and APC_A is average cost of production abroad.

In the maturity phase of the product cycle, labour-intensive production would mean lower manufacturing costs abroad and would thus stimulate direct investment in order to protect the market established through exports.

Other contributions in a similar comparative static vein have come from Horst, Hirsch and Aliber;[44] while in 1985 Buckley and Casson presented a model which related the optimal timing of a switch to direct investment to the costs of servicing the foreign market, demand conditions in that market and host market growth.[45] The model, shown in Figure 1.5, illustrates the behaviour of costs (fixed plus variable) for exporting, licensing and foreign direct investment as volume increases.

With exporting, variable costs are high, including variable production costs as well as transport costs internationally and tariff payments: fixed costs will depend on investment in distribution systems, but would be lower than with foreign production. By contrast, foreign direct investment in manufacturing has high fixed but low variable costs, and with this differential cost pattern the firm would switch to investment as market size grows. In the example given in the diagram, licensing is not a preferred alternative at any point, given the assumed combination of relatively high fixed costs (costs of policing the licence plus the licensees' fixed production costs) with moderate variable costs (lower than with exporting because of the avoidance of transport and tariff costs, etc.). There is thus a suggestion that exporting, licensing and foreign direct investment are in ascending order of fixed costs

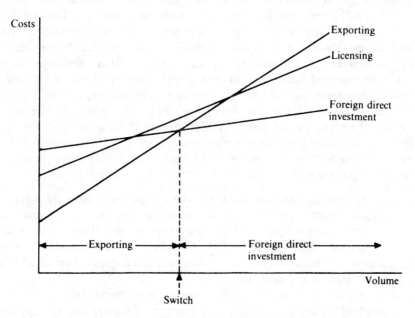

Figure 1.5 The choice between exporting, licensing and foreign direct investment. Source: Buckley, P.J. and Casson, M. (1985), *The Economic Theory of the Multinational Enterprise*, Macmillan, London.

and descending order of variable costs. It is accepted that this is not an invariable rule and would be most likely to apply when the firm was investing abroad for the first time. In fact a model such as this needs to be strongly empirically based to establish the nature and level of fixed and variable costs for the different market-servicing methods and to take market growth, etc., into consideration.

Most recently, the work of economists has appeared to move closer to the approach of business strategy and policy authors, especially in considering strategic and dynamic issues in the choice of process. Dunning, for example, recognises the need to incorporate the strategic behaviour of firms into his eclectic model.[46]

The stages-of-development approach

The analysis of international supply choice has been approached from a different direction, namely, that of stages of development, in work which was initiated in Scandinavia. This 'internationalisation model' suggests an incremental, evolutionary approach to foreign markets with companies gradually deepening their involvement as they gain experience, their perceptions of risk change, and so on. The original research was that undertaken by Johanson and Wiedersheim-Paul in 1975 into the international behaviour of four large Swedish MNEs from their early beginnings.[47] The overseas growth of these firms was distinguished by a series of small cumulative steps, and the establishment of a sales subsidiary was preceded by an agency operation in around three-quarters of cases. This internationalisation model has been extended backwards to explain the commencement of exporting: thus the environment and history of the firm, including experience in extra-regional expansion ('domestic internationalisation') are seen as significant influences.[48] The model has also been extended forward to encompass multinational manufacturing operations, as a stage beyond exporting. For example, one author has characterised the internationalisation process as involving three stages:[49]

1. Experimental involvement stage, where exporting is usually marginal and intermittent. Often, only one or two foreign markets are involved, and exporting is indirect. Where the company takes the initiative, it will target its exports to the psychologically closest country, before extending to countries that are more distant psychologically (see also Chapter 1, page 9 and note 9).
2. Active involvement stage, where the company begins to systematically explore export possibilities in a number of foreign markets. Export activities are no longer considered to be marginal business. An export marketing department may be formed.
3. Committed involvement stage, where the company has a long-run commitment to international marketing.

In this latter case, the internationalisation process may continue with licensing and production facilities in foreign markets. And it would be worthwhile including a fourth stage, viz:

4. Global involvement stage, where the company has a broad international spread of activities, and market-servicing methods differ widely in the pursuit of competitive advantage. Co-ordination of such activities may be high within the framework of corporate globalisation strategy.

The uncertainty over the position of licensing in such models should be noted, as is illustrated in Figure 1.6. Indeed there might be a case for suggesting that licensing is most likely to be used in the last stage of the technology cycle consequent on the standardisation of the product or process. At this point the drive to internalise to retain proprietary know-how is reduced.

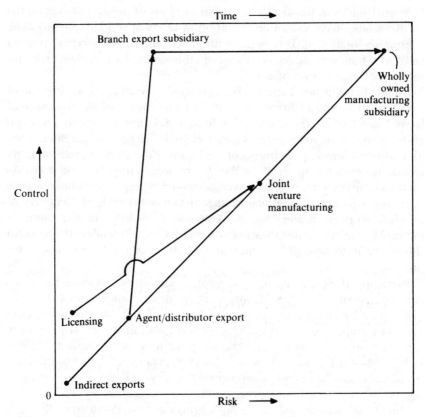

Figure 1.6 Evolution of international supply methods. Source: Root, F.R. (1987), *Entry Strategies for International Markets*, Lexington Books, D.C. Heath and Co., Lexington, Mass., Figure 3.

Evidence from a number of studies exists to support the internationalisation process. Aside from Swedish work which revealed a typical pattern of internationalisation extending from exporting via an agent to the establishment of a sales subsidiary and, finally, to production abroad, Luostarinen and Larimo have produced similar evidence for Finland.[50] Buckley and others, in studies of UK smaller-firm first-time investors and small Continental European investors in the UK, found that only 15 per cent of the combined sample of companies omitted the exporting phase en route to foreign manufacture; and of these one-half were prevented from exporting by the nature of their product – transport costs or a high 'service element' effectively excluded exporting.[51] Despite this evidence, the time period during which a company will remain in any one particular mode may vary quite considerably. For example, Larimo found that before making the manufacturing decision, Finnish firms in his sample had operated in the target country for over twelve years, with a range from one to thirty-six years.[52]

Apart from evolutionary development in terms of method of supply, the Nordic studies have shown an evolution in terms of product offering. The offering to foreign markets began with goods; thereafter, services, systems and know-how were added on a sequential basis until a complete problem-solving package was on offer.[53]

Despite the evidence, there has been growing concern at the assumption of a natural evolution in firms' international expansion. While a number of factors involved in the choice of international supply method are evolutionary in nature, items such as policy changes would produce discontinuities in the operating environment and could, therefore, require a fairly immediate response in terms of the internationalisation method used. As such, a company's development overseas would be expected to be subject to breaks in sequence, the jumping of stages or indeed the reliance on only one or more strategic routes. Again, skills and knowledge in the company increase as the internationalisation process proceeds; this offers the basis for the company to diversify its internationalisation in the later stages of the process.

Reflecting these points, it is possible to cite empirical evidence which scarcely supports the 'stages theory of internationalisation'. For example, a 1983 study by Hood and Young of a sample of 140 American and Continental European subsidiaries in the British Isles found that 44 per cent of them had no involvement in the market prior to direct investment.[54] Similarly a 1984 Australian study revealed that 39 per cent of 228 outward direct investment cases had no pre-existing host-country presence.[55] A speeding up of the internationalisation process was also suggested by the work of Hedlund and Kverneland on Swedish firms entering Japan from the early 1970s.[56]

Research on new trends, particularly as regards high-technology firms, is still in its infancy, but some of the factors of relevance include the following:

1. Cost of R&D and engineering – high-technology products require substantial investment in R&D and engineering. Does this accelerate the internationalisation process so as to achieve rapid global market penetration? And what are the implications for the methods of supply used?

2. Short product life cycles – many high-technology products are also characterised by short product life cycles. Extensive and intensive marketing efforts are required, with simultaneous appeal to various segments. This would seem likely to require a more rapid internationalisation than in the past.

3. For European-based enterprises, the concentration of the market for high-tech products, principally in America but also in Japan, is relevant.

4. Improvements in market knowledge – presumably some of the barriers to internationalisation should have been reduced as companies learn from the experience of others.

5. The education level of high-tech entrepreneurs might be expected to overcome some of the psychological barriers which often exist among would-be international businessmen.

Some exploratory work on this topic was undertaken during 1986 among small, recently established UK high-technology companies.[57] Only one of these companies had been formed before 1970, with the majority being 1980s start-ups. The twenty-one firms in the electronics or biotechnology sectors which were examined, included nine mini-multinationals, with direct investments in both marketing and production, mainly but not totally in the United States. Within the sample firms there were, in addition, a number of outward licensing agreements in West Germany, the USA, India and Australia, one turnkey project and several overseas marketing contracts in which marketing for the UK firm was handled by a larger multinational located abroad. While comparisons are not possible with UK MNEs of the past, it is very unlikely that the latter companies would have gone abroad at such an early stage of their development as the present high-tech firms; or indeed be involved in such variety in their internationalisation methods.

With the empirical evidence showing considerable diversity in firms' internationalisation, the stages-of-development model has come in for substantial criticism. The approach is descriptive rather than explanatory, and in the dynamic and turbulent environment of the 1970s and 1980s it would be hardly surprising to find that firms have to respond more flexibly and react more quickly than when environmental conditions were stable and predictable.

Business-strategy approach

Reviewing the two approaches discussed to this juncture, it can be said that the economics viewpoint stresses rational choice, with an emphasis on the costs and benefits of using internal markets (and achieving control) and recently on the ability to achieve the advantages of internalisation through joint ventures and other collaborative arrangements; while the stages-of-development approach has focused upon the evolution to more direct forms of foreign servicing over time, almost on an inevitable basis. The weakness of the former is its static nature, and the weakness of the latter is its lack of explanation.

The alternative is to take a pragmatic stance stressing the nature of decisionmaking within organisations. In such an approach, companies may indeed follow something like the conventional corporate planning model, as noted earlier in this chapter, even if in the smaller enterprise this is not systematic or documented. However, such a model assumes a 'rational–analytical' approach to business policy, which many writers in the latter literature have argued is inconsistent with the reality of decisionmaking in organisations.[58] Alternative models have thus been developed in the business policy literature such as Simon's 'satisficing' and Lindblom's 'muddling through'.[59] Such models lay stress upon vested interests within the firm, consensus seeking, disjointed approaches to taking decisions and in general the political nature of policymaking.

These concepts are perhaps particularly relevant in the context of international market-servicing decisions, where the signals from volatile foreign environments may be open to various interpretations, where decisionmakers have different perceptions of risk, where political factors in home and host countries need to be considered, and so on. It could, of course, be argued that such problems encourage incrementalism and evolutionary approaches. But at least this perspective brings in additional elements in both internal and external environments which need to be considered, with a stress on risk and perceptions of risk. Among these are the following:

1. Internal environmental factors
   (a) organisational structure and capacity;
   (b) administrative co-ordination inside the firm;
   (c) management culture and attitudes;
   (d) management and personnel resources.
2. External environmental factors
   (a) country risk (political instability, economic fluctuations, currency changes);
   (b) strategies of competitors (including market-servicing strategies).

Introducing such factors allows the possibility of explaining both cautious risk-minimising behaviour and abrupt shifts in international supply methods.

And it is interesting that the work of some economists has been moving in this direction in trying to take a more dynamic approach to mode choice.[60] It is also interesting that when the various approaches discussed above are brought together, a balance between risk, control and motivation emerges: these, it will be recalled, were the key distinguishing characteristics of the alternative international supply methods.

FURTHER READING

1. Oman, C. (1984), *New Forms of International Investment in Developing Countries*, OECD, Paris. This is an important contribution in highlighting the 'new forms' and their incidence in particular developing countries. A summary with some new ideas is Oman, C. (1986), 'Changing International Investment Strategies in the North – South Context', *The CTC Reporter*, No. 22, Autumn, 47 – 50, 55.
2. Readers interested in a brief overview of the topic of business strategy, internationalisation and globalisation might refer to Young, S. (1987), 'Business Strategy and the Internationalisation of Business: Recent Approaches', *Managerial and Decision Economics*, **8**, 31–40. On globalisation, specifically see Hamel, G. and Prahalad, C.K. (1988), 'Creating Global Strategic Capability', in Hood, N. and Vahlne, J.-E. (eds), *Strategies in Global Competition*, Croom Helm, London, 5 – 39. There is also a very clear article by Leontiades, J. (1986), 'Going Global – Global Strategies vs National Strategies', *Long Range Planning*, **19**(6), 96 – 104.
3. The forms of international market entry and development are covered briefly in most international marketing and international business texts. For example:
   Terpstra, V. (1987), *International Marketing*, Dryden Press, New York, 4th edition, Chapter 10.
   Paliwoda, S.J. (1986), *International Marketing*, Heinemann, London, Chapter 4.
   Keegan, W.J. (1984), *Multinational Marketing Management*, Prentice Hall International, Hemel Hempstead, 3rd edition, Chapter 10.
4. See also Buckley, P.J. (1985), 'New Forms of International Industrial Co-operation', in Buckley, P.J. and Casson, M. (eds), *The Economic Theory of the Multinational Enterprise: Selected Readings*, Macmillan, London.
5. For a consideration of the economics approach to international market entry and development consult Buckley, P.J. (1985), 'A Critical View of Theories of the Multinational Enterprise' in Buckley and Casson, ibid.; and Dunning, J.H. (1988), 'The Eclectic Paradigm of International Production: A Restatement and Some Possible Extensions', *Journal of International Business Studies*, **19**(1), 1 – 31.

QUESTIONS FOR DISCUSSION

1. It is suggested in the Summary that 'internationalisation is . . . almost inevitable if corporate expansion goals are to be achieved'. Why is this? Under what circumstances might long-term growth be possible through domestic expansion alone?
2. Environmental factors are commonly divided into broad groupings, such as political, social and cultural, demographic, geographic, political, government and legal, technological, and competitive variables. Identify some of the major features of the present-day world economy within each of these categories, and show how

each will influence the form of international market entry and development strategy employed by firms.
3. Show how the forms of international market entry and development in Figure 1.3 will differ according to the following characteristics:

locus of control (high/low)	time limited (yes/no)
resource commitment (large/small)	space limited (yes/no)
resources transferred (complete/part of package)	payment methods (conventional/ unconventional)

4. Consider some of the similarities and differences in the predictions of the economics, stages-of-development and business-strategy approaches in relation to international market development mode.
5. Assess the circumstances under which several market-servicing methods may be employed together in foreign projects. Provide current examples if possible.

NOTES AND REFERENCES

1. Hood, N. and Young, S. (1979), *The Economics of Multinational Enterprise*, Longman, London.
2. For example, Hood, N. and Vahlne, J.-E. (1988), *Strategies in Global Competition*, Croom Helm, London; Porter, M.E. (ed.) (1986), *Competition in Global Industries*, Harvard Business School Press, Boston, Mass.; Lessem, R. (1987), *The Global Business*, Prentice Hall, Hemel Hempstead.
3. Business International Corporation (1986), *A Guide to Corporate Survival and Growth. The New Thinking*, BIC, New York, June.
4. Oman, C. (1984), *New Forms of International Investment in Developing Countries*, OECD, Paris.
5. The SPRINT programme relates specifically to small and medium-sized enterprises and relates to all aspects of innovation – from invention to the financing and successful marketing of new products and services. The most important thrust concerns the promotion of transnational exchanges of technology. The BRITE (Basic Research in Industrial Technologies for Europe) initiative has the objective of encouraging cross-frontier co-operation among firms of all sizes within the Community in industrial R&D projects. ESPRIT (European Strategic Programme for Research and Development in Information Technology) was adopted in 1984 as a five-year programme to fund collaborative research between companies and other bodies in member states of the EC in five areas of information technology. EUREKA is yet another EC programme for promoting collaborative projects in fields of advanced technology including information technology and telecommunications, robotics, materials, advanced manufacturing, biotechnology, marine technology and lasers: the scheme was launched in November 1985.
6. Jones, S.F. (1984), *North/South Countertrade*, Special Report No. 174, The Economist Intelligence Unit, London.
7. Snowden, P.N. (1987), 'International Equity Investment in Less Developed Countries' Stockmarkets: The Replacement for Bank Lending?', *National Westminster Bank Quarterly Review*, February, 29–38.
8. Adapted and extended from Johnson, G. and Scholes, K. (1984), *Exploring Corporate Strategy*, Prentice Hall, Hemel Hempstead, Fig. 7.1. See also Glueck, W.F. and Jauch, L.R. (1984), *Business Policy and Strategic Management*, McGraw-Hill, New York, 4th edition.

9. The concept of 'psychic distance' was developed first in Scandinavia. See, for example, Vahlne, J.-E. and Wiedersheim-Paul, F. (1977), *Psychic Distance – An Inhibiting Factor in International Trade*, Working Paper 1977/2, Centre for International Business Studies, University of Uppsala.

10. On the concentration v. spreading issue, see BETRO Trust Committee (1976), *Concentration on Key Markets*, 2nd edition, Royal Society of Arts, London.

11. Wind, Y. and Perlmutter, H. (1977), 'On the Identification of Frontier Issues in International Marketing', *Columbia Journal of World Business*, 12, 131–9.

12. Buckley, P.J. and Casson, M. (1985), *The Economic Theory of the Multinational Enterprise*, Macmillan, London. The actual quotation is in Buckley, P.J., Mirza, H. and Sparkes, J.R. (1987), 'Direct Foreign Investment in Japan as a Means of Market Entry: The Case of European Firms', *Journal of Marketing Management*, 2(3), 241.

13. Anderson, E. and Gatignon, H. (1986), 'Modes of Foreign Entry: A Transaction Cost Analysis and Propositions', *Journal of International Business Studies*, 17(3), 1–26.

14. It is in fact worth questioning this generalisation. Construction exporters engaged in building large infrastructure projects are subject to very substantial risk – at the extreme leading to project cancellation. Exchange-rate factors, import controls, etc., represent further risks.

15. The term 'exportise' is used in seminars for exporters run by the Bank of Scotland.

16. See Millman, A.F. (1983), 'Licensing Technology', *Management Decision*, 21(3); and Etele, A. (1985), 'Licensing and the Pricing of Technology', *Management Decision*, 22(3).

17. See Brooke, M.Z. (1985), *Selling Management Services Contracts in International Business*, Holt, Rinehart and Winston, London.

18. Brooke, M.Z. and Buckley, P.J. (1982–86), *Handbook of International Trade*, Kluwer, London.

19. United Nations Centre on Transnational Corporations (UNCTC) (1983), *Transnational Corporations in World Development, Third Survey*, New York. Please note that the United Nations have now published *Transnational Corporations in World Development. Trends and Prospects*, 1989.

20. Wright, R.W. (1981), 'Evolving International Business Arrangements', in Dhawan, K.C., Etemad, H. and Wright, R.W. (eds), *International Business: A Canadian Perspective*, Addison-Wesley, Don Mills, Ontario.

21. Buckley, P.J. (1983), 'New Forms of Industrial Co-operation: A Survey of the Literature with Special Reference to North–South Technology Transfer', *Aussenwirtschaft*, 38(2), 195–222.

22. Related types of arrangement in natural resources include production sharing contracts and risk service contracts.

23. Oman, C. (1984), *New Forms of International Investment in Developing Countries*, OECD, Paris.

24. Sukijasovic, M. (1970), 'Foreign Investment in Yugoslavia', in Litvak, I.A. and Maule, C.J. (eds), *Foreign Investment: The Experience of Host Countries*, Praeger, New York and London.

25. For example, Harrigan, K.R. (1984), 'Joint Ventures and Global Strategies', *Columbia Journal of World Business*, Summer, 7–16; Connolly, S.G. (1984), 'Joint Ventures with Third World Multinationals: A New Form of Entry to International Markets', *Columbia Journal of World Business*, Summer, 18–22.

26. Evidence is cited in Young, S., Hood, N. and Hamill, J. (1988), *Foreign Multinationals and the British Economy*, Croom Helm, London, Chapter 2.

27. National Economic Development Office (1987), *Corporate Venturing. A Strategy for Innovation and Growth*, NEDO, London.

28. Davidson, W.H. (1982), *Global Strategic Management*, John Wiley, New York.
29. Anderson, E. and Gatignon, H. (1986), 'Modes of Foreign Entry: A Transaction Cost Analysis and Propositions', *Journal of International Business Studies*, 17(3), 1–26.
30. Stern, L.W. and El-Ansary, A. (1982), *Marketing Channels*, Prentice Hall Inc., Englewood Cliffs, N.J., cited in Anderson and Gatignon, 'Modes of Foreign Entry: A Transaction Cost Analysis and Propositions', 6.
31. Discussed fully in Buckley, 'New Forms of Industrial Co-operation', 202–5.
32. 'Depackaging' means that instead of taking the entire package of resources through the MNE, the host government tries to obtain only the particular elements which it requires, e.g. technology. 'Repackaging' entails assembling resource components from different sources.
33. Porter, M.E. and Fuller, M.B. (1987), 'Coalitions and Global Strategy', in Porter (ed.), *Competition in Global Industries*. See also, Buckley, P.J. and Casson, M. (1987), *A Theory of Co-operation in International Business*, University of Reading Discussion Papers in International Investment and Business Studies No. 102, January.
34. *Financial Times* (1987), 'Technology Transfer', 10 November. The year referred to was 1986.
35. See Buckley, 'New Forms of Industrial Co-operation', 205–7.
36. For a review of early contributions, see Hood and Young, *The Economics of Multinational Enterprise*, Chapter 2.
37. Buckley, P.J. and Casson, M. (1976), *The Future of the Multinational Enterprise*, Macmillan, London.
38. Subsequently published in Ohlin, B., Hesselborn, P.O. and Wiskman, P.M. (eds) (1977), *The International Allocation of Economic Activity*, Macmillan, London.
39. Dunning, J.H. (1988), 'The Eclectic Paradigm of International Production: A Restatement and Some Possible Extensions', *Journal of International Business Studies*, 19(1), 1–31.
40. Ibid., 3.
41. Casson, M. (1982), 'Transaction Costs and the Theory of the Multinational Enterprise', in Rugman, A.M. (ed.), *New Theories of the Multinational Enterprise*, Croom Helm, London; Rugman, A.M. (1985), 'Internationalization is still a General Theory of Foreign Direct Investment', *Weltwirtschaftliches Archiv*, September; Hennart, J.-F. (1982), *A Theory of Multinational Enterprise*, University of Michigan Press, Ann Arbor; Teece, D.J. (1983), 'Multinational Enterprise, Internal Governance and Market Power Considerations', *The American Economic Review*, 75(2), 233–8.
42. Beamish, P.W. and Banks, J.C. (1987), 'Equity Joint Ventures and the Theory of the Multinational Enterprise', *Journal of International Business Studies*, 18(2), 1–16; the quotation is from p. 4.
43. Vernon, R. (1966), 'International Investment and International Trade in the Product Cycle', *Quarterly Journal of Economics*, 80, 190–207.
44. Horst, T.O. (1971), 'The Theory of the Multinational Firm – Optimal Behaviour under Different Tax and Tariff Rates', *Journal of Political Economy*, 79(5), 1059–72; Hirsch, S. (1976), 'An International Trade and Investment Theory of the Firm', *Oxford Economic Papers*, 28, 258–70; Aliber, R.Z. (1970), 'A Theory of Direct Foreign Investment', in Kindleberger, C.P. (ed.), *The International Corporation*, MIT Press, Cambridge, Mass.
45. Buckley and Casson, *The Economic Theory of the Multinational Enterprise*, Chapter 5.
46. Dunning, 'The Eclectic Paradigm of International Production. . .', 6–8.

47. Johanson, J. and Wiedersheim-Paul, F. (1975), 'The Internationalization of the Firm: Four Swedish Cases', *Journal of Management Studies*, **12**(3), 305–22.
48. Wiedersheim-Paul, F., Olson, H.C. and Welch, L.S. (1978), 'Pre-export Activity: The First Step in Internationalization', *Journal of International Business Studies*, **9**, Spring/Summer, 47–58.
49. Cavusgil, S.T. (1980), 'On the Internationalisation Process of Firms', *European Research*, **8**(6), 273–81.
50. Luostarinen, R. (1979), *The Internationalization of the Firm*, Acta Academic Oeconomicae Helsingiensis, Helsinki; Larimo, J. (1985), 'The Foreign Direct Investment Behaviour of Finnish Companies', paper presented at the 11th European International Business Association Conference, Glasgow, 15–17 December.
51. Buckley, P.J., Newbould, G.D. and Thurwell, J. (1979), 'Going International – The Foreign Direct Investment Behaviour of Smaller UK Firms', in Mattsson, L.G. and Wiedersheim-Paul, F. (eds), *Recent Research on the Internationalisation of Business*, Almquist and Wicksell, Stockholm.
52. Larimo, J. (1985), 'The Foreign Direct Investment Behaviour of Finnish Companies', paper presented at the 11th European International Business Association Conference, Glasgow, 15–17 December.
53. Luostarinen, *The Internationalization of the Firm*, 95–105. See also Hornell, E. and Vahlne, J.-E. (1982), *The Changing Structure of Swedish Multinational Companies*, Working Paper 1982/12, Centre for International Business Studies, University of Uppsala.
54. Hood, N. and Young, S. (1983), *Multinational Investment Strategies in the British Isles: A Study of MNEs in the Assisted Areas and in the Republic of Ireland*, HMSO, London, Part 4, Chapter 1.
55. Bureau of Industry Economics (1984), *Australian Direct Investment Abroad*, Australian Government Publicity Service, Canberra.
56. Hedlund, G. and Kverneland, A. (1984), *Are Establishment and Growth Patterns for Foreign Markets Changing? The Case of Swedish Investment in Japan*, Institute of International Business, Stockholm School of Economics.
57. Young, S. (1987), 'Business Strategy and the Internationalization of Business', *Managerial and Decision Economics*, **8**(1), 31–40.
58. See Hogwood, B.W. and Gunn, L.A. (1984), *Policy Analysis for the Real World*, Oxford University Press.
59. Simon, H.A. (1960), *The New Science of Management Decision*, Prentice-Hall, New York; Lindblom, C.E. (1979), 'Still Muddling. Not Yet Through', *Public Administration Review*, **39**, 517–26.
60. Nicholas, S.J. (1986), *Multinationals, Transaction Costs and Choice of Institutional Form*, University of Reading Discussion Papers in International Investment and Business Studies No. 97, September; Casson, M. (ed.) (1986), *Multinationals and World Trade*, Allen and Unwin, London.

2

IDENTIFYING OVERSEAS OPPORTUNITIES

SUMMARY

1. Poor country/market choice can have far-reaching effects on the firm. A lot of money, management time and other resources of a firm are expended in entering and developing a new market, all of which are wasted if the company has to withdraw at a later stage. Company profits are reduced and failure is evident.
2. The situation is compounded where the company fails to identify suitable countries/markets. Resources that could have been used to develop more promising opportunities yield a low return on investment in difficult countries/markets. The lack of a systematic country/market screening system for a company can lead to poor performance and profits.
3. Country/market screening methods range from the extremely complex and costly to the simple and easy to use. The most comprehensive systems require data to be collected and analysed on a large number of variables for each country. This entails considerable expense over a period of weeks or months. Other methods are quicker and cheaper as they employ more subjective criteria and less information has to be collected.
4. Many firms do not carry out much, if any, market research and do not use a country/market screening system. For these companies, the 'rational-analytical' approach to decisionmaking mentioned in Chapter 1 is inconsistent with the reality of decisionmaking. Decisions can be dominated by highly subjective factors such as decisionmakers' personalities, expectations, perceptions of risk and uncertainty as well as lack of information.
5. There is evidence that as companies become more committed to international markets the nature of decisionmaking changes, becoming highly systematic and informed. Also studies have shown that successful firms do use country/market screening methods of various types and have systematic, methodical approaches to markets outside their home country.

INTRODUCTION

For a company considering internationalisation, the first step is the evaluation of the marketability of the company's products outside its home base and, associated with this, the choice of market or markets to enter. The two issues are directly related, of course, since a country screening process will soon make it clear whether or not sales possibilities can be ruled out because of, say, taste or regulatory differences, the strength of competition, and so forth. The question of whether countries identified as promising prospects can be serviced profitably will, however, require more detailed investigation as part of the process of deciding on entry strategies, setting up distribution and the like. At this stage, the company probably has in mind the export form of internationalisation, although as it iterates towards the decision to go abroad, this view may of necessity have to change. In any event, there are about 160 countries that could be considered and evaluated with vast amounts of information available (even if highly costly to collect and analyse). Collecting appropriate information can have an important role in reducing perceptions of risk in international operations arising from managers' lack of familiarity with overseas markets and the higher level of uncertainty in international business. But the company has to be selective.

In reality, the problem is not so great as it appears: executives in most enterprises will have their own preferences, predilections and biases which correctly or incorrectly will dramatically reduce the number of potential target countries. To give an illustration, in a study of medium-sized electronics companies in the UK, the managing directors of one firm commented that they originally had several ideas for a new business, but the vital criterion for choosing which product to launch was that it should have a chance of succeeding in the US market.[1] Immediately, the number of target markets is reduced to one!

The difficulty with basing country selection on hunch or personal preference is that it stands a good chance of being wrong, to be followed by costly withdrawal. Acorn Computers' withdrawal from the US market in 1984 was estimated to have cost £6m. The company, which had sales of £93m, of which more than 90 per cent were in the UK, blamed the aggressively competitive reactions of Apple, the American computer company, and delays in obtaining product approval from the American Federal Communications Commission (FCC): 'A change in rules by the FCC meant the company had to modify its computers. This delayed entry into the market by nearly eight months and the changes were made after it had spent more than £500,000 on promotion.'[2]

To try to reduce the likelihood of costly mistakes, identifying suitable market opportunities should, therefore, be an integral component of the international marketing process. In an ideal situation, the marketing planning process identified in Figure 2.1 would be undertaken and would emerge from the company's overall business strategy as discussed in Chapter 1.[3] The formalised marketing planning process depicted in Figure 2.1 has four phases. Phase 1 is the preliminary analysis and screening of countries, matching data on home- and host-country constraints with an analysis of

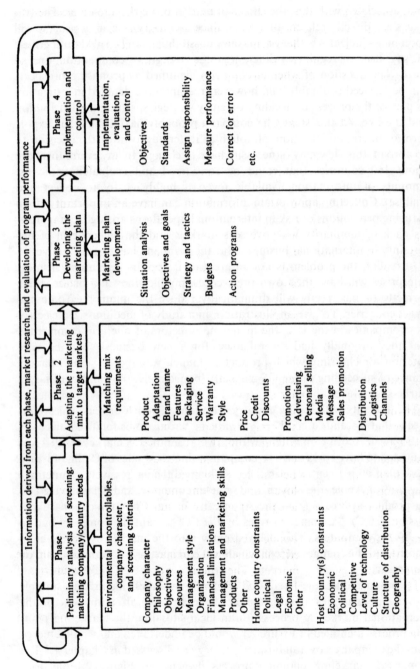

Figure 2.1 International marketing planning process. Source: Cateora, P.R. (1987), *International Marketing*, 6th edition, Irwin, Homewood, III, Exhibit 3-3.

Information derived from each phase, market research, and evaluation of program performance

Phase 1
Preliminary analysis and screening: matching company/country needs

Phase 2
Adapting the marketing mix to target markets

Phase 3
Developing the marketing plan

Phase 4
Implementation and control

Environmental uncontrollables, company character, and screening criteria

Company character
Philosophy
Objectives
Resources
Management style
Organization
Financial limitations
Management and marketing skills
Products
Other

Home country constraints
Political
Legal
Economic
Other

Host country(s) constraints
Economic
Political
Competitive
Level of technology
Culture
Structure of distribution
Geography

Matching mix requirements

Product
Adaptation
Brand name
Features
Packaging
Service
Warranty
Style

Price
Credit
Discounts

Promotion
Advertising
Personal selling
Media
Message
Sales promotion

Distribution
Logistics
Channels

Marketing plan development

Situation analysis

Objectives and goals

Strategy and tactics

Budgets

Action programs

Implementation, evaluation, and control

Objectives

Standards

Assign responsibility

Measure performance

Correct for error

etc.

company characteristics and requirements. In Phase 2, the firm assesses the requirements for adapting the various marketing mix element, product, price, promotion and distribution, to meet the needs of the target markets identified. Phases 3 and 4, concern the development, implementation and control of marketing strategy in individual markets.

COUNTRY/MARKET SCREENING METHODS

This section attempts to review the alternative methods which are available for screening countries and markets. The distinction between countries and markets is an important one because, firstly, real market differences may be unrelated to political boundaries (the Scandinavian countries are treated as a relatively homogeneous market by some firms); and, secondly, small and medium-sized firms do not have the resources to develop profitable operations on a national scale in the largest countries. For example, most companies would be ill-advised to treat the whole of the USA as one market, but would do better to develop on a regional (and not necessarily state) basis, recognising that each area is a market in its own right, and, indeed, comparable in size with countries elsewhere.

A formal approach

Typical of the highly systematic data-sifting approach associated with formal marketing planning is that illustrated in Figure 2.2.[4] It has been indicated that this book is primarily concerned with smaller and medium-sized companies and new entrants to foreign markets. Such firms are unlikely to follow this type of approach to country/market screening which is more usually associated with experienced exporters and multinational firms. The value of considering this, nevertheless, lies in showing how a formal, systematic approach would be employed, and in setting the standard against which the more superficial evaluation procedures can be judged.

Stage 1: Preliminary screening criteria
Here the firm is seeking criteria which will eliminate some countries from the list of 160 or so possible markets. The criteria are ones that make countries of no interest to the firm. Two types of attributes are distinguished:

1. Restrictions or bans on the sale of goods such as the Arab boycott of companies trading with Israel.
2. Specific criteria drawn up by the company for the elimination of countries. These may be product-related as in the case of motorcycle and crash helmet manufacturers who decide that the prohibitively expensive insurance against customers' lawsuits in the United States

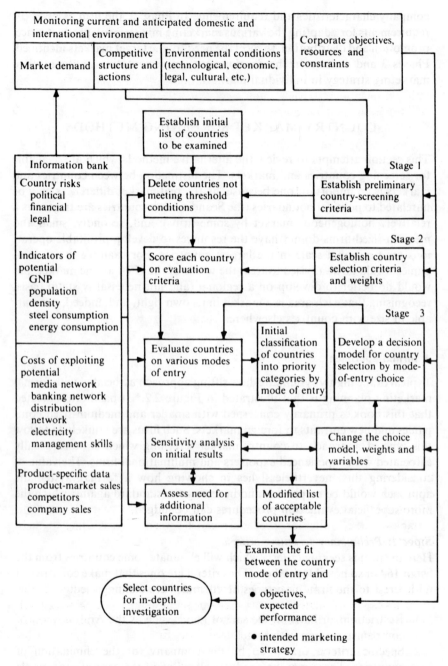

Figure 2.2 A formal approach to country/market screening. Source: Douglas, S.P. and Craig, C.S. (1983), *International Marketing Research*, Prentice Hall Inc., Englewood Cliffs, N.J., Figure 4.2

precludes consideration of that country. Religious and cultural reasons may limit markets served. Sales of alcohol and pork will be limited in Muslim countries. The key point is that the criteria are grounds for dropping a country from the list. Companies in the same industry may not use the same criteria, as the outlook of management and their attitude towards risk-taking will vary from firm to firm. Another criterion used by companies to eliminate countries is political risk. Companies tend to avoid countries judged a poor political risk, preferring to operate in 'safe' countries.

Stage 2: Selecting variables and determining weights for evaluating countries
The company has to select and weight variables relevant to the selection decision. Four types of variables should be considered:

1. The market potential and growth of the country and of the specific product market.
2. The strength of potential competition.
3. The risks associated with operating in a given national or product market. These might be:
   (a) political factors, e.g. internal political stability;
   (b) legal factors, e.g. restrictions on ownership;
   (c) financial factors, e.g. foreign exchange risk and the rate of inflation;
   (d) the costs of operating in a country, e.g. labour costs, tax rates and investment grants.

Once these variables have been selected, management should weight them; depending on management perceptions, of course, the same variable may have different weights in different companies. Weights can be assigned in different ways. One method is for managers to judge criteria themselves and then meet as a group to finally agree on weightings. The weights can be expressed using a number of methods, from rank ordering to interval scales. Although no market entry strategy will be determined at this stage, the variables in the evaluation procedure can be weighted according to their importance for different entry modes.

Stage 3: Country evaluation
With the relevant information gathered and the weightings assigned, the countries can be evaluated. If more than one set of weights is used, whichever set gives a country the highest score should be used. The resultant rank ordering of countries is examined and a list of countries which will be researched in more detail is drawn up. There is no hard-and-fast rule about how many countries would be evaluated at this stage. Much depends on the objectives of the firm, the specific criteria used, and, inevitably, the time and resources available.

One final check should be made on the weightings before detailed research begins. Sensitivity analysis can be used to assess the effects of changes in weighting values on the rank ordering of countries, especially to identify where small changes result in a major change in the rank ordering. It is at this point, of course, that management need to link the quantitative evaluations to any relevant qualitative information of which they are aware (the stress is on 'relevant' qualitative information rather than hearsay or personal bias).

Screening for small and medium-sized enterprises

Technique no. 1

Although small and medium-sized companies could not expect to undertake such an elaborate and costly country/market screening process as that outlined in the preceding paragraphs, Douglas, Craig and Keegan have proposed a modified form of the above based on access to secondary data sources. This would need to be 'customised' to specific company circumstances, so that, for example, a firm marketing minicomputers might be concerned with the number of banking and financial institutions and associated variables; whereas a firm marketing expensive knitwear would be interested in purchasing power, climate, distribution channels, and so forth. Douglas, Craig and Keenan suggest that a two-stage process could be handled in the following way.[5] The first stage is a subjective evaluation based on the use of preliminary screening criteria for the elimination of a number of countries. The second stage involves evaluating market opportunities in more detail using indicators, considered specific to the industry, as follows:

1. Market size and growth potential.
2. Competition.
3. Risk associated with operating in a given national or product market.
4. Factors relating to the costs of operating in the country.
5. Access and availability of channels of distribution and media.

Useful indicators of risk could be the number of coups in a country, or the likelihood of a government coming to power that would restrict business activities. Indicators of the cost of operating in a country could be the stage of development of transport systems, the cost of labour and availability of skills. Table 2.1 lists some of the relevant indicators of market potential.

Countries could be evaluated on the types of indicators listed below in several ways. Minimum levels could be set and countries not meeting these could be discarded. Alternatively, countries could be weighted on each criterion to produce an aggregate score for each country and thus establish a rank order of countries. The company then chooses one or more countries to investigate in detail. It is important for the company to check that countries selected appear to be consistent with the initial management objectives set. Where this is not the case, it is likely that the indicators chosen are not sufficiently relevant to the company or the specific product market.

Table 2.1 Business and market environment indicators

Indicators of market potential

1. Demographic characteristics
   size of population
   rate of population growth
   degree of urbanisation
   population density
   age structure and composition
   of the population

2. Geographic characteristics
   physical size of a country
   topographical characteristics
   climate conditions

3. Economic factors
   GNP per capita
   income distribution
   rate of growth of GNP
   rates of investment to GNP

4. Technological factors
   level of technological skill
   existing production technology
   existing consumption technology
   education levels

5. Socio-cultural factors
   dominant values
   life-style patterns
   ethnic groups
   linguistic fragmentation

6. National goals and plans
   industry priorities
   infrastructure investment plans

Source: Douglas, S.P. and Craig, C.S. (1983), *International Marketing Research*, Prentice Hall, Inc., Englewood Cliffs, N.J.

Technique no. 2

Even the above approach can be too complex and an example of an even simpler method is given in Figure 2.3. This shows the results of a market screening process undertaken to identify, in a preliminary way, market opportunities for Scottish architects abroad.[6] The assessment was carried out using desk research related to four main factors:

1. General economic indicators.
2. Levels of construction activity.
3. Levels of economic and political risk.
4. Competition.

The matrix in Figure 2.3 categorises countries by ease/difficulty of competing in the foreign market and by the level of risk in each market, producing six groups of countries, with Saudi Arabia, United Arab Emirates (UAE), Hong Kong, Brunei and Malaysia as the most promising group in this particular instance. In these latter countries a significant number of Scottish and UK architects, engineers and other consultants are already active. Although competitive pressures are still great, in these markets Scottish entrants would start off with the advantage that not only are fellow countrymen already present, but these countries are generally favourably disposed towards the UK. By contrast, despite low risk, many European countries would present considerable difficulties for market penetration: the architects' profession is strong in these nations and their skills match those of the UK profession. Japan, South Korea and Brazil were regarded as even more difficult because of strong protectionist policies, meaning that foreign consultants would be used only when no local skills existed.

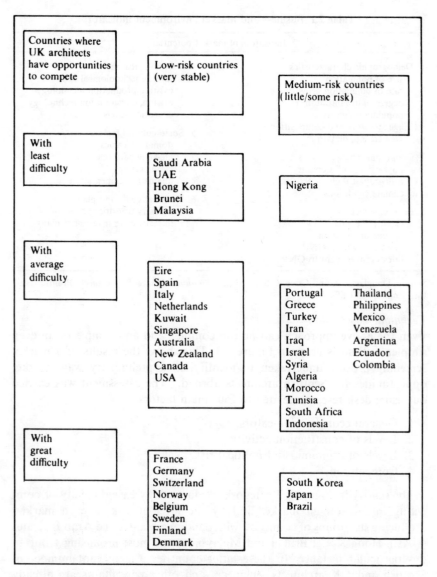

Figure 2.3 Countries where potential for construction and general economic factors are most favourable. Source: Scottish Development Agency (1986), *The Marketing of Scottish Architects – Worldwide*, SDA, Glasgow.

Technique No. 3

For the smaller company, a simple yet effective approach to market selection is the 'simple elimination' method proposed by Cannon and Willis.[7] What the company does is to eliminate countries successively according to certain criteria until a small group is left. The criteria fall into four groups:

1. Company-specific factors.
2. Economic evaluation.
3. Market conditions.
4. Competitive evaluation.

Company-specific factors.   These criteria reflect the preferences and characteristics of the management. The type of criteria could include the following:

1. English is an acceptable business language.
2. The country does not have a different working week, e.g. Saturday to Wednesday in Muslim countries.
3. Close proximity to the home market. To give an illustration, a UK manufacturer of adjustable shelving for houses, shops and factories prefers to export to markets close to its home country because the shelving is a heavy steel product that is price sensitive and costly to ship. The company exports mainly to EC countries closest to the UK like Belgium, the Netherlands, Germany and France. Some exports go as far afield as Hong Kong but distant markets are best served by local manufacture (see Exhibit 2.1).

EXHIBIT 2.1
SUCCESS FROM A SIMPLE PRODUCT

A small British company with a chequered history of high-technology work is now finding life-saving export success in a simple product line found in most houses, shops and factories.

The company is Savage Industries, long known as a manufacturer of aircraft navigational equipment. But in recent years, it has abandoned such work and has shifted its resources into the full-scale manufacture of adjustable shelving.

The shelving, produced under the corporate name of Spur Systems International, and a small number of associated products, last year accounted for a turnover of £3.6m, nearly 37 per cent of which came from Continental sales.

The company's success is somewhat fortuitous. For many years, Spur adjustable shelving was manufactured only as a secondary item to subsidise development of high-technology equipment.

But as Mr David Brown, the company's recently appointed chief executive, said, the general jobbing of components for the engineering business became impractical; Savage Industries put its efforts into reorganising itself around its shelf-making Spur unit, bringing to an end nearly five decades' work on the engineering field.

A private company under the chairmanship of Mr Nicholas Savage, son of the founder, the company is based at Watford, where it has a factory and administrative staff of ninety-seven.

Exhibit 2.1 continued

The number of employees is 25 per cent fewer than fourteen months ago, and this is a direct result of the reorganisation begun in 1979–80 with a £600,000 re-equipment and modernisation of the production plant.

The setting up of a new management team under Mr Savage began in 1980. This has recently been rounded off with the appointment of Mr Brown as chief executive, and Mr F.R. Holloway as marketing director.

Because Spur shelving is basically a weighty steel product that is price-sensitive and costly to ship, the company thinks of direct exports largely in terms of those EC countries closest to the UK, such as the Netherlands, Belgium, where Spur has been active for many years, and Germany and France, both of which are newer markets.

There have been a few one-off deals with retail concerns in Switzerland, Austria and even Hong Kong, but these further-flung markets are thought best served through local manufacture of Spur products under licence. The company is seeking such opportunities in the longer term.

The success of Spur's product on the Continent has come at a time of widespread modernisation of the retail trade and the boom in the do-it-yourself (DIY) market.

Although adjustable shelving is nothing new, the company feels its own double-hook brackets and rails, probably the most durable in the trade, will enable it to increase its sales.

Mr Brown pointed out that the Dutch market most closely resembles that of the UK, with 75 per cent of Spur's sales going to supply shelving to the retail trade and 25 per cent to the DIY consumer. The exact opposite is true in Belgium, often described as the most house-proud nation in Western Europe.

The company is aware of the dangers of over-centralisation of supply, and over-concentration on a single product line.

It has recently set up subsidiaries in the Netherlands and Germany and, after considerable debate, decided to boost its sales efforts in France. Along with Germany, France is a potentially rich market, but its buyer groups are more tightly organised, making it tougher to enter in a big way.

The company has learned the importance of reliability of supply. It maintains warehouses in Europe and tops up its inventory from Watford once a month.

Equitable pricing is also important – this was not easy to achieve in the last year with the volatility of sterling, though Mr Brown says the current softer rate of exchange against Continental currencies is 'just about right'.

As a result of a recent Dutch acquisition, Spur is putting a strong marketing effort into Robox, a multi-purpose wall-storage system, largely for hanging any DIY handyman's tools. Spur unveiled Robox at last month's hardware exhibit in Utrecht and in recent weeks, at exhibitions in Cologne and Birmingham.

Other products now being sold by Spur are sorting trays often used in medical centres and workshops and marketed under the name Spur Kit, and Alu-Spur, a single-hook aluminium adjustable shelf bracket produced under licence from a US company.

Mr Brown sees the UK market as steady, but predicts a rise in turnover to £4m this year, as a result of stronger Continental sales.

Sales volume, he hopes, will climb 10–20 per cent next year, on the assumption the recession has begun to ease and more discretionary spending money is in circulation.

Source: *Financial Times*, 23 February 1982.

Using the first criterion, namely 'English as an acceptable business language', Figure 2.4 illustrates how countries are reduced in number; and if more than one criterion is used then the list is reduced further.

Economic evaluation. Usually there will still be too many countries at this stage, so economic criteria relevant to the company will further shorten the list. Figure 2.5 shows the effect of applying one such criterion, viz. 'advanced developed economies'.

| 149 members of
the UN | *Eliminate*
COMECON, China, Indo-China, France, Spain, Portugal, former French, Spanish and Portuguese possessions, Greece, Turkey, Middle East, South America, Indonesia |
| | *Leaves*
Australia, Canada, Benelux, Bangladesh, Eire, India, New Zealand, Pakistan, Scandinavia, USA, West Germany, former British possessions in Africa, Hong Kong, Singapore, Korea, Japan, Taiwan, Malaysia |

Figure 2.4 Using the criterion 'English as an acceptable language'. Source: Cannon, T. and Willis, M. (1985), *How to Buy and Sell Overseas*, Hutchinson, London.

149 members of the UN		
	Company-specific criterion (Fig. 2.4) leaves in all the countries where English is the acceptable business language	*Eliminate* Bangladesh, India, Pakistan, former British African possessions, Korea
		Leaves Australia, Canada, Benelux, Eire, New Zealand, Scandinavia, USA, West Germany, Singapore, Japan, Taiwan

Figure 2.5 Using the criterion 'advanced developed economies'. Source: Cannon, T. and Willis, M. (1985), *How to Buy and Sell Overseas*, Hutchinson, London.

Market conditions.   Here the company applies criteria that would seriously hinder or make market entry impossible. The types of criterion could include the following:

1. The strengths of the currency versus sterling (for a UK exporter).
2. Tariff barriers.
3. Import restrictions/import licenses.

Competitive evaluation.   This stage involves a more detailed examination of markets to establish how easily the firm could compete with other companies in the market. The types of criterion could be as follows:

1. Compatible technical standard.
2. Product competitiveness versus established firms.
3. Feasibility of servicing the market competitively.

The results of this process are shown in Figure 2.6, with, in this instance, the firm being left with three priority areas for detailed investigation: Benelux and West Germany, Norway and Denmark, and Eire.

This system has been designed specifically for the small company with limited resources but with a commitment to international business. The

| Company-specific criterion (Fig 2.4) leaves in all countries with English the acceptable business language | Economic criterion (Fig. 2.5) leaves in all advanced developed economies | Market conditions criterion leaves in all strong currency markets | *Eliminate* Singapore, Japan, Taiwan *Leaves* Benelux, Eire, Norway, Denmark, West Germany | These then broken down into three priority areas: 1. Benelux and West Germany. 2. Norway and Denmark. 3. Eire. |

Figure 2.6 Using the criterion 'compatible technical standards'. Source: Cannon, T. and Willis, M. (1985), *How to Buy and Sell Overseas*, Hutchinson, London.

information on the criteria in this example is easily found by using any reasonable library and by contacting an organisation such as the British Overseas Trade Board (BOTB) in the UK. A comprehensive world atlas provides much of the data, and again taking the UK as an illustration, the Technical Help for Exporters (THE) organisation, contacted direct or through the BOTB, will provide advice on product standards, with the BOTB itself able to supply the rest of the data required.

THE KEY VARIABLES

Turning briefly to consider the key influencing variables in such country/market screening activities, it is obvious from the foregoing discussion that market size and growth allied to the strength of competition will be likely to emerge as crucial. On that basis the top country importers and the rate of growth of their imports will provide good first approximations of where market opportunities lie (see Tables 3.1 and 3.2 in the next chapter). Nevertheless, the importance of such variables can be misleading for the firm, firstly, because of the difference between countries and markets as explained earlier; for the small firm which is likely to be selling to a small niche, national market trends may be inappropriate. Secondly, the likelihood is that other international firms will be drawn to similar markets, suggesting strong competition.

Where the results of country/market screening are ambiguous, then almost certainly a firm will choose the psychologically closest country for its initial export foray, as a risk-minimising strategy. The concept of 'psychic distance' was discussed in Chapter 1, pages 9 and 32. It is interesting to consider how attitudes of, for example, British businessmen have changed over the years as the country's links with Europe, through membership of the European Community, have strengthened. Until the 1960s, Commonwealth countries such as Australia were certainly viewed as psychologically closer than Continental Europe.

As regards important variables which may receive inadequate consideration when deciding which markets to exploit and which to avoid, it has been suggested that marketing personnel give inadequate attention to vulnerability to exchange-rate developments. To illustrate the point, take the case of a British manufacturer deciding to set up a distribution network in the USA in the first half of the 1980s. Given the high value of the dollar, the US market would have seemed to be highly attractive to many non-US firms. But the consequence of a possible fall in the market value of the dollar should have been taken into account along with the short-run attraction of the market. The depreciation of the dollar which in fact occurred in 1987 and 1988 made domestic US producers far more competitive. Having decided to enter a market, moreover, international firms should always develop contingency plans to deal with exchange-rate movements. It should not be left until the exchange-rate change occurs to start thinking about what the most appropriate response should be.

MARKET SCREENING: EMPIRICAL EVIDENCE

The time and money required to collect the complex information which at least the sophisticated systems require, is more than many firms have available or are prepared to commit. As is evident from the review of the export behaviour literature in Chapter 3, many companies that export are not systematic in their approach to market selection. Firms may not carry out market research or may choose only markets that are close, either in a geographical or in a psychological sense, and so severely limit the number of countries they are prepared to consider. There are also instances when government promotion organisations have advised firms to concentrate on a region which in fact may not be suitable for the firm.

In Chapter 1, reference was made to the 'rational-analytical' approach to decisionmaking and to evidence that this approach is inconsistent with the reality of decisionmaking in organisations. Inasmuch as the use of systematic market screening is part of the 'rational-analytical' approach, it is also true that methodical market screening is not widely used, even on an informal basis.

Typical of research findings in this area is a survey of British exporters commissioned by The Market Research Society and The Institute of Export in the United Kingdom.[8] This was a mail survey of members of the Institute of Export and obtained over 650 responses, representing more than 40 per cent of companies belonging to the Institute. Companies were asked how they assessed their main areas of opportunity, i.e. their most promising markets. As Table 2.2 reveals, most used an 'increase in orders' as a basis for assessing areas of opportunity (71 per cent), while more than half (54 per cent) felt that an 'increase in enquiries' would be a sound basis to judge markets by. Next, 43 per cent said market research undertaken by their own firm was used in this evaluation process; but when the other results are taken into account, e.g. only 6 per cent said market visits were made by export personnel, this alleged 'company market research' is open to a wide variety of interpretations.

In any event, only firms with a turnover of over £50m. commissioned much in the way of market research, and companies whose sales were less than £7.5m purchased negligible amounts. Further, companies searching for country/market information would have been hampered in many cases by lack of foreign language capabilities. Some 25 per cent of firms agreed that there was no one in their export department who would be able to make sense of a foreign newspaper and only a bare majority (54 per cent) were fluent in French.

Table 2.2 Basis of assessment of main areas of opportunity
(per cent)

Increased orders	71
Increased enquiries	54
Market research carried out by their own firm[a]	43
Export Intelligence Service (BOTB)	9
Visits by export personnel	6
Professional market research	4
Syndicated multi-client studies	3
Internal information	3
External information	2
Other	7

[a] Open to a wide variety of interpretations.
Source: MRS/Institute of Marketing Survey (1984). Summarised in
Heald, G. and Stodel, E. (1984), *The Market Research Society News-
letter*, June, 20–1.

Studies show that companies generally do not adopt a systematic and rigorous approach to political risk assessment and evaluation.[9] Indeed, much political analysis is superficial and subjective, with firms avoiding countries they believe to be risky. Companies seem to rely mostly on internal sources of information for data on environmental and political risk analysis.

A number of reasons why firms do not use information relevant to the country selection decision have been identified:[10]

1. Many managers are not aware of information sources, or worse, see no need to use them.
2. In spite of the vast amount of data available, some market research questions remain unanswered. Secondary data sources are excellent for general information but specific information, say, on particular markets may be unavailable or out of date.
3. Given the limited amount of time usually available for research, management may decide it is not worth while searching for additional information.
4. Although some information is free or provided below cost, some secondary data sources are very expensive and may mean a company decides not to buy even though the data are relevant.
5. Decisionmaking styles differ; and associated with these will be wide differences in the extent to which managers rely on systematic information in decisionmaking. Other managerial factors concern the role of internal politics within a company in the use of information; thus data may be distorted or withheld if they fail to support the views of a particular executive or interest group within the enterprise.

Further evidence for the 'non-rational' view of management decision-making comes from a model of decisionmaking styles, developed by Cavusgil and Godiwalla based on a review of empirical evidence.[11] They contend that decisions tend to be dominated by highly subjective factors. Decisionmakers' personalities, expectations, lack of information and perceptions of risk and uncertainty all influence decisionmaking. However, as Table 2.3 suggests, the nature of decisionmaking may change as a firm becomes more committed to international markets. It is only in the later, more committed stages of internationalisation that highly systematic and informed decisionmaking is evident. Thus the authors contend that the nature of the search process, the dominant decisionmaking mode and the typical decisionmaking skills utilised change as a company becomes more international.

In a separate personal interview study of seventy American companies of varying size, Cavusgil portrayed researching foreign markets in the following way:[12]

In most of the firms we studied, the process of analyzing foreign market opportunities was fairly unstructured. How important managers considered foreign market opportunity analysis depended on how important they considered exporting. That is if they attached a low emphasis on exporting, they attached a low level of importance to the analysis.

The process usually had evolved from one person's handling the job or a series of exporting 'change agents'. Many companies employed experienced international marketing people who had a good grasp of the potential for their industry in different countries of the world. Others found it difficult to hire or train individuals for international positions.

Apart from some experienced exporters, companies did not use a sequential screening process to screen countries – instead they developed their own methods for estimating foreign market potential:

1. Using existing distributors as a source of information about developing market opportunities.
2. Directing promotion to prospective distributors or other customers.
3. Participating in overseas trade fairs and shows.
4. Following major contractors around the world.
5. Particularly for consumer goods, using trade audits for assessing market potential.

Over-reliance on secondary data, statistical methods and market research agency reports have been identified as a key difference between American and Japanese approaches to country/market assessment. Johansson and Nonaka identify 'the informed hands-on market research' approach of Japanese managers who prefer to visit markets and see for themselves and talk directly with key people, as a major reason for their success.[13] Some Japanese companies are reported to have eliminated a strong division of labour between market studies and product design. Creative engineers handle both tasks. Such engineers are sent on long, international journeys each year to study market needs and competitors. More generally, there is

Table 2.3 Characterisation of the stages in the internationalisation process

	Stage 1	Stage 2	Stage 3	Stage 4	Stage 5	Stage 6
Stages in the internationalisation process	No involvement abroad	Pre-involvement	Reactive involvement to unsolicited opportunities	Limited experimental involvement	Active involvement	Full-fledged and perpetual involvement
Venture awareness/interest	None	Low	Sporadic	Moderate	High	Intense
Nature of search process	No search		Limited selective search		Intensive venture search. Greater resource commitment to search	
Dominant decisionmaking	Absence of international decisionmaking	Disjointed, incremental			Formal, structured planning and decisionmaking	
Typical decisionmaking skills utilised	None	Passive	Reactive	Intuitive and problem-solving	Proactive and entrepreneurial	Highly systematic and informed decisionmaking

Source: Cavusgil, S.T. and Godiwalla, Y.M. (1982), 'Decisionmaking for International Marketing: A Comparative Review', *Management Decision*, **20**(4).

substantial agreement that personal visits to foreign markets are an important part of the later stages of market assessment.

In spite of evidence for the subjective and non-rational nature of much of decisionmaking, studies have shown that company success is associated with a methodical approach to market selection.[14] In a UK study of winners of the Queen's Award for Export Achievement, the authors took a random sample of a hundred companies for a mail survey plus eight personal interviews giving a sample size of forty-eight. The larger firms in the survey emphasised the role of forward planning in their success, whereas smaller firms relied 'on the "feel" of the overseas markets gained by personal visits to these countries as substitutes for more sophisticated and formalised plans adopted by larger firms'.

In a mail and personal interview survey of active and passive or non-exporters, the BOTB prepared a profile of the attitudes of successful and less successful exporters.[15] For selecting markets, successful exporters used a ranking process according to rational criteria, whereas the unsuccessful exporters spread their efforts too thinly, going for high-cost/risk markets too soon, and self-evidently they did not adequately assess markets before entry.

The discussion on identifying overseas opportunities in this chapter has primarily been directed to the export mode of internationalisation.The link between country/market screening methods and method of entry is reviewed in some detail in Chapter 7. It is true, of course, that the techniques described here might lead to the identification of attractive market prospects but also reveal the inability of serving a particular market by exports because of, say, tariff restrictions. In such circumstances the firm may then be drawn into the consideration of alternative entry methods. As a prelude to what follows in later chapters, it is worth observing, however, that firms use a wide range of market entry modes in promising markets but tend to rely on exporting for less promising markets. Goodnow and Hanz compared one hundred countries on fifty-nine variables and developed three groupings of nations labelled 'hot', 'moderate' and 'cold'.[16] 'Hot' countries had stable governments, good market prospects and were generally favourable markets to do business in. The group comprised most of the Western developed economies, plus Japan. 'Moderate' countries included Latin America and the industrialising South East Asian nations among others. At the opposite end of the continuum to hot countries, and therefore poor business prospects, were the 'cold' countries, including most of Africa and India. The market entry modes of 250 American companies were then studied, revealing increased use of exporting plus correspondingly less use of manufacturing in 'cold' countries; conversely in 'hot' countries, firms use exporting less often in favour of other supply modes. Not surprisingly, countries classified as 'moderate' in the first part of the study also had a range of entry modes in the middle of the continuum in the second part of the study.

FURTHER READING

1. Readers interested in the international market research issues underlying country/market selection should refer to Douglas, S.P. and Craig, C.S. (1983), *International Marketing Research*, Prentice Hall, Inc., Englewood Cliffs, N.J. This text is a detailed comprehensive guide to international market research.
2. For a less comprehensive but much shorter discussion of international market research issues read:
   Terpstra, V. (1987), *International Marketing*, Dryden Press, New York, 4th edition, Chapter 7.
   Keegan, W.J. (1984), *Multinational Marketing Management*, Prentice Hall International, Hemel Hempstead, 3rd edition, Chapters 8 and 9.
   Other international marketing and international business texts also discuss international market research.
3. For a guide to a much simplified country/market selection process read:
   Cannon, T. and Willis, M. (1985), *How to Buy and Sell Overseas*, Hutchinson, London.
   Douglas, S.P., Craig, C.S. and Keegan, W. (1982), 'Approaches to Assessing International Marketing Opportunities for Small and Medium-Sized Companies', *Columbia Journal of World Business*, **17**(3), 26–32.
4. The evidence on the use of market research is fragmented but useful commentary includes:
   Gilligan, C. and Hird, M. (1986), *International Marketing*, Croom Helm, London, Chapter 3.
   Piercy, N. (1982), *Export Strategy: Markets and Competition*, George Allen & Unwin, London, Chapter 4.
   Cavusgil, S.T. (1985), 'Guidelines for Export Market Research', *Business Horizons*, November–December, 27–33.

QUESTIONS FOR DISCUSSION

1. Reference was made earlier in the chapter to the costs of incorrect market selection. What are these and what could be the implications for different sizes of company?
2. Describe the 'formal approach' to country/market screening proposed by Douglas and Craig. What are its drawbacks?
3. Summarise the major variables influencing the choice of EC countries as export markets for shelving, drawing on the case of Savage Industries in Exhibit 2.1. What does this company regard as the most important factors in successful exporting?
4. Outline the reasons why many firms do not systematically screen countries/markets.

NOTES AND REFERENCES

1. Modiano, P. and Ni-Chionna, O. (1986), 'Breaking into the Big Time', *Management Today*, November, 82–4.
2. Crisp, J. (1984), 'Acorn Pulls out of U.S. Market', *Financial Times*, 6 December, 4.

3. Cateora, P.R. (1987), *International Marketing*, 6th Edition, Irwin, Homewood, Ill.
4. Douglas, S.P. and Craig, C.S. (1983), *International Marketing Research*, Prentice Hall Inc., Englewood Cliffs, N.J.
5. Douglas, S.P., Craig, C.S. and Keegan, W.J. (1982), 'Approaches to Assessing International Marketing Opportunities for Small and Medium-Sized Companies', *Columbia Journal of World Business*, 17(3), 26–32.
6. Scottish Development Agency (1986), *The Marketing of Scottish Architects – Worldwide*, SDA, Glasgow.
7. Cannon, T. and Willis, M. (1985), *How to Buy and Sell Overseas*, Hutchinson, London.
8. For a summary of this report see Heald, G. and Stodel, E. (1984), *The Market Research Society Newsletter*, June, 20–21.
9. Kobrin, S.J., Basek, J., Blank, S. and La Palombara, J. (1980), 'The Assessment and Evaluation of Noneconomic Environments by American Firms: A Preliminary Report', *Journal of International Business Studies*, 11(1), Spring/Summer, 32–47; and Kobrin, S.J. (1979), 'Political Risk: A Review and Reconsideration', *Journal of International Business Studies*, 10(1), Spring/Summer, 67–80.
10. Piercy, N. (1982), *Export Strategy: Markets and Competition*, George Allen & Unwin, London.
11. Cavusgil, S.T. and Godiwalla, Y.M. (1982), 'Decision-Making for International Marketing: A Comparative Review', *Management Decision*, 20(4), 47–54.
12. Cavusgil, S.T. (1985), 'Guidelines for Export Market Research', *Business Horizons*, November–December, 27–33.
13. Johansson, J.K. and Nonaka, J.K. (1987), 'Market Research the Japanese Way', *Harvard Business Review*, May–June, 16–22; see also Cunningham, M.T. and Spigel, R.J. (1971), 'A Study in Successful Exporting', *European Journal of Marketing*, 5(1), Spring.
14. Cunningham and Spigel (1971), 'A Study in Successful Exporting', *European Journal of Marketing*, 5(1), Spring.
15. British Overseas Trade Board (1987), *Into Active Exporting*, BOTB, London.
16. Goodnow, J.D. and Hanz, J.E. (1972), 'Environmental Determinants of Overseas Market Entry Strategies', *Journal of International Business Studies*, Spring, 33–50.

3

EXPORTING IN INTERNATIONAL MARKET DEVELOPMENT

SUMMARY

1. Exporting differs from other foreign market-servicing modes in that it has the strong support of government through both macroeconomic and microeconomic policy measures. For similar reasons firms have a greater awareness of exporting, and fairly comprehensive statistics assist the export task.
2. Small firms who start to export have a number of advantages compared with larger firms. They can react quickly to market opportunities; can co-ordinate the administration of exports easily; the management teams are often stable; they can acquire detailed knowledge of customers; and can call on governmental and other export support organisations for advice and training.
3. However, not all firms should export, as not every company has the necessary interest in or the commitment and the competitive advantage to succeed in exporting. If companies assessed the benefits of exporting before they started, the likelihood of costly failure would be reduced.
4. Firms start to export for a variety of reasons. In many cases an unsolicited order is the stimulus. This implies an unplanned, haphazard approach to international markets initially, which, if it continues, may lead to failure in foreign markets. Other stimuli external to the firm include chambers of commerce, industrial associations, banks, government agencies and other firms.
5. The most important internal stimulus is the top management of a firm. Various studies have shown that the quality and the commitment of management is a crucial determinant of success in exporting. Without the willingness to regard exporting as a long-term growth strategy a company runs a serious risk of failure.
6. Barriers to exporting have been identified. However, firm size, operational problems, finance, lack of information and the like have not stopped committed companies developing their exports.
7. There are a range of direct and indirect export distribution channels, each with their own advantages and disadvantages. Using an indirect channel, a firm can export with little or no effort on its part, although sales will be limited. If direct channels are used, potential sales are greater but more of the firm's resources are committed to the market. Research on distribution channel selection provides reasonably strong evidence that channel choice is situationally determined.
8. The advice usually given to exporters is to concentrate on a few countries/markets, but there is a case to be made in certain circumstances for spreading sales over a large

number of countries/markets. A firm should analyse the company, product, market and marketing factors that apply to its own situation before deciding whether to concentrate or spread.

9. International industrial marketing strategies are a function of a wide range of variables that affect the relationship between buyer and seller. An approach for analysing these relationships is discussed and a distinction is made between the formal organisation of a company and the informal organisation (the range of interpersonal contacts between supplier and customer staff).

INTRODUCTION

The central theme of this book is that exporting is only one of a range of methods that may be utilised in penetrating and developing markets abroad. This chapter, the first of a series dealing with the different options, focuses specifically, however, on the export route, with especial attention being given to the development process both from the standpoint of a company new to exporting and the experienced exporter.

Before moving to a discussion of the firm-level, managerial dimensions in exporting, it is important to draw attention to some important differences between exporting and other foreign market-servicing modes. Trade, both exporting and importing, has been at the core of the debate over economic development and the macroeconomic management of national economies for several centuries. No economic policy issue has an older intellectual history of dispute than that of free trade versus protection. The eighteenth century was the era of mercantilism, with import restrictions, export subsidies and monopolistic trading companies designed to operate to swell the gold stock in national treasuries. Adam Smith refuted the doctrine of mercantilism, arguing that 'Britain should by all means be made a free port ... that there should be no interruption of any kind to free trade ... and that free commerce and liberty should be allowed with all nations and for all things'.[1] Debates on the role of trade in the welfare of individual nations and the world as a whole have continued through to the present day, with conflicting theories being used to support the case for either free trade or protection as circumstances change. To illustrate the point, the principles underlying the establishment of the GATT (General Agreement on Tariffs and Trade) derive from the claimed advantages of free trade. On the other hand, the growth of quantitative restrictions, voluntary export restraints, orderly marketing agreements and the like are justified by recourse to concepts such as 'fair trade' and reducing the costs of transition from protection to free trade. In terms of the economic development of industrialising nations, too, there is continuing controversy over the relative merits of outward-oriented versus inward-oriented industrial development strategies. The former, involving realistic exchange rates, low tariffs and the avoidance of quantitative restrictions on imports, combined possibly with export incentives (applied uniformly to all exporters) have been shown by the World Bank to be associated with superior economic performance since the 1960s.[2]

In virtually all countries, therefore, macroeconomic discussions still emphasise trade, balance of payments and exchange-rate issues, and stock markets and foreign exchange markets react quickly to the monthly economic indicators on visible and invisible trade, etc. In developed countries, at least, the need to encourage exports via macroeconomic (e.g. exchange-rate policy) and microeconomic (e.g. exporter support services) measures is accepted unquestioningly.

The growth of the multinational enterprise has focused attention on the macroeconomic effects (including balance-of-payments impacts) of outward direct capital flows. But the issue has never received the same attention as that devoted to exports and trade generally. Many governments have equivocal attitudes to the macroeconomic and microeconomic benefits from establishing wholly owned subsidiaries or joint ventures abroad, and indeed to contractual arrangements such as licensing. On occasion, a belief in the favourable effects of outward direct and portfolio investment has contributed to major policy initiatives such as the abolition of exchange controls by the UK in 1979. Conversely, alleged negative balance-of-payments effects from multinational operations have led to restraining policy measures at times in the USA. In general, nevertheless, there is rather limited overt policy attention to outward direct investment; in fact at the micro-level the absence of training and assistance programmes may be a major hindrance to the firm faced with the alternative of using the non-export route or being excluded from foreign markets.

The policy emphasis on trade emerges in another form, namely in the availability of reasonably up-to-date export and import figures by commodity for the majority of countries in the world, unlike the situation for other forms of market servicing. A company looking for guidelines as to the fastest-growing markets and products can readily obtain this information (see, for example, Tables 3.1 and 3.2, which show the top thirty exporters in the world for the years 1970, 1980 and 1986, and import growth for selected high-technology products). Continuing from the theme of Chapter 2, it is apparent that a crude form of targeting and country selection is possible merely from such data.

Statistical information, by comparison, is very poor on non-export methods of foreign involvement (which, of course, would make it difficult to devise sensible policies, even if there was interest in so doing). Using the models of internationalisation and foreign market servicing, it should be clear that countries and industries differ both in their involvement in international business and in the methods of overseas market penetration employed. Before concluding these introductory remarks, therefore, there is merit in drawing attention to some of these differences. Using data for the major multinational companies worldwide (the sample comprised approximately

Table 3.1 World's leading exporters of manufactures in 1970, 1980 and 1986 (billion dollars, % share, and rank)

	1970			1980			1986		
	Value	Share	Rank	Value	Share	Rank	Value	Share	Rank
Germany, Fed. Rep.	29.9	15.7	1	162.1	14.8	1	213.0	14.9	1
Japan	17.9	9.4	3	122.7	11.2	3	201.9	14.1	2
United States	28.4	14.9	2	139.5	12.7	2	147.3	10.3	3
France	13.1	6.9	5	81.2	7.4	5	90.2	6.3	4
Italy	11.0	5.7	6	65.1	6.0	6	85.2	6.0	5
United Kingdom	15.5	8.1	4	81.8	7.5	4	77.7	5.4	6
Canada	8.2	4.3	8	30.4	2.8	9	53.1	3.7	7
Belgium–Luxembourg	8.6	4.5	7	44.4	4.1	7	50.1	3.5	8
Netherlands	6.6	3.5	9	37.0	3.4	8	45.6	3.2	9
Taiwan	1.1	0.6	23	17.4	1.6	14	36.2	2.5	10
Switzerland	4.6	2.4	12	26.6	2.4	10	35.0	2.4	11
Hong Kong	2.3	1.2	16	18.0	1.6	13	32.4	2.4	12
Korea, Rep.	0.6	0.3	26	15.6	1.4	16	31.9	2.2	13
Sweden	5.1	2.7	10	24.0	2.2	11	30.8	2.2	14
USSR	5.0	2.6	11	19.5	1.8	12	25.0	1.7	15
Spain	1.3	0.7	22	14.9	1.4	17	20.5	1.4	16
Austria	2.3	1.2	16	14.5	1.3	18	19.7	1.4	17

China, Peoples Rep.	0.3	0.2	30	3.0	0.3	30	13.6	1.0	18
Singapore	0.4	0.2	27	9.0	0.8	23	13.3	0.9	19
Finland	1.5	0.8	20	9.9	0.9	21	13.2	0.9	20
Denmark	1.8	0.9	18	9.1	0.8	22	12.2	0.9	21
Brazil	0.4	0.2	27	7.5	0.7	24	11.8	0.8	22
Hungary	1.6	0.8	19	7.5	0.7	26	9.6	0.7	23
Yugoslavia	1.0	0.5	24	6.5	0.6	29	8.3	0.6	24
Ireland	0.4	0.2	27	4.6	0.4	20	8.2	0.6	25
Poland	2.5	1.3	15	11.7	1.1	28	7.9	0.6	26
Romania	0.9	0.5	24	6.0	0.6	27	7.5	0.5	27
Norway	1.4	0.7	21	5.9	0.5	19	6.8	0.5	28
German Dem. Rep.	3.7	1.9	13	13.6	1.2	15	–	–	n.a.
Czechoslovakia	2.9	1.5	14	17.5	1.6		–	–	n.a.
Total of above	180.2	94.5		1,026.5	93.7		1,347.0	94.1	
World trade of manufactures	190.7	100.0		1,095.0	100.0		1,431.0	100.0	

Source: GATT, *International Trade*, 86–87, Geneva.

Table 3.2 World imports of some high-technology products, 1973–84 (billion dollars CIF and percentages)[a]

SITC Rev.2[b]	Products	Values				Shares in manufactures				Annual average rates of change	
		1973	1979	1983	1984	1973	1979	1983	1984	1973–79	1979–84
792	Aircraft and parts	4.9	15.2	20.6	22.0	1.5	1.7	2.0	1.9	20.4	6.7
75	Office machinery and data processing equipment	7.2	22.3	38.5	49.9	2.2	2.5	3.8	4.5	20.6	17.5
772+773	Electrical transmission and distribution equipment	4.8	15.4	20.0	21.2	1.5	1.7	2.0	1.9	21.4	6.6
764+776	Telecommunication equipment and electronic components	5.7	25.7	40.0	50.5	1.8	2.9	3.9	4.6	28.3	14.5
87+774	Professional and scientific instruments	6.6	17.6	23.6	25.2	2.1	2.0	2.3	2.3	17.7	7.4
541	Medicinal and pharmaceutical products	7.4	12.2	15.2	15.3	2.3	1.4	1.5	1.4	8.7	4.6
713+714+716+718	Engines and turbines	7.1	25.9	32.1	34.5	2.2	2.9	3.2	3.1	24.1	5.9
761+762+763	Radio and television receivers, recorders	6.7	14.1	19.0	21.5	2.1	1.6	1.9	1.9	13.1	8.8
	Total of above	50.5	148.4	209.0	239.0	15.7	16.7	20.6	21.7	19.7	10.0
	All manufactures	322.1	888.3	1,015.9	1,102.5	100	100	100	100	18.4	4.4
	All commodities	522.5	1,530.9	1,736.4	1,833.1	–	–	–	–	19.6	3.7

[a]Excluding the Eastern trading area.
[b]Standard International Trade Classification, Second Revision.
Source: GATT, *International Trade, 85–86*, Geneva.

350 MNEs), Stopford and Dunning calculated the contribution of exports and overseas production to total sales, and the results are shown in Figures 3.1 and 3.2.[3] In the country patterns in Figure 3.1, the axes show foreign content as a percentage of worldwide sales – where foreign content comprises export sales + sales from overseas production; and overseas production as a percentage of foreign content – sales from overseas production in relation to total foreign sales (exports + sales from overseas production). The arrows show changes between 1977 and 1981. As the figure shows, the large UK multinationals were about on a par with their French and

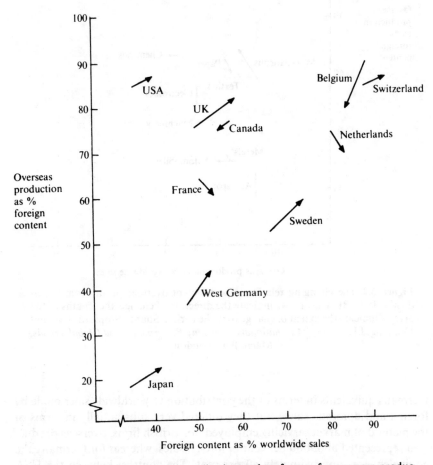

Figure 3.1 Trends in internationalisation and preference for overseas production, by country, 1977–81. The arrows indicate the direction of change; the lengths of the arrows indicate the extent of change over the period. Source: Stopford, J.M. and Dunning, J.H. (1983), *Multinationals. Company Performance and Global Trends*, Macmillan, London.

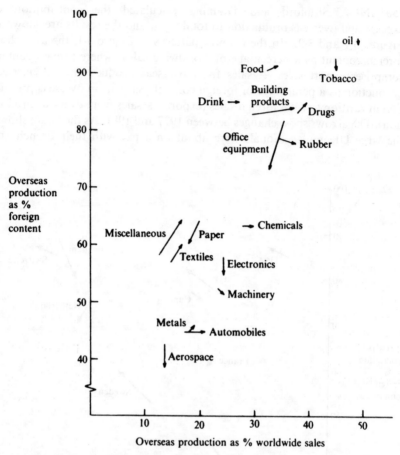

Figure 3.2 The changing relative importance of overseas production, by industry, 1977–81. The arrows indicate the direction of change; the lengths of the arrows indicate the extent of change over the period. Source: Stopford, J.M. and Dunning, J.H. (1983), *Multinationals. Company Performance and Global Trends*, Macmillan, London.

German equivalents in terms of the contribution to worldwide sales made by foreign and domestic sales. But they differed very substantially in terms of the method of market servicing employed: for British firms, overseas production represented about 80 per cent of foreign sales, whereas for Germany the equivalent was approximately 40 per cent. The contrast between the USA and Japan was most striking, confirming the attraction for Japanese companies of supplying foreign markets by exports from Japan because of the low cost and high quality of production in Japan allied, until recently, to a competitive exchange rate.

Figure 3.2 undertakes a similar type of approach, this time referring to industry patterns. The axes show overseas production as a percentage of worldwide sales – sales from foreign subsidiaries as a percentage of worldwide sales; and overseas production as a percentage of foreign content – as before. One of the explanations for the country pattern observed in Figure 3.1 is obviously the industry mix in different countries: some industries are heavily multinational such as the raw material and extractive sectors (foreign investment in extraction, mining, etc.), food and drink (foreign investment because of taste differences between markets, high transport costs, perishability), drugs (legislation, etc.), and office equipment (market-related factors, protection of proprietary know-how).

Dunning's 'eclectic theory' discussed in Chapter 1 is especially interesting here in showing how the balance between OLI variables alters the preference for exporting as opposed to outward direct investment. Clearly patterns of foreign sales for different countries and industries would differ when licensing was taken into consideration, but especially when small and medium-sized enterprises were included (since the latter are much more export-oriented in their internationalisation); little evidence is yet available on these topics.

The remainder of this chapter relates to firm-level dimensions of exporting. The following section on starting to export emphasises that exporting is not suitable for every company. Firms should assess their export potential and be quite clear that exporting requires long-term commitment. Following on from this, the chapter focuses upon barriers to exports, characteristics of successful exporters and research on international industrial marketing.

STARTING EXPORTING

For a small company particularly, exporting can be seen as either an opportunity or a threat. If its motives are short term or related to personal idiosyncrasies of executives, or if no country/market assessment is carried out, exporting may well represent a threat. On the other hand, many small firms shy away from exporting believing that they lack resources and expertise or in general terms are not suited to such a risky venture; whereas in reality, size may not be a hindrance if the company is competitive and committed. In comparison with large firms, small enterprises have a number of advantages:[4]

1. The small firm can react quickly to export opportunities.
2. It can be easier to co-ordinate the administration of exports.
3. The management of a small company is often quite stable. Hence foreign buyers can deal with the same people over a period of time, getting to know each other and building up a business relationship.

4. With close knowledge of customers may come the incentive to deal efficiently with them, something larger companies may not be noted for.
5. Although in the first instance a small company often does not have people with export experience, there are export support organisations in most countries that will give advice and training in export procedures.

There are threats, however, as exporting may not suit every firm and the drain on small company resources in the event of a costly foreign market failure could jeopardise the entire future of an enterprise. As has been suggested by the British Overseas Trade Board (BOTB) in the UK, the unprepared potential exporter may find encounter the following problems:[5]

1. The export opportunity usually appears when a firm is struggling within the domestic market.
2. There is usually no correlation between the size and capability of the firm and the scale of the opportunity.
3. The larger the opportunity, the more likely it is that the firm is deluded into thinking they can win the business.
4. The closer one gets to the opportunity, the more illusory it becomes.

The key features underlying the comments above are that for the firm to be successful, it has to be committed to exporting and has to be reasonably organised and prepared in its approach to foreign markets.

Why firms start to export

Studies on export behaviour have shown that there are a variety of reasons why firms start exporting. Bilkey and other researchers concerned with the initiation of the export process have tended to focus on the effects of change agents, either external to the firm or internal within the firm.[6] External change agents include chambers of commerce, industrial associations, banks, government agencies and other firms. The latter appears to be overwhelmingly the most important external agent and includes firms that buy out smaller companies and then encourage them to export, foreign importers and export agents. Studies by Simpson and Kujawa and others have asked companies what first stimulated them to start to exporting.[7] In many cases, the firm's first export order was unsolicited, and in some studies, 70 or 80 per cent of companies reported that their first order was unsolicited. Hence for a lot of companies the start of their export experience is not planned in any formal way but simply arises, seemingly by chance; and certainly for companies that fail in their export efforts it would seem that quite often a haphazard and *ad hoc* approach to exporting had continued.

It is also evident from the literature that the internal change agent tends to be a member(s) of the firm's top management who is interested in and enthusiastic about exporting.[8] Several studies have identified management characteristics as an important factor in the export initiation process. Cavusgil found that export behaviour appears to be explained by four factors, including the expectations of management and the strength of managerial aspirations, concluding that: 'variations in export activity can be explained, to a significant extent by organisational and management characteristics. Expansion of export activity among the firms studied is clearly related to management's expectations concerning the effects exporting will have on firm's growth, market development and profits; technology orientation of the firm; management attitudes towards risk taking and desire to develop new markets; and the extent of resource allocation to exporting as exemplified by systematic exploration of foreign market opportunities, and the formulation of a fixed export policy.'[9]

Bilkey argued that four factors were related to whether or not management took the initiative in exporting:[10]

1. *Management's impression* of the overall attractiveness of exporting as an abstract ideal, independently of whatever particular contribution exporting might make to its own firm. Note the latter cannot be known by management until they explore the feasibility of exporting or gain export experience.

2. The degree of the firm's *international orientation*. Some studies suggest that this is determined by the firm's background and traditions and by the foreign attitudes of its top management. Bilkey notes in one study that the foreign attitudes of top managements correlate, in turn, with whether or not they had studied a foreign language in school; whether or not they had lived abroad sufficiently long to have experienced cultural shock; and whether or not that foreign experience was attractive. The managers' ages are also relevant, younger ones tending to be more internationally minded than older ones.

3. Another determinant is management's *confidence in the firm's competitive advantage*. This is measured as a composite involving management's perception of whether or not the firm's products have unique qualities; management's perception of whether or not the firm has technological, marketing, financial or price advantages; whether or not the firm possesses exclusive information about a foreign market or customer; whether or not the firm has a patented product; and whether or not the firm has an efficient distribution network.

4. A fourth determinant of whether or not management takes the initiative in exporting is *adverse home market conditions*, causing management to explore exporting as a means of ensuring the firm's survival. The relationship of this initiative to general economic conditions varies greatly among firms, because of the differential impact of macroeconomic conditions at any given time on particular industries.

DEVELOPING EXPORTS

This section discusses barriers to developing exports, with subsections dealing with a variety of such barriers ranging from size, through finance, information and operational problems to the important topic of distribution channels. It should be pointed out that several studies of exporters and non-exporters have found that the latter perceived significantly more serious obstacles and barriers to exporting than did exporting enterprises; and so this section which highlights the difficulties should not lead to the positive side – the opportunities in overseas markets – being overlooked.

Firm size

There is no strong evidence to say that apart from the smallest firms, size need be a barrier to exporting. But empirical results published for the UK indicate that 'the percentage of all firms which export tends to increase with the size of firm measured by turnover. In the less than £1 million turnover band, 14 per cent of manufacturing firms and 3 per cent of VAT-registered firms in non-manufacturing sectors export. In the £100m band, the corresponding figures are 72 and 35 per cent.'[11]

Operational difficulties

Once a company has resolved its strategic export problems, it still has operational difficulties to overcome. A number of studies have investigated operational problems like documentation to see if these are perceived as barriers. The Small Business Research Trust survey results summarised in Figure. 3.3 reveals that for British exporters finance/delays in payment (26.2 per cent) were the most serious obstacle followed by export paperwork (14.4 per cent), market information (14.4 per cent) and product suitability (14.3 per cent).[12]

A related and more comprehensive survey by the British Overseas Trade Board commented, however, that

> The list of items under 'Operations' is indeed formidable but the impression gained was that they did not present a significant barrier to exporting in practice, though the prospect of administrative problems may well deter some non-exporters and passive exporters from exporting.

The report continued:

> It was quite striking that the successful exporters in our sample, almost without exception, dismissed such matters as customs' procedures and export documentation as nothing more than an administrative nuisance, which once the learning process had been gone through, were easily dealt with by routine office procedures and the use of intermediaries such as forwarding agents. Non-

Per cent of mentions

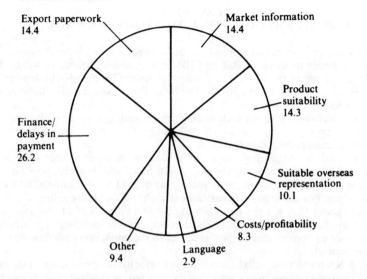

Figure 3.3 The greatest difficulties in exporting. Source: Small Business Research Trust Survey (1987), in British Overseas Trade Board, *Into Active Exporting*, BOTB, London, 5.

exporters and occasional passive exporters not properly organised do find the complexities of bills of lading... and other documents baffling or burdensome at first, but soon discover that if what cannot be dealt with by an intermediary is given the same practised and meticulous treatment as the more familiar cheques or VAT invoices used in domestic business, then the difficulties soon disappear.[13]

Finance

Although finance is seen as a major barrier to exporting, both by active exporters and passive or non-exporters, these two groups perceive the problems of finance in different ways. For the active exporter the main problem is the financing of exports, in other words, the increased drain on working capital that developing the market takes. By contrast, the passive or non-exporter is more aware of possible credit problems and delays in payment and is not keenly aware of the drain on working capital that developing export markets in fact entails. For the experienced exporters, credit risks would seem to be minimal in the developed markets of the world, although in certain developing countries, especially Nigeria, India and Latin America, severe payment delays have been reported.

In a period of floating exchange rates, exchange risk is a major issue. It was argued in Chapter 2 that exchange-rate forecasts should have an important

EXHIBIT 3.1
EXPORT FINANCE – HOW TO AVOID THE ANGUISH

Nineteen eighty-seven was a proud year for C & K Software, a small, Somerset-based supplier to users of IBM and IBM compatible computer networks. In July it was one of the winners of the Export Award for Smaller Businesses, a competition backed by the British Overseas Trade Board and a number of private sector organisations.

But it was also a year in which sterling rose sharply against the dollar and the strong export performance which had gained C & K its award began to produce some painful side effects.

'We took a hammering', says Andy Kenton, finance director and joint founder of the five-year-old company. 'We based our business plan on the pound at $1.60. By the end of the year it was over $1.80. We suffered a loss of £40,000 on our earnings and that came straight off our bottom line.'

Set against C & K's pre-tax profit of £600,000 on sales of £1.35m last year this looks bad but not disastrous. But the company was spending large sums on computer equipment and on new premises so the impact on cash flow was far more serious.

C & K's problem was that it worked out a price list for its products in sterling and converted these prices into dollars at what it thought was a sensible exchange rate. But as the pound firmed against the dollar through the year C & K's US sales were worth progressively less when converted back to sterling.

Kenton says he discussed ways of hedging his currency risk with his bank manager but was unable to find a solution. 'I don't have firm contracts which I can take along to the bank to arrange currency cover', he explains. 'We call on people and persuade them to take our products on a 30-day trial. At the end they may sign a contract. I can't forecast what my sales will be.'

Currency fluctuations have been a source of anguish for exporters ever since the breakdown in the early 1970s of fixed exchange rates. For most of the intervening years British companies have been faced with a decline in the value of sterling, which has tended to benefit exporters, but sterling's strength for much of the past year has added a new dimension to the problem.

Managing currency fluctuations is difficult enough for the larger company; Pilkington, the glass-maker, last week revealed that currency movements wiped £26m off its profits. For the small exporter, with even fewer resources with which to manage its foreign exchange risk, the problem is magnified.

A survey carried out in April by the CBI revealed that currency fluctuations was one of the major problems facing small exporters.

British companies have traditionally solved the problem of volatile currencies by pricing their products in sterling – leaving their customers to take the currency risk.

However, sterling's declining role as a trading currency and increased competition from foreign companies prepared to quote in the local currency has meant fewer British exporters can afford to do this.

Smaller companies are, however, partly protected from these pressures because they often operate in niche markets where there is little competition and price is not a major factor in the buyer's thinking.

Exhibit 3.1 continued

Procal Analytics, a Peterborough-based maker of equipment for analysing gases and liquids with turnover of just over £500,000 makes 70 per cent of its sales abroad and prices its products in most markets in sterling.

'We don't think that pricing in sterling has lost us any orders but we keep in close touch with our agents about this,' says Chris Daw, managing director. The only market where Procal has been forced to quote in another currency is Japan, where it prices in dollars.

The company does not try to hedge against possible exchange losses on its Japanese business because its margins are high enough to absorb currency movements and Japan is only a small part of its business. But Daw also feels that hedging the risks would complicate an otherwise straightforward trade deal. 'We like to keep it simple here,' he says.

However, not all research agrees with the findings of the CBI's report. A study published just over a year ago by the British Overseas Trade Board did not rate currency exposure a major problem. Graham Bannock, a consultant and author of the report, believes small companies have become quite sophisticated in dealing with fluctuating currencies.

It is also true that some exporters like to take a chance on the way currencies will move. Hedging currency exposure not only limits the risks; it also removes the chance of a windfall profit.

But what some businessmen regard as a reasonable punt looks, to those more familiar with currency markets, suspiciously like taking an unacceptable risk.

'Too many small companies take risks when they shouldn't', warns Stuart Bremner, a manager at Barclays Bank's George Street Branch in Luton, which handles a lot of export finance business. 'They are prepared to take a view on a currency or they are frightened of what they see as the intricacies of hedging. I don't recommend it.'

For companies which want to minimise their risks two of the most common options available are:

● Forward exchange contracts: these allow an exporter to fix the rate at which future payments in foreign currency will be converted into sterling, regardless of what happens to the exchange rate in the meantime.

This is the most common form of currency hedging. It has the advantages of simplicity – for both customer and bank – and does not normally involve the customer paying a charge in advance. The cost of the deal is covered by the rate the bank is ready to agree to for the future purchase of the currency.

The drawback of such contracts is that the exporter (or importer) is committed to supplying the currency agreed. If the export deal is cancelled for any reason he will have to buy the foreign currency at the going rate in the currency market.

● Option forward contracts: these also allow an exporter to fix in advance the rate at which his bank will buy a foreign currency but which permit the customer to deliver the currency any time between two agreed dates rather than on one specified date.

These are particularly useful for exporters which do not know when they will receive payment. However, because the bank does not know precisely when it will receive the foreign currency, options are more expensive than forward exchange contracts.

Exhibit 3.1 continued

> Unlike a forward exchange contract, which must be fulfilled even if the export deal does not go through, an option forward contract can be allowed to lapse if currency movements are favourable. For this reason option contracts involve the payment of an advance fee by the exporter.
>
> 'Options are a bit technical but I can see them becoming as popular as forward exchange contracts,' says Bert Alldis, chief manager in Lloyds Bank's customer services treasury division.
>
> One company to negotiate an option contract was Prism Instruments, a St Ives, Cambridgeshire-based supplier of equipment for testing electronic components. It paid a fee of just under 4 per cent for an option contract from Barclays to cover the currency risk on $100,000 of sales to the US.
>
> Prism, which has annual sales of £1.5m. and a workforce of 43, had previously priced all its exports in sterling. But to break into the US market and persuade a reputable local distributor to stock its products it had to price in dollars, Robert French, financial controller, explains.
>
> This contract, which was negotiated on the advice of Prism's venture capital backer, Managed Technology Investors (MTI), meant Prism could guarantee a fixed price to its distributor for eight months. It has also meant that, despite sterling's rise against the dollar, Prism was not forced to raise its US prices.
>
> The problem for the small company is that it often does not have the expertise in-house. And, while banks have been re-organising branch networks to target business customers, they do not always succeed in channelling advice to the small company.
>
> The banks are reluctant to put together the more complex packages such as option forward contracts for exporters doing only small amounts of business.
>
> But whatever the problems, as companies like C & K Software have found, doing nothing can also be costly.
>
> Source: *Financial Times*, 21 June 1988.

role in country/market screening; once in the market the company has to manage its currency risk or take a dangerous gamble on the way currencies will move. Exhibit 3.1 discusses the problems faced by some small British exporters because of exchange-rate volatility in the recent past.

Finance questions emerge directly or indirectly in exporting (and other market entry and development modes) in other ways too. For example, shortages of hard currency may require countertrade arrangements (see Appendix 5.2). Again, leasing is an important technique for the exporting of expensive equipment such as heavy machinery, aircraft, computers, etc. For the lessee, the ability to obtain such high-priced equipment at low annual cost and the availability of maintenance services under the terms of the lease contract are strong arguments in favour of leasing. For the exporter (lessor) flexibility over the form of pricing and finance may give the company a competitive marketing edge, although there are still exchange risk problems relating to the currency specified in the lease terms. Some countries provide support to exporters engaged in leasing: for example, the Export-Import Bank of the United States provides comprehensive guarantee coverage to US companies undertaking leasing activities abroad or to firms that import American equipment for leasing to their customers.

Information

Research in the UK has uncovered an interesting pattern in the sources of information used and in attitudes towards these sources:[14]

> At the bottom of the nursery slope, smaller non-exporters use a very wide range of sources: their friends and business acquaintances, their bank, trade association, chamber of commerce, their trade press, the libraries, and for start-ups, their enterprise agency; but put some emphasis on official sources. Higher up on the slope of export experience and corporate growth, firms seem to place more emphasis on personal visits to markets and intermediaries such as buying houses; they also become increasingly selective about the source of information they approach. Experienced exporters rely principally upon their representatives or subsidiaries or other sources of information overseas, including foreign trade press, and on personal visits. Generally speaking, they disdain the use of official sources of information (other than statistics) and are sceptical of advice given by banks and professional advisers on export matters. The only information problems that experienced exporters admit to concern, for example, intelligence on competitors' prices and forthcoming new products.

It was also noted in the study that the successful exporting companies valued personal experience above all else; and in some instances experience gained with other companies, notably multinationals, was the principal factor in the success of the respondents' present companies.

Other barriers

The chief barrier in this category is the lack of skilled personnel which places limits on the expansion rate of the company; but it is not the lack of people skilled in export procedures so much as the shortage of people who have a knowledge of the particular company and its products. In the view of some respondents in the survey, it was much easier to train somebody in export procedures than it was to make them familiar with the company and its products for export markets. A further barrier was the complex procedures for reclaiming taxes and duties on imported raw materials which were to be processed and subsequently exported.

Other studies have found a variety of factors perceived as barriers to exporting, of which a report by the National Federation of Independent Businesses in America in 1985 is typical. Firms cited 'red tape, better opportunities at home, difficulties in finding customers and the complexity of exporting'.[15]

Distribution channel choice

From the perspective of this book, distribution channel choice is perhaps the most crucial export issue. Thus export distribution channels themselves vary

Table 3.3 Export modes

Export Mode	Characteristics	Advantages	Disadvantages
Indirect Export houses	There are a number of types of export house but the most commonly understood is the organisation that buys from a firm and sells abroad on its own account	May handle all aspects of the export operation	Little market control or information. Limited sales
Confirming houses	Act on behalf of foreign buyers who pay them on a commission basis. The confirming house guarantees payment to the exporter on shipment of the goods	As above but also guarantees payment	As above
Buying houses	Acting on behalf of clients like foreign department stores, buying houses purchase from domestic manufacturers	As above but the domestic manufacturer is approached by the buying house and need have no involvement in exporting other than supplying the order	As above
Piggybacking	The firm sells its goods abroad through the overseas sales distribution facilities of another, usually larger firm	The domestic firm has access to resources of an experienced exporter, who in turn has the benefit of a wider product range and increased sales	Finding a suitable partner. The domestic company's product may take second priority. Growth may be impeded by existing arrangements

Direct

	Description	Advantages	Disadvantages
Agents	There are several types of agent: some will sell only one company's products; other agents will sell products from a number of companies, some of which may be competing. An agent does not take title to the goods, is usually a national of the country concerned and is paid on a commission basis	More market control and information than with channels mentioned above. Permanent presence in the market. Costs of agency are related to sales	May sell more than one company's products. Agency agreements can be difficult and expensive to terminate
Distributors	The distributor takes title to the goods and therefore earns his revenue from his mark-up on the product rather than commission	Like the agent, knows the local market. Able to provide after-sales service. More control of market	Costs of termination are high should exporter's market development plans require new channels
Direct selling	Sales representatives operating from the home country may be used in foreign sales territories	Detailed knowledge of the company and its products. High level of market control and information	Suffer from a lack of market knowledge, increased travelling time and, depending upon the country, language problems
Local sales offices	These may be staffed either by representatives from the home market or from the foreign market	Perceived as a commitment to the market. Easier for local companies to deal with the exporter. Flexible and can accommodate growth	Problem of choosing appropriate personnel for the sales force. Domestic reps may be reluctant to move overseas; local reps have less company knowledge but more country/market know-how

in terms of the control/cost dichotomy in a similar manner to the continuum of foreign market-servicing modes from exporting to joint ventures and wholly owned subsidiaries.

In Chapter 1, indirect and direct methods of exporting were discussed briefly. This section expands on the characteristics and advantages and disadvantages of the most important forms of export distribution channels and reviews evidence on how companies select particular distribution channels. A summary is provided in Table 3.3.

Quite often there is confusion over the characteristics possessed by particular distribution channels. For instance, on occasion no distinction is made between an agent and a distributor, when in fact there are fundamental differences. An agent does not own the goods and is paid mainly on commission, whereas a distributor takes title to the goods and earns his revenue from a mark-up. So when discussing distribution channels, it is necessary to be very clear from the outset exactly what a term means.

Export houses
Export houses handle a large amount of export trade. About a fifth of exports from the UK go through these institutions, which have their origins in colonial days and generally offer a wide range of services to companies who want to sell their goods overseas. Many export houses act as export managers, taking over the entire problem of exporting from a manufacturer. The most common form of export house buys from a company and then sells abroad on its own account. The firm may have approached the export house in the first instance about the possibility of foreign sales but that is the extent of its involvement in exporting. The export house handles the entire export operation, including distribution and selling.

The main advantage of using an export house is that a firm need not be involved in any aspect of the export operation. Apart from some minor changes, perhaps to the product, the labelling or the packaging, exporting via an export house can be as straightforward as selling to the domestic market. There are drawbacks, however, principally the lack of control over distribution and marketing abroad, with the volume of export sales being dependent on the performance of the export house. The image and reputation of a product in a market established by an export house may not be what the firm would have wanted. This becomes important if the company subsequently becomes a direct exporter when it may find its attempt to increase sales hampered by a product image and reputation at odds with what the firm would have wished to establish in the first place.

Confirming houses
Exporters may contact confirming houses in the first instance, even though the latter normally act on behalf of the foreign buyer. In theory, confirming houses offer the best of both worlds for the exporter, for the confirming house guarantees payment to the exporter on shipment of the goods. It is

usually the buyer who pays for the service, plus any interest if a loan or long credit is involved.

Confirming houses usually include in their service all arrangements for insurance and shipment of the goods to the foreign clients. The transaction, however, is still between the manufacturer and the foreign buyer as principals, with the confirming house acting as an intermediary with subordinate functions. Confirming is often one of the services offered by buying houses. The advantages and disadvantages of confirming houses are similar to those of the export house, except when export houses sell a firm's products on a commission basis and the manufacturer is still liable for any bad debts. In this instance, a confirming house offers an exporter the advantage of guaranteeing payment.

Buying houses

So far the onus has been on the manufacturer to find buyers for his product. However, there are organisations from overseas which seek out suppliers by going directly to manufacturers to negotiate with them. The manufacturer is not required to have any representation overseas, yet when the deal is concluded, he is an exporter. Buying houses usually serve a particular country or group of countries where they have been established for a long period. Although the pros and cons of a buying house for a firm are similar to those of export and confirming houses, a buying house has the added advantage that it will approach a manufacturer in the first place. The export behaviour literature lays great stress on the role of unsolicited export orders in initial overseas sales; and, obviously, buying houses may have an important role in such a process.

Piggybacking

This involves an agreement between two companies whereby one firm may sell its goods abroad through the overseas distribution facilities of the other, usually the larger firm. From the perspective of the latter, piggybacking takes place for a number of reasons:

1. The exporter may sell the domestic firms' products because they complement his product range, and this facilitates a wider competitive offering to the market.
2. Foreign customers may have experienced a desire for products that the exporter cannot supply from his own range.
3. Piggybacking offers the opportunity of lowering unit distribution costs.

The advantages for the domestic company are that it can use an established exporter's distribution channels, giving immediate access to a foreign market and reducing risks. On the other hand, finding a suitable piggyback partner may be difficult; the domestic company's products may take second priority to the existing exporter's product line; and future market development may be impeded by a piggyback arrangement that has become outdated.[16] Anecdotal evidence indicates that in the late 1980s, piggybacking was used fairly commonly by small high-technology electronics and bio-technology companies seeking rapid foreign market distribution but lacking the resources and expertise to undertake this activity on their own account.

Agents

Using an agent in a foreign country represents a form of direct representation for the exporter. In the same way that two export houses may offer a widely differing range of services even though they are ostensibly the same, the services offered by agents differ from one to another. Three types of agent may be identified: exclusive, semi-exclusive and non-exclusive. For the exclusive agent, the agreement is with him alone. In effect, the agent is the company abroad. The semi-exclusive agent will handle one firm's goods along with the non-competitive goods of other companies as well. The non-exclusive agent will handle a variety of goods, some of which may be competing. An agent is usually a national of the country concerned, is paid on a commission basis and does not take title to the goods.

The advantages of using an agent are that the exporter has control further down the chain of distribution. The agent is closely linked with the exporter who can, therefore, be better informed about the local market. Finally, the agent, being paid on a commission basis, does not cost the exporter anything if he is not selling – no sales, no commission.

In most cases, the exporter and the agent sign a contract specifying the obligations of both parties. Reflecting the comments above, unless the contract is an agreement for an exclusive agency, the exporter should be prepared for the fact that his agent will be selling the products of more than one company. Given the contractual arrangement, should the agent prove unsuitable or the exporter wish to change his method of distribution at a later date, substantial costs in legal fees and compensation may be incurred in terminating an agency agreement.

Distributors

A distributor, unlike an agent, is prepared to accept the risks involved in the purchase of the product, thereby taking responsibility for sales in the market. Distributors are frequently used when after-sales servicing is required. The latter may require a considerable commitment of resources on the part of the exporter's foreign partner, and it is usually a distributor, with his capital invested in the exporter's product, rather than an agent, who is more suitable.

A distributor, like an agent, knows the local market structure, customs and conventions, etc.; and will likely have extensive business contacts as an existing supplier to the relevant trade or industry – usually being a specialist in that area. The principal disadvantage of a distributor arrangement derives from the lack of flexibility should market conditions alter or the exporter's market development plans change in the future. The costs of termination can be substantial, and even greater than for the equivalent agent's situation, because distributors are likely to handle higher sales volumes and provide more services in the market.

Direct selling – sales representatives
Like any of the other institutions in the channel of distribution, sales representatives have a dual function of distribution and selling. In this case, however, the emphasis changes to selling as opposed to distribution. Direct selling using sales representatives is not necessarily just the province of the larger companies. It is quite possible to replace agents cost-effectively, with one or possibly several representatives. Take, for example, three agents doing £200,000 business each, being paid, say, 15 per cent commission; the £90,000 paid to the agents in commission fees would be sufficient to fund one or two representatives in some overseas markets. Employing a representative who is a company employee has several advantages. One is his specialised product knowledge. He knows the latest developments in the company. He knows all aspects of the company much better than any export house, agent or distributor would do. He feels more closely identified with the company and it is much easier to communicate with the sales rep. He can also possibly supply better feedback, for example, on competitors' activities. And, in fact, when organising sales territories, it is often the case that the internal distances in the domestic market are as large or larger than travelling to major centres of industry in adjacent countries.

A number of factors favour direct selling: the ease of air travel means that most of the capital cities of Europe, for example, are within an hour or two's flying time of each other; high air fares, deriving from the cartel operating in European airlines, are a problem, but expenditures are at least tax-deductible.

There may be problems with foreign languages, although it is also true to say that some countries like Belgium and Switzerland use more than one language, which can limit the effectiveness of agents and distributors. Travelling time, of course, reduces effective working time as compared to an agent or distributor who is located in the market. It also takes time to build up contacts, especially for a representative who is not a national. Continuity is a further problem, as transfers and resignations mean that the new rep coming in has to renew personal and business relationships with existing and potential customers.

Local sales office
This is popular with foreign customers as it is a sign that the exporter is committed to the local market. The problem for the exporter is who do they send out? Do they send out their best salesmen, and how long do they send

them out for? Three years, five years? It may well be that the sales representative sees the overseas office as a backwater away from headquarters where he runs the risk of being bypassed in the promotion race. There is, in fact, a good deal of resistance by sales personnel to staffing local sales offices abroad, and it may well be that the best men do not want to go. Consequently, it would be worth while recruiting nationals of the country concerned to be part of the sales force in foreign markets. Regarding the size of the office, this is dependent on actual sales and sales aspirations. That said, there is a reasonably large investment of company money and time in starting up a sales office. And it would normally be a case that a company would have some export sales experience first and have tested the market thoroughly in an endeavour to ensure that establishing a local office abroad was worth while.

Empirical evidence

As discussed in Chapter 1, models of export development have implied increasing commitment to export markets moving from indirect exports to direct exports as a firm progresses through the stages. In Bilkey's six-stage model below, the experimental exporter is more likely to use indirect export modes than the experienced exporter.[17] The hypothesised stages are as follows:

1. The firm is unwilling to export and would not even fill an unsolicited export order. This could be through apathy, or because it was busy doing other things, etc.
2. The firm fills unsolicited export orders but does not explore the feasibility of exporting.
3. The firm explores the feasibility of exporting.
4. The firm exports experimentally to one or a few markets.
5. The firm is an experienced exporter to its foreign markets.
6. The firm explores the possibilities of exporting to additional markets.

Linked with the notion of creeping commitment to a market, as defined by type of distribution channel used, is a view of channel choice as involving a balance between market control and information and the commitment of company resources. In Figure 3.4, the indirect channels of distribution, namely, export, confirming and buying houses and, to a lesser extent, piggybacking provide low market control and information but involve little commitment of resources. Direct export channels successively represent more market control and information but require more resources and are commensurately more risky. The direct channels are believed to be utilised in the latter stages in the internationalisation process.

This model and others have been criticised for being too deterministic and general.[18] According to such authors, not all firms go from stage to stage,

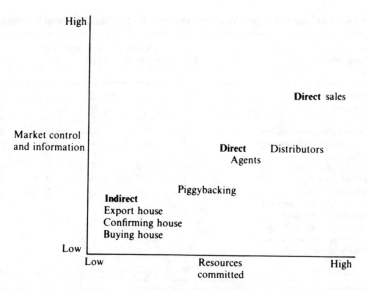

Figure 3.4 Market control and information versus resource commitment.

from low to high commitment. Table 3.4 is taken from a survey by Turnbull of twenty-four companies operating in France, Germany and Sweden using seventy-two separate export structures. It shows that the frequency of occurrence of the various organisation structures does not link to the degree of international orientation (as measured by the proportion of sales turnover accounted for by exports) in an evolutionary manner.[19]

Considering the data in the table, fourteen companies in the low international orientation category had established sales offices and direct sales representation, when the stages theory would suggest agents and distributors. Further, in this category some companies had set up manufacturing or sales subsidiaries. Turnbull explains this as the need for the companies – in the telecommunications industry in this case – to have access and a presence in the foreign markets regardless of international orientation.

Turnbull concludes that: 'the stages theory has merit in its use as a framework for classification purposes rather than for an understanding of how companies internationalise which can be achieved only through a knowledge of the environment within which they operate. It is their environment that determines the nature of their strategies.'[20]

In a study of high-technology firms in the electronics and chemical industries, Ayal and Raban concluded that for those sorts of companies much of the internationalisation literature, including the stages work, was irrelevant.[21] Again, Rosson and Reid analysed choice of export mode in terms of situational analysis.[22] In their view, there is no one correct strategy: the choice of export mode depends on the foreign market opportunity,

Table 3.4 Frequency of export organisation structure by international orientation

Export organisation structure[a]	International orientation[a]				Total
	Low	Medium	High	Very High	
No organisation	2	0	0	0	2
Distributor only	4	0	0	5	9
Agent only	0	0	2	1	3
Direct sales representation only	2	2	0	0	4
Distributor/agent and sales rep.	1	1	8	3	13
Sales office only	1	2	0	0	3
Sales office and sales rep.	14	7	5	0	26
Sales subsidiary only	3	0	3	3	9
Sales subsidiary and distributor/agent and sales rep.	1	0	0	0	1
Manufacturing subsidiary and distributor and sales rep.	1	0	0	0	1
Manufacturing subsidiary and sales office and sales rep.	1	0	0	0	1
Total	30	12	18	12	72

[a] Low = less than 25 per cent of sales turnover is from foreign markets
Medium = 25–49 per cent
High = 50–74 per cent
Very High = 75 per cent or more
Source: Turnbull, P.W. (1987), 'A Challenge to the Stages Theory of the Internationalisation Process', in Rosson, P.J. and Reid, S.D. (eds), *Managing Export Entry and Expansion*, Praeger, New York, 35.

the firm's resources and the type of product; in short, it is situationally determined.

SUCCESSFUL EXPORTERS

A number of studies have sought to identify what makes some exporters successful and others not.[23] One of the most recent studies drew up a detailed profile as outlined in Table 3.5.[24] The overriding characteristic of successful exporters was considered to be the quality of the management, a long-term commitment to export development and respect for the customer. The operational issues were considered as less important in success, but even here there were differences between successful and less successful firms: the latter were highly concerned about issues such as credit risks, currency problems, technical standards, etc., but, perhaps through ignorance, their response was commonly to 'do nothing'.

Exporter profiles

Government export promotion organisations around the world have tried over the years to direct their efforts towards firms that are most likely to

Table 3.5 Profiles of attitudes of successful and less successful exporters

	Successful	Less successful
Key issues		
Find right distributors	Regard this as the prime issue. Board director involvement in vetting	Respond to inquiries. Expect to be found easily via directories, embassies, etc.
Commitment to export	Regard exporting as inevitable and necessary in a growing business. Persistent, professional and go forward to their customers. Concern of company	Insular, unprofessional, unware of issues. Exporting seen as solution to problem of part of company only
Learn by doing	Assume responsibility for in-house expertise on the whole process of exporting. Automatically assume mistakes will be made	Overwhelmed by early obstacles and blame others. Defeatist
Selectivity in markets	Ranking process according to rational criteria, progressive focus	Spread effort too thinly, go for high cost/risk markets too soon. Restrict efforts to passive response to unsolicited enquiries
Financial investment	Prepared to look at projected returns on long-term basis.	Exporting seen as gamble with spare cash. Short-term view
Long-term horizon	Several years' effort necessary to lay foundations for solid success. Expect hiccoughs.	Expect quick results with meagre resources
Confidence	Do not export until confident of success. Control growth	Start too soon in haphazard way. Take on too much
Respect for customer	Assume the customer will be at least as good a businessman as you are. Careful study of his needs and sensitivity to them	Adopt 'take it or leave it' attitude. Underestimates the customer
Attitudes to intermediaries	Use advisers at start of export process, but thereafter only very selectively	Either over- or under-rely on external advice. Insufficient range of potential advice sought
Fast communications	Use telephone, fax, telex, electronic mail as appropriate	Rely on letters. Unaware of importance of speed of response
Less important issues		
Languages	Simply part of looking after the customer. Normal in-house skill	Overestimate importance leading to excessive timidity or ignore altogether

Table 3.5 (cont.)

	Successful	Less successful
Credit risk	Regard as worse than domestic in general. Use of ECGD, Letter of Credit, proper investigation, etc. Obvious exceptions (some LDCs)	Fear of risk prevents action
Export documentation and procedures	No problem to professionals. Handled expertly in house or by forwarding agent externally	Lack of professional approach: try to cut corners
Export pricing	Accept that market determines the price and exporter has to control costs. Quote in foreign currency where customer requires it. Hedge if necessary. Aware of volume/unit cost relationships	Inflexible attitude. Try to price at UK levels plus freight. Worry about currency problems
Export staff recruitment	Good people can be trained in-house	Believe good people are very difficult to find and prohibitively expensive
Technical standards/ legal systems	Can be a non-tariff barrier but usually surmountable	Overestimate importance
Organisation of export function	May have separate export organisation or not, but whole company committed to export. Usually separate staff handle detailed documentation	Exporting not integrated sufficiently with total business
Payment delays	Generally similar or better than UK. Some exceptions (LDCs)	Believed to be a high cost of exporting

Source: BOTB, *Into Active Exporting*, 30–1.

respond to government help. Attempts have been made to compile profiles of characteristics of such companies, especially with the aim of identifying potential exporters.[25] For instance, Cavusgil, Bilkey and Tesar developed a profile of firms highly likely to export, using four characteristics. Firms with this profile had managements possessing very favourable expectations regarding the effect of exporting on their firm's growth; planned to develop their firm's markets; had annual sales of one million dollars or more; and had favourable expectations regarding the effect of exporting on their firm's market development.[26] There is a debate in the literature about how useful this exercise is. Reid characterises the export development process as a complex phenomenon only understood with reference to key variables like the firm, competition, management and environment, and questions the role of profiling.[27] Cavusgil, from perhaps a more pragmatic standpoint, sees a basic profile as helpful in developing export potential.[28]

Market concentration v. spreading

Chapters 1 and 2 have both referred to the country/market selection process. Factors such as market size and growth, the level of competition and psychological closeness were all shown to be significant factors. What was not discussed, however, was the question of the number of countries/markets to export to. This topic has been researched in some detail, culminating in a debate *inter alia* on market concentration versus spreading.[29]

The BETRO Trust Committee has suggested that established exporters will often find that their best markets number between five and ten, and imply that it is upon these that efforts should be concentrated; for new exporters it is proposed that concentration on five or six export markets provides a route to success.[30] The arguments in favour of concentration include the following:

1. Concentration on key markets limits the span of control for dealing with problems, and reduces administration.
2. The firm will gain better market and agent knowledge.
3. There will be more opportunity to compete advantageously on non-price factors rather than relying on price competition.
4. There should be less distraction from important tasks because of small markets and smaller orders; and sales should be improved with higher-quality selling.

Some of the assumptions in market concentration can be questioned. It is assumed that markets can be selected in an optimal way. This relies on the availability of information, on an ability to use it and also on the belief that the markets selected are stable. So there is a danger of concentrating on the wrong markets. A study by Hunt of export management in medium-sized engineering companies in the UK made this point: that practical limitations had led to unfavourable regional specialisation, compared with overseas competitors.[31] There is also the question of market dependence, resulting from reliance on significant market shares in a small number of exports; conversely, the advantage of a spreading and low market share strategy lies in maintaining a low international profile. Finally, it might be questioned whether concentration should relate to products or markets. It has been suggested that the Japanese have concentrated on products rather than geographical areas and that this has been one of the factors in their success in international marketing. A survey of German exporters produced a similar finding: product concentration offers competitive power through specialisation on customer needs and hence the company should not restrict markets in a geographic sense.

Turning to the practicalities of the situation, Table 3.6 presents a checklist for comparing market concentration and market spreading. The first step in

Table 3.6 Checklist for comparing market concentration and market spreading

A. The company's present position
1. Export sales
2. Export markets and market shares ⎫
3. Market numbers ⎪
4. Allocation of efforts between export markets ⎬
5. Is the market strategy of the company market concentration or market spreading, i.e.
(a) exporting to less than twelve markets; ⎫ Market
(b) exporting to more than twelve markets, ⎬ concentration
but concentrating efforts on five or six of the markets; ⎪
(c) exporting to more than twelve markets, and ⎫ Market
not concentrating efforts on a few areas? ⎬ spreading

B. Spreading or concentration
6. Where does the company fall on each of the following factors?

Factors favouring market spreading	Factors favouring market concentration
(a) Company factors	
Managers see dependence on a few key markets as a high risk – which they do not wish to accept	Managers do not see dependence on a few key markets as a high risk – or accept the risk – or small market numbers are seen as less risky
Little export market knowledge or ability to choose 'best' markets	Adequate market knowledge and ability to pick the 'best' markets with an acceptable expectation of reliability
An objective of growth by market development	An objective of growth by market penetration
Early or mature stages internationalisation	Middle stages of internationalisation
Others, e.g. company policy, group market allocations, manpower	
(b) Product factors	
Limited, specialised applications	Extensive, mass-market uses
Low volume	High volume
Non-repeat purchase good	Repeat purchase good
Standard product saleable in many markets	Product requires substantial adaptation to different market requirements
Early in the product life cycle (to gain volume rapidly) or late in the product life cycle (to take whatever demand remains)	Middle stages of the product life cycle, when the market is maturing
Others, e.g. supply limitations, product perishability, transport problems	
(c) Market factors	
Small markets – specialised segments	Large markets – high-volume segments
Unstable markets	Stable markets
Many similar markets throughout the world	Limited number of comparable markets in the world
New or declining markets	Mature markets
Large markets are disproportionately competitive	Large markets are not disproportionately competitive – or if they are, the company can cope with competitors
The company cannot compete effectively on the main competitive base used by other suppliers	The company can compete effectively against competitors on their terms
Established competitors have large shares of major key markets	Major, key markets are not dominated, but divided among many competitors

Table 3.6 continued

Low buyer loyalty to supply sources	High buyer loyalty to supply sources
Barriers to entry of major key markets, e.g. tariffs, non-tariff barriers	No barriers to entry of major key markets – or the barriers act can be overcome
Others, e.g. multinational customers buying worldwide, international trading agreements, restrictive agreements with existing distributors	

(d) *Marketing factors*

Incremental marketing communication costs (personal selling, advertising, promotion, publicity) for additional markets are low, e.g. direct mail, catalogues, shared international advertising	Incremental marketing communications costs (personal selling, advertising, promotion, publicity) for additional markets are high, e.g. extra salesmen, new sales offices, local advertising and promotion
Incremental order handling costs for additional markets are low, e.g. taking up slack in fixed administrative resources	Incremental order handling costs for additional markets are high, e.g. extra personnel, facilities, etc.
Incremental physical distribution costs for additional markets are low, e.g. taking up slack in existing systems using outside contractors, billing physical distribution (PD) costs to customers	Incremental physical distribution cost for additional markets are high, e.g. requiring extra facilities
Incremental after-sales service costs for additional markets are low, e.g. taking up slack in existing service facilities	Incremental after-sales service costs for additional markets, e.g. new facilities are needed, or uneconomical use of existing systems
Net incremental pricing costs (price lists, invoice processing, etc.) for additional markets are low, e.g. where there are opportunities for premium prices in minor markets	Net incremental pricing costs (price lists, invoice processing, etc.) for additional markets are high, e.g. where local currencies have to be used, where a world price level prevails

C. Implications

7. Does the balance of situational factors in B above suggest that market spreading or market concentration is more appropriate to the company's needs?
8. Is the strategy actually pursued by the company compatible with the conclusions reached in B above?
   If our present strategy does not match our analysis of the full range of situational factors, should we consider changing:
   by reducing market numbers;
   by increasing market numbers;
   by changing the way efforts are divided between markets?
   For example, is it possible to group markets into categories, with different types of marketing efforts and costs, i.e.

Groups	Marketing efforts	No. of markets	Sales per market
A	Intensive	Few	High
B	Medium	Several	Moderate
C	Low	Many	Low

9. What would be the consequences of any changes arising out of the answer to Question 8 to:
   Sales
   Costs
   Cash flow
   Competitive reactions?
10. What actions should be taken by the company?

Source: Piercy, N. (1982), *Export Strategy: Markets and Competition*, George Allen & Unwin, London, 104–7.

the process is to check the company's present position by identifying existing export markets and the relative degree of effort devoted to exploiting these. Thereafter it is suggested that the enterprise should evaluate itself, taking account of a series of factors as follows.

Company factors
Naturally the attitudes and knowledge of the management are considerations, as are the firm's objectives, for example whether to develop many country markets, which may be necessary owing to the nature of the product. It is also suggested that companies might consider spreading in the early stages of internationalisation which is, in fact, contrary to much of the advice given by business advisers.

Product factors
How specialised the product is, whether it is a high or low volume product and so on, all influence the choice of country/market. A manufacturer of a specialised low-volume product like desalination equipment will be more inclined to sell in many markets.

Market factors
It is not always easy to disentangle market factors from product factors. Market factors include whether the market is a specialised one, perhaps with small segments in many countries; the nature of competition; and the ease of access to major markets.

Marketing factors
The point here is that it is sometimes possible to win small market shares for relatively low marketing expenditures. This situation favours market spreading. Where firms have to commit large marketing expenditure such as that necessary to establish a foreign distribution network then market concentration is favoured.

In the last section of Table 3.6 some questions are raised about concentration and spreading for the company to answer. Note particularly the example of market categories used in item 8 of the table, as the concentration/spreading argument is not simply about selling to a few markets or to a large number, but how much effort goes into all the markets a company serves.

INTERNATIONAL INDUSTRIAL MARKETING

An important body of research on international industrial marketing has been generated by the International Marketing and Purchasing Group (IMP).[32] Much of international industrial marketing utilises forms of exporting and the work of the IMP Group has added significantly to the knowledge of how companies in industrial markets develop their international activities and what has contributed to the success of companies. The IMP approach recognises two important features of industrial marketing. The first is that buyers and sellers are active participants; neither is passive. Secondly, the buyer/seller relationship exhibits a complex pattern of interaction which means that there is often a close relationship between the parties, and such relationships are frequently long-term and stable, enduring for many years.

Figure 3.5 depicts the major variables influencing industrial marketing as interpreted by the IMP group. In essence the view is that a wide range of variables affect the relationship between the buyer and seller, and to understand and analyse such industrial markets it is necessary to look at more than individual transactions between companies. The four groups of variables are as follows:

1. The elements and processes of interaction which include individual transactions between companies.
2. The characteristics of the parties involved both as organisations and individuals.
3. The environment within which this interaction takes place including geographic and cultural distance.
4. The 'atmosphere' surrounding the interaction. The atmosphere is built up by the specific episodes of exchange and by the long-term process of interaction with suppliers. The atmosphere can be described in terms of power/dependence in the relationships, the degree of conflict and co-operation, and the overall 'social distance' between the parties arising from mutual attitudes and perceptions.

Out of the IMP research came a number of key findings relating to country/market strategy and marketing strategy within countries:

1. The most successful companies in the study recognised the need for an international orientation and for commitment to the foreign market. Customers have to believe their foreign supplier is committed to their country and their company in the long term.
2. The interaction between the customer and supplier is more intensive in those markets perceived as socially and psychologically close to the supplier. This is all very well but there is a danger here. Social and psychological distance can be overcome by investment in the market, so should suppliers continue to operate with the 'closest' markets or should they develop more 'distant' markets?

The work of the IMP Group is highly relevant to the theme of distribution channels discussed earlier. It was apparent from the research, for example, that British firms often exhibited less commitment to a market than their

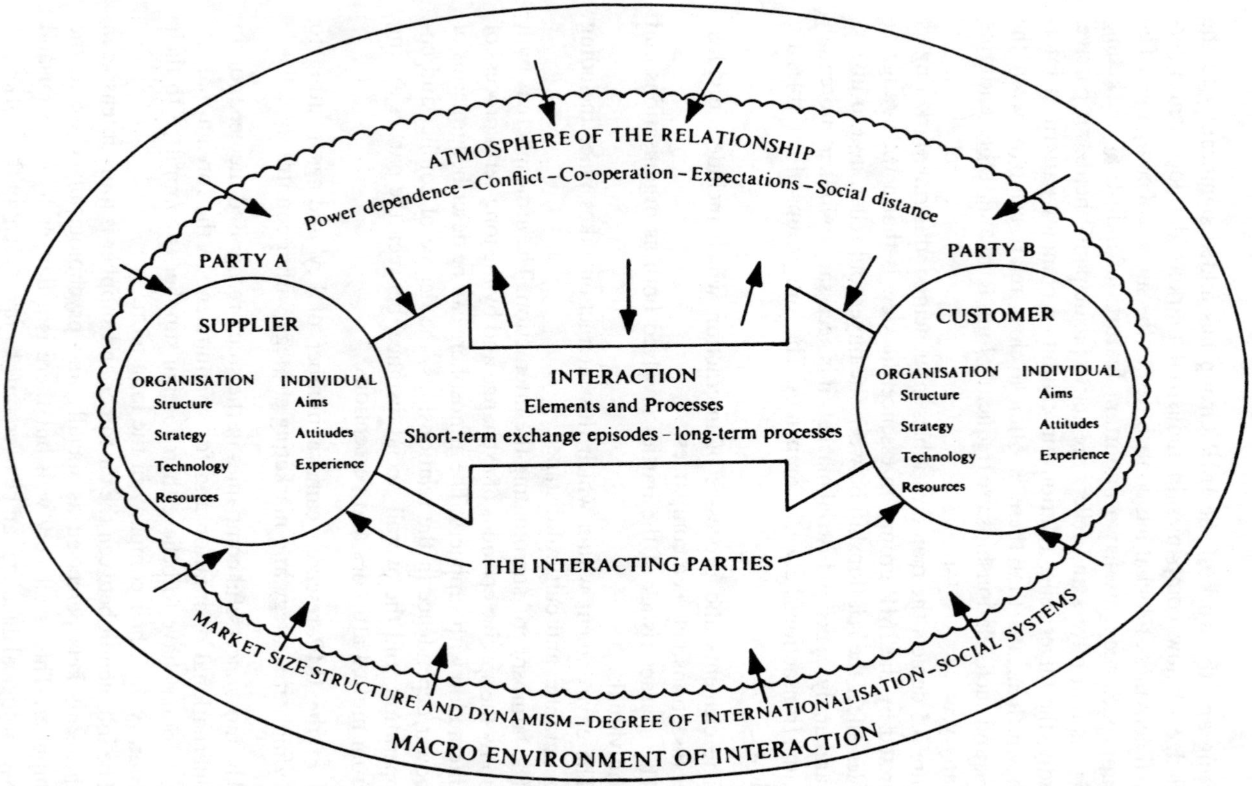
ATMOSPHERE OF THE RELATIONSHIP
Power dependence – Conflict – Co-operation – Expectations – Social distance
PARTY A
SUPPLIER
ORGANISATION
Structure
Strategy
Technology
Resources
INDIVIDUAL
Aims
Attitudes
Experience
INTERACTION
Elements and Processes
Short-term exchange episodes – long-term processes
PARTY B
CUSTOMER
ORGANISATION
Structure
Strategy
Technology
Resources
INDIVIDUAL
Aims
Attitudes
Experience
THE INTERACTING PARTIES
MARKET SIZE STRUCTURE AND DYNAMISM – DEGREE OF INTERNATIONALISATION – SOCIAL SYSTEMS
MACRO ENVIRONMENT OF INTERACTION

Figure 3.5 The nature and scope of supplier–customer interaction. Source: Turnbull, P.W. and Valla, J.P. (1986), *Strategies for International Industrial Marketing*, Croom Helm, London, 5.

competitors as they did not use sales subsidiaries and other high-commitment modes so frequently. This, in the opinion of the IMP Group, has hampered the effectiveness of their industrial marketing abroad. Of equal importance, however, is the distinction which was drawn between the formal organisation (the use of sales subsidiaries) and informal organisation, as manifested in the range and intensity of interpersonal contacts between supplier and customer staff. The informal marketing interaction often represents considerable investment and operating cost. It is argued that these resources and costs should be planned and managed and not allowed to develop by chance in a haphazard way. Exhibit 3.2 comprises three short case studies illustrating some of the variables categorised by the IMP Group in their model of the interaction process, and showing the significance of these interpersonal contacts.

EXHIBIT 3.2
CASE STUDIES

Dorkan Company: an example of sequential interaction strategy for establishing relationships with German customers
The British company 'Dorkan' markets an innovatory process for the manufacture of small castings to the automotive and consumer durables industries. It has developed a sequential interaction strategy for initiating and developing relationships with customers in an attempt to reach the influential members of the customer's decision-making unit. This is undertaken in the knowledge that many customers have had an unfavourable experience in the past of using castings made by this special process.
When entering the German market, the following procedure is followed:

1. First the marketing director establishes contact with the most senior purchasing executive of the customer. No business is negotiated at this stage.
2. He than contacts the buyer, in order to gain access to the customer's engineers who specify the product.
3. A sales representative and engineer from the supplier then take over the account and establish the contacts with the buyer and customer's junior engineers.
4. The sales representative progressively raises his contacts to senior buying and older engineering staff who were previously opposed to the new process.
5. The supplier offers to quote for a trial order and sends over technical staff to liaise with the customer's engineers and buyers in the correct choice of a trial component.
6. At the trial contract stage, supplier's quality control, engineering and marketing staff visit customers to ensure that the trial is conducted satisfactorily.
7. If a contract is likely to be placed, the customer's buyers, engineers and quality inspectors are invited to visit the supplier's factory.

Exhibit 3.2 continued

The interaction strategy is based on a prepared plan using the rules of etiquette in each country, with a matching of status levels in the two organisations. An attempt is made to build up strong professional and social links between matched functions. The resistance to innovation amongst older staff is recognised by ensuring that there is acceptance of the innovation at a low level in the organisation and a strong reputational link at the top level.

Brown Company: the use of organisation mechanisms for co-ordinating and controlling personal contacts between suppliers and customers
The contacts between two trading organisations may originate between marketing and purchasing departments but may subsequently evolve to a complex network of interfunctional contacts. Brown Ltd attempts to control relationships with some important customers by appointing a senior account executive to co-ordinate and control the information exchange between the two companies. His function as the sole point of interaction with customers can be represented as follows:

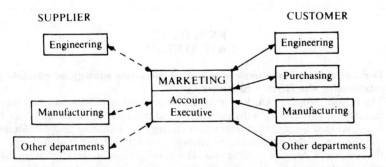

All direct contacts with customers, involving communications, negotiations, adaptations, etc., are handled by the account executive of the marketing department.

Several similar organisational forms were found, especially among capital plant suppliers, who often had special projects or contracts departments developing custom-built product offerings to suit particular customers' needs. A marketing executive, who invariably had a strong technical background, usually acted as the direct personal contact with the potential customer.

In many large automotive component manufacturers a product-development team often undertook special work in collaboration with a customer and a single person was responsible for all personal contacts between the team and the customer.

A wide variety of other forms of co-ordinating and controlling interorganisational personal contacts were found to be operated by suppliers but rarely was this something which was unilaterally decided upon by the supplier. Usually it was a structure evolved jointly by supplier and customer.

Pace Chemicals: a power-dependence strategy with an Italian customer
Pace Chemicals, a British supplier of speciality pigments, has been dealing with an Italian paint manufacturer for over 25 years, but until recently has been only one of several suppliers used by the customer. The technical superiority of Pace's products had been offset by its poor delivery record. In order to

Exhibit 3.2 continued

strengthen the base for a more successful attack on the Italian market, Pace decided to give priority to an improvement in its production batch scheduling system. Once this was achieved, the supplier then set out to make the customer increasingly dependent on the technical features of the product. Through a series of joint product development projects financed by Pace, the customer made adaptations to his manufacturing process. Extensive exchange of technical and commercial information between supplier and customer was initiated by Pace to increase the reputation for trust, collaboration and expertise that it had with the customer. The main basis for the eventual customer dependence on Pace as the sole supplier was through the following:

● The special product advantage over competitors' offerings.
● The large customer technical adaptations achieved by the supplier.
● The supplier's technical competence in seeking out customer application problems and providing the customer with a marketing advantage for its paints.
● The establishment of openness and trust in the relationship by extensive technical and commercial information exchange.

Source: Turnbull, P.W. and Valla, J.P. (1986), *Strategies for International Industrial Marketing*, Croom Helm, London, 200–3.

MANAGING THE EXPORT PROCESS

The objective in this section is to discuss the kinds of activities that will help a company to successfully develop its exports, from the initial assessment of the company itself to the establishment of a successful export operation. Underlying the successful development of exporting as a supply mode is the commitment of the top management in the company to the export venture. Without devoting sufficient resources, especially management time, the chances of success are much reduced.

Step 1: Company assessment
How has your company become interested in exporting? Many firms become interested in exporting by chance. It may be the receipt of an unsolicited order, spotting a market opportunity while on holiday abroad, etc. Such a haphazard start to exporting is not necessarily a weakness in itself but if this approach to export markets continues, the chances of success are significantly lower than if a more planned and organised approach is adopted. It is true that small and medium-sized firms frequently do not have formal, written plans for business development. Nevertheless, the more successful exporters do have an organised and professional approach towards their markets and customers.

The aim here is for management to assess whether or not the company should export. It is perfectly feasible in some cases for a company to restrict its activities to the domestic market. Not every company has to go international. Appraising the most suitable options will depend on an analysis of the company's strengths and weaknesses, objectives and ambitions. The checklist in Table 3.7 sets out the sort of questions the management of a small firm should consider before exporting. By completing the checklist, management should have a clearer idea of the benefits of exporting, and gauge whether starting to export is a suitable option for company growth. Thus high scores for a number of the criteria would be suggestive of significant benefits from selling abroad.

Although some motives like utilising excess production capacity have driven many companies into exporting, sometimes in a haphazard and disorganised manner, if a company assesses its present situation and the likely benefits of exporting, the chances of success are much greater.

There are steps a company can take which should increase the chances of successfully developing exports. These can be summarised as follows:

1. Be committed. Look upon exporting as part of a growing business, a concern for the whole company. Research thoroughly before you start and show the same commitment thereafter.

Table 3.7 Checklist to measure the benefits of exporting

	Very important				Less important
	5	4	3	2	1
Export sales will offset a lack of growth in the domestic market					
Export markets will help exploit the full potential of my products, services, technology					
Export sales will help improve gross margins and profitability					
Export sales will help reduce dependence on the domestic market					
Export sales will help reduce units costs					
Export sales will contribute to R&D costs					
Export activity will help keep me up to date on international changes in technology, products and servicing levels					
Export sales will help utilise excess production capacity					
Export sales will help synchronise fluctuations in production schedules					
Export sales will help synchronise fluctuations in revenue patterns					
Export sales will help secure jobs					

Source: BOTB (1986), *Exporting for the Smaller Firm*, 7.

2. Build up your confidence. Do not start too soon and in a haphazard way. Begin when you are confident of success. Do not take on too much.
3. Do not expect a quick return. Exporting should not be treated as a gamble with spare cash; the firm should go for longer-term returns.
4. Look to the longer term as it takes several years' effort to build success. Expect to make mistakes.
5. Do not be surprised if you seek advice from a number of organisations at the start. Companies usually seek advice from a wide range of intermediaries in the beginning but become increasingly selective as their export experience grows.
6. Learn by doing. The export process can present problems and errors will be made. Endeavour to build up in-company expertise on the whole export process.
7. Respect your customer. Study your customer and his needs.
8. Communicate fast. Speed of response is vital. Use telephone, telex, fax and electronic mail when you can.

Step 2: Utilise available help
There are a large number of organisations that can help companies at all stages of export development. The intention here is to mention briefly organisations that can assist, regardless of country.

Most governments sponsor an export promotion organisation of some kind. They usually provide a wide range of services and really ought to be contacted by any company considering exporting. Although experienced exporters use official organisations less, there may still be benefits for them in using government-sponsored organisations.

Trade associations and chambers of commerce offer free advice and help, and often organise trade missions to foreign markets.

The international sections of banks give advice to exporters as well as providing financial services, including arranging payment procedures, covering foreign exchange risk and financing export business.

Insurance of credit and sometimes political risk is available from private insurance companies, and some governments sponsor such insurance.

Freight forwarders may help with transport and documentation. For a fee, all the export documentation and paperwork will be handled. When a company is interested only in indirect exporting, some forms of export house or export management companies will handle all aspects of exporting.

Particularly of help to exporters from developing countries are the advisory services of the United Nations.

Most exporters work with other organisations on a day-to-day basis. The additional complexity of international business puts stress on working closely and efficiently with banks, freight forwarders and the like.

Step 3: Country/market selection and concentration/spreading decision
When an enterprise is undertaking an assessment of the possible benefits from exporting in step 1, some preliminary consideration may be given to potential markets. However, this needs to be formalised utilising the screening procedures outlined in Chapter 2. More than this, the exporter should also be considering how many markets to focus upon. Most times a new exporter is given advice to concentrate his efforts on one or a few markets, but as suggested earlier there are circumstances where selling to a larger number of countries/markets is appropriate, especially as the exporter gains experience. The point to note is the necessity to analyse the relevant factors in Table 3.6 in favour of market concentration or spreading. The firm's resulting strategy is 'situational' in that it is appropriate for the company's situation, and not the result of following blanket advice to concentrate on markets.

Step 4: Market entry strategy formulation
The choice of country/market and market entry mode are to an extent interdependent. A market with large potential may warrant a sales subsidiary, whereas a small market may be served by an agent or by indirect export modes. In some markets, a combination of modes, perhaps with sales representatives working with a local agent, are judged the most appropriate.

Once a mode has been selected, it can be difficult and costly to change. There may be agency contracts to terminate and there is always the time and effort required to set up replacement distribution arrangements.

The company has to evaluate alternative modes of entry and development, and the checklist in Figure 3.6 provides a framework for the analysis.[33] From the perspective of this chapter, the assumption is that market entry is largely restricted to the export route, where the entry modes available range from export houses through to overseas sales offices. Similar types of checklist relating to the wider choice of exporting, entering into non-equity contractual arrangements or utilising foreign direct investment and production overseas are presented in Chapter 7.

Step 5: Export strategy formulation
It is at this stage that all the previous analyses of the foreign market(s) are drawn together into an export plan for the company (see Figure 3.7). The export plan would include objectives, timetable for implementation, target market(s) and appropriate strategies for these markets. The competition will have been assessed and a view taken on the likely reaction of competitors to the exporter's entry into the market.

Step 6: Export operations – delivery and payment
For the new exporter especially, delivery and payment present problems, although help is available, as the comments in step 2 have indicated. It is

1. What alternative entry modes are available for our product in the foreign market?
2. What are the advantages and disadvantages of each mode?
3. What alternative entry modes are used by importers of major competitive products?
4. Should our firm use different entry modes for various products and/or market segments in the market?
5. What are the costs of the different alternative entry modes?
6. How much working capital will be needed by alternative entry modes?
7. How much control does our firm wish to maintain over the marketing of our product in the market?
8. What types of pre- and post-sales services will the intermediary need to provide with our product?
9. Will the mode of selling our product need to change over time? If so, in what ways?
10. How will distribution methods for our product be different from those used domestically?
11. What are the major problems that relate to distance and communication?
12. What logistical elements are important for the market?
13. Is our firm willing to maintain the responsibility for shipping the product to the foreign market?
14. What type of reputation does our firm want reflected by the intermediary handling our product in the market?
15. What kinds of information will be needed from our intermediary?
16. What are the legal issues that must be considered?
17. What financial resources are needed by the intermediary?
18. What complementary products should the intermediary handle?
19. Will the intermediary be allowed to handle competitive products?
20. What are the various issues that need to be included in the working agreement with our intermediary?

Figure 3.6 Export market entry strategy formulation. Source: Darling, J.R. (1985), 'Keys for Success in Exporting to the US Market', *European Journal of Marketing*, **19**(2), 22.

evident from the export behaviour literature that although the operational aspects of exporting are seen as a barrier by companies not committed to exporting and by inexperienced exporters, documentation and the like need not be a deterrent for committed companies. The checklist shown in Figure 3.8 for delivery and payment emphasises the need for an organised approach to export operations and for continuing to monitor progress, a theme underlying the next step.

Step 7: Evaluation and control
It is only to be expected that the plans drawn up for penetration of a foreign market will be altered in the light of experience in the market. The company will make mistakes and will have to reappraise some of its original decisions.

---

1. Executive summary : Overview of plans for the foreign market
2. Introduction : Why company should do business in the foreign market
3. Part I: A statement of foreign market commitment
4. Part II: The background/situation analysis:
   (a) Overview of market opportunity
   (b) Primary target market segments
   (c) Analysis of competitive situation
   (d) Assessment of product potential
   (e) Established market entry mode
   (f) Operational strengths and weaknesses
   (g) Resources of firm to be allocated
   (h) Organisational structure for market
5. Part III: Strategic marketing plan for foreign market:
   (a) Identified marketing goals
   (b) Product analysis and selection
   (c) Warranties and other product services
   (d) Pricing and other terms of sales
   (e) Channel(s) of distribution to be used
   (f) Shipping and other transportation means
   (g) Warehousing and other logistical needs
   (h) Market information system needed
   (i) Methods of advertising and promotion
6. Part IV : Operational budget and pro forma financial statements
7: Part V: Implementation schedule and timetable
8. Part VI: Procedures for evaluation and control, including periodic operational/ management audits

---

Figure 3.7 Developing an export strategy. Source: Darling, J.R. (1985), 'Keys for Success in Exporting to the US Market', *European Journal of Marketing*, **19**(2), 27.

In one sense, the initial export plans and programmes are just the start of business in a market; much more time, effort and expense will be required to realise the firm's goals.

Concluding comments – managing the export process

Exporting is more complicated than domestic business and the firm should monitor accuracy of documentation, delivery times, cash flow, profits, intermediary performance and the like to see where problems occur and correct them. Also, the firm's analysis of the market at time of entry will become out of date as market conditions change. The company, in evaluating existing plans and preparing new ones, ought to be aware of changes in the market and how they may affect its own operations.

Notwithstanding these cautionary remarks, the fact remains that companies have an awareness of exporting, which they will frequently not have

Setting up

Decide whether to use an export administration company and, if so, which of these points they will cover

Find a good freight forwarder

Talk to your postal services representative

Talk to your Chamber of Commerce

Talk to an international specialist from your bank

Obtain a simplified documentation set if possible

Check if you can take further advantage of other export services such as those of a government export body

At the market research stage

Check competitors' delivery terms (ex works to delivered)

Check competitors' currency of sale (probably buyer's currency)

Check competitors' terms of payment (30, 60, 180 days, Letter of Credit, etc.)

Check normal methods of transport and obtain quotations

Check if subject to special controls or financial arrangements, such as for processed foodstuffs, or textiles

At the quotation stage

Consult your freight forwarder and bank as necessary

Quote delivery terms and include these costs in the price

Quote in suitable currency

Specify a suitable method of transport

Quote the terms and methods of payment clearly

When the order is received

Check that the terms are as quoted and all delivery, paperwork and payment requirements can be met

Arrange cover against foreign currency fluctuations and default

When the order is ready – or preferably beforehand

Contact the forwarder to arrange transport and insurance

Allow time to complete and process the documents, especially for special certificates or methods of payment where other organisations are involved

Use the most appropriate simplified documentation

At regular intervals until payment is in your bank account

Check progress of payment and other commercial factors such as the customer's total indebtedness to you

Check cumulative costs of interest, both from date of invoice and back to the date of receipt of order

Figure 3.8 Checklist for delivery and payment. Source: Adapted from BOTB checklist. (Continued on p. 106.)

When payment has been received

Check whether the intended margin has been realised after deducting all costs and overheads

Review the success of the transaction and what points to improve on next time

Costpoints – fees, charges and other costs

Carriage to point of delivery

Insurance to point of delivery

Fees for forwarder's export services

Fees for import services (if selling delivered)

Fees for special documents, e.g. stamping Certificates of Origin

Refunds or levies for certain processed foods

Interest charges on credit sales, or discounts/fees on bank's up-front settlements

Bank fees for services debited to you

Insurance against default by customer

Communications costs – airmail, telex, telephone

Time costs at up to £10 per day for each £1,000 p.a. salary

Figure 3.8 continued

for other forms of international business. And returning to the theme of the introduction to this chapter, governments' desires to stimulate exports mean that virtually all countries operate export promotion policies (to supplement macro and industrial policy) in support of overseas trading enterprises. The instruments of export promotion include reply-on-request and information services, assistance with overseas missions and trade fairs, as well as direct management support to exporting companies on an individual basis. Although studies show a high level of dissatisfaction among firms using such export services, the fact remains that government policies are likely to reinforce the belief that exporting is the 'normal' first step into international markets. [34]

FURTHER READING

1. For the smaller firm a useful commentary on the problems of starting exporting is Willis, M. (1985), *Exporting for the Smaller Firm*, BOTB, London.
2. Several reviews of the export behaviour literature have appeared over the years. Two recent studies are Bradley, F.M. (1987), 'Nature and Significance of International Marketing: A Review', *Journal of Business Research*, 15(3), June, 205–19; Kedia, B. and Chhokar, J. (1986), 'Factors Inhibiting Export Performance of Firms: An Empirical Investigation', *Management International Review*, 26(4), 33–43.
3. For further commentary on the spreading/concentration issue, see Piercy, N. (1982), *Export Strategy: Markets and Competition*, George Allen & Unwin, London. This book puts forward arguments against market concentration, while IMR (1978), *How British Industry Exports*, Industrial Market Research Ltd, London, illustrates the need to concentrate on markets.

4. A full discussion of international industrial marketing strategy in Europe with inter-country comparisons and implications for strategy is given in Turnbull, P.W. and Valla; J.P. (1986), *Strategies for International Industrial Marketing*, Croom Helm, London.

QUESTIONS FOR DISCUSSION

1. Firms have started exporting in response to a variety of stimuli. What are they and do they have implications for a company's success in exporting?
2. Comment has been made to the effect that committed exporters recognise barriers to exporting but are usually able to overcome them. Do passive or non-exporters perceive barriers in the same way and why are barriers a disincentive for such companies?
3. What are the weaknesses in the market concentration argument and why is a situational view of country/market selection advocated?
4. What are the characteristics of the main export modes? Why is it said that the choice of export mode depends on foreign market opportunity, firm's resources and type of product?
5. How would you distinguish between the formal and informal organisation and why is it important for international industrial marketing?

NOTES AND REFERENCES

1. Smith, A. (1776, Glasgow edition, 1976), *An Inquiry into the Nature and Causes of the Wealth of Nations*, Book IV, Chapter III, 488–98.
2. World Bank (1988), *World Development Report 1987*, International Bank for Reconstruction and Development, New York.
3. Stopford, J.M. and Dunning, J.H. (1983), *Multinationals. Company Performance and Global Trends*, Macmillan, London.
4. British Overseas Trade Board, (1986), *Exporting for the Smaller Firm*, BOTB, London. See also Cannon, T. and Willis, M.D. (1985), *How to Buy and Sell Overseas*, Hutchinson, London.
5. *Financial Times*, 10 March 1987, page 16.
6. Bilkey, W.J. (1978), 'An Attempted Integration of the Literature on the Export Behaviour of Firms', *Journal of International Business Studies*, 9(1), 33–46.
7. Simpson, C.L. and Kujawa, D. (1974), 'The Export Decision Process: An Empirical Inquiry', *Journal of International Business Studies*, 5, Spring, 107–17; Cook, D. (1987), 'The Queen's Award for Export Achievement. The First 21 Years: An Evaluation', in Proceedings, Marketing Education Group, Bradford; BOTB (1985), *Success in Japan*, BOTB, London; Turnbull, P.W. and Valla, J.P. (1986), *Strategies for International Industrial Marketing*, Croom Helm, London.
8. For example, see Cavusgil, S.T. and Nevin, J.R., (1981), 'Internal Determinants of Export Marketing Behaviour: An Empirical Investigation', *Journal of Marketing Research*, **28**, February, 114–19.
9. Cavusgil, S.T. (1984), 'Differences Among Exporting Firms Based on their Degree of Internationalisation', *Journal of Business Research*, **18**, 195–208.
10. Bilkey, 'An Attempted Integration of the Literature on the Export Behaviour of Firms', 33–4.
11. British Overseas Trade Board (1987), *Into Active Exporting*, BOTB, London.

12. The Small Businesses Research Trust Survey (1987), in BOTB, *Into Active Exporting*.
13. BOTB, *Into Active Exporting*, 6.
14. Ibid., 11.
15. *Financial Times*, 10 March 1987.
16. Paliwoda, S.J. (1986), *International Marketing*, Heinemann, London, 61–2.
17. Bilkey, 'An Attempted Integration of the Literature on the Export Behaviour of Firms', 40.
18. Rosson, P.J. and Reid, S.D., 'Managing Export Entry and Expansion: An Overview', in Rosson, P.J. and Reid, S.D. (eds), *Managing Export Entry and Expansion*, Praeger, New York.
19. Turnbull, P.W. (1987), 'A Challenge to the Stages Theory of the Internationalisation Process', in Rosson, P.J. and Reid, S.D. (eds), *Managing Export Entry and Expansion*, Praeger, New York.
20. Ibid., 37.
21. Ayal, I. and Raban, J. (1987), 'Export Management Structure and Successful High Technology Innovation', in Rosson, P.J. and Reid, S.D. (eds), *Managing Export Entry and Expansion*, Praeger, New York.
22. Rosson and Reid, *Managing Export Entry and Expansion*, 16.
23. See, for example, Bilkey, W.J. (1982), 'Variables Associated with Export Profitability', *Journal of International Business Studies*, 13, Fall, 39–55; and McFarlane, G. (1978), 'Scots Queen's Award Winners Don't Excel', *Marketing*, April, 27–32.
24. BOTB, *Into Active Exporting*, 30–1.
25. See, for example, Cavusgil, S.T. (1987), 'Firm and Management Characteristics as Discriminators of Export Marketing Activity', *Journal of Business Research*, 15, 221–35.
26. Cavusgil, S.T., Bilkey, W.J. and Tesar, G. (1979), 'A Note on the Export Behaviour of Firms: Exporter Profiles', *Journal of International Business Studies*, 10(1), 91–7.
27. Reid has written several papers on this theme; see for example, Reid, S.D. (1987), 'Export Strategies, Structure and Performance: An Empirical Study of Small Italian Manufacturing Firms', in Rosson, P.J. and Reid, S.D. (eds), *Managing Export Entry and Expansion*, Praeger, New York.
28. Cavusgil, S.T. (1984), 'Organisational Characteristics Associated with Export Activity', *Journal of Management Studies*, 21(1), 3–22.
29. For a detailed discussion, see Piercy, N. (1982), *Export Strategy: Markets and Competition*, George Allen & Unwin, London.
30. BETRO Trust Committee (1976), *Concentration on Key Markets*, 2nd edition, Royal Society of Arts, London.
31. Hunt, H.G. (1969), 'Export Management in Medium-sized Engineering Firms', *Journal of Management Studies*, 6(1), 33–44.
32. Turnbull, P.W. and Valla, J.P. (1986), *Strategies for International Industrial Marketing*, Croom Helm, London.
33. Adapted from Darling, J.R. (1985), 'Keys for Success in Exporting to the US Market', *European Journal of Marketing*, 19(2), 17–30.
34. See, for example, Barrett, N.J. and Wilkinson, I.F. (1985), 'Export Stimulation: A Segmentation Study of Australian Manufacturing Firms', *European Journal of Marketing*, 19(2), 53–72; and Seringhaus, F.H.R. (1987), 'Export Promotion: The Role and Impact of Government Service', *Irish Marketing Review*, 2, 106–16.

4

LICENSING AND FRANCHISING IN INTERNATIONAL MARKET DEVELOPMENT

SUMMARY

1. Successful licensing-out is usually dependent on the company securing legal protection for its intellectual property rights (patents, trade marks, designs, trade secrets and know-how). But obtaining protection is expensive and factors such as counterfeiting represent major problems. The legal framework of licensing also relates to the technology-transfer policies pursued at national and international level which, *inter alia*, seek to eliminate the restrictive business practices frequently incorporated into licensing contracts.
2. Recent evidence on the strategic reasons for licensing by US companies identified as the three top-ranked factors: country regulations or political risk; transport or tariff barriers inhibiting exports; and licensing as a means of rapid entry into a market.
3. Characteristics of licensing enterprises and licensing agreements include: mostly process industries and otherwise R&D-intensive sectors involved; licensing activities usually generated by requests from potential licensees; lead-times of around one year or longer; technologies being licensed still actively used by licensors; while highly profitable, licensing costs can be substantial; main problems relate to the formation of the contracts and to country regulations and laws; major growth is forecast but joint ventures and technology sales may develop more rapidly.
4. The process of establishing a licensing agreement should begin with a technology audit and licensing memorandum. After the signing of the licensing agreement, co-operation in implementation will be necessary and the licensor needs to carefully monitor the agreement.
5. The two types of franchising identified are 'product and trade name' franchises and 'business format' franchising. In general franchising involves the provision of a wider package of services than licensing, and a continuing direct association between the parties to the agreement.
6. The issue of protecting legal rights arises in franchising, with protection being sought for the 'image package' through registered trade marks.
7. Reasons for franchising include the opportunity to expand businesses internationally on a far larger scale, with greater speed and with much reduced capital requirements. Problems for the franchisor include lack of full control over the franchisee and the possible creation of competitors.

INTRODUCTION

To this point in the book much of the emphasis has been on the export route to market entry and development. The discussion now turns to the whole range of alternative international market-servicing methods, beginning in this chapter with licensing and franchising. The chapter is written primarily from the viewpoint of an international licensor or franchisor, but licensing-in or cross-licensing may be important components in firms' growth strategies and, therefore, some consideration is given to these issues too. When looking at the data on licensing, it becomes evident that the preponderance of activity is that which takes place within the multinational firm across national boundaries; that is, when a parent company licenses its subsidiaries to undertake certain activities abroad.[1] Given the orientation of this book, however, the focus is upon licensing between independent companies as would more typically be the case in smaller and medium-sized enterprises. Having said that, it must be recognised that equity participation by licensors in licensee firms is not uncommon – around one in seven firms in one international survey reported that they took equity participation in the enterprises to which they licensed – and the phenomenon is growing.[2]

It is not possible to obtain comprehensive or reliable information on the extent of licensing and franchising activity worldwide. A global figure of £14 bn in international licensing payments has been cited for 1978, but this includes relationships between parents and majority-owned affiliates as well as arm's-length transactions; using US data as a guide, the former represents about 70 per cent of the total.[3] What is clear is that licensing activity has been growing rapidly and not simply as a response to protectionism and the regulation of foreign direct investment. Other factors include an expansion in the licensing of research results from the universities; the recent emergence of small, high-technology firms lacking the resources to penetrate international markets by other means; rising R&D costs and shortening product life cycles again requiring rapid moves into markets overseas; the avoidance of duplication in R&D spending by licensing-in or cross-licensing; and the emergence of industries such as semiconductors and biotechnology where licensing is recognised as a fact of life.[4] In short, licensing has increasingly become a means of helping enterprises survive and compete within a rapidly changing international industrial environment.

Franchising activity also has shown dramatic growth. The term 'franchising' was derived from the French, meaning 'to be free from servitude' but in fact franchise activity was almost unknown in Europe until the beginning of the 1970s; and the concept was popularised in the USA where over one-third of retail sales are derived from franchising, in comparison with 5–10 per cent in the UK. Internationally, US firms have also been in the vanguard of franchise developments, and the potential for expansion is reflected in the fact that there are still only around 30,000 US-franchised outlets outside America, compared with half a million inside the United States.[5]

LICENSING-OUT

What to license?

At its narrowest, a licence has been described as merely permission given by one firm to another to allow the latter to engage in an activity otherwise legally forbidden to it.[6] This definition is derived from the fact that patents or trade marks are legally sanctioned monopolies or rights proprietary to a company. In fact, as will be shown, 'pure licensing' of this sort is relatively rare, and a broader concept where licensing may involve any transfer of technology or other intellectual property is preferred. It is useful, therefore, to begin by considering those categories of intellectual property that can be licensed.

Patents

A patent is the form of intellectual property which comes most immediately to mind in licensing. A patent is a public document issued by a government that grants to its owner the right to exclude others from making, using or selling an invention described in the patent for a period of up to twenty years. It protects a concept rather than the appearance of a particular article and so may cover 'everything from a machine to a method of clearing fog, everything from agricultural techniques to treating the human body'.[7]

The legal position will be discussed at greater length later, but it is generally accepted that patents provide the best protection available for a technical concept, although they are of limited duration, expensive and subject to considerable delays in being issued. Moreover, weak patents could result in the release of information about technology, while offering only limited protection.

Designs

Unlike patents, design protection is limited to the appearance of a good and so the article must have features such as a shape or pattern which appeal to the eye. Like a patented invention, a design must be registered when it is new. Protection normally exists for about fifteen to twenty years as for patents.

It is rare for design protection to be used in licensing except as part of a total package because protection is limited to appearance. Nevertheless, in industries such as furniture, automobiles and some electronics products, where design is an important marketing aspect, licensing can be useful. On the other hand, because of delays in registration, design protection is of little value in fast-moving fashion industries.

Other more specific forms of intellectual property in design relate to copyright and design copyright. As pointed out in Chapter 1, copyright has become an issue in technological licensing with the need to protect computer programs and other information-transfer systems. Essentially copyright comes into existence automatically without any legal procedure, providing published material is clearly marked with the international copyright legend:

© Name of copyright owner, year of first publication.

For material which is unpublished so as to maintain secrecy, as with computer programs, 'copyright reserved' or some similar statement is required. Assuming such procedures are followed, as soon as copyright material is published in a country which is a member of the relevant international treaty or convention, it is protected in other member countries.

The general rules for protection of copyright also apply to design copyright, which may apply as follows. Where an article or good is copied by reverse engineering, and that article was produced from drawings under copyright, then such a copy is deemed to be an infringement of the copyright of the original drawing. This is important in regard to such items as spare parts: courts have tended to find an implied licence in sales agreements or patent licences so as to permit the licensee to make certain spare parts. This doctrine of design copyright has been developed in countries such as the UK, New Zealand, South Africa and Hong Kong.

Trade marks
A trade mark represents an identification of the goodwill of a business and its reputation, taking the form of an identifying symbol (word, logo, design or other identifying feature, e.g. stripes on a shoe or item of clothing). If goods are of a clearly different type, the same trade mark may be used on them and this possibility has been exploited fully by some manufacturers, e.g. Coca Cola, Laura Ashley. As with patents, the extent of trade mark protection is dependent on individual laws, but three criteria will be evaluated: the trade mark must be distinctive, it must not be deceptive and it must not clash with any other mark.

The right to use trade marks may be more important in many licence agreements than patents or know-how, particularly in those cases where a successful product with a well-known brand name is the subject of the agreement. Furthermore, trade marks have an indefinite life, unlike patents, and are therefore of great value. Because of this the transfer of rights to use a trade mark are normally carefully controlled by the licensor. Similarly, quality control is important, to ensure that the licensor's product reputation is not impaired by poor-quality products emanating from the licensee.

Trade secrets and know-how
These types of intellectual property, which may be encompassed within the general term 'confidential information', are commonly included as part of a licensing contract enabling the licensee to assimilate transferred technology and facilitate the development and learning process. Trade secrets may include designs, specifications, engineering drawings, control systems, software and technical information and other items such as marketing information,

customer lists, etc. 'Know-how' is often applied to knowledge which cannot easily be transferable from the people possessing it, that is human skills and craftsmanship.

In relation to trade secrets, the question for the company may be whether to keep technology to itself rather than to disclose it in a patent application or copyright document. What may happen is that sufficient information to carry out the process or produce the good may be patented, while core technology is retained as a trade secret. Concerning know-how, there are obvious problems of definition and transfer. Thus once know-how has been transferred it is virtually impossible to recover it. In consequence, any clauses requiring the return of know-how are of little value, and the licensing contract may instead require that the licensee ceases to manufacture in a particular area if the agreement is terminated.

In summary, there are a range of intellectual property rights, each of which tends to merge into the other. The choice of which of the property rights is most suitable for any licensing package has to be made carefully, taking into consideration the legal protection afforded and the fees involved in taking out and renewing patents, etc., compared with the expected return from the licence.

The legal framework of licensing

Protecting intellectual property rights[8]
As the above comments have implied, the use of licensing in overseas markets may depend on the company first securing legal protection for its intellectual property rights in the countries concerned. Registration of patents and trade marks not only provides some protection to the licensor, but may indeed be necessary to obtain a licensee, given that some of the latter are extremely reluctant to license unpatented technology. Nevertheless, the legal considerations must all the time be viewed within the wider commercial and strategic context of penetrating international markets profitably, and so registration is not an end in itself.

Patents. The patent laws of individual countries have a very diverse history, and reflecting this, national patent laws differ widely with respect to degree of novelty, duration (from five to twenty years), patentability (sometimes only process patents are allowed, in other cases patents are excluded for particular products such as pharmaceuticals), renewability, time period for commercial utilisation (if not used, the patent may be lost), and so on. In the UK, British patents date from 1852 and provide statutory protection for up to twenty years for a technical concept.

There is no such thing as a world patent and in general it is necessary to apply for a separate national patent in each foreign country in which protection is required. However, regional systems, in particular the European Patent Convention (EPC), allow a company to file a single application for the countries which are party to that convention. The EPC came into force in 1977 with nine members, now increased to thirteen (the EC except for Ireland and Denmark, together with Austria, Sweden, Switzerland and Liechtenstein). A patent issued by the EPC is effective for twenty years, but once granted the European patent is interpreted and enforced in national courts. The advantage in a European filing is, therefore, in avoiding the duplication in dealing with separate national patent offices.

The other form of international patent co-operation is the Patent Co-operation Treaty (PCT) which became effective in 1978, although its predecessor, the Paris Convention on international patent rights, has a long history back to 1883. The Paris Convention provides, *inter alia*, for the filing of a patent application in the company's home country which then gives international priority for a period of twelve months. The PCT, ratified by around forty countries at present, extends this principle, so that not only the original filing but also preliminary examination can be obtained with a single application before it becomes necessary to file multiple foreign applications; and the priority period has been extended to twenty months. It is still necessary to file in individual countries and failure to do so within the specified period may mean a permanent loss of patent rights.

It should be added that filing is not the same as securing protection at the national level, which will entail further delay; and this raises the question as to whether licensing will be possible while a patent application is pending. Certainly the licensor company would wish to make full use of its 'patents pending' position.

Bringing the points discussed above together, the company possessing technology which it is considering licensing into overseas markets has basically three sets of decisions to make:

1. Whether to seek international patent protection. Foreign filing is expensive – about £500 per country to start, including patent fees and translation costs; together with maintenance fees year by year after that. In making the decision the company should also assess whether patent protection is preferable to keeping knowledge as a trade secret, and whether patent infringement can be detected and patent rights enforced.
2. Assuming the firm decides to go ahead with patenting, in which countries should patent applications be made? Clearly this is a question of market prospects and whether or not licensing is to be used as a method of market entry and development.
3. Finally, the company must decide on the patenting route to follow as between: national all countries; European Patent Convention in Europe and national elsewhere; Patent Co-operation Treaty and national for non-European nations. This is related to the point above, but as a guide

to inventions with substantial prospects from European enterprises, a European application together with registration in USA and Japan might seem sensible.

Trade marks.[9] The legal position with regard to trade marks is rather different to that for patents. In common-law countries (the UK, USA and other countries whose legal system derives from English law) the first person to use a trade mark is entitled to the rights in it and the mark may be used without registration. Even so, registration is probably advisable as it serves as a warning to other parties that the trade mark may not be used. In civil-law countries (Continental European nations and their former colonies, and other countries where rules of law are embodied in a legislative code) the trade mark right generally comes into existence upon registration.

The registration of trade marks in most countries is the function of the patent office or an equivalent government body, and registration must be undertaken in each country when protection is required. Under the terms of the Paris Convention, registration in one country provides priority for a period of six months in another ninety or so countries which are parties to the convention.

Trade mark registrations must be renewed at intervals of seven, ten, fourteen or twenty years depending upon the country concerned. Subject to various conditions, such as showing that the trade mark is in use at the renewal date, a trade mark acquisition can be maintained indefinitely. Examination procedures for trade mark applications vary: strict procedures are involved in the UK, somewhat less stringent requirements exist in the USA, Germany and France, and in other countries registration may almost be a rubber-stamping exercise; the latter may create problems if it comes to defending the trade mark in court proceedings. A number of problems may arise for the unsuspecting firm in the area of trade marks. Given the position in civil-law countries, where first registration gives exclusive rights, a company could find that its trade mark has already been registered in a foreign country by another firm (sometimes deliberately to prevent entry), in which case the former company will have to buy its trade mark from the foreign firm if it wishes to gain access to the market or change the mark.

Trade marks may be lost if they slip into generic usage, e.g. aspirin, nylon. And the problem of counterfeiting has come to be of almost epidemic proportions in many countries because of weak administration of trade mark laws, inadequate penalties and, indeed, general lack of concern by the authorities. The fact that some of the worst offenders are not members of the Paris Convention does not make the position any easier (the issue of counterfeiting is reviewed in Appendix 4.1).

Designs, trade secrets and know-how. The legal position with respect to designs is somewhat similar to that for trade marks and is thus not discussed further here. With trade secrets and know-how, the decision has been consciously taken to refrain from patenting. The licensor must, however, attempt to incorporate safeguard clauses into any licensing contract to prevent the licensee using or disclosing trade secrets during the period of the licensing agreement or subsequently.

Before concluding this section, it is worth pointing out that the protection of intellectual property rights, through possession of a solid patent, etc., is not what it used to be and not simply because of counterfeiting. Factors undermining patents as barriers to entry include shorter product life cycles, and large numbers of product adaptations within cycles. Moreover, increasing international competition means a great likelihood of inventions being discovered almost simultaneously in different locations. Costly legal battles may then occur, as in the biotechnology industry, as companies seek to secure their patents for particular technological breakthroughs.

Government regulations and licensing
The protection of intellectual property rights is one component of the legal framework within which licensing takes place; the second component concerns the policies pursued at national and international level towards licensing as a mode of technology transfer. The underlying basis of the legal system for protecting intellectual property rights is that of providing the entrepreneurial incentive for research and development and the commercialisation of technology, nationally and internationally, that would otherwise be lacking.[10] However, from the perspective of developing countries, in particular, there is a view that the system of protecting intellectual property rights (and the process of licensing generally) inhibits local innovation and the development of indigenous technological capacity; creates large payments for imported technology; and is associated with restrictive business practices which both increase the cost and reduce the market potential for the licensed product. There are also special concerns relating to trade marks, given the link to advertising expenditures designed to support foreign-branded items and the likelihood of inhibiting local competition. Such views have been constrained by pragmatism, and the realisation that long-run returns to innovative firms must be sufficient to cover R&D expenditures, and that the world technology market is imperfect; but they do, nevertheless, provide a backcloth to the regulation of technology transfers through licensing and other means.

The legal framework for regulating licensing and technology transfers derives mainly from policies pursued by host countries, especially developing nations, and by international organisations such as the United Nations. Within developing countries, policies towards licensing are part of the overall regulation of technology transfer which also encompasses the control of foreign direct investment (joint venture laws, etc.) and different types of contractual arrangements. This association is important because foreign-equity participation may be prohibited or severely constrained, in which case licensing may represent the only route to obtaining a presence in a particular country. In post-war Japan, for example, government policy discouraged foreign investment, using licensing as the means of obtaining technology. The Japanese government carefully screened licensing proposals, channelling technology into key industrial sectors and using its bargaining strength in negotiating terms with licensees: the outcome was the acquisition of 3,200 licences from foreign licensors between 1950 and 1964.[11] In India, similarly, approvals by the Foreign Investment Board give strong preference to licensing: it has been indicated that of several hundred foreign industrial collaborations approved each year, only 15 per cent involve foreign-equity participation and even then the latter is not normally allowed to exceed 40 per cent. It is because of such restrictions that licensing is important as a way into closed markets.

Initial approaches to licensing policy in developing countries focused on regulating the remuneration for technology and trade marks along with the duration of the agreements and restrictive business practices.[12] Rules were established for rates of royalty payments for technical know-how, patents and trade marks (dependent on whether sales were directed towards domestic or export markets, whether the licensor had substantial equity participation in the proposed venture, whether lump-sum fees were involved along with sales-related royalties, etc.); the payment of guaranteed royalties; the treatment of imported components and parts for the calculation of the sales base for royalty payments; and the frequency and method of payment of royalties and fees. The regulations of countries such as Brazil, India, Malaysia, Mexico, the Republic of Korea, the Philippines and Andean countries followed this type of approach.

Restrictive business practices that countries seek to avoid in licensing agreements (as well as in joint venture contracts) include:

- tied purchases of raw materials and parts from the licensor or suppliers designated by the licensor;
- restrictions regarding the volume, the sale or resale prices or the structure of production;
- restrictions on the handling of competitive products or the use of competitive technology concurrently;
- stipulations requiring improvements in technology made by the licensee to be made available free of charge to the licensor without reciprocal obligations;
- stipulations requiring the licensee or joint venture to export its products through the licensor or agents designated by him;
- stipulations permitting the licensor to regulate or control the management of the licensee company . . . ;
- and stipulations that exclude national laws and jurisdiction for purposes of dispute settlement.[13]

To implement such rules in developing countries, screening agencies commonly exist. In some countries the same agency is responsible for screening both foreign investment and technology-transfer arrangements, whereas in other areas different agencies are responsible for the two activities. As the formality of screening and monitoring has increased, the approach to the regulation of licensing arrangements has changed. Much more emphasis is placed upon the identification of national technological needs, the evaluation of alternative technologies and suppliers, the building up of indigenous technological skills and generally a more systematic approach to licensing and technology transfer. Still, there is great variety in the nature and severity (from the viewpoint of the licensor) of rules, as the examples shown in Exhibit 4.1 illustrate. As the author of the extract in Exhibit 4.1 notes: 'Assuming that the primary concern of the developing nation is the rapid acquisition and development of state-of-the-art technology, it is ironic that approval mechanisms often discourage technology transfers altogether.'[14]

EXHIBIT 4.1
EXAMPLES OF TECHNOLOGY TRANSFER
RULES IN SELECTED COUNTRIES

Argentina

On 12 March 1981, Argentina enacted Law No. 22.426. This law governs transfers of technology and trade marks. Technology is defined as patents, industrial designs and models, and any technical know-how for manufacture of a product or rendering of a service. The Argentine delegate at the UNIDO/LES Meeting on Technology Transfers to Developing Countries stated that, although software does not come under present technology transfer rules, all proposed laws subject it to technology transfer regulation.

Agreements between related parties (such as parent – subsidiary corporations) must be submitted for approval by the National Institute of Industrial Technology (INTI). Those between unrelated parties do not require approval and are valid as of the date provided in the agreement but must be registered with INTI. Technology transfer agreements are not void for failure to obtain INTI approval or registration. Without such approval or registration, however, royalty expenses by the technology recipient are not deductible and fees received by the technology owner are taxed at full rate.

China

In China, laws and regulations relating to technology transfers are still being developed. For the most part, such laws as have been enacted have not been tested by litigation. The Ministry of Foreign Economic Relations and Trade (MOFERT) or its designated agency must approve technology transfer agreements. The Foreign Economic Contract Law, effective as of 1 July 1985, sets forth requirements for contracts between Chinese and foreign entities. The Regulations on Administration of Contracts for Acquisition of Technology were promulgated on 24 May 1985. These regulations provide that the technology recipient will not disclose confidential information within the scope and time period agreed to between the parties. The duration of technology transfer agreements is ten years, but agreements may be extended with approval.

Exhibit 4.1 continued

Certain use limitations are disfavoured and their scope will be particularly scrutinised by MOFERT. These are restrictions regarding improvement of the technology by the recipient, requirements for exchange of improvements of the technology, sales channels or export markets, and use of the technology after termination or expiration of the agreement.

India

The Indian emphasis is upon the absorption, adaptation and dissemination of technology transferred from foreign sources. Not all technology is eligible for transfer into India. If the technology is eligible, the parties may proceed to negotiate an agreement and to submit it for governmental approval. The permissible term of the agreement is five years with exception for agreements involving highly sophisticated technologies. The determination of permissible duration is based upon the time needed for absorption and adaptation of the technology. Regardless of the actual contract duration, royalties may be paid for no more than five years and generally must not exceed 5 per cent. Lump sum payments are permitted. The rights of the recipient to sublicense the technology and to export to all other countries is encouraged.

Venezuela

Technology transfer agreements must be approved by and registered with a Venezuelan governmental agency. If an agreement is not approved and registered, it may be void and unenforceable and payment of royalties and fees under the agreement prohibited. The agency may require that agreements be modified before approval is given. Generally, requirements of confidentiality of proprietary technical information may not extend beyond the lesser of the term of the agreement or five years. In some cases, however, the Venezuelan Government may approve extensions of confidentiality for up to fifteen years.

Source: Hurley, D. (1987), 'National Limits to Technology Transfer', *Les Nouvelles*, **22**(2).

The discussion above has emphasised the position in developing countries, but, as the example of China in Exhibit 4.1 reveals, a similar perspective on licensing exists in the Eastern Bloc countries and the People's Republic of China. Aside from enacting legislation establishing the conditions for licensing deals, China has also been attempting to improve the framework and climate for licensing through its Patent Law of 1 April 1985, the establishment of a network of patent offices, government-approved patent agencies, and the setting up of a judicial system for settling disputes concerning intellectual property rights.[15] In the Soviet Union, licensing has been handled by the foreign trade company Licensintorg since 1962. Compared with the position in most developing countries, however, Licensintorg is a licensor as well as a licensee, and a similar two-way licensing process is evident in some other COMECON countries such as Hungary.[16]

Aside from the regulations of individual countries, various United Nations agencies together with other international organisations such as the World Bank, International Labour Office (ILO) and OECD have been involved in formulating proposals for multilateral controls over technology transfers (as well as in assisting developing countries in devising appropriate science and technology policies and improving their bargaining position). Particularly relevant here are the UNCTAD-instituted discussions on codes of conduct for technology transfer and guidelines for restrictive business practices. A code on the latter was adopted by the UN General Assembly in 1980 whereas there is as yet no agreement on a code for technology transfer. For the foreseeable future, thus, it seems that the locus of significant policy formulation will be the national level.

The exception to the above generalisation concerns the position of licensing agreements under EC competition law. Article 85 of the Treaty of Rome (which set up the EC) prohibits restrictive agreements and, therefore, exclusive agreements which prevent parallel imports back to the country of the licensor are banned. The implication, according to Lowe and Crawford, was 'that licensing within the EC (and the US) means effectively setting up a competitor'.[17] However, in 1984 the EC passed a regulation for patent licence agreements allowing for territorial protection as follows:[18]

1. Licensor and licensee can agree for the term of the contract to neither manufacture nor distribute the products under patent protection in the other party's territory.
2. Between licensees, mutual protection of this type is allowed for five years from the date when the product has first been marketed in the EC. After that time the licensees may be prevented from pursuing an active sales policy in the territories of other licensees.
3. Once, however, the products have been put on the market in one member country they must freely circulate throughout the Community.

This would seem to provide some protection, and similar legislation was enacted in 1988 in relation to know-how licensing and franchising. This enabling legislation has to be considered together with EC efforts to encourage licensing and other forms of technology transfer and industrial collaboration through a variety of programmes (see Chapter 1, Note 5).

When issues relating to the protection of intellectual property rights and host-country-oriented regulations are taken alongside legislation that may emerge from home countries (principally US export controls on technology transfers to the Eastern Bloc) it becomes very clear that the would-be licensor faces a legal and regulatory minefield. And yet these self-same regulations in developing countries, for example, can be a prime reason for licensing, as the next section shows.

LICENSING STRATEGY: THEORY AND PRACTICE

Chapter 1 reviewed three approaches to the issue of mode of international market entry and development – contributions from economics, the stages-of-development approach and the business-strategy approach. When considering the economics literature, the concept of internalisation has considerable relevance to the decision to engage in multinational operations rather than to license an independent firm abroad. Because the market for technology is very imperfect (as the previous section has shown, there are difficulties in protecting and enforcing intellectual property rights, as well as in trying to identify licensees, negotiate licensing contracts, etc.), there will be an incentive for the company to internalise as much as possible its technological advantage. Foreign direct investment will normally be preferred since the owner of the technology is in a position to capture all the returns from proprietary know-how. The empirical evidence does tend to support this broad proposition: for example, Davidson and McFetridge, in a regression study of 1,200 intra-firm and market technology transactions undertaken by US firms during the period 1945–78, concluded that the probability of internal transfer was greater *inter alia* for more R&D-intensive companies, and for newer technologies and technologies with few previous transfers.[19] Protection of proprietary knowledge in R&D-intensive enterprises thus underlies decisions to operate through affiliates rather than through licensing abroad.

Yet this and other research has revealed that firms may employ several different modes simultaneously in foreign markets, so clearly other factors are involved. The stages-of-development approach to market servicing suggests a sequential progression towards wholly and majority-owned affiliates abroad, but the position of licensing is uncertain. The latter does not require substantial resource commitment, either capital or management (although the costs in terms of establishing the licensing agreement, monitoring the agreement and protecting industrial property rights should not be overlooked);[29] and may be a more effective means to penetrate markets than through exports. This would indicate that licensing might be an attractive option for the firm in the early stages of overseas expansion. On the other hand, in some presentations of the internalisation model, the licensing option is predicted for the end of the technology cycle, consequent on the standardisation of the product and process.

Given the widely differing environmental and competitive conditions facing firms in international markets, aside from differences among companies themselves, it would, in fact, be unsurprising to find licensing being used in a more flexible way than the above comments would indicate. Talking about (probably large) US firms, one author notes:

> The theoretical generalization that multinational firms will prefer 'internalization' via direct investment over the sale of technology via licensing is a proposition that needs to be examined with greater circumspection in the emerging climate for international business . . . Recognizing that across the board policies can be sub-optimal, some companies are beginning to make entry strategy decisions on a case-by-case basis, formally including licensing as a possibility. In the extreme, a few firms periodically review the strategy decision for every combination on their product/country matrix.[21]

Among smaller and medium-sized companies a project-by-project approach would, in fact, be likely to be very much the norm.

Changing the focus to the empirical evidence available on the explanations for licensing, Table 4.1 summarises the results of fifteen studies undertaken over the period 1971–81. The majority of, but not all, the studies relate to US firms and to multinational enterprises, and so it is necessary to be slightly cautious in interpreting the results. A distinction is made between firm-level, industry/product-level and country-level variables to maintain the link with Dunning's eclectic theory (Chapter 1).

Considering the country-specific factors first, the observations in the previous section on the legal framework of licensing are confirmed in the evidence relating to environmental constraints on foreign direct investment. However, it is not simply restrictions on investment *per se* but the requirements for equity sharing with local partners, restrictions on dividend repatriation (because they are incorporated into a licensing agreement, royalty payments have a stronger claim on foreign exchange in host developing countries) and generally high political risk which will encourage licensing. At the same time the exporting option may be ruled out by high transport costs or trade barriers. Overall, the indication is of licensing as a market development mode in closed (and small) markets.

At the firm level, evidence was cited previously to show that R&D-intensive firms would prefer to internalise their newest technologies. And the results in Table 4.1 do not contradict this conclusion, except in the suggestion that even research-intensive firms may agree to license in areas where investment is difficult or risky, because the company is confident of its technological lead and discounts the possibility of investment or eventual licensee competition. Small firms, lacking the resources or expertise for overseas investment, and large firms, exploiting diversification possibilities, may also use the licensing route. Finally, licensing may be a valuable and continuing source of earnings, especially where auxiliary business is created or where the licensee becomes dependent on the licensor. In this latter instance a very high proportion of the licensee's business may be generated by the licensed product(s) and permission to use a foreign trade name is critical to marketing success.

The industry/product-level factors quoted in Table 4.1 also have relevance to the internalisation thesis. The idea that the more mature, standardised products within the firm are amenable for licensing accords with the model. But in R&D-intensive industries such as pharmaceuticals, chemicals, synthetic fibres, etc., licensing is common as a form of reciprocal technology exchange: to take the example of synthetics, the technology is such that the possibilities for modifying a basic generic structure, such as nylon or polyester, over time and improving its performance are nearly endless; licensing and cross-licensing then become important, given that the market size may be too small to justify investment in optimally sized plants without creating

Table 4.1 Conditions under which licensing may be preferred strategy (summary of studies undertaken over period 1971–81)

Strategic concept	Conditions
Firm level	
Licensor firm size	Licensor firm too small to have financial, managerial or marketing expertise for overseas investment Licensor firm too big (see below)
Research intensity	Licensor firm will remain technologically superior, so as to discount licensee competition in other markets
'Choosing' competition	With a patent about to expire, licensing gives a head start to a licensee firm favoured by present patent holder. (May be illegal in some countries)
Creation of auxiliary business	Even if direct royalty income is inadequate, margins on components to or from licensee can be handsome (in the extreme, e.g. licensing automobile assemblers, licensing is tantamount to disguised imports). Other auxiliary business can be turnkey plants, joint bidding with licensee, etc.
Diversification and product-line organisation in licensor firm	Especially in large diversified firms, with divisional attention focused on the 'product imperative', a centralised examination of the product/country matrix reveals neglected market penetration possibilities via licensing (especially where considerable diversification puts a constraint on the financial and managerial resources available for equity ventures overseas)
Perpetuation of licensee dependency	Even without or beyond the licensing agreement, effective licensee dependency maintained by trade marks, required components, or licensee hunger for technical improvements
Industry/product level	
Product cycle standardisation	Obsolescing products considered for licensing Imminent technology or model change Increasing competition in product market
High rate of technological turnover	Change so rapid, and technologies so perishable (e.g. semiconductors) that even with equally proficient licensees, a design or a patent may be transferred with little fear of significant competition
Reciprocal exchanges of technology	Licensing as a valuable tool for obtaining technology or market rights, in industries characterised by high R&D and market development costs and product diversity (e.g. pharmaceuticals, electricals, chemicals)
Product v. process technologies	Licensing opportunities in auxiliary processes (e.g. galvanising in the steel industry, or anodising aluminium) even if the basic product technologies not licensed
Country level	
Environmental constraints on foreign direct investment or foreign investment income	Government regulations restricting foreign direct investment to selected sectors only High political risk in nation Market uncertain or volatile, licensor lacking in requisite marketing abilities, or market too small for foreign investment
Constraints on imports into licensee nation	A high ratio of transport costs to value for item Tariff or non-tariff barriers

Source: Contractor, F.J. (1985), *Licensing in International Strategy*, Quorum Books, Westpoint, Conn., Table 20.

excess capacity. Similarly, if technological change is very rapid, then fears of losing proprietary know-how to licensees may be unfounded.

While this summary of the empirical evidence is very useful, it is obviously not possible to ascertain from the table the relative importance of particular factors. It is useful, therefore, to complement this information by more up-to-date research evidence from Contractor which investigated the strategy role of licensing in American companies.[22] In general, it was apparent that there was a wide range of strategic reasons for using licensing; but the first-ranked factor was the country's regulations or political risk which inhibited the formation of majority-owned affiliates. The second-ranked factor was transport or tariff barriers making exports difficult. These environmental factors thus suggest the use of licensing when alternative strategies fail. In rank order, other important variables were as follows: licensing as a means of rapid entry into a market; licensing when it is possible to divulge details concerning a process without harming company competitiveness; the expectation of receiving technology or improvements back from the licensee; and licensing as a strategy when products or processes are older or standardised.

To quote Contractor himself, 'in general, the main motivation of licensing remains short- to medium-term income generation as opposed to longer-term objectives such as market development'.[23] Other authors, on the other hand, have argued that licensing should be viewed as a long-run relationship and that it is dangerous to regard this type of arrangement as a makeshift solution. In such a situation a vicious circle may develop in which a badly planned licensing agreement which is not maintained leads to failure, and this in turn produces scepticism about the value of licensing in general – a scepticism that may spread to other companies that have not used this mode. Supporting this view of licensing as a long-term possibility are Buckley and Davies, who suggest that licensing can fit into an optimal worldwide strategy or that it is a viable alternative to other international market development modes in a world of institutional or economic constraints.[24] IBM's decision in 1988 to license out all patents associated with its new line of personal computers may be cited as a case in point. Within the global strategy of IBM, the decision could be seen as an attempt to increase the likelihood of the design evolving into an industry-wide standard; and to forestall the development of low cost 'clones'. Many practitioners take a similar position, arguing that companies deciding to license must recognise that they are making a long-term commitment that cannot be turned on and off with the cycles of the economy. As Silvia concludes, 'Licensing is a lot more than a short-term tactic for immediate income. It has to be a basic business strategy . . . management must be fully committed to doing the technology transfer right.'[25] In this regard, the case of Lee Cooper shown in Exhibit 4.2 is interesting: after initially getting into licensing in an *ad hoc* way, the company has used this approach to develop a truly international brand.

EXHIBIT 4.2
LICENSING AS A PLANNED BUSINESS STRATEGY-THE CASE OF THE LEE COOPER GROUP PLC

Lee Cooper is a British jeans and casual wear manufacturer which first began producing clothes in 1908; the company went public on the London Stock Exchange in 1959 and in 1986 had sales of £140m. While highly internationalised, the company's foreign direct investment activities were limited by policy decision to Western Europe and North Africa (international subcontracting) with all other markets served through licensing arrangements.

Lee Cooper became involved in trade mark licensing in 1972, almost by accident, and this initial operation in New Zealand was set up without any formal licensing agreement. It was only several years later, by which time the company had five licensees, that a clear licensing strategy was devised by Lee Cooper. A subsidiary was formed specifically charged with responsibility for overseeing the existing licensees and seeking out and acquiring and managing new ones; and broad guidelines were laid down concerned with geographical and marketing policy. In essence, licensing has been used as a market penetration strategy into countries where the market size or demand for jeans was limited; where the market was closed to imports; or where geographical distance or a culture gap (Japan being a case in point) created problems for alternative methods of servicing markets. In addition, the company negotiated licences in Barbados and Canada, where a part explanation related to a desire to understand the North American market prior to a more direct push into the United States. By 1987, therefore, Lee Cooper had twenty-four active licences in some nineteen countries worldwide.

The following country examples are presented in alphabetical order and relate to the position as at 1987.

Australia
Foreign direct investment and exports were not considered to be viable in this market due to geographical distance and competition from the Far East. The licensee perceived of Lee Cooper as being an international brand and, therefore, licensed the trade mark; by 1987 the agreement was into its third five-year term with the same licensee.

Barbados
As the centre for its Caribbean operation, licensing was deemed to be the most appropriate strategy for two reasons. Firstly, the CARICOM market had 5 million people. Secondly, with the predominant American influence and number of tourists, it was seen as a means of gauging prospects in the USA. The licence agreement was in its second five-year term.

Canada
A recently negotiated licence, it was also felt that much could be learned about marketing in North America.

Czechoslovakia
After thirty-six months of negotiations a six-year agreement was signed, which was then extended for an additional nine years. This was the first consumer goods licence between the UK and Czechoslovakia, and is generating royalties at a level in excess of £1m. per annum.

Exhibit 4.2 continued

Egypt
This agreement was viewed as successful notwithstanding the difficulties of operating in a developing country, and cultural problems. Payment was made according to prevailing black-market exchange rates.

Finland
One of the group's oldest licensing relationships. Exporting would have been difficult because of protectionism. The licensee was the market leader in Finland and the country represented a good base for exporting into the USSR.

Greece
While the Greek market was lucrative and allowed access to Bulgaria, the licensing experience was not viewed as a total success. Repatriation has been difficult, mainly because of substantial 'bureaucrat-created delays'.

Hungary
Reflecting similar experiences in Czechoslovakia, the group have found that after protracted negotiations initially, the licensing agreements have been successful. A second agreement for a five-year term was recently signed.

Japan
As the only realistic method of market entry to bridge the culture gap, licensing was extremely lucrative in view of the relative strength of the yen.

Malaysia
A marketing decision was made to license rather than invest directly.

Norway and Sweden
Licensing agreements were used to maintain a market presence after divestment of subsidiaries. Essentially the markets were felt to be too small to justify capital investment.

Pakistan
The licensing agreement was part of a larger package that included the building of a factory.

Singapore
As well as the importance of the market place, the view was taken that licensing in this region supported the view of Lee Cooper as an international corporation.

Tunisia
Licensing came about through the minority partner in an export-oriented manufacturing plant. This was the only means of gaining access to an otherwise closed market. Repatriation of royalties was difficult initially as the government viewed the technology transfer to have taken place in the main plant.

Turkey
Foreign direct investment and exports had not been considered, when the licensee approached Lee Cooper with a view to reducing his dependence on existing export programmes. The licensee was heading towards market leadership after three years.

Exhibit 4.2 continued

North Yemen
Licensing developed after contacts and introductions through the British Embassy.

Yugoslavia
The first licence agreement in Eastern Europe. Royalties relate to both technology and trademarks.

Source: Cooper, M.A. (1987), *Trademark Licensing Around the World*, paper delivered at Licensing Executives Society Conference, Edinburgh, Scotland, 3 July; Cooper, M.A. (1987), *Manufacturing Under Licence: Licensor Aspects of International Expansion: The Decision-Making Process*, paper presented at the First European Licensing and Franchising Conference, Glasgow, Scotland, 15–16 June.

CHARACTERISTICS OF LICENSING ENTERPRISES AND OF LICENSING AGREEMENTS: EMPIRICAL EVIDENCE

Following on from the empirical evidence quoted in the previous section, the aim here is to review the various studies that have considered the characteristics of companies involved in licensing and the nature of licensing agreements. The cautions which were indicated above apply with even greater force here: the surveys of licensing which have been undertaken generally use membership of the Licensing Executives Society (LES) as a sampling frame, immediately orienting results towards firms which do license; sample sizes vary; licensing activity sometimes relates to domestic as well as international licensing; and only one of the studies cited, that published by the OECD on international licensing in 1987, is based on a sample of licensors from several countries, the others referring either to US or British licensors.[26] Notwithstanding these points, it is useful to establish what generalisations, if any, can be made on the nature of licensing enterprises and the agreements they operate.

Characteristics of licensing enterprises

Licensor size and sectoral distribution
The issue of firm size was discussed implicitly in the context of the theoretical explanations for licensing: if most transferable technology is possessed by large firms, then the incidence of licensing would be higher among such enterprises, particularly where foreign direct investment is not possible or desirable. Conversely, since licensing does not involve substantial capital or management resources, it could be favoured as a market entry and development strategy by smaller firms. American evidence suggests that small and medium-sized enterprises (SMEs) are more heavily involved in licensing-out,

even although the large firms have a somewhat greater number of technology transfers.[27] One British study indicated small-firm involvement in licensing to range between 5 and 9 per cent of the total population of SMEs, although the licensing companies were clustered in the higher SME employment size bands (101–500 employees compared with 100 and fewer employees); no comparable figures were available for larger companies.[28]

As to sectoral distribution, the chemical, pharmaceutical and health-care industries are strongly represented in licensing, as are other processing industries such as rubber and plastics. There are also indications that electronics and transport are important sectors for licensing. In the main these are fairly R&D-intensive industries, of necessity, otherwise the licensing possibilities would not arise; and the link between R&D spending and licensing is confined by data at the firm level.

Licensing and other international market development modes
Survey evidence points to the fact that licensing is only one of a variety of market development/technology transfer modes used by many companies.[29] This fits with the notion that firms need to be flexible according to circumstances, and that the various modes are, in some instances at least, complementary rather than competitive. It may suggest, in addition, that once firms have the expertise and experience gained in one form of international technology transfer, this may give them confidence to engage in other forms. It is true, nevertheless, that it is the large licensors which are dominant in activities such as turnkey plants, management contracts and joint ventures; whereas among smaller licensors, modes which involve limited resource commitment, such as reciprocal exchange agreements and the contracting-out of marketing or distribution may be more significant.

Income from licensing
Revenues from licensing-out would be expected to be small in relation to companies' sales (although the contribution to profit would be much higher) and this is borne out in the data. In one survey of British licensors, where the focus was medium-sized enterprises, only one in twenty firms received in excess of 5 per cent of turnover from licensing.[30] In a wider international study of mainly large enterprises, licensing income was rarely greater than 1 per cent of sales; this proportion was derived from an average number of fifty licensing agreements per enterprise and an average value per agreement of almost $250,000.[31]

Characteristics of licensing agreements

Source of licensing activities
Unlike some of the empirical results, there is a good deal of unanimity in the findings relating to source of licensing activities. The conclusion was that

licensing activities were usually generated by requests from potential licensees abroad. In other words, companies which have marketable technology are largely passive in the licensing process, because they are unaware of the possibilities and/or lack the skills to license-out. For the licensee, by comparison, active approach may stem from a realisation of product or technological weaknesses and a requirement to find external solutions, of which licensing in one. Although there is no information on the subject, the expectation might be of an active approach when licensors are seeking to enter developing countries.

Lead-times in establishing licensing agreements
There is an extensive literature on the subject of success and failure in innovation, the time lags between invention and innovation, etc., which are outside the scope of this book. What is interesting here is the relationship, for example, between patent applications, patent issues and the licensing of patents. Research on thirty-three large US firms came up with the following conclusions:[32] about one-fifth of internally generated ideas were filed in the form of patent applications; and most filed applications resulted in issued patents; but few patents were subsequently licensed; and few licences generated much income. The lowest time delay in moving from patenting to licensing was minus one month, in a case where the first licensee was established prior to the granting of the patent. The other extreme was forty-one months, a typical time delay being approximately thirteen months. This corroborates other evidence relating to Eastern Europe, where technology transfer deals may take one to three years typically, with no returns for five years. As will emerge later, the length as well as the complexity of negotiations are regarded as major problem areas in licensing.

Age of technology being licensed
The OECD survey of international licensors reported that over 90 per cent of technologies that were being licensed were still being actively used by the licensors (the proportion was, however, lower for US licensors). A similar result emerged in one British study, although in neither case was a distinction made between the geographical location of the licensee.[33] In regard to the latter, Contractor's work on agreements between US firms and arm's-length recipients has indicated significantly older technologies in developing countries, as one of a number of important differences between licensing contracts in industrialised and developing nations, which will be discussed in following paragraphs.[34]

Basis of licences
It has been noted that licensing may relate to a variety of types of intellectual property, some of which, such as patents and trade marks, may be protected by legal registration. Some comments were also made on the issue of whether or not licensees would be prepared to enter into agreements relating to, for

instance, unpatented technology. Once again the results are fairly clear cut: the majority of transfers take the form of some combination of patents and know-how; know-how licensing alone is probably second in importance (but well behind the patent/know-how combination), although in developing countries, trade marks, often together with know-how, assume substantial significance. Licences relating to patents or trade marks or copyrights alone tend to occur in a very small proportion of cases. From the perspective of lessons for would-be licensors, these findings suggest that 'the marketable technology possessed by companies extends beyond that which is immediately identifiable because of patent coverage. This emphasises the importance of carrying out an audit of the company's technology to identify those skills or know-how which may be unrecognised or unused, but which have market value.'[35]

The content of the licensing package: goods and services provided
The implementation of licensing arrangements works most satisfactorily when transfers occur between firms of roughly comparable technological sophistication. However, where the recipient firm is technologically inferior, then the satisfactory conclusion of a licensing deal will require, aside from manuals and blueprints, etc., the provision of assistance in the form of licensee training, in general and production management and overall personal interaction with the licensee. Such technical services are very commonly provided with licences, and especially with licences to developing countries. Thus the lower the level of industrialisation of an economy, the greater the volume of attendant services that have to be provided to the licensee to accompany patent rights, design and specification.[36] The same research, it might be added, found that non-affiliate (arm's-length) licensing was more common in advanced nations; this reflects, in part at least, the ability of companies in these countries to assimilate licensed technology without the need for a long-term equity relationship with the licensor.

Aside from technical services, raw materials or components, production machinery and finished products are fairly commonly supplied as part of licensing agreements.

The content of the licensing package: elements in agreements
The extensive incidence of restrictive clauses in licensing agreements in developing countries has been widely discussed and documented. A 1977 survey of US enterprises found that whenever it was legal or feasible to do so, firms would incorporate a variety of restrictive clauses in their agreements with non-affiliated firms.[37] The most common clauses related to territorial limitations on manufacture and grant-backs from licensees (where the licensor obtains any technology impovement free of charge). In a more recent study in four South East Asian developing countries, clauses dealing with export restrictions and tied purchase of inputs were included in a substantial

minority of contracts; while 'confidentiality' clauses and clauses restricting the rights granted to licensees (both of these affect the domestic diffusion of technology) were included in half or more contracts.[38]

In so far as it is possible to judge, some of these elements in agreements such as limits on exports, and limitations on field of use or field of sale (together with exclusivity provisions) were about as common in developed as in developing countries.[39]

Payments and returns in licensing agreements
The contents of the licensing package discussed above are of major import-ance when evaluating returns in licensing agreements, but clearly other factors – royalty fees and other forms of payment, and transfer costs – must be considered. The major payment methods and the practicalities of negoti-ation are reviewed more fully in the next section, and the comments here are restricted to a review of the empirical evidence on payments and returns.

Following Contractor, in a typical bargaining model the licensor has a minimum or floor price comprising the direct costs of effecting the transfer, plus the opportunity costs of doing so (e.g. loss of market opportunities).[40] The licensee has a maximum or ceiling price that he is prepared to pay which can be either the costs of developing the technology independently; or the cost of obtaining the technology from an alternative supplier; or the in-cremental returns (or cost savings) derived from using the techno-logy – whichever is lower. The actual price will be somewhere between the licensor's floor and the licensee's ceiling, with the outcome being indetermi-nate or depending on relative bargaining power and negotiating expertise.

Empirical evidence from a survey of US firms provided the results shown in Table 4.2. The first ranked factor was the amount of technical and other services provided, indicating that transfer costs are important determinants

Table 4.2 Factors considered in setting the 'price' or 'returns' of an agreement

Rank	
1	Depends on amount of technical and other services provided to licensee
2	Industry norms (e.g. uniform royalty %)
3	Licensee's market size and profitability
4	Take what is available (since firm is restricted from market anyway)
5	Varies with R&D expenditure
6	Returns must at least equal returns from exporting or direct investment
7	Less for old and obsolescent technology
8	Less when patent is expiring
9	Grantbacks
10	Patent coverage

Source: Root, F.R. and Contractor, F.J. (1981), 'Negotiating Compensation in International Licensing Agreements', *Sloan Management Review*, 22(2), Table 1.

of the licensor's floor price. The second and third ranked factors suggest that the licensor considers the licensee's ceiling price by taking into account the price of alternatives and the possible value of the technology to the licensee. (It should be noted that the idea of a 'going rate' for pricing technology has emerged as being of substantial importance in other studies in the UK and USA.)[41] The relatively low ranking of R&D expenditures confirms that these are mainly regarded as sunk costs, although the licensor might use the information as a guide to the licensee's costs of developing the technology on his own.

Turning to the transfer costs and returns, Contractor estimated the ratio of returns to costs (discounted at 15 per cent) at 35.0 for licences in industrialised countries, and 13.7 and 8.0 for licences in Eastern Bloc nations and developing countries respectively. Therefore even if actual transfer costs set a floor price to these agreements, actual returns are many times the level of these costs. Further analysing some of the differences between industrialised and developing country licences, it was found that technical costs were substantially higher in the latter, whereas legal costs were greater in industrialised nations, possibly due to greater patent coverage. Interestingly, total returns were higher in patented technologies.[42]

It is necessary to stress, nevertheless, that the costs of licensing should not be underestimated. Table 4.3 presents a breakdown of costs of licensing-out

Table 4.3 Relative costs of licensing overseas (per cent)

Breakdown of total costs of licensing overseas	
Protection of industrial property	24.8
Establishment of licensing agreement	46.6
Maintenance of licensing agreement	29.0
	100.0
Breakdown of establishment costs	
Search for suitable licensee	22.8
Communication between involved parties	44.7
Adoption and testing of equipment for licensee	9.9
Training personnel for licensee	19.9
Other (additional marketing activity and legal expenses)	2.5
	100.0
Breakdown of maintenance costs	
Audit of licensee	9.7
Ongoing market research in market of licensee	7.2
Back-up services for licensee	65.0
Defence of industrial property rights in licensee's territory	11.0
Other	7.1
	100.0

Source: Carstairs, R.T. and Welch, L.S. (1981), *A Study of Outward Foreign Licensing of Technology by Australian Companies*, Licensing Executives Society of Australia, Canberra.

by Australian firms, distinguishing between the three major groups of costs, viz. protection of industrial property, establishment of licensing agreement and maintenance of the agreement. Establishment costs were the major component, and within this, communication between involved parties accounted for nearly half of the total, with licensee search being another significant element. Regarding maintenance costs, back-up services for the licensee were the biggest component by far.

Problems associated with licensing-out activities

Two sets of difficulties emerge in the establishment of licensing agreements, the first relating to the formation of the contracts (identifying licensees, negotiating, etc.) which is very much a process of personal interaction; and the second to the regulations and laws of licensee and licensor countries. The two are linked, of course, since country restraints have been shown to cause substantial delays, if not, indeed, preventing or terminating agreements.[43] The first group, however, reflect the difficulties of the parties in reaching agreement over issues such as the items to be included in the licence, payments for the technology, etc., commonly exacerbated by lack of expertise and experience among the negotiating personnel on both sides, financial problems in the companies, and so forth.

The second group of problems are country-specific, and the disincentives to licensing in recipient countries, as established in one study, are shown in Table 4.4. The largest set of disincentives by far were in developing countries, with a variety of factors but especially foreign exchange controls on royalty payments or other fees, prior government approval for agreements and inadequate protection of industrial property rights being mentioned very frequently by licensors.[44]

In Eastern Europe, licensing enterprises perceived fewer problems overall, but the same three major groups of factors were cited as posing particular disincentives. Although fewer disincentives again were perceived in industrialised nations, a different set of problems were identified, including anti-trust or competition laws on licensing agreements, withholding or value-added taxes on licensing income and government export regulations.

Turning to disincentives to licensing in the country of the licensor, controls on exports in high-technology sectors; inadequate enforcement of domestic intellectual property rights on process patents and subsequent exports to the home country following licensing; and home country anti-trust regulations were emphasised. In the latter context, EC and US regulations were commonly cited as influencing licensing activity, but new Community legislation on block exemptions for patent licensees was viewed as being helpful.

Regarding international arrangements, the World Intellectual Property Organisation (WIPO – the organisation that co-ordinates the Patent Co-operation Treaty's activities) and WIPO model licensing agreements were

Table 4.4 Disincentives to licensing in country of licensee[a] (per cent[b])

Issue	Area		
	Industrialised countries	Eastern Europe	Developing countries
Inadequate industrial property rights protection	15	36	75
Competition laws	45	6	21
Government regulations			
prior approval, registration, notification	18	45	80
local purchase of raw materials	10	28	59
local purchase of machinery, etc.	5	24	55
import quotas	8	20	57
export regulations	22	32	52
Exchange controls on royalty payments or fees	14	45	88
Taxes on licensing income	29	28	62

[a] Study based on the international licensing activities of a sample of European, Japanese, United States and other enterprises.
[b] Percentages based on 106 responses for industrialised countries, 94 for Eastern Europe and 109 for developing countries.
Source: Organisation for Economic Cooperation and Development (1987), *International Technology Licensing: Survey Results*, Paris, August, Table 40.

viewed favourably. The authority of the publications was regarded as helpful in the drafting of contracts and especially in gaining acceptance of essential clauses in contracts. Licensors in the OECD sample did not appear to be particularly aware of or concerned about UNIDO and UNCTAD guidelines and proposals, such as the draft Code of Conduct on the Transfer of Technology.

Future prospects for licensing activity

Various comments have been made in this chapter about the growth of licensing in recent years and future prospects in the light of much changed global environmental and competitive conditions. Surveys of licensors confirm these conclusions: in the OECD study around 60 per cent of licensors reported increased licensing activity over a three-year period to the late 1980s, with growth being most apparent in high-technology as opposed to mature-technology sectors. For the future, too, companies were bullish about licensing prospects, although it is interesting that some other forms of international investment and technology transfer were foreseen to expand perhaps even more rapidly than licensing; this was the case, for example, for joint ventures and technology sales.

Concluding remarks on empirical evidence

Within the constraints of data availability, the empirical evidence does reveal something of the diversity and complexities of licensing. It is not an international market development mode to be entered into lightly, given the time required to enter into agreements and the problems created by the legal and country-regulatory envelope within which licensing takes place. Nevertheless, the licensing mode can be very profitable and an important complement to or alternative to other methods of foreign market servicing. There is no simple answer to the question of whether licensing is mainly used as an entry mode to closed markets and for short-term reasons, as opposed to longer-term strategic and market development reasons. It can be both, depending on size of firm, nature of industry and technology and the environmental conditions facing the enterprise. Irrespective of motive, however, the need for a planned, systematic and committed approach would seem to be essential.

PLANNING AND MANAGING LICENSING AGREEMENTS

The intention in this section is to focus upon the practical activities to be undertaken when setting up licensing agreements – from planning through to the signing of contracts and working with licensees. The recommendation is that the licensor with marketable technology takes the initiative in the international licensing process, despite the fact that the empirical evidence has shown that commonly this is not the case. The focus is upon technology licensing, but the principles apply equally, for example, to licensing of trade marks.

Step 1: Technology audit
The objective of this preparatory stage is to identify all usable technology in the company – current and active technology, mature and obsolete technology, dormant or partially developed technology. Although the costs of such an audit may be high, the outcome will be a profile of the company's technology portfolio available for licensing-out (the process might also draw attention to gaps in the technology portfolio which could be filled by licensing-in). Questions of protecting intellectual property rights through patents and trade marks will also need to be considered at as early a stage as possible, given delays in approval procedures in different countries.

Step 2: Establishing the planning framework
With a portfolio of technologies, a variety of international market entry and development options and a large number of country alternatives, it is important for the prospective licensor to have a framework within which the licensing process will be undertaken. The selection of a target country will

have been approached along the lines of that set out in Chapter 2, and the entry mode decision as discussed in Chapter 1. Along with the results of the technology audit, these decisions represent the starting point for planning the company's licensing strategy in a particular country, as set out in Figure 4.1. The 'global strategic context' represents the stage of considering licensing within the firm's international activities as a whole (even if it is not a global company as such), and of bringing together the parties within the company who will be affected by and involved in the licensing process and licensing negotiations. From that stage detailed implementation issues are involved, but it is useful to have a reference point, such as Figure 4.1, which the licensing team can refer to as negotiations proceed.

Step 3: Preparing a licensing memorandum[4 5]
The purpose of the licensing memorandum is to provide a succinct and accurate description of what is on offer from the licensor. It may be assumed that evaluation of such a licensing submission will often be undertaken by decisionmakers in the potential licensee firms who do not have a highly technical background and are busy. Licensing memoranda would usually include the following sections:

Section	Contents
Executive summary	Major points
Description and brief history of licensor	Credentials of licensor and factors leading up to the invention or development to be licensed
A summary of the technology	Non-technical description of business advantage to the licensee; technical analysis, photos, samples, etc., might be appended
Reference to the intellectual property rights	Existence of patents or pending patent applications including reference to presumed breadth and enforceability; conditions desired by licensor in trade mark licensing; descriptions of types of know-how, means of making this available to licensees and availability of trouble-shooting and consulting services
Economics of licensee business	Cash flow and profitability analysis on a variety of assumptions. Reference to actual performance of technology elsewhere in the world will improve credibility

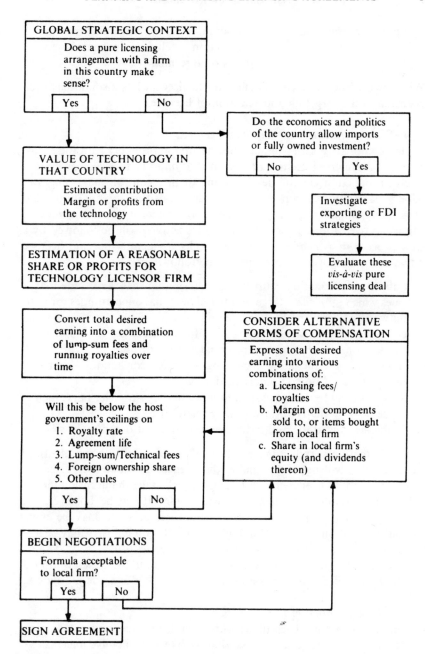

Figure 4.1 Steps in planning for negotiations. Source: Contractor, F.J. (1985), *Licensing in International Strategy*, Quorum Books, Westpoint, Conn., Figure 4.

| Suggested transactions | Proposed business formula for the transaction including proposals for terms of agreement. |

With the evidence of such a document, the licensor has a sound basis for proceeding to the targeting and selection of licensees.

Step 4: Search strategies and targeting licensees
This step comprises a series of activities beginning probably with the establishment of a preferred licensee profile, in relation to factors such as market strength, production capabilities including quality control, marketing and general managerial competence, financial position, reputation and compatibility/empathy (given that a licence arrangement involves a working relationship over a long period of time). This activity will be followed by a search process in which the enterprise seeks to identify specific licensee candidates, making use as necessary of the following:[46]

1. Published information sources, e.g. licensing journals and trade magazines which publicise a large number of potential opportunities for both outward and inward licensing. Sifting can be a time-consuming and costly activity, however, and it is often unclear as to whether the product on offer has had commercial success or not.
2. Intermediaries, including technology-transfer consultants, 'marriage bureaux' based on computerised databases.
3. Trade fairs and exhibitions, including technology-transfer fairs (such as those held by the Dworkowitz organisation).
4. Embassies and trade and industrial development organisations.[47]

The information search process, when taken together with the identified licensee profile, will hopefully enable the licensor to make a targeted approach to potential licensee candidates (at which stage the licensing memorandum will be sent to the latter for consideration). It may be, however, that the information is too general for this purpose, or there may be many potential applications of the technology, or the relevant industry may be very diverse. In such cases consultants may have to be used in a more detailed investigatory capacity; alternatively the firm could publish a description of the technology offered for license in relevant licensing or trade journals.

Step 5: The negotiation process
Once initial contact has been made with suitable licensees and one or more have expressed interest, a process that is likely to involve increasingly detailed negotiations will follow, including at some stage face-to-face negotiations. Issues of concern to the licensee might include the following:[48]

1. Technical queries about the operation and effectiveness of the technology, on its own and in comparison with alternatives (a demonstration

of the technology in use is important in creating a favourable impression).

2. Financial and cost matters that impact upon profitability or risk to the licensee.
3. Environmental problems and other regulatory issues.
4. Evaluation of the coverage and enforceability of intellectual property rights being offered for license.
5. Availability to the licensee of assistance to get the project started and of follow-up assistance in later years.

Given the fact that partners' mutual trust and confidence in licensing arrangements need time to develop, some gestation period is nearly always necessary, especially in international licensing where the parties may come from very different cultural backgrounds. The need is all the greater when lengthy and difficult negotiations may have been undertaken to reach agreement on the licence.

The level and nature of royalty rates will be one obvious centre of attention in negotiations.[49] The norm would comprise a first down-payment, plus progress payments and royalties (perhaps including a minimum royalty) as indicated in Chapter 1. The minimum royalty is effectively a guarantee that some minimum income will be received by the licensor for giving up his selling rights. Running royalties may operate at a constant rate, although in some cases royalties may decrease with volume, providing an incentive to the licensee to increase sales and market penetration. In rare cases royalties could increase with output, enabling the licensor to share in cost reduction associated with economies of large-scale production.

Other methods of payment include lump sums with no running royalty; schemes for converting royalties into equity; management and technical fees; and a variety of methods of counterpurchase as found in dealings with Eastern Bloc countries (see Chapter 5). Along with methods of payment, payment definitions must be very clear concerning 'sales', currency of payment (and the treatment of foreign exchange risk), who pays withholding tax or value-added tax, etc.

Licensors' views on the factors influencing the price in licensing negotiations were discussed in the previous section on empirical evidence, and some of the variables likely to increase or decrease licensing agreement compensation are listed in Appendix 4.2. If there is substantial political risk, as might be the case in some developing countries, high up-front payments would be desirable along with a shorter time-scale for the agreement. On the other hand, if the market is large and the licensee is well-positioned to develop a substantial market share, then royalty rates would be lower and up-front payments reduced.

Apart from royalties and fees, negotiations between licensor and licensee will centre upon a variety of non-price aspects including the issues of exclusivity, technical rights, reciprocal agreements on technological advance, and the supply of components and machinery. The provision of exclusivity is a common clause in licensing agreements. This allows the licensor, subject to the legal position within the country (see the earlier comments on EC law and the issue of parallel imports), to control competition by limiting the nature and number of suppliers by market area. Exclusivity is as much in the licensee's as the licensor's interest, and will usually be associated with higher royalty rates. Territorial restrictions, of course, represent an important component of exclusive agreements. Access to any technological advances made by the licensee – so-called grant-backs – will be another area for negotiation. Grant-backs can be difficult to define and enforce but may be traded off against lower royalty payments. As the empirical evidence showed, such non-price aspects, as with the provision of goods and services as part of the licensing package, are very common.

Step 6: The licensing agreement
Assuming that the main points have been agreed upon at the negotiation stage and signed as 'heads of agreement', the licensing contract is then drafted, usually by the licensor. An illustration of specimen heads of agreement is shown in Appendix 4.3.

Step 7: Monitoring licences and working with the licensee
The licensing contract is only the beginning of the agreement, since co-operation in implementation through the provision of technical and managerial assistance, etc., is likely to be very necessary; and the licensor needs to monitor the agreement carefully. Even if there is no intentional disregard of the contractual terms, errors have been found to occur very frequently in royalty payments, and reporting and auditing procedures, therefore, need to be established.[50] What may be even more problematic are the difficulties which arise from deliberate flaunting of licensing terms, from minor infringements through to large-scale counterfeiting.

Organising for licensing out

In many ways, licensing, like the new product development process to which it is related, is an important test for corporate organisation and communication. Thus, licensing requires inputs from the R & D unit, which may be the vehicle to accomplish the transfer of technology. The marketing department is involved in assessing market potentials and in any product/marketing know-how transfers in licensing agreements. Production personnel may be called upon to assist the licensee in manufacturing problems, and there must be effective and efficient support from the legal and patent departments of the company.

While relating only to one company – British Telecom – the activities to be handled within the scope of licensing-in and licensing-out are highlighted in Figure 4.2. In this instance all operations were undertaken by an Intellectual Property Unit (IPU) which acted as a corporate co-ordinator. While individual divisions within British Telecom may negotiate independently of each other with licensees, the IPU's role ensures that there is no possibility of conflict and the company presents an undivided corporate position to potential clients.[51]

Clearly only a minority of firms are in a position to tackle licensing in such a co-ordinated way. Factors that will influence the organisation of licensing activity include size of firm; the significance of licensing-out or licensing-in to the company and/or the overall extent of internationalisation of the enterprise (where the question of licensing as a mode of entry compared with the alternatives is important); the approach to licensing (pro-active or reactive); and the organisation structure of the firm as a whole.

The small-firm sector is far from homogeneous, and in high-tech smaller enterprises where technology transfer and other forms of internationalisation are of crucial concern, licensing may have an important role within the

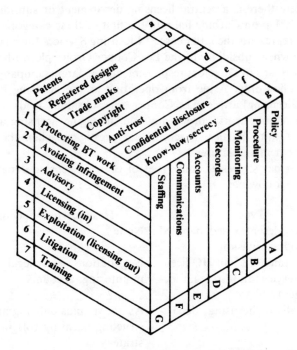

Figure 4.2 Activities involved in licensing. Source: British Telecom Intellectual Property Unit, 1987.

organisation and be an integral part of strategic planning. In one recently formed small US company in the electronics interconnection business, for example, the R & D, licensing, product development and model shops were linked under a single umbrella organisation dubbed the Advanced Technology Group.[52] An identifiable licensing function was set up to find new licensees, service and monitor existing licensees and generally market new technologies which were constantly being developed. More typically, perhaps, small-firm licensing-out is *ad hoc*, often resulting from approaches made by licensees, and there is no licensing function as such.[53] It is often stated that irrespective of the formal organisation, there is still a need for licensing to have the equivalent of a 'product champion'; that is, an experienced executive with good product and company knowledge, who has the confidence of management at all levels and the stature to represent the company in negotiations. It should be possible to earmark such a person within small as well as large businesses, and thereby facilitate a more systematic approach to licensing.

Within larger enterprises, there is a wide spectrum of activity, from the case where there is no licensing department and licensing is simply seen as a fortuitous add-on within one or more divisions in the firm; to the other extreme where there is a central licensing department or subsidiary. Until fairly recently Union Carbide fell into the first of these categories, whereas Lee Cooper represents the latter case.[54] Licensing Services International Ltd is a wholly owned subsidiary of the Lee Cooper Group plc, with a separate independent Board of Directors responsible to the parent company on group corporate policy only. Aside from operating as the licensing (principally trade mark licensing) arm of Lee Cooper, this subsidiary is also engaged in outside consultancy work – processing and managing licensing agreements on behalf of third parties – a recent and prestigious client being Aston Martin, the car manufacturer.

Contractor has suggested four types of central licensing departments as shown in the following:

Type	Headquarters' function
1. Entirely decentralised; handled by product division	None
2. Decentralised; small HQ licensing service and/or legal department	Negotiations and legal advice; monitoring; accounts
3. Centralised licensing department	As above, plus defining and constructing licensing role in overall strategy
4. Centralised licensing department as a profit centre	As above, plus allocation of licensing income to divisions after deducting department expences.

Study of US firms found that type 2 or type 3 organisation dominated, the conclusion being that licensing executives 'must be able to appreciate the strategic alternatives to licensing. . . and take a top management view. . . [And] this means, for the licensing executive, a need to superimpose on the nitty-gritty of negotiating agreements, reading foreign laws or collecting royalties, the larger view of licensing's place in the overseas expansion of the company'.[55]

LICENSING-IN

As was pointed out in the introduction, the emphasis in this chapter is on licensing-out. Much of what has been said, however, can be turned around and applied equally well to licensing-in. As the empirical evidence shows, many licensing agreements actually stem from approaches by licensees; and there must be a suspicion, at least in regard to small-firm licensing-in in developed countries, that a prime motive underlying this is declining demand for existing products. This would suggest that the licensee is at an immediate disadvantage in negotiations and general relations with the licensor. In a similar vein, there are instances where licensing-in is used as the easy option, with the licence being renewed regularly and the licensee becoming heavily dependent on the technology supplier. A considered and 'panic-free' approach in licensing-in is thus advocated.

For the firm considering inward licensing, Table 4.5 summarises the advantages and disadvantages to be weighed up before embarking upon this route to development, as opposed to alternatives such as developing technology internally or purchasing it essentially fully developed. Then Table 4.6 provides advice on what to do and what not to do when acquiring intellectual property.

FRANCHISING

It is generally agreed that the first franchise ever established was by the Singer Sewing Machine Company in the USA in 1863. The main growth period for the US franchising industry was, however, after the Second World War; and domestic expansion was followed by international expansion, as US franchisors identified opportunities in Europe and elsewhere where the franchising concept was late in catching on. In the early 1980s, it was estimated that there were 295 international franchisors based in the USA, with a total of 23,500 outlets abroad.[56] Of the latter total, about 25 per cent were in Europe, 20 per cent in Japan and 30 per cent in Canada. While domestic franchising has been growing rapidly in Europe, to date internationalisation has been proceeding more slowly.

Table 4.5 Advantages and disadvantages of licensing-in

Advantages	Disadvantages
1. Is an approach for buying time; it can result in faster commercial production and market entry, or assist in gaining market share and/or improving profitability if the licensee is already a participant in the industry.	1. Is an investment in the current state-of-the-art technology of the licensor at best, rather than in technology which will be superior to all others.
2. Can be significantly less expensive than internal development and can eliminate or reduce the firm's commitment in staff and costly facilities.	2. May create substantial problems in translating the technology to the licensee's operations, particularly if the licensor is located in a foreign country with language and cultural differences.
3. Can have much less risk than internal development.	3. May require significant scale-up, resulting in additional costs and delays in commercialisation.
4. Can provide specialised knowledge and skills that are beyond the capability of the licensee to develop in a reasonable time and enable the technology function to focus on projects where it has the greatest competence and highest odds of success.	4. Does not necessarily result in the in-depth technical knowledge and training of personnel gained from internal development.
5. Can generally provide for continuing technical assistance from the licensor through the licence agreement; and may result in access to new developments from the licensor and, in some instances, from its other licensees through technological 'pool' arrangements.	5. May require grant-back of improvements made by the licensee. These improvements may flow from the licensor to other licensees who are competitors of the firm making the improvements.
6. May avoid a patent or trade secret dispute or a costly effort to circumvent existing patents.	6. Can have adverse effect on morale of the R&D staff, who may interpret licensing-in of technology as a vote of no confidence.
7. May permit use of a trade mark or result in immediate market recognition based on the good reputation of the licensor.	7. May require the licensee under exclusive licences to bear the cost of policing the market for infringement and of subsequent litigation if required to resolve a dispute.
8. May stimulate the licensee's technological development and help overcome a 'not invented here' attitude. Relying solely on internally developed technology is introspective and can be costly. A sophisticated licensing staff can also act as technological 'gatekeepers' by monitoring outside developments.	8. Could be so expensive that the cost of the licence is a significant drain on the business.
9. Is sometimes easier to 'sell' management on investing in proven technology from outside than in an internally developed technology.	

Source: McDonald, C.W. and Leahey, H.S. (1985), 'Licensing has a Role in Technology Strategic Planning', *Research Management*, **28**(1), 35–6.

Many of the principles of licensing apply equally well to franchising, which, however, usually involves the provision of a wider package of services to the franchisee than would be the case with licensing and a continuing direct association between the parties to the agreement. It must be admitted that there is still a lively debate about the precise differences between the two types of agreement, and one view of these is presented in Table 4.7 (on p. 148). Two types of franchising have been identified. The first is 'product and trade name' franchising, as, for example, when Coca Cola sells its syrup, along with the right to use its trade mark to independent bottlers (franchisees). The second type is 'business-format' franchising which involves not only a product or trade mark but also marketing strategies, operating procedures and quality control; and continuing liaison and interchange between franchisor and franchisee.[57] Restaurants, hotels, personal and business services, etc., are examples of sectors using business-format franchising.

The issue of protecting legal rights arises in franchising as in licensing. Patents are rarely a significant part of a franchise, and legal protection will mainly be sought for the 'image package' of the franchisor, namely, names and designs and distinctive features of the operation, through registered trade marks. A trade mark is not necessarily just a word or an easily defined symbol but can relate to the design of the article or service and, therefore, may be applied to the colour and styling of the premises and products, shapes of shop fronts, and so on. This is seen clearly in the common styles of premises, colour schemes and layout of Pizza Hut, Wimpy or McDonald's restaurants, and the like. It is the case that many franchises exist with weak trade marks, but this can lead to encroachment by third parties and former franchisees and creates problems when trying to persuade new franchisees to pay the package of up-front fees, management fees and running royalties.

Why would a company wish to franchise overseas as opposed to internalising its ownership advantages through foreign direct investment (the exporting option is out, at least as regards service activity, since many business services are non-tradable internationally)? And what is the explanation for the concentration of franchising activity in consumer service products? Referring to the hotel industry, Dunning and McQueen argue that equity investment is not necessary to ensure control, unlike the situation in manufacturing and resource-based industries.[58] Rather, day-to-day operation of hotels and long-term production and marketing strategy may be controlled by contract – either management contracts or franchising. Conversely, the hotel management company may be unwilling to invest in hotel ownership because it has little expertise in property development, or ownership is regarded as risky, or because of the high capital requirements. Quality control may also be ensured without equity investment in other consumer services such as fast foods. The situation is different in 'higher-technology' service sectors like banking, accounting, consulting and advertising. The exclusive possession of proprietary information is one of the major

Table 4.6 Do's and don'ts in licensing-in

	Pre-acquisition	Initial in-house studies	Organising for exploitation	Managerial consideration	Financial consideration	Legal consideration	Decision-making
Do's							
Study internal technical, marketing and financial needs	×	×					
Study external markets	×	×					
Analyse competition	×	×					×
Determine ultimate consumer opinion		×					
Develop interdisciplinary team			×	×			
Adopt strategic plan			×	×			×
Find product champion & put him in charge			×	×			
Set up a new venture group				×			
Provide a balanced organisation				×			
Use techniques of successful entrepreneurially oriented companies				× ×	×		
Develop realistic capital needs					×		
Study patent-antitrust implications					×	×	
Determine legal restrictions on marketing and fund transfer				×		×	
Analyse government regulatory environment				×		×	
Acquire know-how plus patents					×	× ×	
Enlist strong management support				× ×			
Require frequent management questioning				× ×		×	
Have and maintain enthusiasm, patience and persistence							× ×
Face facts and have courage to terminate							

Don'ts

Believe in-house market surveys without objective outside market studies

Back new technology too far from existing product lines

Spread organisation too thinly

Expect quick positive results

Allow existing production and marketing to kill project with negative inputs

Allow not-invented-here attitude to prevail

Allow in-house research to suffer from licensing-in or purchase of technology

Allow legal advisers to be exclusive negotiators

Use licensing-in for defensive or market control purposes only

Allow creative scientist or engineer to dominate

Allow negative financial department input to overweigh other positive factors

Source: Marcy, W. (1979), 'Acquiring and Selling Technology: Licensing Do's and Don'ts', *Research Management*, **22**(2), 18–22.

Table 4.7 How licensing and franchising differ

Licensing	Franchising
1. The term 'royalties' is normally used.	1. Management fees are regarded as the most appropriate term.
2. Products, or even a single product, are the common element.	2. Covers the total business, including the know-how, intellectual rights, goodwill, trade mark and business contacts. (Franchising is all-encompassing, whereas licensing concerns just one part of the business.)
3. Licenses are usually taken by well-established businesses.	3. Tends to be a start-up situation, certainly as regards the franchisee.
4. Terms of 16 to 20 years are common, particularly where they relate to technical know-how, copyright and trade marks. The terms are similar for patents.	4. The franchise agreement is normally for five years, sometimes extending to ten years. Franchises are frequently renewable.
5. Licensees tend to be self-selecting. They are often an established business and can demonstrate that they are in a strong position to operate the licence in question. A licensee can often pass his licence onto an associated or sometimes unconnected company with little or no reference back to the original licensor.	5. The franchisee is very definitely selected by the franchisor, and his eventual replacement is controlled by the franchisor.
6. Usually concerns specific existing products with very little benefit from ongoing research being passed on by the licensor to his licensee.	6. The franchisor is expected to pass on to his franchisees the benefits of his ongoing research programme as part of the agreement.
7. There is no goodwill attached to the licence as it is totally retained by the licensor.	7. Although the franchisor does retain the main goodwill, the franchisee picks up an element of localized goodwill.
8. Licensees enjoy a substantial measure of fee negotiation. As bargaining tools, they can use their trade muscle and their established position in the marketplace.	8. There is a standard fee structure and any variation within an individual franchise system would cause confusion and mayhem.

Source: Perkins, J.S. (1987), 'How Licensing, Franchising Differ', *Les Nouvelles*, **22** (4), 157.

sources of advantage to banking firms, for instance, encouraging internalisation through foreign direct investment. Servicing multinational manufacturing companies requires multinational banking operations if personal and confidential relationships are to be nurtured and maintained; and internalisation may overcome other imperfections in international financial markets.[59]

At the practical level, the franchisor has the opportunity to expand the business internationally on a far larger scale, with greater speed and with much reduced capital requirements. Take the example of Holiday Inns, approximately 87 per cent of which were franchised in 1987.[60] The concept of the founder was of a chain of hotels providing consistent and reliable quality accommodation and a referral or reservation system connecting them. The use of franchising enabled this concept to be fulfilled on a scale and at a speed that would have been impossible otherwise. In the mid-1960s the company was opening a Holiday Inn every two and a half days. Of course to make the franchise viable a company such as Holiday Inns has to invest heavily in its support facilities – sophisticated marketing, advertising and computer technology. The reservation system entails satellite linkage of nearly 700 reservation terminals in the two reservation centres, plus 250 terminals in the offices of travel agents and 20,000 terminals in airline reservation offices internationally, to the computer centre in Tennessee, USA.

Problems for the franchisor are similar to those of licensing, including lack of full control over the franchisee and the possible creation of competitors, and so the identification and selection of partners becomes a crucial issue. One early study on the problems experienced by US firms in establishing franchises in foreign countries identified the following major factors:[61]

Problems encountered	Percentage of sample ($n = 52$)
Government or legal restrictions	59.6
Difficulty of recruiting enough qualified franchisees	44.2
Lack of sufficient local funding	36.5
Difficulty of controlling franchisees	36.5
Difficulty of redesigning the franchise package to make it saleable to franchisees in foreign markets	28.8
Trademarks and/or copyright obstacles	28.8

Building up the business to the point where an international name has been created – itself a requirement to attract franchisees – is a major undertaking, moreover, as the experience of McDonald's, the US fast-food chain has shown.[62] The company's entry into different markets has been marked by costly mistakes – in Canada in 1970, McDonald's had to pay $6m. to buy back rights for which they had been paid $70,000 three years earlier; the British operation, a joint venture with an American franchisee, lost $10m. in the first five years. The conclusion that was reached was that local franchisees must be allowed total marketing freedom (in terms of items on the menu list, location of stores, etc.), but, on the other hand, the parent company should have complete control over operational and managerial procedures. Reflecting. the former point, at least, one study reported that one-third of franchisors had 'altered' logos, promotional and colour themes and architecture in foreign markets.[63]

The experience of the major franchising companies reveals one further lesson which concerns flexibility over entry methods into foreign markets. Hackett, in a survey of eighty-five US franchisors, found that only two-thirds of foreign operations were totally owned by franchisees; the remainder were either wholly owned by the franchisors or involved joint ventures with local interests.[64] For a potential franchisee, taking a franchise may be quite risky until the concept and brand name is known in the country. Therefore, franchising may be more common in the later stages of the firm's market development in any particular country. To illustrate the point, McDonald's entry into Eastern Europe in 1988 involved a 50/50 joint venture with Genex, Yugoslavia's biggest general trading enterprise.

FURTHER READING

1. Readers wanting a brief introduction to licensing issues and practicalities (although not specific to international licensing) should consult; Lowe, J. and Crawford, N. (1984), *Technology Licensing and the Small Firm*, Gower, Aldershot; the book is only 115 pages in length.
2. F. J. Contractor has undertaken some of the best work in this field and for serious study of licensing the following books are essential reading:
   Contractor, F.J. (1985), Licensing in International Strategy. *A Guide for Planning and Negotiations*, Quorum Books, West point, Conn., especially Chapters 5–9.
   Contractor, F.J. (1981), *International Technology Licensing: Compensation, Costs and Negotiation*, D.C. Heath and Co., Lexington, Mass.
3. Recent empirical evidence derived from a survey of licensing companies is in Organisation for Economic Co-operation and Development (1987), *International Technology Licensing: Survey Results*, OECD, Paris.

QUESTIONS FOR DISCUSSION

1. Discuss some of the problems a company might experience in licensing the manufacture of brand-name clothing in the Far East.
2. To what extent are the predictions of the economics, stages-of-development and business-strategy approaches borne out in the empirical evidence cited in Table 4.1?
3. Assuming you are the potential US licensor of air conditioning control technology,
   (a) outline the steps you would take to identify a licensee in Britain;
   (b) what terms would you try to incorporate into the licensing contract to maximise your financial returns from the deal?
4. Using the examples of a brand-name sports shoe manufacturer (licensor) and a fast-food restaurant (franchisor), show how licensing and franchising differ.
5. Do you believe that licensing-in represents a feasible long-term development strategy for a company? Discuss, in relation to the alternative development approaches such as in-house R & D, acquisitions, and other forms of corporate collaboration.

NOTES AND REFERENCES

1. For a discussion of why multinational enterprises license abroad, see Telesio, P. (1984), 'Foreign Licensing in Multinational Enterprises', in Stobaugh R. and Wells, L.T., Jr. (eds), *Technology Crossing Borders*, Harvard Business School Press, Boston, Mass.

2. Organisation for Economic Co-operation and Development (1987), *International Technology Licensing: Survey Results*, OECD, Paris, 23.

3. Contractor, F.J. (1985), *Licensing in International Strategy*, Quorum Books, Westpoint, Conn., 37.

4. See Rosenblum, J.E. (1985), 'Licensing Second-Source Suppliers', *Les Nouvelles*, 20(2), 93–4; Ostrach, M.S. (1985), 'Biotechnology Licensing Issues', *Les Nouvelles*, 20(3), 101–4.

5. Calingaert, M. (1987), 'Policies for the Future: The USA', paper presented at the First European Licensing and Franchising Conference, Glasgow, Scotland, 15–16 June.

6. Contractor, *Licensing in International Strategy*, 6.

7. The quotation and the following discussion draw on Baillie, I.C. (1987), 'Workshop on Intellectual Property (Licensing Aspects)', paper presented at the First European Licensing and Franchising Conference, Glasgow, Scotland, 15–16 June.

8. This section draws on University of Manchester in association with Licensing Executives Society (UK and Ireland) (1986), *Recent Developments in International Patenting*, Papers CP 86/1, University of Manchester; Ryan, W.T. and Bonham-Yeaman, D. (1982), 'International Patent Cooperation', *Columbia Journal of World Business*, 17(4), 63–6.

9. Parkes, A.J.A. (1987), *Trade Marks, Patents and Copyright*, Irish Export Board, Dublin; see also Root, F.J. (1987), *Entry Strategies for International Markets*, Lexington Books, D.C. Heath & Co., Lexington, Mass., Chapter 4.

10. Contractor, F.J. and Sagafi-Nejad, T. (1981), 'International Technology Transfer: Major Issues and Policy Responses', *Journal of International Business Studies*, Fall, 113–35.

11. Tsurumi, Y. (1980), *Technology Transfer and Foreign Trade. The Case of Japan, 1950–1966*, Arno Press, New York.

12. United Nations Centre on Transnational Corporations (1985), *Transnational Corporations in World Development: Third Survey*, UN, New York, 51.

13. Ibid., 68.

14. Hurley, D. (1987), 'National Limits to Technology Transfer', *Les Nouvelles*, 22(2), 52.

15. Shaojie, C. (1987), 'Effect of PRC's Open-Door Policy', *Les Nouvelles*, 22(2), 75–8.

16. Solovykh, D.A. and Voinov, I.L. (1986), 'Licensing Into/Out of USSR', *Les Nouvelles*, 21(4), 169–71.

17. Lowe, J. and Crawford, N. (1984), *Innovation and Technology Transfer for the Growing Firm*, Pergamon Press, Oxford, Chapter 2.

18. The regulation concerned is Regulation No. 2349/84. Drauz, G. (1987), 'Policies for the Future: The Commission of the European Communities (EC)', paper presented at First European Licensing and Franchising Conference, Glasgow, Scotland, 15–16 June.

19. Davidson, W.H. and McFetridge, D.G. (1985), 'Key Characteristics in the Choice of International Technology Transfer Mode', *Journal of International Business Studies*, 16(2), 5–21.

20. See, for example, Telesio, P. (1977), 'Foreign Licensing Policy in Multinational Enterprise', DBA dissertation, Harvard University; Contractor, F. (1981), *International Technology Licensing: Compensation, Costs and Negotiation*, D.C. Heath & Co., Lexington, Mass.; Teece, D.J. (1977), 'Technology Transfer by Multinational Firms: The Resource Cost of Transferring Technological Know-How', *Economic Journal*, **87**(346), 242–61; Carstairs, R.T. and Welch, L.S. (1981), *A Study of Outward Foreign Licensing of Technology by Australian Companies*, Licensing Executives Society of Australia.
21. Contractor, *Licensing in International Strategy*, 80.
22. Ibid., Chapter 6.
23. Ibid., 127.
24. Buckley, P.J. and Davies, H. (1981), 'Foreign Licensing in Overseas Operations: Theory and Evidence from the UK', in Hawkins, R.G. and Prasad, A.J. (eds), *Technology Transfer and Economic Development*, JAI Press, Greenwich, Conn.
25. Silvia, W.F. (1985), 'Case Against Licensing', *Les Nouvelles*, **20**(1), 7.
26. OECD, *International Technology Licensing: Survey Results*. The other studies are cited in the references which follow. The sample comprised 119 licensors broken down by nationality as follows: Europe 51, Japan 16, USA 43, Other 9.
27. Contractor, *Licensing in International Strategy*, 101. The sample comprised 241 US companies and a total number of agreements in excess of 100. See also OECD, *International Technology Licensing*, 12.
28. Lowe and Crawford, *Innovation and Technology Transfer for the Growing Firm*, 164. See also Ford, D. and Jongerius, C. (1986), *Technology Strategy in British Industry*, BASE International, Milton Keynes, 7.
29. OECD, *International Technology Licensing*, 18–19; Ford and Jongerius, *Technology Strategy in British Industry*, 4.
30. Ford and Jongerius, *Technology Strategy in British Industry*, 14.
31. OECD, *International Technology Licensing*, 12–14.
32. Roberts, E.B. (1982), 'Is Licensing an Effective Alternative?', *Research Management*, **25**(5), 20–4.
33. OECD, *International Technology Licensing*, 25; Ford and Jongerius, *Technology Strategy in British Industry*, 19.
34. Contractor, F.J. (1980), 'The "Profitability" of Technology Licensing of US Multinationals: A Framework for Analysis and an Empirical Study', *Journal of International Business Studies*, Fall, 40–63.
35. Ford and Jongerius, *Technology Strategy in British Industry*, 11.
36. Contractor, F.J. (1980), 'The Composition of Licensing Fees and Arrangements as a Function of Economic Development of Technology Recipient Nations', *Journal of International Business Studies*, Winter, 47–62.
37. Contractor, *International Technology Licensing: Compensation, Costs and Negotiation*, 61.
38. Cited in United Nations Centre on Transnational Corporations (1987), *Transnational Corporations and Technology Transfer: Effects and Policy Issues*, UN, New York, 44.
39. Inferred from the results in OECD, *International Technology Licensing*, 31.
40. This approach is discussed in various places including Contractor, *International Technology Licensing*, Chapter 3.
41. For example, Ford and Jongerius, *Technology Strategy in British Industry*, 16, and an equivalent survey in the USA.
42. Contractor, 'The "Profitability" of Technology Licensing by US Multinationals', 56–8.
43. OECD. *International Technology Licensing*, 36.

44. Ibid., 34. To quote the OECD, 'a considerable number of respondents gave details of other problems which they encountered. Most of these firms emphasised: problems in developing countries including "corruption" and "silly and unrealistic" regulations, compulsory disclosure and automatic transfer of unpatented know-how, short licensing periods, and poor quality control when required to locally purchase components, machinery and services; and expansion by licensees from developing countries into other markets, due for example to non-acceptance of territorial limitations on sales, or disregard of other elements of licences and patent protection.'

45. Goldscheider, R. (1984), 'The Art of "Licensing Out"', *Les Nouvelles*, **19**(1), 84–9.

46. Lowe and Crawford, *Innovation and Technology Transfer for the Growing Firm*, Chapter 5. The following list is taken from the licensor's perspective. If a licensee was undertaking a similar search process he might like to consider institutional sources of information, e.g. research associations, government laboratories and universities.

47. With the national interest in technology transfer, industrial development organisations, even in developed countries (e.g. Scottish Development Agency, Industrial Development Authority – IDA – in the Republic of Ireland), will do all they can to assist licensors.

48. Goldscheider, 'The Art of "Licensing Out"', 88.

49. Millman, A.F. (1983), 'Licensing Technology', *Management Decision*, **21**(3), 3–16.

50. Axelrod, I.L. (1987), 'Monitoring Licenses, Royalty Payments', *Les Nouvelles*, **22**(1), 41–2. The author reported royalty payment discrepancies occurring in 80 per cent of royalty and licensing investigations.

51. The Intellectual Property Unit of British Telecom comprises four divisions: Patent Advisory Division, Corporate Licensing Division (licensing-out), New Ventures Division (licensing-in, acquisitions, joint ventures and collaborative research), Education and Marketing Division (encouragement of technology auditing by BT managers and ensuring full common use of technology). Source: Milligan, A.P. (1987), *Licensing: A Pro-Active Approach*, MBA Dissertation, Strathclyde Business School, September.

52. Nunes, T. (1986), 'Licensing and the Small Business', *Les Nouvelles*, **21**(2), 85–6. The company was Advanced Circuit Technology Inc.

53. See Lowe, J. and Crawford, N. (1984), *Technology Licensing and the Small Firm*, Gower, Aldershot, Chapter 6.

54. The Union Carbide case is discussed in Silvia, 'Case Against Licensing', 20–2.

55. Contractor, F.J. (1985), *Licensing in International Strategy*, Chapter 7, p. 171.

56. Kacker, M.P. (1985), *Transatlantic Trends in Retailing: Takeovers and Flow of Knowhow*, Quorum Books, New York.

57. Calingaert, M. (1987), *Policies for the Future: The USA*, paper presented at the First European Licensing and Franchising Conference, Glasgow, Scotland, 15–16 June.

58. Dunning, J.H. and McQueen, M. (1982), 'The Eclectic Theory of the Multinational Enterprise and the International Hotel Industry', in Rugman, A.M. (ed.), *New Theories of the Multinational Enterprise*, Croom Helm, London, Chapter 5.

59. For a general discussion of service multinationals, see Boddewyn, J.J., Halbrich, M.B. and Perry, A.C. (1986), 'Service Multinationals: Conceptualization, Measurement and Theory', *Journal of International Business Studies*, **17**(3), 41–57.

60. Ashman, R.T. (1987), *The Way Ahead for Franchising and Licensing*, paper presented at the First European Franchising and Licensing Conference, Glasgow, Scotland, 15–16 June.
61. Walker, B.J. and Etzel, M.J. (1973), 'The Internationalization of the US Franchise System: Progress and Procedures', *Journal of Marketing*, 37, April, 38–46.
62. Calingaert, M. (1987), *Policies for the Future: The USA*, paper presented at the First European Licensing and Franchising Conference, Glasgow, Scotland, 15–16 June.
63. Hackett, D.W. (1976), 'The International Expansion of US Franchise Systems: Status and Strategies', *Journal of International Business Studies*, Spring.
64. Ibid., 69–70.

APPENDIX 4.1

COUNTERFEITING

Counterfeiting involves the imitation of a product or service, without the permission of the legal owner, and the packaging of it to look like the original, with the result that the consumer is misled. Within this broad definition, at least five different types of activity have been identified:

1. *Outright piracy.* False product in the same form and same trade mark as the original. Records and tapes are common examples.
2. *Reverse engineering.* Stripping down the original product and then copying it, underselling the original manufacturer – a common phenomenon in the electronics industry.
3. *Counterfeiting.* Involves altering the product's quality without altering the trade mark. Clothing companies such as the international jeans manufacturers suffer heavily from this.
4. *Passing off.* Modifying both product and trade mark, adapting a trade mark that is similar in appearance, phonetic quality or meaning to the original product. All that is normally associated with the product is copied.
5. *Wholesale infringement.* This involves the questionable registration of famous brand names overseas rather than the introduction of faked products. In countries where the principle of first registration is practised rather than prior use this abuse can take place.

The first signs of large-scale commercial counterfeiting appeared in the 1950s when Japan became notorious for producing counterfeit goods. Hong Kong took over from Japan in the 1960s and 1970s, to be joined since then by Taiwan, South Korea, Thailand, Malaysia, Indonesia, the Philippines, Mexico and Brazil. All these countries have been cited for their lack of protection in areas of product and patent infringements. The products and services involved are wide ranging: electrical appliances, electronics, audio and video tapes, computer programs, toys and sports goods, auto accessories and parts, chemicals and pharmaceuticals, textiles and clothing and books, are all counterfeited. And the more famous the brand name, the greater the incentive; Cartier, Christian Dior, Ford Motor Company, Stanley Tools, Johnnie Walker whisky, Gordons gin, Apple computers, and so forth. Estimates of the value of world trade accounted for by counterfeited goods range from 2 to 5 per cent.[1]

The enormous incentive to counterfeiting arises from the buoyant demand for prestigious, heavily advertised products with strong brand names and the shortage of such products in many foreign markets. The facilitating factor, however, is the inadequacy of home and host country and international legislation in restraining the expansion of counterfeiting activity and/or weak enforcement measures. At host nation level, some countries may not be signatories to international patent or copyright treaties; again, even if lawsuits are filed for patent or copyright infringement, prosecution may be rare and the laws themselves weakly enforced when they do exist. The other problem may derive from the failure of companies themselves to register trade marks, patents or copyrights in countries they view as unimportant to growth, encouraging a secure sellers' market for counterfeit products to develop; once the domestic market is saturated, the counterfeit goods will start appearing on the export market. In home countries such as the USA and EC, too, legislation may be outdated or inefficient in combating counterfeiting.

There are signs of a more pro-active approach to counterfeiting emerging. Under pressure from foreign governments and companies (particularly of the USA), various Far Eastern countries are toughening intellectual property laws and increasing fines and prison terms for violations: Taiwan, Singapore and Indonesia fall into this category, although it remains to be seen how vigorously the laws will be implemented.[2] On the positive side is the recognition by governments such as Taiwan that counterfeiting is damaging to the country's image, and the fear that foreign firms will be deterred from investing in high-technology processes or products if the latter can be stolen with impunity. Such actions have been matched by legislation in developed countries: in the USA, the Trademark Counterfeiting Act of 1984 made trading in goods and services using a counterfeit trademark a criminal rather than a civil offence and established stiff penalties; in Britain the first major review of intellectual property and innovation for thirty years took place in 1986, the objective of which was, in part, to strike back at countries copying British products.[3] Since 1979 the USA and the EC, along with Japan, Canada and other developed countries, have been attempting to persuade the members of the General Agreement of Tariffs and Trade (GATT) to adopt an anti-counterfeiting code. Opposition from developing countries has, however, prevented much progress on this proposal and prospects for improved trade mark and patent protection emerging from the current Uruguay Round of negotiations in the GATT do not seem favourable.

Of course the companies which are victims of counterfeiting have also been active. Employment of special investigators, an active strategy of prosecution, timely registration of intellectual property rights and a variety of security systems to protect branded merchandise can all have an impact. Collective company action can improve the situation further, as when Swiss watchmakers charged fifty Hong Kong companies in 1983 with pirating Swiss designs (a year of negotiations led to an out-of-court settlement concerning designs, copyright and patent rights). More generally, in 1978 the International Anti Counterfeiting Coalition was formed to lobby for stronger legal sanctions worldwide. And under the auspices of the International Chamber of Commerce a Counterfeiting Intelligence Bureau (CIB) was established in 1983.[4]

For all this, the profits from counterfeiting are so great as to provide a continuing massive incentive to the activity. Success in anti-counterfeiting measures in one country may only lead to new country entrants, with the economic development gains encouraging passive if not active connivance of governments.

Notes and references

1. Harvey, M.G. and Ronkainen, I.A. (1985), 'International Counterfeiters: Marketing Success Without the Constant Risk', *Columbia Journal of World Business*, Fall, 37–44.

2. (1987) 'Indonesia Approves Tough Copyright Law', *Indonesian Development News*, **11**(1), September/October.
3. Department of Trade and Industry (1986), *Intellectual Property and Innovation*, HMSO, London.
4. Kelly, R. (1985), 'A New Initiative to Control International Counterfeiting', *The Crown Agents Review*, **2**, 24–6.

APPENDIX 4.2
LICENSING AGREEMENT COMPENSATION

Table A4.2.1 lists some of the factors that influence licensing agreement compensation (a + indicates an increase in compensation and a − indicates a decrease in compensation in relation to each factor).

Table A4.2.1 Variables influencing total licensing agreement compensation

Size of market	+
Competition faced by licensee	−
Transfer costs	+
Opportunity costs to licensor	+
Exclusivity granted to licensee	+
Years since patent registered	−
Strength and defensibility of patent	+
Age of technology	−
Export possibilities for licensee	+
Alternative sources for similar technology	−
Commercial proof of production viability	+
Internationally known trade mark	+
Inclusion of performance guarantees	+
Requirement of present and future technologies developed by licensor	+
Inclusion of other income sources for licensor (e.g. supply of components)	−

Source: Contractor (1981), *International Technology Licensing: Compensation, Costs and Negotiation*, D. C. Heath and Co., Lexington, Mass.

APPENDIX 4.3
ILLUSTRATION OF SPECIMEN HEADS OF AGREEMENT

Table A4.3.1 gives an example of specimen heads of agreement for the case of a small UK company with an innovative product, being faced by a large American enterprise with a major share of the US market.

Table A4.3.1 Specimen heads of agreement for licence negotiation

Heads and contents	Licensor action
Introduction Heads of agreement intention is to record all negotiations prior to formal licence negotiations. They provide an agenda under which the standard factors going into the final agreement can be discussed, but have no legal standing.	Send confidentiality letter to licensee prior to negotiations.
Parties to the agreement Description of both licensor and licensee, including location, operations etc.	n.a.
The agreement Specification of the objectives of the negotiations, viz. that the licensor undertakes to grant the licensee the exclusive or non-exclusive rights to manufacture and distribute his products or use his process in particular markets over a particular time.	Emphasise (1) that licensee should pursue the agreement to best of his ability; (2) that subject is a licence agreement not an agency partnership or joint venture.
The licensed properties Description of the product(s)/process(es) and/or technologies under consideration. These would be appended to the heads of agreement as a list.	Define the subject of the agreement in general terms at this stage. Final, detailed list should go to licensee on final agreement.
Obligations of the parties Licensor states that it is the owner of the technology under consideration and that it will take the necessary steps to transfer that technology to the licensee. Licensee states that it will use its best endeavours to maximise the income accruing to its use of the licensed properties.	Endeavour to reduce any commitment to protect industrial property while ensuring that licensee has responsibility for this in his own market.
Markets Description of those markets in which licensee will have rights to exploit the product.	Account must be taken of EC law forbidding restrictive market clauses.

Technical assistance
Description of the methods by which the technical assistance shall be imparted to the licensee by describing
   the numbers of personnel involved
   their duties at licensee's premises
   the time they will spend
   the information they will impart.
	Avoid *commitment* to provide the licensee with a working plant, i.e. this is the objective of the agreement, but it should not be the licensor's responsibility except under suitable remuneration conditions. Specifics left to licence agreement.

Compensation
Initial description of the method by which compensation will be arrived at, with possible methods as
   fixed fees prior to transfer of technology
   other lump sum payments at transfer
   royalties and minimum royalties.
	Details of possible royalties and fees appear on separate attachment. The company would be unwise to be too specific on the price of the licence until extra information has been obtained on licensee's projected sales and cost volume ratios.

Table A4.3.1 (cont.)

Heads and contents	Licensor action

The licensor to specify how and where compensation is paid with particular reference to
output definition on which royalties are levied
taxation conventions
currency of compensation
location of payment of compensation
licensee records of output
licensor auditing of output.

Licensor should, however, begin to explore licensee reaction to a front ended fee, although the amount of money involved will depend very much on the factors emphasised in the licence royalty analysis.

A clearer idea of licensee's projected sales and the cost/volume ratio for making this product will be required to calculate reasonable royalty rates.

Agreement duration
Agreement length defining those factors also pertinent to the time the agreement remains in force, viz.
patent life normally to last for the life of the agreement or until patent expires, whichever is the sooner
other industrial property to last for life of the agreement.
termination obligations–who shall have the right to terminate, and when? How much notice shall be given?
renewal clauses after specified time period.

There are dangers in agreeing to a very long-term licence agreement. However, a short term (particularly if there are substantial tooling costs) may not be acceptable to the licensee. A five-year agreement, with sufficient clauses for termination should contract be broken, would therefore be a reasonable compromise. This would depend entirely on minimum royalty rates being acceptable. Otherwise, a renewable agreement (yearly) would be necessary.

Exclusivity
Depending on the technology under consideration, the markets involved and the willingness of the licensee to pay reasonable minimum royalty payments, exclusivity can be negotiated. In general, the licensor seeks to maximise his income from licence agreements in that market. Hence the decision to grant exclusive or non-exclusive licences will be based upon his evaluation of the commercial factors involved.

To define areas of restriction. This probably means an exclusive agreement in the USA for primary uses with possible sub-licensing agreements outside the USA for non-primary purposes. This would exclude areas covered by a UK licence. Possible provisions for separate licensing for non-primary uses of products may be discussed.

Protection of the licensed properties
Statement by the licensee that he will to the best of his ability protect the licensed properties from unauthorised use by others and to acknowledge the ownership of those properties as directed by the licensor (through the use of marks on products, etc.).

It is important that the licensee keeps all pre-contract negotiations secret and confidential. Should a prototype pre-contract production run be required, this could be done under an option agreement which would contain clauses designed to ensure secrecy.

Protection of property rights will vary depending on legal system under which agreement is drawn up. The licensor should endeavour to ascertain that this will be under UK law.

Grant backs/grant forwards
Generally all improvements to the product/process designed by licensor or licensee to be notified to the other party as appropriate. Rights to be granted to licensor/licensee on a reciprocal basis.

Reciprocal agreement would normally be sought and this would be particularly important if the licensee decided to enter markets not presently covered by the licensor, with amendments or improvements to the products.

Table A4.3.1 (cont.)

Heads and contents	Licensor action
Parts and supplies Licensor will provide licensee with initial stocks of parts and other supplies to allow licensee to enter production as quickly as possible. Licensee has right to purchase completed goods from licensor to allow initial market evaluation and/or penetration. Licensor may seek to insist that licensee purchase parts from him on a longer term basis.	Advantageous to seek licensee purchase of parts as one method of remuneration. Relative bargaining strength of licensor may not allow this, however.
Other clauses Disputes, not amenable to settlement between the two parties shall be settled by an arbitrator agreed by both parties, under International Chamber of Commerce Rules or under the national laws of the territory in which the dispute arose.	Advantageous for the licensor to have any disputes settled under his national law.

Source: Reproduced from Lowe, J. and Crawford, N. (1984), *Innovation and Technology Transfer for the Growing Firm*, Pergamon Press, Oxford, 151–4.

5

CONTRACTUAL ARRANGEMENTS IN INTERNATIONAL MARKET DEVELOPMENT

SUMMARY

1. A characteristic of a number of the contractual modes of international market entry and development is that they are commonly found in combination; moreover, the arrangements primarily apply to relationships in developing countries and the Eastern Bloc. International subcontracting is different in that the products manufactured are earmarked for export, either back to the home country or to third-country markets.
2. Management contracts are most common in public utilities, tourism (e.g. hotels) and agriculture in developing countries, as part of a package comprising other arrangements. The management firm's duties are similar to those a foreign company performs in running an overseas subsidiary.

   Motives for management contracts vary, but defensive reasons still dominate – relating, for example, to a method of entry into otherwise closed markets, and guaranteeing sources of raw materials and components. Many conflicts have arisen between the parties to management contracts, which can only be solved by building up mutual interest and trust.
3. Turnkey contracts represent arrangements whereby one party is responsible for setting up a plant and putting it into operation, and have been used by some countries to establish entire industrial complexes, especially in the heavy industry and basic materials' fields. Various 'turnkey plus' contracts have been introduced by developing countries to improve the ability of local managers and workers to run the plants and to assist with the marketing of plant output.
4. International subcontracting activity relates to the production of components or the assembly of finished products, primarily in a developing or Eastern Bloc country. Inputs are provided by the principal, with the finished product then being re-exported. The attractions in international subcontracting lie in low labour costs for assembly activities, reinforced both by home-country legislation (offshore processing rules) and host-country incentives (through export processing zones).
5. The term 'industrial co-operation agreement' (ICA) is used to apply to the variety of contractual arrangements utilised by Western companies in dealings with the Eastern Bloc nations. For the Socialist enterprises, the advantages of ICAs are seen in terms of access to Western machinery, technology and management know-how, along with marketing and exporting possibilities (through countertrading). Western partners gain market access and other advantages, although facing bureaucratic procedures, inconsistent quality and delivery delays, as well as countertrade problems.

6. Countertrading is quite often associated with forms of contractual arrangements, although not exclusively so. The main modes of countertrading include barter, counterpurchase, buy-back or compensation, offset and switch trading. While the impetus for countertrading has come principally from Eastern Bloc and developing nations, enterprises from industrialised countries may be prepared to offer counter-trade possibilities to gain competitive advantage.

INTRODUCTION

The previous chapter considered licensing and franchising as international market development modes used by firms independently of other types of contractual and collaborative arrangements. However, a characteristic of these contractual modes is that they are commonly found in combination, and this is especially true of management contracts, turnkey arrangements and industrial co-operation agreements which are considered in the present chapter. To illustrate the point, in one study of market entry modes in the Middle East, over 80 per cent of sample firms were reported to be involved in more than one type of contract at a time. For example, turnkey contracts automatically included a management contract as well as licensing.[1] International subcontracting, which is also discussed here, is rather different from the other contractual forms in that the motive is not host-country market entry or development, but low-cost assembly or manufacture in the host country for export back to the home nation or into third-country markets.

Less detail is presented on these different activities than was the case for licensing and franchising, partly because of information deficiencies, and partly because some of the issues are fairly common, such as planning the arrangements, negotiating with partners, problems experienced, etc. One distinguishing feature is that the contractual arrangements reviewed in this chapter primarily apply to relationships in developing countries and the Eastern Bloc, where an important issue concerns their use as alternatives to substantial direct investment. For example, in theory at least, the management contract eliminates from the 'package' transferred by the multinational enterprise the equity and possibly loan capital and the basic control that this provides, but leaves intact the technology and management needed to produce and market a product.

MANAGEMENT CONTRACTS

As noted in Chapter 1, a management contract represents 'an arrangement under which operational control of an enterprise (or one phase of an enterprise) which would otherwise be exercised by a board of directors or managers elected and appointed by its owners is vested by contract in a separate enterprise which performs the necessary management functions in return for a fee'.[2] The predecessor to the management contract was the management agency of the nineteenth century, when British companies in India, for instance, made agreements with local princes and maharajas to develop and manage businesses for them.[3] The modern management contract is of much more recent date, and within the definition above are a range of different types of contracts for management services. Under a 'pure' management contract, the parent company provides management services to a foreign project without ownership, receiving a fee for its contribution. Frequently, however, management contracts are combined with some other form of agreement, including the following:

1. Technical assistance services or turnkey arrangements, with a separate contract to cover these aspects.
2. Licensing agreements, complementing the transfer of the licensed technology with the expertise to use it.
3. Sale of capital goods, which may need special instructions to facilitate their use.
4. Production-sharing arrangements, particularly in East–West trade.
5. Joint ventures, and indeed the distinction between management contracts with a small equity stake and minority joint ventures tends to be blurred in any event.

As a management contract *per se*, the management firm's duties are similar to those a foreign company performs in running a subsidiary, and include the following:

1. General management: overall corporate planning; organisation and personnel planning.
2. Financial administration: financial analysis; planning and budgeting; borrowing; control over liquid assets; accounting.
3. Personnel administration: job descriptions; recruitment; promotion and job evaluation; replacement of expatriate personnel by indigenous staff.
4. Production management: materials management; purchasing; maintenance; quality control including laboratory tests.
5. Marketing (may also include sales promotion, distribution, dealer relationships and advertising).

The human resources provided within the management contract commonly consist of field staff working directly on the project throughout the contract period and certain temporary, principally specialist staff who may be seconded for specific tasks. In addition the management company will provide support functions and corporate capabilities. The aim of a management contract is to transfer foreign corporate know-how to the domestic staff of the project so that the latter will be able to run the operation after a period of time. Thus some contracts specify deadlines by which a certain number of host-country personnel are to replace expatriate staff; others provide for checks to be made on progress towards such replacement.

Basic details concerning management fees and length of contract term were given in Chapter 1, pages 14–15.

Management contracts are used in four major sectors: industrial; service industries/public utilities; tourism; and agriculture.[4] Two examples are presented in Exhibits 5.1 and 5.2. In the industrial sector, they are used to operate various mining projects, oil exploration and refining, heavy engineering and steel and aluminium plants. Sugar refineries and pulp and paper mills are also operated through management contracts, as are enterprises manufacturing agricultural implements, textiles, chemicals, etc. Management contracts have been operating in service sectors for the longest period of time, principally involving developing public utilities in transportation, power, telecommunications, medical care, port management and finance. In tourism, international hotel chains and airline companies make use of management contracts to develop and operate local hotels and host-country airlines. In fact, the management contract is the single most important method of conducting foreign business used by the international hotel groups: 1980 data show that almost one-third of rooms in foreign-owned hotels were operated under management contracts, a figure which rose to nearly two-thirds in hotels in developing countries.[5] Finally, management contracts are common in agricultural projects such as livestock, irrigation schemes and plantations. Brooke suggests that the *pure* management contract is most commonly found in the service industries, including tourism.[6]

It should be noted that construction management contracts are not conventionally included within 'management contracts' as discussed here, although they are not too dissimilar: in construction, management contracting applies to the case where:

> a client for a construction project enters into a contract with an external management organisation which then operates as the project's Management Contractor with responsibility for the management and coordination of the design and construction phases of a project . . . A management contractor does not normally undertake any of the construction work on site. He provides management services to control and coordinate all site activities, which are sublet to other (construction) contractors on a competitive basis.[7]

Regarding the companies providing the management service, these are usually firms in the same line of business as the local enterprise to be managed. Manufacturing corporations, for example, may be prepared to sell their managerial expertise to foreign project buyers. Engineering consultancy firms provide management expertise along with their preparatory studies, design and supervision work. One interesting example relates to public-sector agencies, some of which have offered their management expertise on a worldwide basis. For instance, the North Western Electricity Board in Britain handled the management of the electricity supply system of Riyadh

EXHIBIT 5.1
BOOKER AGRICULTURAL INTERNATIONAL LTD

Booker Agriculture International Ltd (BAI) is a subsidiary of a well-known group involved in tropical agriculture (both crops and animal rearing) and sells technical and management expertise as a package to its clients. The three main activities, which shade into one another, are consultancy, technical assistance and management contracts. The last two differ in the responsibilities undertaken. Technical assistance projects do not imply a separate organisation or the permanent secondment of staff; the contractor is only responsible for the individual performance of the staff seconded to the overseas client. In the case of management contracts the contractor is responsible for the venture which he or she manages.

BAI finds management contracts profitable in their own right and has never been involved in legal disputes or had to resort to arguing over the terms of a contract. Normally the clients are developing local industries for local markets and this, in the company's view, makes for an easier business relationship. At the same time the company insists on the following characteristics:

1. The contractor has full management responsibility for the contract venture whose chief executive is always one of BAI's executives. This firm exercise of authority is, however, tempered by the contractual rights of the local board. The chief executive reports both to the board and to head office.
2. Head office maintains a staff of high-calibre experts to provide important monitoring and support services. They are available to go at short notice to any project that is in difficulties (the company pointed to the lack of such support as an important reason for failures in management contracts in other companies).
3. Nothing is allowed to dilute the key task of training local staff.
4. Remuneration is by a fixed fee (indexed if possible) up to the start of commercial production after which a proportion of the fee is commuted to payment by results. The company is often willing to invest in a proportion of the equity of a project which it is invited to manage. This is regarded as a demonstration of its commitment to success.
5. Expatriate staff, in addition to the general manager, are always highly qualified and permanent employees of the parent company. They will be moved to other posts when the contract ends or when they are replaced by local nationals.
6. On principle, trade between the contract ventures and other divisions of the parent company is not encouraged, but in practice there is some buying and selling.

BAI represents a company that has gone further with basic management contracts than most, and that has developed distinctive policies through experience.

Source: Brooke, M.Z. (1985), *Selling Management Services Contracts in International Business*, Holt, Rinehart & Winston, London, 68–9.

EXHIBIT 5.2
HOSPITAL ENTERPRISES LTD

Hospital Enterprises Ltd incorporated the International Health Management Group (IHMG) and the Hospital Equipment and Provisions Company (HEPC). The major shareholder was a government-backed investment institution (75 per cent) and four private investors, each with 6.25 per cent of the shares. The aim of the company was to sell the expertise built up in the country over thirty years of operating public health schemes.

The Middle East Military Hospital
IHMG's contract with the ministry of defence of the client country was for the provision of a management consultancy for a period of three and a half years, and contained the following provisions:

1. Advisory services. The development of policies and procedures for medical, nursing and support departments.
2. Provision of computer services. The installation of equipment to cope with all aspects of hospital administration from financial accounting and controls to patient information systems.
3. Personnal services. The recruitment of personnel and the development of a personnel policy for staff.
4. Training services. The provision of training programmes for indigenous personnel in both the Middle East and Europe.
5. Purchasing services. The provision of a supplies and purchasing service as agents.
6. Accountancy advisory services. The objective was to accumulate and communicate financial and statistical data in a form suitable for decisionmaking, including the establishment of procedures and the preparation of budgets; accounting controls and reporting systems were to be designed and installed.

IHMG maintained a minimum staff of sixty personnel in the host country and thirty-five in Europe during the period of the programme. The staff of the hospital was approximately 1,300.

The host government saw two principal advantages in this contract:

1. Control was retained over the level of service provided for the patients and over the expenditure, while the services were operated with the advice of IHMG.
2. The cost was lower than in a total turnkey contract without loss of any advantages of such a contract.

Another project
A second project involved the provision of medical services for a large plant in another country. The facility comprised a general hospital of twenty beds, with special facilities for dealing with trauma patients, and two outlying clinics with four beds each together with laboratory and X-ray facilities located 50 and 80 miles from the central hospital. IHMG and HEPC provided under the contract the following services:

1. The supply of all medical equipment and furnishings.
2. Detailed equipment, engineering and layout advice to the other contractors involved in the project.

Exhibit 5.2 continued

  3. Consolidation, shipping and installation and commissioning on site of all
     items supplied.
  4. Full engineering support for the equipment for a period of two years.

Source: Brooke, M.Z. (1985), *Selling Management Services Contracts in International Business*, Holt, Rinehart & Winston, London, 242–3.

city; and the Nigerian railway system was, for a period, managed by the Indian railway administration.[8]

Empirical evidence

Some of the earliest work on the motives for and performance of management contracts was that undertaken by Gabriel in 1967 on four American companies.[9] The motives behind the management contracts varied: in one case, the US firm wanted to generate additional transport business to support its international transport operations; in another two instances, direct profitability was the prime motive; and in the final case the motivation was a desire to acquire experience to undertake similar projects in other countries. In all instances the relationship between the parties continued after the end of the first management contract period; and although the bargaining power of the four firms declined, the expatriates were able to exert control beyond the terms of the legal contracts into planning and policy formulation issues. One interesting observation which is relevant to companies considering this form of activity, however, was that: 'The degree of involvement on the part of the contractor's senior management was reported to be at least as broad and deep as in the case of a conventional direct investment.'[10]

Some preliminary work based on interviews with British firms using management contracts was prepared in 1975.[11] It was concluded that an increasing number of firms were using management contracts for offensive reasons, namely to gain new markets or to improve their competitive position, but a wide range of motives were identified, including: the capital required for a particular venture was too great; investment risks were too high; the company was anxious to secure a market for its products or to secure a supply of raw materials; or it wanted to protect an equity investment or support a joint venture; finally, in some countries, management contracts were the only method of involvement acceptable to the governments concerned. Problems identified included disputes between the foreign and local enterprises on issues of training and technology transfer, and conflicts over objectives when the foreign company has an equity stake as between financial returns and the host government's concern with the social gains.

Sharma studied a number of Swedish management contracts in the chemicals, pulp and paper and drug sectors, focusing mainly on control and returns aspects.[12] Concerning the latter, a distinction was made between direct and indirect financial returns and strategic returns. The direct financial returns took the form of management fees which were fixed for the period of the management contract and were largely independent of the financial results achieved by the local companies. Three sources of indirect financial returns were found: firstly, returns from technical consultancies provided, relating, for example, to assistance on selection of suitable production technology and design of machinery; secondly, export orders for the Swedish companies which were nearly all equipment manufacturers; and, thirdly, marketing fees. The strategic returns were considered in terms of internationalisation (overseas experience, which could be exploited subsequently in other markets), international marketing expertise and the establishment of listening posts. For the three pulp firms studied, the latter took the form of gaining knowledge and information about the tropical pulp industry, and its technical and economic feasibility, etc.; while one of these companies also gained access to forest raw material for its Swedish mills. Ranking these various returns, the management fee was of relatively minor significance, with a good deal more importance being attached to the indirect financial returns and the major returns being strategic.

The most comprehensive work on the subject is that of Brooke, who identified the following major uses of management contracts:[13]

1. Support for other contractual arrangements – here the management contract is entered into as part of a deal which involves licensing, franchising, turnkey or other arrangements.
2. The supplier type – in this case, the motive for a management contract is to support an existing market following moves towards protectionism. Licensing, direct investment or management contracts may then be employed, with, for many companies, the contract as a last resort.
3. The purchaser type – the contracted company wishes to guarantee its sources of raw materials or components and the management contract with a mining or petroleum extraction company (often owned by a developing-country government) may be a means of ensuring this.
4. The part-owner approach – in this instance a management contract is linked to a minority equity stake (the latter perhaps following indigenisation measures in a host country).[14] The management contract can be a means of ensuring that control systems, marketing knowledge and other expertise are used by the affiliate.
5. The consultancy type – the contracting company is in the business of providing management services in its own right. Such arrangements may go under the term 'technical assistance agreements'.

6. The business extension type–this refers to the use of management contracts to enter otherwise closed markets.
7. The consortium approach–in large-scale projects, one partner company may be under contract for the management, which is likely to include funding, control, staffing, purchasing, marketing and general consultancy services.

The first four items listed above represent defensive uses of management contracts and were considered to be more common on the whole than the aggressive or pro-active uses. Because of the variety of motives for entering into management contracts, the mixed nature of many deals (in which management contracts are only supportive of joint ventures, turnkey contracts, etc.) and the limited experience of (some) firms and countries in operating management contracts, it is hardly surprising that problems have been experienced. Viewed from the perspective of the host developing country, some of these difficulties are as follows:

1. Conflicts can arise when the management company has a profit link to the enterprise, which may mean an emphasis on efficient operation, e.g. meeting production targets and deadlines, as opposed to other contractual obligations such as training local personnel.
2. Similarly, where the interests of the management company are primarily in the sale of inputs of machinery or related technology rather than the contract itself, the potential for problems exists.
3. The issue of control is also a possible source of conflict. Irrespective of the degree of control provided for in the contract, in the initial stages of the relationship the host country might not have the technical capability or know-how to handle the planning, control and evaluation functions. On the other hand, the host nation's managerial capabilities will gradually increase and lead to strains as they seek to re-exert control.
4. Country owners have been dissatisfied with the lack of project autonomy from the home offices of the management company.
5. The management company remains a foreign firm, and some countries may prefer a shorter-term consultancy arrangement.
6. With management contracts (as with turnkey projects) there is a strong link to aid provided by multilateral agencies such as the World Bank and government-to-government assistance. Particularly with the latter, disputes may arise where aid is 'tied', say to the employment of a contracting company from a particular country, contrary to the preference of the host government.

Some of these possible conflict areas cannot be resolved by contractual terms, and the management company for its part may be highly frustrated by the 'difficult environments' in which they are frequently operating with management contracts. As was suggested in the case of licensing, the solution must be found in terms of developing a partnership by building on mutual interest and trust.

Despite the problems, management contracts are considered to have become far more common in recent years, albeit from a very small base. It is speculated that management contracts account for about 1 per cent of the total value of remittances across frontiers as a result of knowledge agreements between separate enterprises. This is slightly deceptive because of their industry and country concentration, the latter including both developing countries and Eastern Bloc states (where management contracts are common as part of industrial co-operation deals). It has been concluded that the take-off point for management contracts will come

> when this method of business is recognised as an option in the corporate strategy and not just as a special case . . . At present, the main purpose of management contracts has been to support other means of conducting business and to defend markets under threat. Licensing, franchising and minority holdings are underpinned by an arrangement which assures that adequate management skills are made available.[15]

TURNKEY CONTRACTS

The turnkey contract was developed during the 1930s in the United States by capital goods producers with the objective of increasing sales. Internationally, the first turnkey contracts were operated in an East–West context in the 1960s, to be followed by various contracts in developing countries towards the end of the decade. But the major boost to this form of activity came with the oil price rises of the 1970s, when some of the OPEC countries used turnkey operations to establish entire industrial complexes.[16] Given that these projects are usually very large, they do not offer opportunities for small or medium-sized companies operating alone. But this does not prevent a number of smaller engineering-contracting firms forming joint ventures to pool their resources, technology and expertise to bid for international turnkey projects.

The turnkey contract represents a contractual arrangement whereby one party is responsible for setting up a plant and putting it into operation. Specific responsibilities of the contractor vary but usually include

> responsibility for supply and establishment of the works, plants and facilities on a turnkey basis, including supply of technology and know-how, basic design and engineering, supply of complete plant and equipment, design and construction of civil works, complete erection of plant and equipment and commissioning of the total plant facilities up to the stage of start-up . . . Depending on the nature of the plant and the technology involved, the turnkey contract may be either the owner of the technology or the main supplier of machinery or

a transnational engineering organization. Sometimes, several corporations may combine in a consortium to take up turnkey responsibilities for major projects, such as a steel plant or a large petrochemical unit. While the overall responsibilities of establishing a plant to the stage of commissioning and start-up would rest with one party, the turnkey contractor would, in turn, subcontract various elements of the operations to a number of subcontractors.[17]

As the above remarks suggest, turnkey projects are concentrated in heavy industry and basic materials, including chemicals; thermal, hydro and nuclear energy plants; iron and steel; hydrocarbons; and construction materials (e.g. cement and glass). Textiles, food processing, paper, water treatment and mining are other industries where turnkey activity has been significant. Significantly, therefore, they are related to activities which commonly fall within the government or quasi-governmental sector.

From the corporate viewpoint,

a turnkey contract ensures that equipment can be installed, tested and adjusted to operate in the total system in accordance with performance specifications. It also allows the firm to establish a medium-term presence in what is generally a growing market for its equipment. Finally, the turnkey operation allows the corporation to trade directly in the resource in which it has its greatest comparative advantage – its own unique package of corporate skills.[18]

Offsetting such advantages are the various problems encountered frequently by companies participating in this type of operation. The list which follows relates specifically to the Canadian situation, but many of the points have wider applicability, especially for the smaller enterprise:

1. Market knowledge. Poor representation of companies in financial institutions like the World Bank, through which many of these projects emerge.
2. Political marketing. The need for high-level political support in the selling process when major projects are at stake.
3. Lack of negotiating experience. Aggressive project development teams from Japan and elsewhere may 'camp' on projects until they are won. What is required is continuous top-executive involvement throughout the whole period from feasibility study to contract.
4. Skills transfer. The delivery of an equipment-oriented turnkey package (albeit as specified by the client) may fail to provide the skills needed for independent system operation and maintenance after the 'key has been turned'. What are, therefore, likely to follow are *ad hoc* patch-up programmes involving combinations of operating contracts, management contracts and/or technical assistance programmes. As Wright and Kobel note, 'bitterness and recriminations often result. Apart from the direct financial losses involved, there is considerable risk that the corporation–host nation relationship will weaken the company's future market in the area.'[19]

5. Risk exposure and financing. Issues which arise here include the large size of the projects; the long time required to complete them; the expensive and risky bank guarantees required, for instance, by the governments of Middle East countries; and, related to a point above, the competitive financial support provided by governments. (Appendix 5.1 discusses the whole issue of export credits and refers to some of the problems which have occurred in bidding for international projects.)

From the other side, according to the United Nations Centre on Transnational Corporations (UNCTC), a turnkey arrangement could have a number of advantages for developing countries:[20]

1. Ownership and control of the plant or project is retained in the hands of the owner/purchaser in the post-contract stage.
2. Responsibility for the project lies with a single party, viz. the turnkey contractor, and the owner/purchaser is relieved of the responsibility for any elements in the contract which could be the cause of poor performance.
3. Related to the above, time may be saved in putting projects into operation. With both design and construction being the responsibility of one enterprise, parts of each can take place simultaneously and disputes can be minimised.

On the other hand, several disadvantages may present themselves:

1. The cost of a turnkey contract may be higher than the cost of contracting the various elements of the project separately.
2. The checks and balances that exist when various responsibilities are assigned to different parties are missing in the turnkey contract. This is especially the case where the contractor is also the equipment supplier.
3. Because of the minimum participation by the owner/purchaser in the contract, the latter does not gain the necessary familiarity with the plant. Consequently, problems may arise in the post-commissioning period, especially with complex facilities such as petrochemical and fertiliser plants (as compared with, say, cement or sugar manufacturing units). This is the reverse side of the issue discussed previously in relation to problems encountered by contractors. The outcome has been that other requirements have been incorporated into contracts, such as product-in-hand requirements (see below); in other instances, some developing countries have been pressing firms supplying plants under turnkey arrangements to take (minority) equity stakes in the projects, offering lucrative incentives such as long-run oil supply contracts.
4. Turnkey contracts may not be the most appropriate arrangements where the creation of a technological service capability represents an important objective in developing countries. In consequence, some

countries have limited the participation of MNEs to only those stages of project implementation where local expertise is not available. This is the reverse of the situation referred to above, and principally applies in the more advanced developing economies such as Brazil, India, Mexico and Korea.

Because of difficulties perceived by developing countries, such as those above, standard turnkey contracts may be replaced by a variety of 'turnkey plus' operations. Thus 'product-in-hand' contracts are turnkey operations in which the contractor's responsibilities end only when the installation is completely operational with local personnel. Product-in-hand contracts include provisions whereby the contractor has a responsibility for preparing local management and workers to run the installation. These may entail additional technical or training services or responsibilities for plant operations for a short period of time (six months perhaps) after start-up.

Another form of modified turnkey contract is the 'market-in-hand' agreement. Here the project contractor is required to give assistance in or take responsibility for the sale of at least part of the project's output. This type of arrangement begins to merge into the industrial co-operation activities which are discussed later in the chapter, and countertrading (see Appendix 5.2).

As is clear from the foregoing remarks, turnkey contracts can take many forms, each project being unique in one way or another. This fact plus the size and complexity of deals (including the financing packages, which are likely to involve soft loans, subsidised credits, payment by means of countertrades, and so on) means that negotiations will be very time-consuming and require sophisticated legal back-up. Partners from several developed and/or newly industrialised countries may be involved in a single project. Establishing a complete and defensible contract is a must in such circumstances. Especially important may be issues pertaining to contract violations and procedures for resolution of disputes; although no legal agreements can fully account for the political risks of contract revocation, compulsory renegotiation and the arbitrary calling of bank guarantees, such as were experienced in a number of countries following the oil price slump (and consequent impact on industrial development plans) of the early/mid-1980s.

The turnkey plus contracts, in particular, represent forms of technology transfer into developing countries, and as such the attitude of international companies has been ambiguous. For some, the concept of technology transfer is seen as something that contributes to the creation of new opportunities, and for a technology transfer programme to work a great deal of additional effort must be put into it. The changing demands of developing nations are also affecting the traditional structure of industries such as construction. For example, a Middle East client could deal direct with a contractor and have no technical dealings with consulting engineers until project completion. Because of mistrust or problems with contracts, consulting engineers are still employed to monitor turnkey projects, although on a much restricted basis. Thus the market for traditional consulting engineering services is much reduced.[21]

There is a dearth of empirical information on turnkey contracts specifically, but it is important to recognise the importance of developing- as well as developed-country firms in this business. One study investigated project exports in the civil construction and industrial fields; these project contracts ranged from general building contracts requiring relatively simple civil engineering, e.g. housing projects, to turnkey contracts which incorporated licensing and technical assistance agreements for continuous process technologies, e.g. petrochemical projects.[22] Industrialised-country contractors dominated in contracts for power and process plants (mostly on a turnkey basis). However, while the most successful area of activity for developing nations was the co-ordination of manufacturing plants and general buildings, several developing country firms ranked among the top turnkey contractors – at least for projects other than power or process plants, viz. projects involving a great deal of construction. In the study as a whole, Korea was the frontrunner among developing countries, with more foreign contracts than all other nations together. And the most successful developing country firm was Hyundai Engineering and Construction Company Ltd.

CONTRACT MANUFACTURING/INTERNATIONAL SUBCONTRACTING

In international subcontracting (otherwise known as contract manufacturing), a principal places orders with a subcontractor in a developing or Eastern Bloc country to produce components or assemble finished products with the inputs it provides. The final product is then exported to be marketed by the principal, either in its home market or international markets more generally.

The nature of international subcontracting may vary along the following dimensions:

1. The type of firm giving the subcontract, as between a producer, retailing organisation, trading company or sometimes an importer or wholesaler.
2. The technical aspects of production. Here a distinction can be made between the subcontracting of processes (as in semiconductor assembly) and the subcontracting of whole products.
3. The business relationship between principal and subcontractor. Some definitions of international subcontracting restrict the meaning to a relationship between distinct undertakings in different countries; and certainly if the foreign enterprise has more than just a minority holding

in the subcontractor, the arrangement is little different from conventional foreign direct investment ('export platform' investments and 'international sourcing' are the terms applied to this type of foreign investment activity).

Other aspects of the business relationship relate to whether or not physical equipment is provided for the subcontractor; whether technical assistance is included (if technology or technical assistance is part of the arrangement, this may be formalised in a separate licensing/ technical assistance contract); and the nature of orders placed, as between long-term, short-term or single-batch orders with no guarantee of renewal.

4. The location of the principal. The type of subcontracting arrangement that is most common is that between enterprises in developed and developing countries; but principal firms from countries such as Hong Kong are also very active, especially in the clothing industry, with operations in other states in the Far East as well as in locations such as Mauritius.

5. Products involved. Mainly electrical and electronic goods, and textiles and clothing.

International subcontracting is believed to have been developed first by the Japanese general trading companies or *sogo shosha*, Mitsubishi, Mitsui, Marubeni, Sumitomo, etc. in Hong Kong, Korea, Taiwan and Singapore.[23] In the late 1960s/early 1970s around three-quarters of their purchases were then exported to the United States commonly under originally established Japanese brand names. The spread of Japanese *sogo shosha* buying brought US retail companies and buying groups to the Far East, to be followed by European firms and then developing-country principals. The growth of this phenomenon has been accompanied by a widening of host countries, too, to take in low-labour cost locations in North Africa and elsewhere around the Mediterranean Rim, and Eastern Bloc nations (especially for West German firms).

In terms of orthodox theory, the question arises as to the basis for these contract production relationships, particularly in a low-technology sector such as clothing. Clearly both partners must benefit from the relationship. The principal firm benefits from low labour costs, home government regulations (offshore processing rules of the EC, and US tariff regulations relating to Sections 806.30 and 807.00 of the Tariff Schedule of the USA, whereby goods can be exported from the USA for assembly abroad and then reimported, with import duties being levied only on the value added abroad), and various host-country policies, especially relating to the establishment of export processing zones. The subcontractor obtains market access and marketing expertise, including sales outlets, brand names, publicity, marketing research and design. By entering into a contractual arrangement, the principal firm can ensure a certain amount of control over the operation. In addition, the scale of investment in marketing facilities and brand names represents an important barrier to entry for developing-country producers, and therefore reduces the risks for the principal that a competitor may emerge from subcontracting *per se*. For the principal, other advantages include the small commitment of financial and management resources required, the removal of political and other risks which exist with foreign direct investment, and low switching costs when new supply points are desired for whatever reason.

According to Dicken, therefore, 'subcontracting ... is a kind of half-way house between arm's length transactions on the open-market and complete internalization within the firm ... The subcontracting relationship is *symbiotic* – a technical division of labour between independent firms – in which each partner contributes to the support of the other.'[24]

As noted above, the growth of international subcontracting has been aided by home- and host-country regulations, with export processing zones (EPZs) or free trade zones (FTZs) offering highly favourable investment and trade conditions to export-oriented industries being the major items in the latter category.[25] An illustration relating to FTZs in Turkey is presented in Exhibit 5.3. Before 1966 there were only two EPZs, Kandla (India) and Mayaguez (Puerto Rico). The number of EPZs has expanded very rapidly since the end of the 1960s, covering the Asian, Caribbean and Latin American developing countries particularly but also Africa, the Mediterranean Rim and Eastern Europe; and by the second half of the 1980s there were 175 EPZs with a total employment of 1.3 million, and at least 110 new zones under construction or at the planning stage. From a developing-country perspective, EPZs might appear to offer a mechanism for facilitating export-oriented industrialisation and raising employment levels, but there have been concerns about low wages, low levels of job security, low skill requirements, the reliance on a young, female workforce, constraints on the formation of trades unions, and so forth. Nor have the principal firms been entirely happy, with difficulties arising over alleged low productivity, high employee turnover, delivery delays and poor quality.[26]

A variant of the EPZ/FTZ concept is found in the Chinese Special Economic Zones (SEZs) – comparisons between the two are shown in Table 5.1. Under regulations of 1980, four coastal cities – Shenzhen, Zhuhai and Shantou in Guangdong Province and Xiamen in Fujian Province – were established as SEZs. The zones offer financial incentives to foreign investors, e.g. a 15 per cent corporation tax, with a two-year 'tax holiday' for a new venture and a 50 per cent reduction in the next three years. Furthermore, companies reinvesting their profits for five years can apply for tax exemptions on the reinvested amount. Further tax reductions are applicable to high-technology industries, and there are exemptions from import and export duties.[27] Experience to date reveals considerable concern, at least

EXHIBIT 5.3
FREE TRADE ZONES IN TURKEY

1. **Location of the Turkish free trade zones**
   The FTZs of Mersin and Antalya are within easy access to the largest and best equipped Turkish ports on the Mediterranean Sea. Both ports play a major role in Turkish trade with Europe and the Middle East. Mersin in particular is a major entry point for products destined for Iran, Iraq and the Arabian peninsula. The Mersin FTZ occupies 763,405 sq. metres of land consisting of roughly 115 parcels. The Antalya FTZ encompasses 573,536 sq. metres of approximately 130 parcels of land.

2. **Foreign capital**
   (a) *Limitations.* There is no limitation on the proportion of foreign capital participation within the FTZ.

   (b) *Transfer of profits and capital.* Dividends and profits, as well as the proceeds derived from the full or partial sale and/or liquidation of capital shares by foreign domiciled persons or entities operating within the FTZ, may be added to their existing capital, or transferred to entities or sectors encompassed by the Law for the Encouragement of Foreign Capital No. 6224; or to other FTZs within Turkey, or to other countries, provided that the Regional Free Trade Zone Authority is given due notification and that ownership of the funds can be fully documented.

   (c) *Incentives.* Foreign capital entities operating within the FTZ may benefit fully from all of the incentives described below.

3. **Incentives**
   Turkish and foreign entities possessing an Operating Licence for the FTZs may benefit from the following incentives in both the investment and the production stages of their operations:

   Investment stage
   (a) *Exceptions from taxes, duties and tolls.* Investors may bring into the FTZs any inputs they require from foreign locations without being subject to any taxes, duties or tolls.

   (b) *Export treatment of Turkish-origin inputs.* In cases where investors select to obtain their necessary inputs from the host country, they will be able to obtain such inputs at attractive prices, due to the fact that such goods entering the FTZ will be treated as exports from Turkey.

   (c) *Exemption from export formalities.* If desired by the investor, and subject to approval, goods of less than $500 value may be obtained from the host country without having them subjected to export procedures.

   (d) *Income tax exemption.* The salaries of persons working within the FTZs are not subject to income taxes.

   (e) *Other incentives.* Investors will also be able to benefit from any additional incentives that the Council of Ministers may deem to be appropriate.

Exhibit 5.3 continued

(f) *Payments in local currency.* During the investment phase, payments for rents, salaries, and for services and goods may be made in the form of Turkish Lira.

Production stage

(a) *Exemption from taxes, duties and tolls.* All necessary production inputs can be transported from foreign locations into the FTZ without being subject to any taxes, duties or tolls whatsoever.

(b) *Export treatment of Turkish-origin inputs.* In cases where production inputs are procured from the host country, because of the fact that such transactions will be considered as exports, it will be possible to acquire such inputs at attractive prices.

(c) *Income tax exemption.* No income taxes will be levied upon the salaries of those working within the FTZs during the production stage.

(d) *Exemption of profits from income and corporate taxes.* The FTZ-origin profits of those entities operating within the FTZs are not subject to either income or corporate taxes and duties; nor will their accounts within the FTZs be merged, for tax or any other purposes, with their accounts within the country. FTZ-origin profits and income of corporate and real entities, who are subject to full or limited tax treatment in Turkey will also be exempted from income and corporate taxes, providing that it can be documented in accordance with foreign exchange regulations, that such profits and income have been brought into other locations within Turkey.

(e) *Right to benefit from new incentives.* In cases where new incentives are deemed necessary to enhance the competitive position of the FTZs, existing users will be able to benefit fully from any such adjustments.

4. **Conditions pertaining to the production and flow of goods**

(a) *Customs exemption.* The FTZs are outside Turkish customs jurisdiction. The controls and restrictions entailed by the Customs Law are not applicable within the Zones.

(b) *Imports into Turkey.* Only those goods that cross the FTZs' customs borders and are destined for use inside Turkey are subject to customs regulations and the relevant taxes, duties and tolls. These goods will be subject to import formalities, and pier duties will be levied upon those goods that arrive by sea transport.

(c) *Goods originating from or destined to the FTZ.* The procedures described in (b) above are not applicable for goods that arrive from or are destined to other FTZs, or foreign locations. Nor are they applicable for goods destined from Turkey to the FTZs.

(d) *Applicability of exemptions.* These exemptions are applicable for both the investment and the production stage of FTZ operations.

(e) *Exports from Turkey.* With the exception of goods that are specifically designated as being acceptable, or those valued at less than $500, goods sent to the FTZs from Turkey will be considered as exports, in accordance with existing foreign trade regulations.

Exhibit 5.3 continued

> Goods sent to the FTZs from Turkey will also be subject to procedures specified by relevant export decrees and directives.
>
> (f) *No 'E&D Fund' charge on Turkish-origin goods.* No charge will be made for the FTZ Establishment and Development Fund on goods arriving in the FTZs from Turkey.
>
> 5. **Employment and working conditions**
>   (a) *Minimum wage.* The minimum wage rates determined for Turkey in general are applicable within the FTZs.
>
>   (b) *The work-week and overtime.* The 45-hour work-week and the 270-hour yearly overtime limits are applicable within the FTZs.
>
>   (c) *Employment of foreign personnel.* The employment of foreign managers and specialists is fully permitted for entities operating within the FTZ.
>
>   (d) *Unions and collective bargaining.* Within the general framework of labour laws being applied in Turkey, unionisation of labour and collective bargaining are permissible within the FTZs.
>
>   (e) *Limitation of strikes and lock-outs.* For a period of ten years following the establishment of a FTZ, the strike, lock-out and arbitration provisions specified by Law No. 2822 are not applicable. However, any disputes arising from labour agreements during this period will be subject to the decision of the Superior Council of Arbitration.
>
>   (f) *Procurement of workers.* Operators within the FTZ may or may not, depending upon their preference, procure their personnel through the official Employment and Employee Procurement Agency of the Government.
>
>   (g) *Social security.* All social security regulations are applicable within the FTZs.
>
> Source: Extract from Turkish Government Publication, *Free Trade Zones in Turkey* (n.d. but obtained in 1987).

from the Chinese side, about the performance of the SEZs in terms of their failure to attract sufficient high-technology investment and the level of exports generated.[28] Essentially, China's aims for the SEZs were different from those of the investors, who were less interested in China as an export base than in gaining access to the country's large, untapped internal markets in which to sell their goods. Despite the problems, the Soviet Union has decided to set up similar SEZs which would use hard currency and Soviet labour and could sell products both in the West and in the USSR.

Stress has been placed above on contract manufacturing in developing countries. But if a firm's competitive advantage lies in marketing and service rather than in production, a developed country enterprise may equally contract with a company in another developed nation to undertake manufacture on its behalf. Aside from obviating the need for plant investment,

Table 5.1 Chinese SEZs and EPZs elsewhere: comparisons on selected aspects

	Export processing zones	Chinese special economic zones
Strategic aims		
Socio-political objectives	Not usually	Yes
Emphasis on attracting overseas investment	Yes	Yes
Emphasis on training, technology transfer	Not usually	Yes
Financial/legal		
Relaxation of customs duties	Yes	Yes
Fewer restrictions on profits transfer	Yes	Yes
Lower company taxation	Yes	Yes
'Tax holidays'	Often initially	Initially
Export-oriented production	Usually	Yes, but not totally
Access to local market	Sometimes	Officially restricted
Reduced environmental controls	Often	Uncertain
Planning/geographical		
Physical size	Usually small (many under 100–500 hectares)	Larger than most EPZs
Specific designation of boundaries	Yes	Yes
Restrictions on free movement of goods/people	Usually	Usually
Central zone control/administration	Usually	Yes
Physical site planning/delimitation	Yes	Yes
Social and infrastructure		
Constraints on labour/union organisations	Often	Probably
Greater use of female labour	Usually	Probably
Social infrastructure for workers	Sometimes	In course of construction
Cheap industrial sites in zone	Yes	Yes
Standard factory units available	Often	Yes
Residential facilities for overseas staff	Sometimes	Yes
Recreation facilities for tourism	Rarely	Yes
Hotels included	Rarely	Yes

Source: Phillips, D.R. (1986), 'Special Economic Zones in China's Modernization: Changing Policies and Changing Fortunes', *National Westminster Bank Quarterly Review*, February, Table 1.

contract manufacturing enables the firm to avoid potential labour and other problems deriving from its lack of familiarity with the country. At the same time the firm can advertise its product as locally made, and generally keep control of marketing, something which is not possible with licensing. Difficulties shared with the latter include quality control and the risks of assisting a potential competitor.

While not a manufacturing issue, contractual arrangements may apply to other functional aspects of business such as R&D and marketing. These are discussed in the context of strategic alliances and the Single European Market in the EC in Chapter 7.

INDUSTRIAL CO-OPERATION AGREEMENTS

Contrary to what might be believed, there is a long history of Western involvement in non-trade activities in centrally planned economies. As early as 1920 the government of Soviet Russia passed a law permitting concessionary investments in extractive industries, with foreign investors' repayment in resultant products.[29] Mixed companies (joint ventures) were also permitted; and between 1920 and 1930 the Soviet Union granted 125 investment concessions and 93 mixed companies were established. With the changing internal political climate during the 1930s, there was a gradual liquidation of these investments, with only some technical assistance projects and turnkey arrangements remaining. There then followed a long period when commercial relationships with Soviet and Eastern European markets were very limited, Western companies, indeed, viewing these countries as 'markets of last resort'.[30] The position began to change again in the late 1960s and 1970s when the Soviet Union commenced an ambitious investment programme in its engineering and chemical industries. Foreign direct capital participation was then legalised in Yugoslavia in 1967, followed by Romania (1971), Hungary (1972), Poland (1976), the People's Republic of China (1979) and Bulgaria (1980), providing the framework within which the concept of industrial co-operation has developed to its present level of significance.

While not the subject of the present text, it should be added that the opening of Eastern Bloc markets has been paralleled by a smaller but still significant expansion of Eastern European enterprise activity in the West through wholly owned subsidiaries and joint ventures: the majority of such ventures take the form of trading companies, assembling and marketing products made in the Socialist countries and providing after-sales service to customers; but there are more conventional firms such as Tungsram, the Hungarian producer of light bulbs and car lamps which operates in Western Europe, the United States and some developing countries and is Hungary's biggest earner of foreign currency.[31]

There is no agreed definition of industrial co-operation; indeed it has been argued that what is at issue is not a function or activity but an institutional relationship.[32] The definitional debate is well summarised elsewhere and is not continued here. Following Paliwoda, the working definition to be used is:[33]

> industrial co-operation is generally understood to denote the economic relationships and activities arising from contracts extending over a long period of time (typically 5 to 10 years) between partners belonging to different economic systems, providing for reciprocal transfer of one or more commercial assets (such as technology, know-how, capital, products, marketing and services), to meet specific objectives of the contracting parties. This relationship is usually one in which the Western partner has no equity interest . . .

EXHIBIT 5.4
A CASE STUDY OF A BRITISH ENGINEERING COMPANY ENGAGED IN INDUSTRIAL CO-OPERATION – A DESIGNER AND MANUFACTURER OF MOBILE CRANES

In 1966, the company signed one of the first East–West industrial co-operation agreements, with a Polish foreign trade organisation responsible for the import and export of cranes and other handling equipment; cranes had previously been sold to Poland, but not in any great quantity. The agreement lapsed in 1973 and no new agreement has been subsequently signed, although trade in some of the items covered by the arrangement was continued. The various topics covered by the agreement are outlined below:

1. The British company provided full design and manufacturing documentation for the production of a particular model of crane of thirty tons lifting capacity, available in wheeled and tracked variants.
2. The Polish foreign trade organisation delivered a programme of twenty-three items to the company including chassis and gearboxes to the company's technical specification, for subsequent assembly into various end-items in the company's product range. The Polish-manufactured items were delivered to the company in mutually agreed quantities and at advantageous prices – far cheaper than those quoted by UK suppliers.
3. The company supplied kits of items for use in the crane for which the Polish foreign trade organisation had been provided with design and manufacturing documentation, but which Polish enterprises were unable to deliver (e.g. oil seals, bearings, clutches, etc.). These items were supplied at mutually agreed prices. Some free-issue components were also supplied by the company for assembly into the items delivered to it by the Polish foreign trade organisation (e.g. rams and bearings for assembly into chassis).
4. The co-operation agreement was extended to include the subcontracted production to Poland of twelve complete cranes of a modified version of the type covered by the agreement. This occurred at a time when the capacity of the British company was overloaded.
5. The agreement also specified countries in which each partner had exclusive and non-exclusive marketing rights for the crane covered by the co-operation agreement. The Polish foreign trade organisation had exclusive rights in the socialist countries of Asia and Eastern Europe, and India; while the British company retained exclusive marketing rights in the rest of the world. The Polish partner was also allowed to sell in some other Middle Eastern, African and Asian countries, and Yugoslavia, provided that permission was first obtained from the British company.

In summary, therefore, it can be seen that the co-operation agreement included a range of activities, namely:

(a) A licensing agreement.
(b) Supply of parts to the East European partner.
(c) Provision of parts to the British company's specifications for inclusion in its final product.
(d) Provision by the East European partner of products produced to the British company's specification for subsequent marketing by it.
(e) Exercise of quality control by the British company.
(f) An agreement for marketing and servicing in specified geographical areas.

Exhibit 5.4 continued

The company considered that the major reason for the Eastern European partner entering the co-operation agreement was the rapid absorption of design and production know-how to meet its expanding market needs. Furthermore, the outlay of foreign exchange was minimised, since no immediate currency payment was made for the acquisition of the technological know-how, and attempts are made annually to balance the values of the bilateral trade in components and sub-assemblies. The company itself entered into the industrial co-operation agreement for reasons of cost savings in the production of certain types of sub-assemblies and components, due to cheaper availabilities of Polish skilled labour, capacity and capital resources.

The company, however, met with a number of problems in the implementation of the co-operation agreement. These can be summarised as follows:

1. A tendency for the Polish side to require firm orders a longer time in advance than is necessary in the case of British suppliers. This could sometimes lead to supplies arriving in larger quantities than required (i.e. 'lumpy' supply). Furthermore, delivery lead times for certain items could be very long. It would consequently appear that the cheaper Polish products were purchased at the expense of flexibility in delivery.
2. A tendency for the Polish side to sometimes cancel letters of credit for those items to be supplied by the British company. This could lead to the British company being left with comparatively high stocks due to postponed delivery.
3. The necessity of informing the Department of Industry, at frequent intervals, that the Polish-produced items were still available at a substantial cost advantage. This consequently entailed having to unnecessarily contact a number of British companies to obtain competitive quotations for supplies of relevant items.
4. The final and major problem has been caused by an action by the Polish side, which was viewed by the British company as not in accordance with the spirit of the agreement. The company had put a great deal of effort into the development of a certain Middle Eastern market, which was its exclusive market under the terms of the agreement. Fifty-six cranes had been sold, operators had been trained, and after-sales service had been established. In mid-1976, the company bid for a further 140 cranes, worth approximately £20 m.; the Polish side, however, bid for the same contract, quoting cranes which were the subject of the co-operation agreement, at prices equivalent to approximately 50 per cent of those quoted by the British company. The Polish side was awarded the contract, which subsequently caused an increase in demand on Polish production capacity leading to an unavailability of chassis for the British company. The company consequently attempted to make itself independent from Polish sources of supply for those products previously covered by the co-operation agreement. As a result of this experience, it was the company's view that co-operation agreements in Eastern Europe were best restricted to those product areas in which there is a rapidly changing technology, to prevent unwanted market competition.

Source: Adapted from Hill, M.R. (1983), *East–West Trade, Industrial Co-operation and Technology Transfer*, Gower, Aldershot, 78–81.

The forms of activity included within industrial co-operation can be gauged approximately from surveys conducted by the Economic Commission for Europe, a summary of one of which is presented in Table 5.2. As is apparent, industrial co-operation agreements (ICAs) include several of the forms of contractual arrangement which have been discussed in the previous and present chapters, along with co-production, joint ventures and joint tendering. However, licensing and plant deliveries (effectively turnkey arrangements) are associated in an East–West context with payment via forms of countertrading (see Appendix 5.2). As the tabular data show, co-production agreements were the most common type of ICA in all countries except the German Democratic Republic, Romania and Yugoslavia; in these latter countries plant deliveries or contractual joint-ventures were the preferred modes.[34] A specific project which encompasses a number of these forms of industrial co-operation is presented in Exhibit 5.4.

Regarding the actual numbers and value of ICAs, estimates are very tentative. It has been suggested that the number of ICAs rose from 180 to

Table 5.2 Share of various types of contract in total number of East–West industrial co-operation contracts, by country (per cent)[a]

Country	Total	Licens- ing[b]	Plant delivery[c]	Co-production and specialisation[d]	Subcon- tracting[e]	Joint ventures[f]	Joint tendering or joint projects[g]
Bulgaria	100.0	4.1	12.2	47.0	6.1	22.5	8.1
Hungary	100.0	16.3	7.8	32.2	5.0	27.6	11.0
Poland	100.0	18.6	24.8	31.8	0.9	10.6	13.3
GDR	100.0	4.8	45.2	11.9	4.8	9.5	23.8
Romania	100.0	5.0	12.5	15.0	2.5	55.0	10.0
Czechoslovakia	100.0	19.0	3.8	63.3	—	11.4	2.5
USSR	100.0	3.6	20.3	54.1	0.7	9.8	11.4
Yugoslavia	100.0	4.7	4.4	32.4	2.3	48.1	8.0
Total	100.0	10.0	12.6	38.5	2.7	25.8	10.4

[a]Based on a sample of 1,325 contracts at the end of August 1987.
[b]Supply of licences and know-how, in exchange (at least partially) for products or components.
[c]Supply of plant or equipment, with payment (at least partially) in resultant product or components.
[d]Specialisation by each partner either in the production of certain parts of a final product, which is then assembled by one or both for its own market needs; or specialisation on production of parts of the product range which are then exchanged to complete each partner's range; or co-operation and specialisation involving R&D only.
[e]Either short term or long term, for the delivery of an agreed quantity of finished or semi-finished goods produced through the use of documentation and know-how (and sometimes parts, machinery and equipment) provided by the contractor.
[f]Joint ventures involving production, marketing and R&D.
[g]Joint tendering or joint construction, mainly in developing countries.
Source: Economic Commission for Europe (1987), *Promotion of Trade through Industrial Co-operation. Statistical Survey of Recent Trends in Industrial Co-operation*, UN, Geneva, 21 September.

around 1,000 from the mid-1960s to the mid-1970s, while the total financial value in 1975 was put at $1 bn (equivalent to approximately 2 per cent of the value of total East–West trade).[35] Despite the less favourable economic climate subsequently, it does seem that there has been significant further growth in all major categories of industrial co-operation since then.[36]

Eastern Bloc motives for industrial co-operation

A number of motives have been indicated for the growth of industrial co-operation between East and West, most of which stem from the need for modernisation and greater efficiency, requiring Western technology, production and marketing know-how as well as market access. The industrial co-operation route itself was regarded, rightly or wrongly, as the way to achieve such objectives, as well as others pertaining to the balance of payments. Wilcyznski links the following microeconomic and macroeconomic advantages from industrial co-operation:[37]

1. The possibility of equipping Socialist enterprises with modern Western equipment and machinery without direct expenditure of hard currency.
2. Assimilation of Western technology.
3. Application of Western management techniques and know-how.
4. Achievement of economies of scale resulting from specialisation and production for wider markets.
5. Improvements in production quality since the Socialist enterprise has to meet the requirements of Western buyers.
6. Improvement of supplies to the Socialist domestic market, for products previously unavailable or in short supply.
7. Circumvention of Western countries' import restrictions through countertrading.
8. Establishment of a toe-hold in Western markets using Western partners' marketing channels and expertise.
9. Balance-of-payments gains from import substitution manufacturing and exporting.
10. Generally, 'a disciplining factor . . . prodding the Socialist enterprise to more radical and continuous improvements in its methods of production, management, marketing and overall efficiency'.[38]

Some of the problems which have been noted, by contrast, sound very familiar, including a possible decline in the Socialist partner's own research and development activity, and possible overdependence on the technology of the Western partner, along with difficulties in assimilating transferred technology; problems in Western economies, e.g. inflation tending to be transferred to the Eastern Bloc countries; and exclusion from certain export markets.

Western enterprises' experiences with industrial co-operation

The purpose of this section is to draw out the experiences and lessons from Western firms' involvement in industrial co-operation, summarising the empirical evidence available. Readers should also consult Exhibit 5.4, where motives for the British crane company entering into a co-operation deal with a Polish foreign trade organisation are discussed, as are problems encountered.

At one level, industrial co-operation could be viewed by a prospective Western company as a *fait accompli*, namely the only method of doing business in the East. More positively, there may be a range of advantages which accrue directly and indirectly from ICAs, aside from obvious components such as marketing, technical and market fees (with punctual payment), market access and sales of both products and equipment. These include the following:

1. Point of entry into a number of other Eastern European countries; and indeed into third countries with which the Eastern Bloc country has political and trading relationships.
2. Access to certain raw materials and power resources in Eastern Europe.
3. Access to Eastern European technological know-how in areas where this is relatively well advanced.
4. Access to low-cost labour resources of Eastern Europe, giving possibilities for cheaper sourcing, particularly of less sophisticated or labour-intensive components. This could be especially useful when domestic production capacity was overloaded.

Such possibilities have to be set against the inevitable problems encountered, which stem in part from the political set-up in these countries and the fact that Western companies are dealing with relatively less developed economies. Thus problems frequently mentioned include the following:[39]

1. Cumbersome business relationships and bureaucratic procedures. These pose continuing difficulties, but, in particular, make for very lengthy negotiations (two to four years perhaps) prior to the signing of agreements. Of course negotiations are inevitably more complex than in, say, a conventional licensing agreement, because there are almost always several components to the agreement. The period of time spent negotiating is also increasing the age of the product or process being transferred.
2. Inconsistent quality and delivery delays, which are related partly to lack of awareness of Western customers' needs.
3. Lack of breadth and poor quality of products (especially manufactures) offered for counterpurchase by Socialist enterprises.
4. Length of agreements, which pose problems because of difficulties in predicting future market and cost conditions.

On the basis of work on industrial co-operation agreements in Poland, Paliwoda identified a number of operational issues to be tackled by Western firms,[40] and these are listed in the following paragraphs.

Contractual requirements. Difficulties have arisen over the interpretation of particular clauses in contracts (although this is perhaps inevitable in agreements which when placed on top of each other have a thickness of twenty or twenty-five centimetres!). Price terms and conditions in contracts require careful consideration, with the counterpurchase element being especially important.

Communications. With the centralisation of decisionmaking, good relations with top-level officials are regarded as vital. But problems may still arise because of the variety of ministries or foreign trade enterprises which may be involved where projects cross several functional areas and industry sectors.

Technology gap. The technical and management technology gap necessitates a substantial training commitment which may greatly reduce profit margins on any co-operation venture. In the Polish case, this was exacerbated by the high turnover of the workforce, with people leaving or moving to other positions shortly after training.

Product buyback. Aside from the prices and terms in product buyback agreements, there are fears of creating competitors. In companies dealing with Poland, a part solution was to transfer goods manufactured under licence to the international marketing division of the Western firm prior to distribution to avoid revealing actual markets to the Polish side. Poor quality and erratic delivery have been mentioned previously and were also noted in Paliwoda's work. These problems were regarded as difficult elements to incorporate into agreements other than in terms of penalties for inability to comply with the required standard. Finally, at least in the past, there has been labour union opposition to ICAs which incorporate buyback provisions.

In summary, Paliwoda notes:

> it is important to have every last detail encapsulated in clear, unambiguous language within the contract that is to be signed. A further precaution may be to seek legal arbitration rights for disputes arising out of the contract, under a jurisdiction other than the East European partners. . . In terms of the operational aspects of technology transfer as such, it was found that marketing costs were difficult to accept on the Eastern side, that there was often a problem of higher machine tolerances and that there was also the problem of highly mobile labour. . . Finally, once all the problems had been dealt with, and production begun with co-operation exports to Britain and the West, there was next the problem of import restrictions and certificate of origin problems relating to co-operation trade.[41]

Another author, Artisien, studied contractual joint ventures in Yugoslavia, reaching the following conclusions from his sample of forty-two companies:[42]

1. Firms which took a step-by-step approach, including intermediate stages such as exporting, importing and licensing, were more successful than those which launched directly into joint ventures.
2. Careful evaluation of alternative entry strategies were not, however, usually undertaken, and the decision to form a joint venture stemmed more from the Western firm's existing working relationships with its prospective Yugoslav partner.
3. Confirming earlier remarks, there was wide agreement among firms about the need to spell out precisely in the joint venture contract the rights and responsibilities of the partners.
4. The advantages perceived from operating contractual joint ventures in Yugoslavia included risk sharing and the better local knowledge of the Yugoslav partner; the problems were mainly financial, viz. restrictions on profit and capital transfers and the non-convertibility of the dinar.

CONTRACTUAL JOINT VENTURES AND EQUITY JOINT VENTURES IN THE EASTERN BLOC AND PEOPLE'S REPUBLIC OF CHINA

The following chapter deals with the topic of equity joint ventures specifically, but there is merit at this juncture in making some comparison between the contractual and equity joint venture forms, especially when there is growing interest, backed up by enabling legislation, to encourage the latter in a number of countries in Eastern Europe and China. The formal differences between the two forms were given in Chapter 1 (pages 17–18) and Table 5.3 extends the comparison to a range of operational variables. Romanian legislation on equity ventures goes back, in fact, to 1971 (although production activities were excluded), to be followed by Hungary in 1972, Poland in 1976 and subsequently by other countries, including China (1979). In the main, the approach has been flexible, with regulations being changed in the light of experience. That flexibility is necessary is evident from the fact that equity joint ventures are still a rather small-scale phenomenon: in the mid-1980s the value of the foreign capital inflow into equity joint ventures in Eastern Europe was estimated at $120–$130m., represented by 776 ventures (712 of these in Poland).[43] Apart from their limited extent, it seems that equity joint ventures have not generally achieved the objectives that were set for them. In Poland, Romania, Hungary and Bulgaria, at least, equity joint ventures were seen as focusing on high-tech, high-export activity, but in none

Table 5.3 Comparisons between industrial co-operation and joint equity ventures

Operation variables	Industrial co-operation		Joint equity	
	Possible advantages	Possible disadvantages	Possible advantages	Possible disadvantages
Ownership	None, no company finance involved	Lack of control	49% equity stake	Weakening of company equity base
Venture control	Contractual limitations, plant Eastern responsibility	Limited control	*De facto* control greater than equity share	Inability to reconcile objectives
Venture capital	No capital investment by company	ICA entails acceptance of goods made under licence	Capital and managerial investment	Commitment of company resources
Return on investment (ROI)	Fast	Speed of project rests with Eastern partner	Gradual ROI shows willingness to stay in market	Venture has to achieve profitability first
Risk sharing	Contractual liability only	Diminished risks diminish opportunity for spectacular profits	Half-share only	Eastern partner may refuse to kill-off an unprofitable joint venture
Venture duration	Fixed duration	Renewal or extension requires separate contract	Unlimited	Termination a possible problem
Western company repayment	Hard cash and goods	Adjustment to Western business cycles	Goods made under licence and hard cash	Subject to Eastern taxes
Manufacturing	Extra facility at cost	May flood market eventually	Extra plant at cost	Exposure to risk

Management skills	Limited, contractual obligations	Costs of this transfer may be greater than anticipated	Full access	Too great a dependence on the Western partner
Marketing	Lower-cost goods made under licence	Co-ordination with Western business cycles	Lower-cost goods made under licence	Investment in capital, machinery and management
Market expansion	Western access to COMECON and limited Eastern access to West via partner	Ability to vary deliveries according to demand	Western access to COMECON and limited Eastern access to West via partner	Sales priced only in 'hard' currency
Pricing	Lower costs	Western inability to forecast Eastern expectation	Lower costs	All costs priced in 'hard' currency only
Quality control	Goods to Western quality standards	Free access but geographical distance and cost of quality control	Goods to Western quality standards	Free access but geographical distance and costs of quality control
Research and development	May be included or may lead from an ICA	Dependent upon mutual capabilities	Ability to capitalise on Eastern strengths	Difficulties of co-ordination
Updating of technology transferred	Contractual	Ambiguity of contract act definition	Closer integration	Sharing of current company specific technology

Source: Paliwoda, S.J. (1981), *Joint East–West Marketing and Production Ventures*, Gower, Farnborough, Hants.

of the four countries have these ventures become either technological leaders or important exporters.

Nevertheless, policymakers in the Eastern Bloc still believe in the opportunities associated with the operation of equity joint ventures, and steps are gradually being taken to liberalise the legislation: for example, a new regulation on equity joint ventures was introduced in the Soviet Union in January 1987, the main features of the legislation being: 51 per cent Soviet equity share; a Soviet citizen as chief executive; hard-currency profits to be repatriated only to the extent that exports for hard currency provided a surplus over hard-currency imports; two-year tax holiday with normal 30 per cent rate subsequently and profits remitted abroad subject to a 20 per cent transfer tax.[44] By the summer of 1987, five joint ventures had been created and 250 proposals were pending.[45]

Progress in the People's Republic of China (PRC) was very slow in the years immediately after the approval of a joint-venture law in 1979. Thus, in the period to autumn 1983 only eighty-nine joint venture agreements had been signed (firms from Hong Kong accounting for the largest number of agreements).[46] But the outlook is more optimistic, given the Chinese State Council's approval in 1986 of twenty-two regulations governing joint ventures and new laws giving foreign businessmen working in the PRC a 50 per cent tax reduction. By the end of 1988 7,000 enterprises with foreign capital were reported to have gone into operation.

One study concerning the creation and management of joint ventures in China came up with the following recommendations:[47]

1. To minimise time delays in setting up joint ventures, locate near Beijing – because of exposure and proximity to national decisionmakers. Another important location option involves special economic zones (see earlier comments on export processing zones).
2. Prepare an initial written agreement – this provides a sound starting point for the negotiation process.
3. Know who the negotiators are, and know who the authorities are – at the negotiating table, the front line of negotiators will comprise numerous individuals involved in the eventual operation of the joint venture; 'the authorities' behind the negotiators are the officials in the various state, provincial and municipal ministries and bureaux.
4. Write it down and have patience – a two- to four-year time span has been standard for getting final agreements signed, then there are additional delays associated with the start-up period.

Even then the main problems associated with joint ventures in China seem to be related to the ongoing operation of the enterprise: high costs, the requirement for foreign-exchange balance, and low productivity. Environmental conditions, including Chinese law, poor communications between Chinese organisations, bureaucracy, etc., represent further potential difficulties. Still, there do exist numerous, very successful joint ventures, and the enormous potential of the country means substantial opportunities for companies willing to persevere and take the long view.

FURTHER READING

1. There is a substantial range of material covered in this chapter. Readers may, therefore, like to read Oman, C. (1984), *New Forms of Investment in Developing Countries*, OECD, Paris, for revision purposes. Chapters 1 and 3 are especially useful, but note that joint ventures, licensing agreements and franchising are included in this book as well as other contractual arrangements; and the focus is upon developing countries only. See also Brooke, M.Z. and Buckley, P.J. (1982–86), *Handbook of International Trade*, Kluwer, London.
2. On the subject of East–West trade and technology transfer, the edited volume by Schaffer, M.E. (ed.) (1985), *Technology Transfer and East–West Relations*, Croom Helm, London, has some interesting contributions. And Paliwoda's book is still useful: Paliwoda, S.J. (1981), *Joint East–West Marketing and Production Ventures*, Gower, Aldershot: the book gives attention to the different types of contractual arrangements involved in industrial co-operation agreements.
3. On management contracts, see Brooke, M.Z. (1985), 'International Management Contracts: Servicing Foreign Markets and Selling Expertise Abroad', *Journal of General Management*, 11(1), 4–15.
4. On countertrading, refer to Jones, S.F. (1984), *North/South Countertrade*, Special Report No. 174, The Economist Intelligence Unit, London. Up-to-date issues are covered in the bi-monthly magazine, *Countertrade and Barter*, published by Metal Bulletin Journals Ltd, London.

QUESTIONS FOR DISCUSSION

1. Aside from the management fees involved, what benefits might a Western company or organisation derive from entering into management contracts overseas?
2. Disentangle the various components of the industrial co-operation agreement described in Exhibit 5.4, showing the different types of contractual arrangement involved.
3. A company exporting computer equipment to North Africa is required to enter into a counterpurchase arrangement to the value of 100 per cent of the export order. What advice would you give the exporting firm about the factors to be considered in negotiating the counterpurchase deal?
4. What advantages would a European company derive from undertaking the manufacture of clothing in one of the Turkish free trade zones (see Exhibit 5.3)?
5. Taking the viewpoint of a developing or Eastern Bloc country, what difficulties might be experienced in entering into any contractual arrangements outlined in the chapter?

NOTES AND REFERENCES

1. Farhang, M. (1986), *Dimensions of Market Entry in the Middle East: Behaviour of Swedish Firms*, RP86/5, Institute of International Business, Stockholm School of Economics, May. It should be noted that the range of contractual agreements is

even wider than that covered in this chapter. For example, Oman, C. (1984), *New Forms of International Investment in Developing Countries*, OECD, Paris, draws attention to:

Production sharing contracts. These agreements require a foreign company to undertake exploration in specific areas and, if petroleum or minerals are found, to undertake production in association with the host countries' state-owned enterprise. The contract will relate to a specific period of time, during which the foreign firm will obtain a predetermined share of the physical output once it has recovered its costs. Figures quoted for the production share vary from a 15 per cent host-government share in Chile to an 85 per cent government share in Egypt, although differential tax rates on foreign companies are likely to narrow the differences. In many ways, these contracts are similar to the industrial co-operation/buy-back arrangements which are discussed in the context of counter-trading.

Risk service contracts. Used mainly in the petroleum industry, these are similar to production sharing contracts except that the foreign firm's share of output is paid in cash rather than physical production. Here the burden of risk is placed on the foreign contractor who must provide the investment capital for exploration and production.

2. Brooke, M.Z. and Buckley, P.J. (1982–86), *Handbook of International Trade*, Kluwer, London.
3. Brooke, M.Z. (1985), *Selling Management Services Contracts in International Business*, Holt, Rinehart and Winston, London, 3.
4. United Nations Centre on Transnational Corporations (1982), *Management Contracts in Developing Countries: An Analysis of Their Substantive Provisions*, UNCTC, New York.
5. United Nations Centre on Transnational Corporations (1980), *Transnational Corporations in International Tourism*, UNCTC, New York.
6. Brooke, *Selling Management Services Contracts in International Business*, 331.
7. Construction Industry Research and Information Association (1983), *Management Contracting*, CIRIA, London, 6.
8. Brooke, M.Z. (1985), 'International Management Contracts: Servicing Foreign Markets and Selling Expertise Abroad', *Journal of General Management*, 11(1), 4–15.
9. Gabriel, P.P. (1967), *The International Transfer of Corporate Skills*, Harvard University, Boston, Mass.
10. Ibid., 166.
11. Elison, R. (1975), *Management Contracts*, International Business Unit, UMIST, Manchester, mimeo.
12. Sharma, D.D. (1983), *Swedish Firms and Management Contracts*, Department of Business Administration, University of Uppsala.
13. Brooke, *Selling Management Services Contracts in International Business*, 8.
14. Thus management contracts may be negotiated following complete or partial nationalisation or fade-out requirements which provide for a planned scheme of reduction of equity.
15. Brooke, 'International Management Contracts: Servicing Foreign Markets and Selling Expertise Abroad', 15.
16. Oman, *New Forms of International Investment in Developing Countries*, 16.
17. United Nations Centre on Transnational Corporations (1983), *Features and Issues in Turnkey Contracts in Developing Countries: A Technical Paper*, UNCTC, New York, 6.
18. Wright, R.W. and Kobel, V. (1981), 'Turnkey Projects: Canada's Route to Third

World Markets', *Business Quarterly*, Spring, 46–55. The quote is from p.49. See also, Lecraw, D. and Gordon, N. (1984), 'Turnkey Projects to Spur Exports – A Bidding Model', *Business Quarterly*, Summer, 46–54.

19. Wright and Kobel, 'Turnkey Projects', 52.
20. United Nations Centre on Transnational Corporations (1983), *Transnational Corporations in World Development, Third Survey*, UNCTC, New York, 261–3.
21. Morrow, A. (1985), 'British Consulting Engineering: Where Will it be in 1990?', *Multinational Business*, **3**, 18–22.
22. Sapir, A. (1986). 'Trade in Investment-Related Technological Services', *World Development*, **14**(5), 605–22.
23. For a discussion of the general trading companies see Kojima, K. and Ozawa, T. (1984), *Japan's General Trading Companies: Merchants of Economic Development*, OECD, Paris.
24. Dicken, P. (1986), *Global Shift. Industrial Change in a Turbulent World*, Harper & Row, London, 189–90.
25. This section overall draws on United Nations Centre on Transnational Corporations (1987), *Transnational Corporations in the Synthetic Fibre, Textile and Clothing Industry*, UNCTC, New York; this publication was prepared by S. Young and N. Hood for the UNCTC. EPZs are very similar in many respects to free ports and foreign trade zones; some definitions make no distinction, but to be exact it is probably best to restrict the concept to zones which always include export-oriented assembly and/or manufacturing operations, whereas activities in other types of zones will be wholly or partly trade related (e.g. assembly, storage, transportation, brokerage, insurance, etc.).
   See Robles, F. and Hozier G.C., Jr. (1986), 'Understanding Foreign Trade Zones', *International Marketing Review*, **3**(2), 44–54; Tansuhaj, P.S. and Gentry, J.W. (1987), 'Firm Differences in Perceptions of Facilitating Role of Foreign Trade Zones in Global Marketing and Logistics', *Journal of International Business Studies*, **18**(1), 19–33. There were, for example, 109 general-purpose foreign trade zones and 28 sub-zones in the USA by early 1985.
26. There have been a series of articles published by the ILO into the effects of multinationals in EPZs, especially employment effects, e.g. Hein, C. (1988), *Multinational Enterprises and Employment in the Mauritian Export Processing Zone*, Working Paper No. 52, Multinational Enterprises Programme, ILO, Geneva.
27. Davidson, W.H. (1987), 'Creating and Managing Joint Ventures in China', *California Management Review*, **29**(4), 77–94.
28. *Financial Times Survey* (1986), 'Guangdong', 22 September.
29. Lebkowski, M. and Monkiewicz, J. (1986), *Equity Co-operation Ventures Domiciled in the Socialist Countries. Trends and Patterns*, World Economy Research Institute Working Paper No. 8, Central School of Planning and Statistics, Warsaw, Poland, December.
30. Hill, M.R. (1985), 'Western Companies and Trade and Technology Transfer with the East', in Schaffer, M.E. (ed.), *Technology Transfer and East–West Relations*, Croom Helm, London.
31. Hamilton, G. (ed.), *Red Multinationals or Red Herrings? The Activities of Enterprises from Socialist Countries in the West*, Frances Pinter, London; McMillan, C.H. (1987), *Multinationals from the Second World*, Macmillan, London.
32. Paliwoda, S.J. (1981), *Joint East–West Marketing and Production Ventures*, Gower, Aldershot, Hants, 108, quoting C.H. McMillan.
33. Ibid., p.90. Other definitions are given on pages 108–10 of Paliwoda's book.

34. According to Kogut, the preference for co-production derives from the fact that this type of arrangement most closely resembles foreign direct investment. Kogut, B. (1986), 'On Designing Contracts to Guarantee Enforceability: Theory and Evidence from East–West Trade', *Journal of International Business Studies*, **17**(1), 47–61.
35. Hill, 'Western Companies and Trade and Technology Transfer with the East', 117–18.
36. McMillan, C.H. (1981), 'Trends in East–West Industrial Cooperation', *Journal of International Business Studies*, **12**(2), 53–67.
37. Wilczynski, J. (1976), *The Multinationals and East–West Relations*, Macmillan, London.
38. The quotation is from Hill, M.R. (1983), *East–West Trade, Industrial Cooperation and Technology Transfer*, Gower Press, Aldershot, 176, citing Wilczynski.
39. Hill, 'Western Companies and Trade and Technology Transfer with the East', 119; Hill, *East–West Trade, Industrial Cooperation and Technology Transfer*, 76–7.
40. Paliwoda, *Joint East–West Marketing and Production Ventures*, Chapter 8.
41. Ibid., 189.
42. Artisien, P.F.R. (1985), *Joint Ventures in Yugoslav Industry*, Gower, Aldershot, Chapter 10.
43. Lebkowski and Monkiewicz, *Equity Cooperation Ventures Domiciled in the Socialist Countries. Trends and Patterns.*
44. Ivanov, I.D. (1987), 'Joint Ventures in the Soviet Union', *The CTC Reporter*, **23**, 48–51.
45. The Economist Intelligence Unit, *The World in 1988*, EIU, London, 54.
46. Daniels, J.D., Krug, J. and Nigh, D. (1985), 'US Joint Ventures in China: Motivation and Management of Political Risk', *California Management Review*, **27**(4), 46–58.
47. Davidson, 'Creating and Managing Joint Ventures in China', 78–84.

APPENDIX 5.1
FINANCING EXPORTS AND OVERSEAS PROJECT WORK

Because of the greater risks associated with overseas sales, many firms are reluctant to finance them in the same way that they would domestic sales. Recognising some of the problems faced by exporters, governments have developed various forms of assistance for firms engaged in exporting and overseas project work. 'Supplier credit' is the term used to describe the granting of long-term financing by the supplier to a customer; while buyer credit involves the provision of finance either directly to a foreign buyer, or indirectly through a bank in the buyer's country acting on his behalf. In the latter case, whereas the finance is provided by a bank, or in the case of a major project, possibly a syndicate of banks, in the supplier's country the supplier has no role to play in the final financial arrangements. The exporter will be paid once the relevant supply conditions specified in the contract with the buyer have been fulfilled.

OECD Consensus Agreement on Export Credits

The terms under which supplier and buyer credits can be made available to overseas customers are regulated under the OECD's 'Consensus on Export Credits'.[1] As competitive pressures in world markets increased, particularly in the 1970s, it became apparent that international agreements not to subsidise exports were being circum-vented by offering importers very attractive terms for the financing of their purchases of capital goods and project requirements. Official export credit agencies were offering financial packages characterised by interest rates well below those which would have prevailed in a commercially based market. The high level and volatility of interest rates experienced in the 1970s provided a further impetus to this process. Interest-rate subsidies were supplemented by the lengthening of repayment periods, and by increasing the proportion of the cost of the imports for which finance was made available. The escalation of implicit subsidies led the governments of the leading industrial nations represented in the OECD to seek agreement on the terms on which export financing packages would be made available. Although co-operation in the regulation of export credit, more particularly in the regulation of insurance to begin with, goes back to the establishment of the Berne Union in 1934, finding a basis for agreement on financial terms has not proved to be an easy task. The initial 'Consensus' in 1978, which was not a legal binding agreement but simply an agreed set of guidelines, contained too many loopholes. Negotiations have continued over the last decade and although the latest set of guidelines have overcome many of the initial difficulties, various possibilities for unfair competition remain.

The prevailing 'Consensus' sets limits on the terms and conditions of all officially supported export credits with a duration of two or more years. The following conditions have been agreed:

1. At least 15 per cent of any contract should be paid in cash by the importer.
2. The maximum repayment period should normally be 8.5 years but 10-year periods can be made available for importers in the poorer developing countries.
3. Minimum interest rates, which depend on the duration of the credit and the development status of the borrower's country, should be set every January and July (these interest rates are automatically adjusted in line with the rates prevailing in the five International Monetary Fund (IMF) Special Drawing Rights' currencies).

Various exceptions to these terms have been agreed. Firstly, any country with commercial interest rates below those specified in the agreement can make loans at these rates. This provision was introduced to minimise the disadvantages of the agreement to countries with low inflation and low interest rates such as Germany. Clearly the guidelines, by specifying minimum rates of interest in absolute terms, favour those countries with high rates of inflation and interest. A borrower should consider the rate of interest in conjunction with the expected appreciation or depreciation of the currency. Those countries experiencing high rates of inflation and high interest rates can generally expect their currencies to depreciate, and by setting their interest rates on credits at the minimum level allowed they can subsidise their financial packages in a way which is not available in countries with interest rates below this level. However, it should be noted that there is a feeling in Britain that many buyers focus on the interest-rate cost and tend to neglect the impact of expected exchange-rate changes on the real cost of borrowing. Secondly, more generous terms may be made available to developing countries if the subsidy, or 'grant', element is sufficiently large, and other countries are notified of the intention so that they can match the terms if they wish. To qualify as an exception to the agreed guidelines, the subsidy complement in the financial package must account for at least 25 per cent of the cost of the contract. Such financial packages are referred to as mixed credits, being partly motivated by commercial considerations and partly motivated by the desire to help developing countries.

Mixed credits

Mixed credits is the term used to describe credit packages which include an element of aid: the aid is offered to attract the business to the exporting country. The world recession and the contracting markets of the developing world, following the debt crisis, has encouraged certain industrialised countries to use more of their aid budget for the subsidisation of their exports. When exports become sufficiently subsidised for the transaction to be considered acceptable as a form of aid rather than outlawed as unfair competition is a matter of some controversy. The OECD agreement on the issue specifies a minimum grant component of 25 per cent of the value of the transaction before a concessional credit is deemed to be acceptable.

The Dutch may have been the first to use aid funds in this way but the French were the first to really exploit the use of aid to increase exports and was the first country to include 'Credit-Mixte' as a standard part of its aid programme. Mixed credits have been the subject of considerable controversy in the UK. Industrialists have argued that the terms on which they are made available are not sufficiently generous to allow them to compete with their main industrial competitors, particularly France and Japan, and tend to be allocated too much on the basis of the development contribution without adequate regard being paid to commercial considerations. Development economists on the other hand have argued that mixed credits divert aid from the more pressing development needs of Third World countries. It is suggested that it biases the provision of aid towards more capital-intensive projects and revenue-generating activities in developing countries.

In recent years there has been considerable worldwide over-capacity in those industries involved in large projects. The level of large-project activity in the developing world and the OPEC countries has fallen sharply, in the former as a result of their debt problems; in the latter the slump in oil prices is responsible. Competition on an international basis for the continuing projects is intense. International companies in all countries in the engineering and construction industries are pressing for their governments to provide financial support to enable them to meet or undercut their competitors. In this buyer's market, the financial package which can be made available to the country undertaking a project becomes of critical importance. Developing countries have been increasingly expert in assessing the 'deals' which are available. The project cost is seen to be very sensitive to the interest rate and length of the loans which can be offered to finance the venture.

The financial support for mixed credits in the UK is made available under the 'Aid and Trade Provision' (ATP). Applications for assistance under ATP have to be approved by both the Treasury and the Overseas Development Administration (ODA), one to examine the commercial and the other the development rationale for the government's support. While it has been suggested by Mosley that the time made available to assess the development potential of proposals is totally inadequate, businessmen resent the 'bureaucratic delay' in obtaining the ODA's approval.[2] The greater flexibility and enthusiasm of the French government in dealing with mixed credits is contrasted with the conservative approach of the UK government. The UK government also tends to react to proposals put forward by developing countries, whereas the French plan ahead, and even initiate the consideration of projects in developing countries that might be financed by 'Credit-Mixte'. Businessmen point out that despite the limited funds available under ATP, about 6 per cent of the overall aid budget, it is not unusual for the budgetary allocation to be totally employed.

A high proportion of the funds under the ATP accrue to a small number of companies heavily engaged in international project work. Between 1978 and 1985, nearly one-third of the budget was spent on projects involving four companies, Balfour Beatty, GEC, NEI and Davy Mackie. This has led to criticism of the programme for such firms. The *Financial Times*, in an editorial commenting on an Indian project supported under the ATP facility, posed the question: 'Is this money really designed to help India or is it a covert subsidy to the shareholders and employees of GEC, Babcock Power and other hard pressed British engineering companies involved in this project?'

The typical pattern of negotiations surrounding a proposed project has been well described by Rubner:[3]

> In 1981 three consortia (French, German and British) fought for the privilege of constructing the £1.25 bn. Paradip Steelworks. The Indian government insisted 'of course' on 100 per cent credit financing and derided the applicable consensus rule which demanded a minimum interest of about 8.5 per cent. To the delight of the French and the British, Mannesmann (the German contender) was unable to persuade Bonn to authorise additional foreign aid for the purpose of clinching the deal. Actually, the Indian authorities had been very impressed with the technical details of the German proposal but the financial conditions were more important, which is why they turned down Mannesmann and accepted the offer of a British consortium (in collaboration with the French) led by Davy. Paris immediately authorised export credit in accordance with the Consensus, topping it with aid funds. London helped to make this credit-mixte an appetising dish because the UK government allocated new money to supplement what had already been promised in the Foreign Aid budget in India. An outright grant of £150 m. plus the usual export credit with ECGD (Export Credits Guarantee Department) backing produces an average interest charge of 4.5 per cent.

The use of mixed credits is widely perceived to lead to unfair competition, with the US government being the most vocal critic. Having failed to convince the governments of other industrialised countries of the need to effectively limit the use of mixed credits, the US government has indicated that it is prepared to match the terms offered by other countries competing for the same contracts. Each time the US Eximbank, its export credit agency, has matched the terms of mixed credits offered by a competitor it has done so with considerable publicity to make its intentions quite clear. Typical of Eximbank's response to what it considers to be unfair competition was the assistance provided to Cincinatti Milacron's export of machine tools to Indonesia in 1985. Under the OECD's Consensus Agreement the minimum interest rate should have been 9.5 per cent, but Eximbank offered finance at 6.5 per cent 'to counter the predatory financing by France, and to discourage such future action by foreign governments'.

APPENDIX 5.2
COUNTERTRADING[4]

Background and forms

'Countertrade' is a general term which is applied to a whole range of reciprocal trading activities, the common characteristic of which is that the sale of goods or services to a country is contractually linked in some way to an obligation to buy from that country. The modern era of countertrading began in the 1930s when it was used to assist the German economy out of depression. The system was mainly used in trade with the Middle East and other less developed countries. Following the Second World

War, a variety of international agreements provided for the exchange of goods under bilateral clearing agreements, but after the 1950s the importance of countertrading fell away, except in the Eastern Bloc countries. As will be indicated, the growth in countertrading since the 1970s has been associated primarily with problems in developing countries, including depressed economic conditions, low commodity prices and deepening debt; but as noted earlier in the chapter, countertrading continues to be a major element in industrial co-operation arrangements and is also a factor in China's modernisation plans.

There is a good deal of confusion concerning the terms used to describe the main modes of countertrading, but the most common forms are as follows.[5]

Barter
Pure barter involves the exchange of goods under a single contract, and, in the simplest case, no cash is involved. Problems such as determining and agreeing upon the relative value of traded goods have discouraged interest in barter. In addition, the use of one contract to cover both deliveries and counter-deliveries has been a disincentive.

Western banks are rarely willing to finance or guarantee a transaction in which a creditor's proceeds are contingent upon another party's performance. There are no letters of credit in barter transactions, although the involved parties may obtain parallel bank guarantees in the form of stand-by letters of credit or performance bonds. Though fairly uncommon, barter has been sought by some African and Latin American countries which are oil dependent or have extensive currency restrictions.

Counterpurchase
Under this type of agreement, the exporter sells goods, and contractually agrees to make reciprocal purchases from the country concerned. There are two parallel but separate contracts, one for the principal order – which is paid for on normal cash or credit terms – and another for the counterpurchase, linked by a protocol. Normally, the duration of the transaction is relatively short, say one to three years, and the value of the counterpurchase varies between 10 per cent and 100 per cent of the original export order. Agreements may vary from a general declaration of intent to a binding contract which specifies the goods and services to be supplied, the markets in which they have to be sold and the penalties for non-performance. The goods offered may be unrelated to those exported, and parties unrelated to the sales contract may be involved in the agreement. It is worth noting that if the Western company can find no suitable products for counterdelivery, its obligation may be transferred to a trading house which will dispose of the goods for a commission or discount; these may range from under 5 per cent for easily marketed goods such as raw materials, to as much as 40 per cent.

Buy-back or compensation
In industrial co-operation deals, the sale of technology, equipment, or a plant is linked to a contractual commitment on the part of the seller to purchase a certain quantity of products that are produced or derived from the original sale. These arrangements are commonly known as buy-back or compensation. The arrangements are most common in connection with exports of process plant, mining equipment and similar orders, including turnkey arrangements. Licensing contracts with Eastern Bloc countries may also stipulate buy-back terms. The duration of the transaction can be very lengthy – three or four years up to twenty-five years or longer. Counter-deliveries often total 100 per cent or more of the original sale. Contract negotiations are complex since the Western seller in the deal may be setting up a potential

competitor, and technology transfer, the right to the use of brand names and distribution rights are all involved.

Offset

This may be regarded as another form of industrial co-operation. A condition of exporting some products, especially those incorporating advanced technology (civil/military aircraft or other military equipment) to some markets is that the exporter includes in his final product particular materials, components or sub-assemblies procured within the importing country. Although a long-established feature of trade in defence equipment, offset is becoming more important in other sectors, particularly where the importing country is seeking to develop its industrial capabilities.

Switch trading

Switch transactions are probably the most complicated of the counterpurchase arrangements. The system operates within the context of bilateral agreements, usually between COMECON countries and developing nations. Such agreements are often out of balance, leading to the accumulation of uncleared credit surpluses in one or other country. The manipulation of clearing credits and debits and the trading of the associated goods often involves several countries in a web of complex arrangements; such transactions are known as 'switch' or 'swap' deals because they typically involve switching the documentation and destination of goods at sea. To take an example, Brazil at one time had a large credit surplus with Poland; these surpluses can sometimes be tapped by third parties so that UK exports to Brazil could be financed from the sale of Polish goods to the United Kingdom or elsewhere.

Country involvement and motivations for countertrade

As suggested earlier, the most consistent users of countertrade have been the COMECON countries which have always used bilateral trade among themselves, and have used countertrade extensively with developing nations and to a lesser extent with Western countries (countertrading is believed to represent on average something over 25 per cent of COMECON trade with the West).

Countertrade is relatively limited in trade between the industrialised nations, which undertake over three-quarters of their trade with each other. The exceptions relate to defence, aviation and big high-technology deals, where an element of direct offset has often been involved. Countries such as Portugal and Greece have sought counter-purchase for other large export orders but only on an *ad hoc* basis. Australia and New Zealand require offset for public-sector purchases and these are the only OECD nations with mandatory countertrade requirements.

The major growth in countertrade in recent years has come from the developing countries. Nevertheless, while seeking countertrade arrangements, the number of deals actually undertaken has been constrained by the inability to provide marketable goods for the counterpurchase and the lack of effective organisation.[6] On 2 December 1981, Indonesia, facing an imminent foreign-currency shortage as oil revenues dropped through the floor, became the first industrialising country to introduce mandatory countertrade requirements in respect of all civilian public-sector contracts financed by the state budget and by export credits. A 100 per cent counterpurchase obligation was required and to maximise earnings the Indonesians refused to allow exporters to take back their most saleable products, oil and natural gas. Indonesia has been joined since then by other countries such as Malaysia, which has set up a special countertrade unit, but many other countries still treat such deals on a case-by-case basis. There is no general legislative requirement in Brazil, for instance, although administrative guidance and informal requirements are enforced by government agencies.

Where countertrade is perhaps of most significance is in the oil-producing countries, where in several cases exporters bidding for public-sector contracts may be required to accept oil in exchange for goods. In general, oil barter deals are fairly straightforward, with goods being exchanged for oil. Two extra parties are included in the contract, however, the oil-producing company and the oil-distributing company, and this complicates the issue. The Department of Trade and Industry in the UK in its guidance for exporters on countertrade has noted that three points should be borne in mind:

1. The oil-distributing companies' discount – this may be required since the volume of oil involved even in large contracts will be small in relation to oil purchased under long-term contracts. It is suggested that arrangements should be made for recouping the cost of a discount from the end-buyer.
2. 'Additionality' – the oil-producing companies are likely to specify that bartered oil should be additional to what would be sold anyway. The process of establishing additionality can be lengthy.
3. Oil price – this is subject to change and therefore the basis for determining the price of oil should be clearly specified in the contract. Any management fee should be related to the value of the goods to be provided rather than to the oil to be bought.

While there is a lack of information concerning the significance of countertrade in relation to total world trade, because of secrecy and the fact that the transactions are not separately identifiable in official trade statistics, countertrade perhaps accounts for 15–20 per cent of total world trade (assuming a fairly wide definition of countertrade is used, so as to include bilateral agreements).

Turning to the motivations for countertrade, and considering first the developing and Eastern Bloc countries, reasons include the following:[7]

1. To preserve hard currency and improve the balance of trade. Such problems, in turn, have commonly emerged because of the artificial exchange rates that many countries maintain for their currencies. Products cannot be sold on the world markets at local costs converted into foreign currency at the official exchange rate.
2. Sellers may believe they can expand markets or gain access to new markets by drawing on outside marketing expertise. It has to be asked, of course, whether or not this is the least-cost method of opening up new markets.
3. Manufacturing capabilities may be upgraded by entering into industrial co-operation agreements.
4. For industries in which price maintenance is believed to be important, counter-trade transactions may permit concealed discounting in a period of weak markets, as with oil in recent years. Similar examples can be found in industrial countries, where, with high unemployment and excess capacity, firms have wanted to sell anything that they could above their variable costs – providing normal markets and pricing patterns were not disturbed.
5. Countertrade transactions may provide some additional certainty for producers, so that investment and production decisions can be more efficient.
6. In Eastern Bloc countries, countertrade fits into the system of central planning with its emphasis on physical quantities.

There are some additional points which should be made relating to the types of commodities which may be offered in countertrades. All else being equal, primary commodities would be preferred because they are relatively homogeneous, which makes it easier to determine values and thereby reduces the extra transaction costs and risks associated with the deals. Again, primary commodities are less 'lumpy' than most manufactures, allowing finer adjustment of quantities exchanged; and finally, the commodities are usually sold in large consignments. The converse is, however, that countries lacking such commodities are likely to find difficulties in countertrading.

It is not always the case that the impetus for countertrading has come from the Eastern Bloc and developing countries. Some of the motivations for exporters from the industrialised nations entering into countertrade deals are as follows:

1. To gain prominence in new markets. Countertrade may be a means of showing good faith, enabling the company to establish itself as a reliable trading partner.
2. To gain a source of supply. Especially in compensation transactions, countertrade may be used by a Western company to obtain a long-term, reliable supply of raw materials, components or finished goods.
3. To take advantage of sales opportunities. The company that is prepared to engage in countertrade may gain a competitive edge over one that is not.
4. To reduce tariffs or taxes payable. This may occur in compensation deals where a multinational company exports parts to a foreign plant for assembly and understates the value of the shipment to avoid paying higher tariffs.

Despite these points, the public face (at least) of international organisations, Western governments and Western exporters is opposed to countertrading for the reasons highlighted in Figure A5.2.1.

The mechanics of countertrading[8]

Space forbids a detailed description of contracts, agreements and protocols involved in countertrading, and in any event the variety of arrangements is very wide. For present purposes, what is most important is to identify the various issues that will be involved in agreements, and these are listed below as a kind of checklist, with comment where appropriate:

1. *Time frame* – deals may be completed within a matter of days where two simultaneous shipments are involved, or may take place over a number of years, especially where buy-back and offset are involved.
2. *Percentage of the contract for countertrade and how it is calculated (FOB or CIF)* – the countertrade percentage may vary from single figures to over 100 per cent. Some countries use a stepped system, with the countertrade requirement varying according to type of import. Jamaica is quoted as a country where the countertrade may be more than 100 per cent, since on occasions the countertrade partner is required to take out Jamaican products where the value of the local content of the Jamaican export must be equal to the value of the countertraded import. Regarding the calculation of payment, Eastern Bloc countries generally prefer to buy FOB, and use their own transport and insurance for which they can pay in soft currency.
3. *Pricing* – a specific price may be set where shipments are to take place in the near future and stipulated in the contract; where shipments take place over a period of time, it is usual to express the price in terms of an agreed formula, e.g. the price quoted on a futures market. The question of discounts is very sensitive: it is normal for developing countries to insist on the world price being paid for their products, with a discount being partially 'hidden' within the import price, rather than appearing as a discounted price in the contract. The discount is a function

The viewpoint of Western governments and international organisations

- Represents a dangerous deviation from the principle of multilateral free trade
- Interferes with the proper functioning of trade by disguising price
- Cumbersome, inefficient and has the effect of increasing transaction costs sharply
- May lead to dumping and injury to local companies
- May delay painful economic decisions by enabling a country to live beyond its means of external payment

The viewpoint of the Western exporter

- Costly[a] and may create risk of incurring penalties
- Procedures in many developing countries have not been worked out, causing bureaucratic difficulties
- Problems over the procurement of suitable products
- Difficulties of locating buyers for the goods, especially where there are stipulations of additionality
- The majority of countertrade negotiations do not come to fruition
- Profit margins may need to be reduced to absorb some of the countertrade costs
- Countries may withdraw because they have found cash buyers at the last minute
- Even after contracts have been signed, transactions may not be completed, e.g. *force majeure* may be declared over harvest failure
- Deals in developing countries may be hampered by central banks insisting on foreign-exchange earnings from exports being remitted to the bank rather than being allocated to finance imports

Note: [a]Costs include fees and/or commissions to trading houses or banks; fees to information specialists or specialist consultants; special insurance and banking costs (e.g. operating an escrow account); additional costs to the company arising from staff time on negotiations; air fares and other expenses; adjustment to tender prices to take account of low success rate in countertrade deals (suggested as about 1 in 20); and discount to the final buyer as an inducement to accept the goods.

Figure A5.2.1 Problems in countertrading from the Western viewpoint. Sources: *Financial Times Survey* (1985), 'Countertrading', 6 February; Jones, S.F. (1984), *North/South Countertrade*, Special Report No. 174, The Economist Intelligence Unit, London.

of a variety of factors including world supply and demand, quality, the commission of the specialist broker who may take on the obligation to purchase the goods, and so on.

4. *Types of product* – some countries issue lists of products which are allowed for countertrade, whereas others operate on an *ad hoc* basis. Trading corporations in Eastern Bloc countries are not prepared to offer any of their standard export goods in exchange, and some developing countries are also attempting to insist that countertraded products should not be traditional exports. From the viewpoint of the Western exporter, their interest is at least in keeping the percentage of technical goods as low as possible (since quality variations are likely to be quite substantial).

5. *Additionality* – discussions concerning this and subsequent supervision of the stipulations are likely to cause substantial difficulties; but an additionality policy is necessary for a developing country since otherwise the exporter will usually simply try to substitute countertraded products for conventionally traded products in the same export market.

6. *Assignment and transferability* – with the involvement of major trading houses and banks, it is necessary for contracts to permit the assignment and transferability of obligations to third parties.
7. *Penalty* – countertrade contracts contain a penalty for non-compliance, usually around 10 per cent but as high as 50 per cent (imposed by the Indonesian government).

At the same time there should be provisions for progressive cancellation of a countertrade contract if the goods are not available.

There are a host of other details which need to be considered, including arbitration, mechanics of documentation, maintenance of delivery schedules and separation of payment conditions, possibilities for re-export, use of an escrow account (if used, then it is necessary from an exporter's point of view to ensure that progress payments meet requirements so that the contract can be aborted without loss at any time if payments do not continue to arrive), and so on. Finally there are governmental dimensions to be considered: a UK exporter, for instance, has to obtain Bank of England approval for any deal and the position with the ECGD has to be considered if this form of credit insurance is in the sale.

Organising for countertrading

Part of the complexity of countertrade deals derives not only from the possible variety of such agreements, but also from the number of other different countries as well as organisations which may be involved. The various countertrade players are listed in Figure A5.2.2.

Within Western industrialised countries

- Company (supplier of products/projects to country)
- Government or private information centre
- Consultant/adviser
- Countertrade unit/subsidiary of manufacturing company offering its services to outsiders
- Trading house
- Bank
- Other financial institutions
- Switch specialists
- Lawyer
- Final buyer(s) of countertraded product(s)

Within Eastern Bloc and developing countries

- Designated organisation responsible for countertrade
- Export promotion organisation
- Central bank
- Ministry of trade
- Other ministries (e.g. finance)
- Organisation/company responsible for imports or project
- Supplier(s) or product(s) for export
- Local agents/subsidiary of Western company
- Local representative of trading company
- Local bank

Figure A5.2.2 The countertrade players. Source: Jones, S.F. (1984), *North/ South Countertrade*, Special Report No. 174, The Economist Intelligence Unit, London.

A Western exporting company which is involved in countertrade transactions has to make a decision concerning the handling of its obligations. A number of companies which face recurring demands for countertrade have made the decision to establish an in-house capability, but it has been suggested that an annual countertrade turnover of $10 m is necessary to justify such an in-house countertrade unit.

Where a company's involvement with countertrading is less significant, the enterprise is likely to turn to the services of trade consultants or trading houses. A number of the world's major commodity trading houses play a central role in countertrade. They have created special countertrade units and will sometimes assume the role of principals in transactions on behalf of an exporter by taking title to goods on their own account. There are probably around thirty major trading houses in the world, and four of these are principally important in the world of countertrade. These are: Andre, a grain and soft commodity trading house based in Lausanne, Switzerland, which operates through its Finco subsidiary; Cargill, the US grain and commodity trading house which operates from London and Geneva with its Tradax subsidiary; Metallgesellschaft, a West German metal trading house, has a subsidiary MG Services Inc. operating from New York, London and Hong Kong; finally, the US-based Phibro-Salomon has had a long involvement in countertrading through offices in New York, London and Amsterdam. The suggestion is that these big trading houses are bound to strengthen their grip on the countertrade market because they have the worldwide trading networks necessary to dispose of the goods. This will become more relevant as countertrade deals get larger and the products involved more varied; and associated with this, the larger the deal, the more likely the countertraded goods are to be commodities.[9]

It is important to note that trading houses may be involved in a wide variety of ways, operating as intermediaries on behalf of third parties; as principals and indeed initiators of countertrades (e.g. grain trading companies have been concerned with deals where grain is exported and other commodities taken out as a countertrade); as organisations structuring deals for developing countries, which involve assembling an import package of various products obtained from Western sources and taking out a countertrade package; as receivers of goods procured within countertrade; and so on.

As countertrading has gained in importance and respectability, the banks have been another group of organisations which have been quick to see the opportunities available. Most of the major banks now operate a countertrade unit. The functions that such a unit can undertake may include the following:[10]

1. Advice to client exporters, especially those who have never before engaged in countertrade.
2. Provision of an information bank on countries where countertrade is practised.
3. Guidance on incorporating countertrade proposals into bids and offers.
4. The placing of goods taken in countertrade with trading houses and any users which are clients of the bank.
5. The creation of documentation on special accounts to improve the efficiency of countertrading, e.g. hybrid letters of credit or compensation accounts/escrow accounts.
6. Working with the bank's trade finance departments in the use of the bank's funds and services for countertrades.

In addition, however, some banks offer a full countertrade service, effectively in direct competition with the trading houses. Certain of the banks with the longest involvement are those based in Vienna, a city which has had extensive involvement in East/West trade and countertrade for many years. Banks located there include the Creditanstalt, which offers a full countertrade service through its subsidiary trading and finance company AWT. Again, Centro Bank, which is jointly owned by banks in Italy, Austria, Poland and the UK (Kleinwort Benson), is one of the most successful countertrading operations, using Vienna as a base for handling deals around the world.

There is a variety of other types of organisation which are active in counter-trading. For example, some manufacturing companies which initially created countertrade units for in-house purposes, have since expanded to offer a service to outside bodies. There are several of such industrial groups particularly in Europe, including Voest-Alpine of Austria, Société Generale of Belgium, and another Belgian concern, Devetra, in each case through their subsidiary companies. Then there are a number of companies which, while offering a countertrade service, are switch specialists; and there are a whole host of countertrade advisers and consultants offering services of various sorts, often specialising on particular activities, e.g. credit insurance, etc.

To these commercial concerns must be added the various services provided by Western governments on behalf of their exporters. As suggested earlier, many of the governments have a fairly ambivalent attitude towards countertrading, but in order to avoid competitive disadvantages they have been forced at least to provide guidance for exporters.

Notes and references

1. OECD (1987), *The Export Credit Financing System in OECD Member Countries*, OECD, Paris.
2. Mosley, P. (1987), *Overseas Aid*, Wheatsheaf, London.
3. Rubner, A. (1987), *The Export Cult*, Gower, Aldershot.
4. The major references used in the preparation of this section were: Department of Trade and Industry (1985), *Countertrade: Some Guidance for Exporters*, London, July; *Financial Times Survey* (1985), 'Countertrading', 6 February; Jones, S.F. (1984), *North/South Countertrade*, Special Report No. 174, The Economist Intelligence Unit, London; Verzariu, P. (1980), *Countertrade Practices in East Europe, The Soviet Union and China*, US Department of Commerce, Washington D.C., April.
5. Readers are likely to come across various countertrade terms (aside from references to various forms of countertrading) which are worth knowing: 'Disagio' – the discount required by final buyers of countertraded goods in order to provide a purchasing incentive. 'Escrow account' – an independent or trustee account where cash is held in trust (escrow); it is released when a particular function is performed, such as exports by a country. 'Evidence account' – this is used where countertrading takes the form of a continuous flow of goods between two parties. Since it is unlikely that each import will be matched by an equivalent export at the same time, evidence accounts are kept showing the values of exports and imports. The evidence account must be maintained more or less in balance year by year.
6. See, for example, Welt, L.G.B. (1984), 'Why Latin America is Wary of Barter', *Euromoney*, January, 132–4.
7. Cooper, R.N. (1984), 'Why Countertrade?', *Across the Board*, March, 36–41; Welt, L.G. (1983), 'Straight Cash for Goods? No Longer a Sure Bet!', *American Import/Export Management*, October, 26–27, 44; Banks, G. (1985), 'Constrained Markets, "Surplus" Commodities and International Barter', *Kyklos*, **38**(2), 249–67.
8. Jankovic, P. (1984), 'Compensation Trading', Alcon (Compensation Trading) Ltd., mimeo; Eretson Association Ltd. (1984), 'Countertrade Checklist', London, 11 July.
9. Mills, D. (1985), 'Big is Beautiful in Countertrade', *Euromoney*, January, 144, 148.
10. Bracher, R.N. (1984), 'If Countertrade is Inevitable Make the Best of it', *The Banker*, May, 69–71.

6

JOINT VENTURES AND WHOLLY OWNED SUBSIDIARIES

SUMMARY

1. Equity joint ventures and wholly owned subsidiaries represent the final stage in the implicit spectrum of international supply activity examined in this book. Both partially and wholly owned foreign subsidiaries involve a greater capital commitment by the firm and are, therefore, more risky financially than the alternative supply methods considered in previous chapters. They also give rise to new management problems, as well as to a higher level of political risk. The risks associated with the direct investment mode of entry and the greater commitment of financial and managerial resources will be a particular problem for small to medium-sized enterprises. There are, however, a number of compensating advantages to this entry mode, including greater parent company control, closer contact with the market, deeper market penetration.

2. The term 'joint ventures' has become a generally used one to describe a wide variety of collaborative agreements between firms. Equity joint ventures can be distinguished from other types of international collaboration in three main respects:
   • A capital commitment and a sharing of ownership between two or more partners.
   • The establishment of a separate legal entity ('the child').
   • A sharing of management control as well as ownership.
   Different types of equity joint venture can be identified and these vary with respect to the activity of the venture; the nationality of partners; the ownership arrangement; and the control dimension.

   Equity joint ventures emerged as an important international supply mode during the 1960s, especially by developed-country MNEs in developing nations. There are significant variations between companies, however, in their willingness to use joint ventures, and these are related to technology, nationality of ownership and size.

3. There are a number of potential advantages to be derived from entering into joint ventures. These can be divided into three broad categories, namely, internal uses associated mainly with cost reduction and sharing resources; competitive uses aimed at improving the firms' strategic position; and strategic uses aimed at implementing changes in the firms' strategic postures. Local partners in developing countries may derive major benefits from forming joint ventures with developed-country MNEs, including gaining access to new sources of capital and the transfer of technology, management and marketing skills. Joint ventures between developed- and developing-country firms may be an important factor contributing to the emergence of Third World MNEs.

4. All joint ventures suffer from a substantial failure rate, but the latter is even higher in the case of international joint ventures. Problems arise mainly because of conflict between partners over control of the venture; strategic objectives; and operating policies. The high failure rate enhances the importance of effectively planning, negotiating and managing joint ventures.

5. Despite the growth in non-equity forms of international business and in joint ventures, wholly owned subsidiaries remain the most important international supply mode – at least for larger MNEs. Foreign direct investment in wholly owned subsidiaries is now highly diversified in terms of source countries, and recent years have seen a rapid increase in the inward capital stake in the USA.

6. The main advantages of establishing wholly owned subsidiaries relate to control and competitiveness. The disadvantages are associated mainly with the high level of financial and management commitment and the associated risks. Because of this, the establishment of wholly owned subsidiaries may not be a feasible international supply mode for small companies, although it is one which should be considered at some point in the internationalisation process.

7. As for the other supply methods examined in this book, the effective planning and management of wholly owned subsidiaries is critical to success.

INTRODUCTION

The emphasis in the previous two chapters has been on forms of international market entry and development involving non-equity, contractual arrangements between unrelated concerns. This penultimate chapter examines the final stage in what is an implicit spectrum of international supply activity (see Figure 1.3.), namely, foreign direct investment in partially and wholly owned subsidiaries abroad.

Equity joint ventures (as distinct from contractual forms of joint venture activity discussed in Chapter 5) and wholly owned subsidiaries involve a greater capital commitment on the part of the firm and are, therefore, more risky financially than the alternatives considered previously. In addition, entering foreign markets through direct investment creates new management problems for the investing firm. Effective reporting relationships need to be established between subsidiary and parent company and this may require changes in the formal organisational structure of the firm. Decisions need to be taken regarding the allocation of decisionmaking authority, especially the extent of functional decentralisation in the areas of production, marketing, R&D, finance, etc. To varying degrees, direct investment will involve cross-national transfers of personnel and this will require an effective international human resource management policy to overcome the many problems commonly associated with expatriate employees.[1] Finally, assessment and management of political risk becomes more important in the direct investment mode of entry because of the higher capital stake overseas and the fact that subsidiaries may be subject to close and continuing public scrutiny by host-country governments, especially in developing countries.

The risks associated with the direct investment mode of entry and the greater commitment of financial and managerial resources will be a particular problem for the small to medium-sized enterprises with which this book is primarily concerned. There are, however, compensating advantages to be derived from this entry and development mode. While some degree of shared control may be necessary in joint ventures, both partially and wholly owned subsidiaries permit a higher level of parent-company control than the alternatives considered in previous chapters. This will be especially important for firms with proprietary products or technology. Establishing local subsidiaries may provide close contact with markets and customers, thereby facilitating deeper market penetration and higher market share. Captive export markets may be established through subsidiary purchases of material inputs from the parent company. Direct investment may, in addition, overcome some of the difficulties associated with other entry modes such as host-country import controls, restrictions on royalty payments and the problems of negotiating with agents and licensees. In the long run, direct investment may allow the possibility of establishing global strategies in production and marketing.

As in earlier chapters, both the general literature and the empirical evidence covering these two forms of international business are reviewed, the main focus being on the management aspects of negotiating, implementing and operating equity joint ventures and wholly owned subsidiaries. Although both alternatives involve foreign direct investment, the two need to be considered separately since the planning, negotiation and management of the former differ significantly from those of the latter. It should be noted that much of the evidence cited refers to studies of large multinational firms, with extensive international networks and global strategies. Most of this evidence, however, is equally applicable to smaller and non-dominant international companies entering into joint ventures and wholly owned subsidiaries.

JOINT VENTURES

It is important to define clearly the nature of joint ventures being discussed in this chapter since the term has become a generally used one covering a wide variety of collaborative agreements between firms. For example, Friedman and Kalmanoff in their pioneering study adopted a very broad definition of joint ventures as 'any type of association which implies collaboration for more than a transitory period'.[2] Similarly, Walmsley defined joint ventures as 'the deliberate alliance of resources between two independent organisations in order to mutually improve their market growth potential'.[3] According to Sukijasovic, there are four distinctive features of a joint venture, namely 'a community of interests involving doing business in common, the sharing of profits, the sharing of business risks and losses, and longevity of co-operation'.[4]

Although the pooling of resources and the sharing of costs and benefits are important characteristics of any joint venture, the above definitions are too broad for the purposes of this chapter, encompassing, as they do, most of the non-equity, contractual forms of collaboration discussed previously. This section is concerned with equity joint ventures which involve the creation of a third entity ('the child') through capital commitments by two or more parent companies. The working definition used is that of Harrigan, who defines joint ventures as 'partnerships by which two or more firms create an entity to carry out a productive economic activity and take an active role in decision-making'.[5] Somewhat similar definitions are provided by Tomlinson, according to whom joint ventures involve 'the commitment for more than a very short duration of funds, facilities and services by two or more legally separate interests to an enterprise for their mutual benefit'; and by Beamish, who defines joint ventures as 'shared equity undertakings between two or more parties'.[6] Although some of the characteristics of contractual and equity joint ventures are similar (e.g. pooling of resources, common objectives, sharing of costs and risks, etc.), the latter is distinguishable from the former in three main respects. First, a capital commitment and a sharing of ownership between two or more partners; second, the establishment of a separate legal entity ('the child'); and third, the sharing of management control, as well as ownership.

Although this section examines only equity joint ventures, a wide variety of activity still falls within even this narrow definition:

1. The joint venture may be in manufacturing or in the service sector.
2. Alternatively, it may have a narrower functional focus being concerned with some aspect of marketing, distribution, technology, R&D, etc.
3. The joint venture may be between two developed-country enterprises. More commonly, the joint venture will be between a developed-country enterprise and a local partner in a developing country, or between East and West. In addition, in recent years there has been an increase in the use of joint ventures by developing-country multinationals in their investments in other developing nations (see later).
4. The ownership relationship between parent and child may vary, with each partner having an equal share or with one being in a majority position. Alternatively, it may be a 'spider's web' joint venture linking many firms to one pivotal partner.
5. Finally, joint ventures may vary with respect to the distribution of decisionmaking between partners which will either be shared or with one partner accepting a passive role.

Trends in joint venture activity

According to Harrigan, joint ventures have a long history in international business, being used extensively by the merchants of Ancient Egypt,

Babylonia, Phoenicia and Syria to conduct overseas trading operations, and by the merchants of Great Britain during the fifteenth and sixteenth centuries.[7] The sharing of risks associated with overseas trade during this period was the main motivation underlying the early use of such joint ventures. During the late nineteenth century, joint ventures were used extensively in the development of the US rail network; while in the early part of this century, capital-intensive projects in the mining, oil exploration, metal refining and film production industries were jointly financed by two or more partners in order to share costs and reduce risks.

Most of these early joint ventures, however, took the form of portfolio investments with little or no involvement by investors in the management of the venture partnership. It has only been since the 1960s that equity joint ventures have emerged as an important form of international business, especially by developed-country enterprises operating in developing countries. Thus the proportion of new, wholly owned subsidiaries established by a sample of 180 US MNEs in developing countries fell from 58 per cent before 1951 to 37 per cent between 1961 and 1965, although increasing to 44 per cent in the period 1971 to 1975.[8] Over the same periods, the proportion of minority-owned subsidiaries increased from 11 per cent to 22 per cent and to 28 per cent. The use of joint ventures was even more common for 135 Continental European MNEs surveyed, with the proportion of minority-owned subsidiaries established increasing from 10 per cent before 1951 to 42 per cent in the period 1961–65. Over the same period, the proportion of wholly owned subsidiaries established in developing countries fell from 39 per cent to 19 per cent. A similar tendency has been identified for British MNEs operating in developing countries.[9]

Whereas the motivations underlying early international joint ventures were associated with risk sharing and the combination of financial resources, the growth in joint venture activity during the 1960s and 1970s was less voluntary. During this period, many developing-country governments introduced ownership controls which restricted the degree of foreign-equity participation allowed in local industries, and this was accompanied in many cases by the introduction of severe restrictions on the volume of imports. For developed-country firms, therefore, joint ventures with indigenous partners represented the only feasible method of entering many developing-country markets. According to Stopford and Wells, such joint ventures represented a trade-off between 'the quest for additional resources' and 'the drive for unambiguous control'.[10] Developed-country multinationals obtained several benefits from entering into joint ventures with developing-country partners, including access to indigenous management talent, knowledge of local legislation and market conditions, and market access. The sharing of ownership and control with local partners, on the other hand, complicated the integration of the joint venture entity into the company's wider international strategy. As various authors have shown, even so, it is possible for the multinational to retain control without 100 per cent ownership.[11] For the developing country, the joint venture offered an attractive method of obtaining technology, while at the same time participating in the ownership, management and profits of the venture.

Empirical evidence regarding the current importance of joint ventures in international business is limited and somewhat conflicting. Contractor and Lorange suggest that joint ventures have retained their importance over the last decade or so.[12] Compared with approximately 10,000 wholly owned foreign affiliates, US MNEs have between 14,000 and 15,000 affiliates in which the parent company holds less than 100 per cent ownership. Of the latter, there are around 12,000 affiliates in which the US parent has less than 50 per cent ownership. In other words, the number of minority-owned foreign affiliates is roughly equal to the combined total of wholly owned and majority-owned affiliates. Due to the generally smaller size of minority-owned ventures, however, over two-thirds of the value of US foreign direct investment is still accounted for by wholly owned subsidiaries – even though these subsidiaries are vastly outnumbered by shared equity arrangements. A recent study by Kobrin suggests that there has been no overall increase in the importance of joint ventures established by US MNEs in developing countries.[13] Based on a sample of 162 of the largest and most geographically dispersed US MNEs undertaken in 1985, the study showed that 62 per cent of subsidiaries located in developing countries were wholly owned. By contrast, only 18 per cent were minority-owned. The concentration on the largest US MNEs, however, may have underestimated the importance of joint ventures which, as later arguments will show, may be more common among smaller and less dominant international companies.

Although there is some dispute regarding the overall importance of joint ventures, there can be little doubt that the last decade or so has seen a significant diversification in the use of joint ventures by country and sector. Japanese direct investment in South East Asia – which increased rapidly during the 1970s – has largely taken the form of joint ventures. Host-country ownership controls and the need to spread the capital costs of investing in a number of countries simultaneously explain the preference for less than fully owned subsidiaries. Inward investment in Japan itself is also largely in the form of joint ventures. The People's Republic of China and Eastern Bloc countries are trying to stimulate equity joint ventures, as the previous chapters showed. A similar trend is evident in India and Egypt as discussed in Exhibits 6.1 and 6.2. Joint ventures between developing-country enterprises have increased in importance, with one estimate suggesting that 90 per cent of the foreign subsidiaries of Third World MNEs involve local equity participation.[14] International joint ventures are becoming more important in the service sector, especially in banking and finance.[15] Finally, there has been a significant increase in the formation of 'strategic alliances' between developed-country MNEs.[16] Although many of these take the form of contractual agreements (see Chapter 7), equity joint ventures are becoming more prevalent. According to Porter, the motivations underlying such joint ventures are less tactical (response to government pressures) and more strategic (to improve global competitiveness).[17]

EXHIBIT 6.1
INDIA'S CHILLY?

In 1985, the number of joint ventures between Indian companies and foreigners shot up, and the trickle of foreign investment into the country turned into a sizeable flow. This year, however, the Indian government's warm welcome to foreign companies has chilled.

After Mr Rajiv Gandhi came to power in late 1984, news of his more liberal economic policy (with attendant images of cutting red tape) brought droves of foreign executives to Delhi's grubby Palam airport. They found that some of what they had heard was true. The government was keen to get hold of foreign technology to reduce costs and update outmoded products. It had lifted controls on some industries, and opened up others which had previously been reserved for the public sector (like telecommunications). The laborious process for getting deals with Indian companies approved had been streamlined, and (most important) the bureaucrats were less hostile.

But they still found obstacles in their path. The government rarely allows foreign companies to put their own managers into joint ventures. Patent protection is poor. Foreign equity holdings are in effect limited to 40 per cent, except in companies making the highest technology, which the government will bend over backwards to get. Each technology-licensing deal goes through government boards which may beat the price down even after the foreign and Indian companies have come to an agreement.

Despite this, in 1985, the Indian government approved 1,024 foreign joint ventures, compared with 752 in the previous year. American, West German and Japanese companies making industrial machinery, electronics and chemicals accounted for most of the increase. One quarter of the approvals were for joint ventures in which foreigners took equity; the rest were technology-licensing deals.

Although foreigners are still interested in getting together with Indian companies – the number of applications for joint ventures is still rising – there have been many fewer approvals this year: 355 in the first six months, compared with 440 in the same period of 1985. The foreigners are victims of a battle going on in the government and the bureaucracy between those who want change (and think that foreigners can help bring it about) and those who find the status quo more comfortable. Mr Viswanath Singh, the finance minister, belongs to the first camp; Mr Narayan Tiwari, who was the industry minister until 22 October, when he became foreign minister, to the second. This year, the cautious camp is winning, partly because it is much bigger, and partly because Mr Gandhi is no longer pushing for change as enthusiastically as when he first came to power.

The liberalisers' arguments have also been shaken by the alarming jump in the trade deficit. The Indian government tries to ensure that any joint venture which requires imported parts becomes Indian over a specified period. But that does not always work. The Maruti car, produced by a joint venture with the Japanese carmaker, Suzuki, is now only 37 per cent Indian, not 50 per cent as required by the indigenisation plan.

The status quo lobby is strengthened by support from well-established Indian companies which are not keen to face competition from upstarts working with foreigners. Gillette's factory in India is at last going into production after opposition from big local blade-makers held it up for five years. But Pepsi's attempt to get into the Indian market is still stymied.

Source: *The Economist*, 25 October 1986, 80–81.

EXHIBIT 6.2
EGYPTIAN JOINT VENTURES

Investing

The socialist planning and nationalisation policies adopted by Egypt during the 1950s and 1960s severely restricted the flow of inward direct investment from abroad. Since then the foreign investment climate has improved considerably with the introduction of President Sadat's 1974 'open door' policy and subsequent amendments to this policy.

The Egyptian authorities now actively encourage joint ventures with foreign partners and a range of incentives is available to attract foreign investors back to Egypt. Especially favoured are export oriented and import substitution projects. Targeted sectors include: textiles; tourism; agricultural industries; construction; metals; engineering; and land reclamation. In addition, four free zones have been established at Port Said, Nasr City (Cairo), Al Ameriya (Alexandria) and Port Tawfik. The benefits on offer to companies locating in the free zones include exemptions from local equity participation requirements, exchange control regulations, most taxes, certain labour law regulations and other restrictions on foreign investment.

Seen in conjunction with Egypt's advantages of ample, relatively low cost labour and proximity to major markets in the EC, North Africa and the Middle East, these incentives make the country much more attractive to potential foreign investors. However, as in the case of importing, various obstacles to foreign investment still apply and several foreign owned firms (such as Tootal) have had unpleasant experiences in conducting joint venture operations.

The two main regulatory bodies governing foreign investment in Egypt are the General Authority for Investment and Free Zones (GAIFZ) and the General Organisation for Industrialisation (GOFI). Foreign investors must obtain prior permission from both organisations to make new investments, undertake expansions, remit profits and capital or receive incentives. GOFI evaluates a project's economic viability and then notifies GAIFZ which has final approval.

In evaluating projects, preference is given to joint ventures with Egyptian partners, although foreign companies may be allowed complete ownership in special circumstances.

Although the authorities have recently attempted to speed up the investment project approval mechanism, progress in this area has been slow: foreign investors frequently complain about the lengthy delays in obtaining approval from the regulatory bodies. General Motors, for example, initiated negotiations with the Egyptian authorities in 1983 for the establishment of an integrated automobile plant to supply European markets. In 1987 final approval for the project has not yet been given and there are doubts over its future. Other difficulties facing foreign investors in Egypt include the following:

- The problems associated with managing a joint venture in a state dominated economy.
- Competing imports from the black market.
- Restrictions on imported raw materials, parts and components.
- Competition from public sector enterprises able to sell cheaply on the domestic market because of subsidised inputs.
- Egypt's multiple exchange rate system which can often result in substantial exchange losses for foreign companies.
- Potential for conflict with labour unions.

Source: *Textile Outlook International*, November 1987, 18.

- Government legislation, especially in developing host countries, requiring local equity participation
- The increasing participation of small to medium-sized companies in international business, with joint ventures being used to reduce the capital cost and risks associated with international expansion.
- A greater diversity in the source-country distribution of MNEs and the greater willingness of non-US MNEs to enter into joint ventures.
- The increasing costs of technological development, with joint ventures being used to reduce risks and the costs of R&D.
- The growing intensity of competition, with joint ventures being used for strategic/competitive reasons.

Figure 6.1 Factors contributing to the growth of joint venture activity. Source: Derived from UNCTC (1987), *Arrangements between Joint Venture Partners in Developing Countries, UNCTC Advisory Studies*, No. 2, Series B, UN, New York, 1-13.

A number of factors have contributed to this diversity in the use of joint ventures and these are shown in Figure 6.1. The importance of these influencing factors will be examined in more detail in subsequent sections of the chapter.

While the above discussion points to an overall increase in the use of joint ventures, there remain significant variations in the willingness of different firms to enter into such partnerships.[18] Generally, companies manufacturing standardised products, diverse product lines and those engaged in vertical integration are more willing to enter into joint ventures, especially in developing countries. Joint ventures will provide such firms with access to local sources of raw materials and intermediates, as well as local expertise on marketing, political, economic and cultural conditions. By contrast, firms engaged in high-technology industries and those involved in global or regional integration of production are less willing to enter into partnerships. For such firms, the retention of complete ownership and control of foreign subsidiaries may be necessary to retain control over proprietary information and to allow integration. Such factors partly explain the varying propensities of multinationals from different source countries to enter into joint ventures. Thus, the greater willingness of European multinationals to engage in joint ventures can be attributed to their product and geographical diversification. This has encouraged looser control structures (including joint ventures) since no single product or area is crucial to success. Similarly, the concentration of Japanese foreign direct investment in developing countries in standardised, low-technology sectors (textiles, clothing, metals, etc.) partly explains the high incidence of joint ventures.

Advantages of joint ventures

The preference of many multinationals to retain 100 per cent ownership of their foreign subsidiaries in order to avoid the problems associated with shared decisionmaking has already been identified.[19] Joint ventures, therefore, are frequently seen as a second (or even third) best option, used only when government regulations (ownership and import controls, restrictions on royalty payments, etc.) prevent the establishment of wholly owned subsidiaries, exports or licensing. Indeed, as the next section shows, major problems do arise in the negotiation, planning and management of international joint ventures which often result in a high failure rate.

Despite such difficulties it is becoming increasingly recognised that there are major competitive and strategic advantages to be derived from the successful negotiation of joint venture agreements and that such collaboration may be a preferred option in many circumstances. Connolly, for example, argues that the assets of developed-country MNEs (capital, foreign exchange, technology, management and marketing skills, etc.) and developing-country firms (lower costs, greater familiarity with local markets, etc.) are complementary and that the combination of these assets in a joint venture results in mutual benefits.[20] Similarly, Contractor argues that the loss of control and the sharing of profits inherent in equity joint ventures is more than compensated for by the expertise and capital contribution of the local partner; contacts with government officials; faster entry into the market; and risk reduction.[21] Harrigan argues that joint ventures should not be seen as a hiding-place or as a sign of weakness.[22] Rather, if organised properly, joint ventures can be a source of competitive advantage, a means of defending existing strategic positions against forces too strong for one firm to withstand itself; or as a means of implementing changes in strategic postures (e.g. diversification; access to technology). Joint ventures allow each partner to concentrate their resources in areas of expertise, while enabling diversification into attractive but unfamiliar business areas. Overall, Harrigan concludes that joint ventures are an important strategic weapon in responding to the challenges of global competition.

A recent paper by Beamish and Banks[23] uses the internalisation and transaction-cost paradigm of Williamson to explain the conditions under which joint ventures may be more efficient than wholly owned subsidiaries. According to internalisation theory, firms would have a strong economic incentive to avoid joint ventures (as well as contractual arrangements such as licensing, management contracts, etc.) since these are inferior to wholly owned subsidiaries in exploiting the firm's ownership-specific advantages. Some of the problems associated with joint ventures (and contractual arrangements) include strategic risk, especially the problem of opportunism whereby the local partner may take advantage of the MNE's lack of complete knowledge; the transactions costs associated with writing, executing and enforcing the joint venture contract; and dealing with future uncertainty. In order to remove such difficulties, the firm should internalise the activity through the establishment of a wholly owned and controlled subsidiary.

According to Beamish and Banks, however, joint ventures which conform to certain preconditions and structural arrangements can provide a better solution to these problems than wholly owned subsidiaries. Although there will be transaction costs associated with contract writing, execution and enforcement, these will be more than offset by the enhanced revenue potential deriving from the joint venture. These arise through the potential synergistic effects of combining the complementary assets of the MNE with those of the local partner. While the MNE provides firm-specific knowledge regarding technology, management and capital markets, the local partner provides location-specific knowledge regarding host-country markets, infrastructure and political trends. The pooling and sharing of know-how also reduces the information costs of foreign investment, thereby allowing the MNE to reduce the problem of uncertainty at a lower long-term average cost than in the case of wholly owned subsidiaries. The realisation of these advantages depends on the establishment of an effective joint venture agreement which encourages mutual trust and the long-term commitment of both parties (in order to reduce opportunism); and supportive inter-organisational linkages covering mechanisms for the division of profits, joint decision-making processes, reward and control systems, and the effective pooling of resources.

As for the other forms of international market development strategy examined in this book, the advantages (and disadvantages) of joint ventures can be examined in relation to several key dimensions – financial and management commitment; degree of risk; the extent of control, etc. The potential advantages of joint ventures as identified in the literature are listed below.[24] Some of these are relevant mainly to joint ventures between developed- and developing-country firms, whereas others are more relevant to joint ventures between developed-country MNEs (or indeed between developing-country MNEs).

Financial commitment
Joint ventures may allow for foreign market expansion with reduced capital outlay. This may be especially helpful for small companies with limited financial resources for internationalisation; companies expanding rapidly in several foreign markets simultaneously (as with Japanese investment in South East Asia – see earlier), and for large capital- or technology-intensive projects where costs may be prohibitive for one company acting alone. This last point has been emphasised by Harrigan, with the increasing costs and sophistication of technology innovation required for global competitiveness

being an important motivation for joint ventures between developed-country MNEs.[25]

Synergy
Joint ventures may result in substantial cost savings and greater efficiency through the sharing of resources; the concentration of partners' efforts in areas of expertise; and larger minimum scale efficiencies. Potential synergies arise in numerous ways including the sharing of manufacturing facilities, technology and other physical assets; marketing synergies through the sharing of brand names, products, support services, distribution channels, sales forces and other marketing facilities; procurement synergies through sharing components, raw materials and other supplies, and innovation synergies through the sharing of laboratories, scientific personnel and R&D results.

Management commitment
The planning and negotiation of successful joint ventures will involve a significant commitment of managerial time and resources. The management commitment involved in the subsequent operation of the venture once established, however, may be reduced through the complementarities that exist in the assets provided by the foreign and local partners. For the foreign parent corporation, joint ventures with local partners may result in substantial savings with respect to familiarisation with local markets, business practices and government legislation, access to existing distribution channels, and establishing personal contacts with suppliers, customers and public officials. Management commitment may also be reduced through the specialisation of effort on a functional basis (technology; production; marketing, etc).

Risk reduction
The above savings (financial, synergistic and managerial) imply that joint ventures may be a less risky option than the establishment of wholly owned subsidiaries (see later). Additionally, political risks may be lowered through the involvement of local partners; the promotion of a local image; and established contacts with government legislators.

Control
Joint ventures will allow a greater degree of parent-company control than the non-equity, contractual agreements considered earlier, especially if the local partner adopts a 'passive' role. This may allow a greater integration of the venture into the global strategy of the firm. In 'shared', as opposed to 'passive' joint ventures, the extent of parent-company control will be constrained by the need to involve foreign partners in the decisionmaking process, although as stated previously the parent company may still be able to retain effective control even in minority-owned joint ventures.[26]

Long-run market penetration
Joint ventures may result in a greater long-term penetration of foreign markets than the alternatives considered in previous chapters. Reasons for this include the promotion of a local image; proximity to the market; market knowledge and other advantages provided by the local partner (see earlier); and potential access to government contracts. Furthermore, joint ventures may be used as a means of establishing captive export markets through 'tied' exports of parts, components, equipment, etc.

Other Advantages
Other potential advantages of joint ventures have been identified in the literature. Walmsley focuses on the 'clarity of purpose' which can be achieved through a clear statement of venture objectives during the negotiation process.[27] Similarly, the joint venture can operate unfettered by the problems experienced by the two partners elsewhere in their global activities. Finally, the flexibility of joint ventures has been emphasised, with the venture agreement being negotiated to reflect the desired inputs (capital, technology, etc.) and outputs (division of earnings between profits, royalties, etc.) of both partners.[28] As early as 1974, Drucker stated that 'the joint venture is the most flexible of instruments for making fits out of misfits'. In fairness, he went on to state that it was also 'the most demanding and difficult of all tools of diversification and the least understood' – a comment which is particularly appropriate for later sections on joint venture performance.[29]

The various uses of joint ventures have been classified by Harrigan[30] into three broad categories (see Figure 6.2): *internal uses* associated mainly with cost reduction and the sharing of resources; *competitive uses* aimed at improving the firms' strategic position through forcing their industries' structures to evolve in a favourable manner, pre-empting competitors and developing defensive strategies in mature industries; and *strategic uses* aimed at implementing changes in the firms' strategic postures through access to new technology or diversification. The potential advantages of joint-ventures are examined in Exhibits 6.3 and 6.4.

The above listing of the potential advantages arising from joint ventures has been devised mainly from the perspective of the developed-country MNE. Local partners in developing host countries (as well as the host-country economy) may derive important benefits from entering into joint ventures with foreign firms. These include the contribution made by the foreign MNE in terms of capital, technology transfers, and the transfer of advanced management and marketing skills. According to Connolly, such benefits will improve the competitiveness of developing-country firms, not only in their domestic markets, but also in foreign markets. Joint ventures therefore, could provide an important stimulus to the growth of Third World multinationals.[31]

A. Internal uses
1. Cost and risk sharing (uncertainty reduction)
2. Obtain resources where there is no market
3. Obtain financing to supplement firm's debt capacity
4. Share outputs of large minimum efficient scale plants
   • avoid wasteful duplication of facilities
   • utilise by-products, processes
   • shared brands, distribution channels, wide product lines, etc.
5. Intelligence: obtain window on new technologies and customers
   • superior information exchange
   • technological personnel interactions
6. Innovative managerial practices
   • superior management systems
   • improved communications among strategic business units (SBUs)
7. Retain entrepreneurial employees

B. Competitive uses (strengthen current strategic positions)
1. Influence industry structure's evolution
   • pioneer development of new industries
   • reduce competitive volatility
   • rationalise mature industries
2. Pre-empt competitors ('first-mover' advantages)
   • gain rapid access to better customers
   • capacity expansion or vertical integration
   • acquisition of advantageous terms, resources
   • coalition with best partners
3. Defensive response to blurring industry boundaries and globalisation
   • ease political tensions (overcome trade barriers)
   • gain access to global networks
4. Creation of more effective competitors
   • hybrids possessing parents' strengths
   • fewer, more efficient firms
   • buffer dissimilar partners

C. Strategic uses (augment strategic position)
1. Creation and exploitation of synergies
2. Technology (or other skills) transfer
3. Diversification
   • toehold entry into new markets, products, or skills
   • rationalisation (or divestiture) of investment
   • leverage-related parents' skills for new uses

Figure 6.2 Motivations for joint venture formation. Source: Harrigan, K.R. (1985), *Strategies for Joint Ventures*, Lexington Books, D. C. Heath & Co., Lexington, Mass., 28.

Reasons for establishing joint ventures: empirical evidence

A number of empirical studies have examined the reasons why firms enter into international joint ventures, and the results of these studies have been summarised in Beamish.[32] In his sample of thirty-four joint ventures in developed countries (DCs), Killing divided the reasons for creating a venture

EXHIBIT 6.3
JOINT VENTURES

Advantages and disadvantages

For the overseas investor, a joint venture with a UK partner may offer one or more of the following advantages over 'going it alone':

- Immediate access to the British partner's manufacturing facilities.
- Access to the British partner's business connections – an intangible advantage but one that cannot be underestimated (e.g. for government contracts).
- Access to the British partner's distribution chain – this can greatly speed up market penetration as building a sales/distribution network may cause substantial delays.
- Access to knowledge of the home market, its language and culture – cultural differences can often be perplexing for overseas companies.
- Access to first hand knowledge of UK employment practices, accounting conventions, legal framework and other local business methods.
- Reduced operating costs – because staff and facilities may be shared with other products.
- The ability to run the joint venture with qualified managers and staff – recruitment or secondment of staff is best undertaken in conjunction with a local partner, and the need to divert valuable managerial resources from existing operations may be reduced.
- Reduced capital costs – sharing risks (and rewards) is a sound business principle.

However, the joint venture route is not without its own risks which may include:

- Conflicting objectives of the joint venture partners unless the business is fully thought out in advance.
- Even if objectives are clearly defined, the partnership may not work smoothly or amicably.
- Lack of control compared with a wholly owned subsidiary.
- The risk of establishing a competitor in the long run.
- The local partner may not assign its best people to the venture.
- The possibility of inheriting work practices that are undesirable or alien to the overseas partner.

It is therefore important, when contemplating a joint venture, to consider carefully all the details and to understand the wealth of variations possible on the basic theme. To help in this, a carefully selected company is used to illustrate possible joint venture options. The relative merits and drawbacks are shown in order to assist overseas companies to select the route which is most appropriate to their own circumstances.

Types of joint venture

This document describes three of the many possible ways in which a joint venture involving equity participation may be structured. Though there are many variations, most joint ventures will broadly follow one of these patterns.

Exhibit 6.3 continued

1. The industrial joint venture
In this illustration, the overseas partner puts equity into an existing business, as well as technical expertise.

This presumes that a suitable UK company exists and that the directors and shareholders are willing to admit the overseas partner as a shareholder.

By investing in the equity of the UK partner, the overseas partner is participating in the existing activities as well as the new venture.

This option is likely to be most appropriate where the new product is an expansion of the UK partner's existing range or is closely related to the current products. Hence, there is less flexibility associated with this option compared with the other two.

2. The joint subsidiary
In this option, the British and overseas partners form a new joint operation to make a new product using new technology.

This is the 'conventional' form of a joint venture, where both partners are theoretically equal and the new venture forms a separate entity from either of them.

In practice, a 50:50 ownership structure is open to lack of management decisiveness and the partners may therefore choose a different ratio such as 51:49 to identify the intended leader of the new venture, with the rights of the minority partner defined in the legal agreement.

The joint subsidiary will normally occupy a separate building from the UK partner, or may be on a greenfield site. The latter gives the new venture much greater freedom and autonomy – it is free to choose the most advantageous location, it is not subjected to local constraints such as wage parity, union agreements etc. and it may use the UK partner's sales team (or not) as it sees fit. There is also less scope for argument over how overhead costs are split – all site costs are clearly the responsibility of the new venture.

There is also greater flexibility over the joint venture's product range, which does not necessarily have to be related to the UK partner's existing range.

3. The institutional joint venture
Here, the overseas partner forms a British subsidiary with funding and other forms of support provided by one or more British financial institutions.

The financial institution will, if required provide assistance with recruiting management, recommending professional advisers, obtaining government grants and other operational matters but without seeking leadership.

Source: WINVEST (1986), *Joint Ventures: Routes to a Manufacturing Base in the UK*, Welsh Development Agency, Cardiff, 3.

into three groups: (a) government suasion or legislation, (b) partner's needs for other partner's skills, and (c) partner's needs for the other partner's attributes or assets.[33] Beamish compared his own findings, based on a sample of sixty-six joint ventures in less developed countries (LDCs), with those of Killing and identified significant differences in the motivations underlying the establishment of joint ventures between developed and less

EXHIBIT 6.4
IS IT WISE TO ENTER INTO AN EAST–WEST PARTNERSHIP?

Yang Sze-Kao always felt quiet satisfaction as he walked through his machine room and upstairs into the modest office of his factory in Singapore. He wished that his father were still alive, to see how the family business had developed.

Under the name Ang Seng Pte Ltd, Yang senior had made cheap souvenirs for tourists. Meanwhile, his son had studied for an engineering degree while working in the business. But graduation day had been marred by the father's untimely death.

Yang Sze-Kao had persuaded his younger brother to take on the souvenir side of the business and, with loans from a Chinese bank and grants from the Singapore Development Corp., had worked extremely hard building up a light engineering business that specialized in making submersible drainage and sewerage pumps.

Limited market
The company had been successful, but its market was limited to Singapore and one or two of the other ASEAN countries. Yang was ambitious, and when his cousin Hsieh Yeong-Feong, who was Yang's own age and ran his own family manufacturing business, entered into a partnership agreement with an American manufacturer, Yang began to wonder whether he was fully exploiting the market potential of his highly efficient pumps.

'Our problem here in Singapore is a marketing and not a manufacturing problem,' Hsieh told his cousing when they met at the latter's home. 'We have sophisticated products. We have an intelligent and dedicated workforce. We have active support from government agencies. But how can we really compete in world markets with foreign international companies, many of whom are based in Singapore?

'I will tell you how,' Hsieh said without giving Yang time to reply. 'You must go into partnership with a Western company, as I have done. That way, you get the advantage of both their technical expertise and, more important, their well-established distribution networks.'

Yang thought about his cousin's words but did not react – until, six months later, three things happened in quick succession.

First, Universal Oil Corp. announced that it was beginning to drill for oil in the Far East. Its Singapore office asked Yang if he could develop his submersible heavy duty drainage pumps to cope with special problems the company expected to encounter in mangrove swamps, where it intended to set up initial drilling operations.

Second, a message was received from the Rotterdam Ports Authority in the Netherlands, saying that while they approved of the quality and price of some pumps that Yang was offering for installation in a docks development scheme, they were concerned that the Singapore company could not provide back-up facilities and maintenance in Holland to match what was on offer by Dutch and other EC suppliers.

Third, as though in answer to a small pump manufacturer's prayer, Yang received a call from Dieter Müller, chief executive of Kramer Pumpen, a large German pump manufacturer located in Düsseldorf, suggesting that they explore the possibilities of a partnership in Singapore that would work to their mutual advantage.

Exhibit 6.4 continued

Yang would gain the use of Kramer's European distribution network for certain lines that did not compete head-on with Kramer's best-selling models. Kramer, in return, would gain access to Far Eastern markets where it had not been too successful in the past. Yang would have access to Kramer's first-class research and development know-how and the companies together would set up an R&D facility in Singapore specifically to develop pumps for special uses, such as those required by the Universal Oil Corp.

Separate subsidiary?
Either the two companies could set up a separate subsidiary, in which each would own 50%, Müller suggested, or the German firm could take a 49% interest in Yang's company. Yang would remain as chairman and chief executive and he would have a German nominee as his second-in-command.

In the following weeks, Yang thought about these proposals. He also met Müller, who conveniently was on a world trip, and decided he could get along with the German. He realized, however, that on a day-to-day basis he would not be dealing with Müller but with some other nominee of the German company.

Yang's cousin Hsieh urged him not to hesitate. 'Do you, yourself, have the resources to develop the kind of pump required by Universal Oil?' Hsieh asked.

'Probably,' Yang replied. 'But it would take time.'

'Don't you think the Rotterdam authorities will be more inclined to buy from you if they know you are actively associated with a big firm within the European Community'?

'Possibly,' Yang said. 'I appreciate your concern.'

At first, he was much attracted to the idea of an association with the German company, which would open up prospects of faster expansion in world markets than he could achieve on his own. He was disconcerted, however, when an old and trusted family friend, Hu Wen-Yuan, warned him of the pitfalls of partnership deals.

'Partnerships seldom work,' Hu cautioned, 'particularly when the partners come together from East and West.

'Often what follows the honeymoon is not a happy marriage. There are a hundred ways in which the Western company can avoid supplying you with the technology it really wants to keep to itself. And there will come a time when you want to sell your own products in countries where you will be stepping on the toes of your partner.'

'Surely that can be avoided,' Yang suggested, 'if the partners are aware of the problems in advance.'

'How many couples believe, when they marry, that they will be unhappy?' Hu said. 'When you are thinking of divorce, then you will regret all the energy and effort spent on something that came to nothing.'

Yang respected Hu's judgement. He welcomed his advice, just as he had listened to the advice of his cousin. But it didn't solve his problem.

Should he climb into bed with the German firm or follow a different course – even if it meant risking losing both the Universal Oil contract and the Rotterdam order. If he took up the German offer, should he give the Germans a 49% stake in his own company or should they set up a separate subsidiary? Above all, how could he arrange things so that he would not face disappointment?

Exhibit 6.4 continued

Rather than simply respond to outside pressure, Yang Sze-Kao needs to set objectives more clearly in line with his firm's competitive strengths. It is imperative that he explore more options. And in weighing the costs and benefits of each, he needs to evaluate his firm's changing priorities and opportunities over time.

The sale of 49% to the German firm is attractive only if Yang is in serious trouble, e.g., where the products he is making are about to be replaced by more technologically advanced or otherwise more competitive ones, or where some other 'near disaster' looms. The problems associated with being the chairman and CEO of an operation with a foreign nominee could, however, significantly lower Yang's comfort levels, as well as his motivation.

If the nominee is well-versed in the issues of doing business in Singapore and works well with Yang, then it could be a happy relationship. But the uncertainty involved in probable changes in the representative from the German side, and the inevitability of differences in opinion between the two companies (particularly since they appear to have very similar, as opposed to complementary, product lines), would present Yang with a whole new set of cultural and operational problems. Excluding the possibility that he is contemplating exit from the business, the option of selling 49% of his firm's equity to the German interest would be ill-advised.

Yang should take a look at the possibilities of buying foreign technology, the costs of setting up service facilities in overseas markets and the availability of other distributors for his product.

One of his crucial market requirements is evidently reliable service. The Rotterdam Ports Authority was satisfied with the quality and price of his products, only questioning the availability of back-up and maintenance facilities in the Netherlands. Yang might be able to locate a suitable service organization partner in a field related to, though not in, submersible pumps, but would still have to solve his product development problems.

Pressure to deliver
With two major customers at his door, Yang is under some pressure to deliver. He needs to close these sales, but to do so in a way that will serve his longer-term interests. The option of buying foreign technology would help him close his 'R&D gap', suggesting that the prospects for purchasing technology from Kramer Pumpen for re-export might be explored. It is probably unlikely, however, that a foreign company such as Kramer Pumpen would agree to license its technology and provide a European distribution service network without a greater stake in the ASEAN markets.

Ideally, Yang should go it alone. This option offers the greatest possible rewards, and risks. Numerous Japanese companies have profited handsomely from long-term commitments to building international support networks independently. On balance, however, while going it alone is an option, it would probably require too much time and money for a small pump manufacturer such as Yang.

The joint venture with Kramer Pumpen for a limited scope of products provides the greatest number of advantages to Yang in the short term, and if properly structured and managed, offers longer-term potential as well. Some of the principal advantages include sharing of costs and quick access to Kramer Pumpen's distribution service network; conversely, profits would naturally have to be shared.

Exhibit 6.4 continued

Joint ventures, contrary to the suggestion in the dilemma, have traditionally been excellent conduits for technology flow to the less technologically advanced partner. Again, reference to the Japanese case is in order. Japanese firms have shown considerable skill at accessing foreign technology through joint ventures, at the same time often effectively precluding foreign partners from penetrating the local Japanese market when the foreign company's competitive advantage may have been strongest.

As a result, contrary to his friend's advice, Yang could very well use the joint venture as a means of upgrading his technical knowhow. He should also ensure that assistance on service in third country markets is clearly provided for in the joint venture's charter. One downside issue for him is that Kramer Pumpen could cut into his Asian markets. Further discussion on product scope and territories is called for.

Specifically, the joint venture should allow Yang to develop the specialized pump sought by Universal Oil, and to gain greater credibility in bidding on the Rotterdam project.

Final analysis
In the final analysis, Yang has much to gain, and relatively little to lose, by forming a 50–50 joint venture with the German company. In the best case, the joint venture would take advantage of Yang's greater expertise in the ASEAN market, bringing either Yang's current line, jointly developed products, or Kramer Pumpen products to a wider range of customers.

Yang would also be able to introduce his own products into Western markets via the Kramer Pumpen network.

The long-term viability of the joint venture perhaps depends most critically on the ability of each partner to manage the entry of the other's products into home markets. Yang could avoid a certain amount of potential conflict by advocating co-operation in markets solely outside Singapore.

Operationally, it is important for Yang to keep his joint venture partner somewhat at arm's length to allow for future flexibility should conditions change. Properly structured, the joint venture could leave Yang's options open for marketing other products in Europe or elsewhere. He should also go into the agreement with his eyes open and with the clear understanding that the joint venture may founder one day.

Source: *International Management*, October 1984, 16–18.

developed countries. As Table 6.1 shows, government suasion/legislation is a significantly more important influence on joint venture formation in LDCs compared with DCs, a result which is supported by the evidence of other studies by Janger, Gullander, and Tomlinson.[34] Such political influences on joint venture formation in LDCs ranged from the legal requirement to involve local equity partners, to seeking a competitive advantage in attaining government contracts through taking local partners.

Partners' needs for the associated enterprise's skills were an important reason for establishing joint ventures in both developed and developing countries, although they were more important in the former. The main skills

Table 6.1 Relationships of stage of development to venture-creation rationales

Rationale	Developed country (%)[a]	Less-developed countries (%)[b]
Government suasion/legislation	17	57
Skills needed	64	38
Assets or attributes needed	19	5

[a] Based on sample of 34 joint ventures by Killing.
[b] Based on sample of 66 joint ventures by Beamish.
Source: Derived from Beamish, P.W. (1985) 'The Characteristics of Joint Ventures in Developed and Developing Countries', *Columbia Journal of World Business*, Fall, **20**(3), 14.

required of local partners were knowledge of the local economy, politics and culture. Partner's needs for the other partner's attributes and assets (cash, patents, etc.) were only of marginal importance in developing nations' joint ventures, but were more important in industrialised countries.

A recent study by the UNCTC[35] emphasised the importance of both government legislation and the complementarity of partners' contributions to the formation of joint ventures by developed-country firms in industrialising nations. As regards the former, two types of government policy have been important. First, the introduction by many developing countries – including China, India, Indonesia, Malaysia, Mexico, Nigeria, Pakistan, South Korea and Sri Lanka – of ownership controls whereby foreign MNEs are allowed to establish production operations only in the form of joint ventures with local partners. Second, 'fade-out' agreements where foreign multinationals, already operating in the country, were required to reduce their ownership to a minority position over a period of time or, in some instances, almost immediately. For example, in 1973 the government of India introduced a Foreign Exchange Regulation Act which required MNEs in non-priority sectors to reduce their equity to 40 per cent or less. A similar policy was introduced by the Andean Pact countries under a Foreign Investment Code which required that MNEs with established manufacturing subsidiaries in the Andean Common Market should divest ownership of their subsidiaries to 49 per cent or less within fifteen years. While the UNCTC quotes evidence to suggest that both regulations reduced the flow of inward direct investment to these countries, the legislation has encouraged many MNEs to enter into joint ventures.

In addition to government suasion, the UNCTC argues that the complementary contribution of resources by the partners provides a firm basis for a viable joint venture between developed- and developing-country firms. The major contributions of the MNE is its manufacturing technology, product know-how, patents, business expertise, technical training and management

Table 6.2 Rank ordering of local partners' contributions to the joint venture

Rank	Contribution
1	Knowledge of the political situation, economy and customs of the country
2	General management
3	Access to markets for goods produced in the country
4	Marketing personnel and expertise
5	Local capital
6	Contacts and relationships with governments of host countries
7	Plants, facilities and land of local partners
8	Capability of recruiting local labour and dealing with labour unions
9	Access to local materials
10	Access to local financial institutions

Source: UNCTC (1987), *Arrangements Between Joint Venture Partners in Developing Countries*, UNCTC, New York, 18.

development. For marketing-orientated MNEs, significant contributions may be made in terms of product differentiation, trade marks, brand names, effective marketing programmes and training. The local partner's main contributions include capital, management, knowledge of the local environment and country, contacts with host governments, financial institutions, local suppliers and labour unions and local marketing capabilities. Referring to a survey of a hundred US MNEs, the importance of local partner's contributions were ranked in the order shown in Table 6.2.

Joint venture performance

Despite the potential advantages obtained by both (or more) partners to a joint venture, inevitable tensions do arise in the operation of such agreements which in many cases lead to failure. Such tensions stem from the simple fact that there is more than one parent company. This may result in difficulties with respect to the distribution of decisionmaking power; strategic objectives; and day-to-day operational control. Holton, for example, identifies two main reasons for joint venture failure: first, attempts by one of the partners to retain centralised control; second, disagreements over operating strategies, policies and methods.[36] As regards the first of these, the retention of centralised control may be necessary to integrate the joint venture into the MNE's global strategy. The failure to delegate decisionmaking power, however, will be resented at local level and will create pressures for decentralisation; whereas the MNE will be reluctant to delegate such power because of the interdependencies that exist between subsidiaries in different countries. The distribution of decisionmaking authority between the partners to the joint venture is also addressed by Killing, who argues that most successful international joint ventures occur when one partner is willing to accept a 'passive' role.[37] Tomlinson, on the other hand, argues that dominant control is not a necessary prerequisite for successful joint ventures since the sharing of responsibility is more than compensated for by the other contributions made by the local partner.[38]

A further main reason for joint venture failure concerns disagreements over venture objectives, strategies and management. Holton identifies nine major areas of potential disagreement: strategy; management style, especially the decisionmaking process; financial management; accounting and control methods; marketing policies and practices; production policies and technology transfers; personnel and industrial relations policies; R&D; and government and trade relations. In addition, there may be other differences of opinion regarding the contributions of each party; the distribution of rewards and their composition (profits, royalty fees, etc.); and the time-scale of the venture. Finally, in some countries, joint ventures may run into anti-trust problems.

Joint venture performance: Empirical evidence

Various studies have attempted to measure the stability of international joint ventures and the factors contributing to success or failure.[39] Estimated failure rates range from 30 to 61 per cent depending on region, with joint ventures in developing nations suffering from greater instability than those in developed countries. In addition, joint ventures involving government partners suffer from a higher incidence of failure than ventures with local private enterprises. The latter is explained by the fact that local private enterprises are better equipped than governments to supply skills essential to successful joint ventures.

In terms of the factors influencing joint venture success or failure, most research has focused on the control–performance relationship. Killing provides evidence that shared-management joint ventures underperform when compared with dominant-parent ventures, in which one parent plays a strong decisionmaking role and the other partner a minor one.[40] Independent joint ventures (in which the venture management team were highly autonomous from both parents) had the highest performance level of any of the three main types of venture. Janger, on the other hand, found little relationship between control and performance in shared and dominant joint ventures;[41] while opposite findings to those of Killing, as already stated, were reported by Tomlinson, who claimed that higher levels of return were obtained from joint venture investments with a more relaxed attitude toward control.[42]

A recent study by Kogut examined the mortality rate among joint ventures (both domestic and international) and the reasons for joint venture success or failure.[43] According to the author, joint ventures undergo a life cycle of creation, institutionalisation and eventual termination – which may be the result of either dissolution of the partnerships or full acquisition by one of the partners or by a third party. Based on a sample of 148 domestic and international joint ventures entered into by US companies, no less than 60 per cent had been terminated within a life cycle of six years. Of these, 57 per cent were dissolved, with 43 per cent being fully acquired by one parent or by a third party. International joint ventures suffered from a higher mortality rate than domestic joint ventures, with 68 per cent being terminated within a six-year period (the equivalent figure for domestic ventures was 56 per cent).

As far as the reasons for joint venture mortality are concerned, Kogut developed four main hypotheses deriving from previous research in this area. These were as follows:

H1: Dominant joint ventures are more stable than shared joint ventures.
H2: Joint ventures formed between firms which differ significantly in size are less stable because many additional problems arise.
H3: Concentrated settings will be more attractive for joint ventures because firms operating within oligopolies can focus on mutually desirable goals with greater ease.
H4: Ventures with a partner who has market access are more stable because access is a more desirable advantage than technology.

None of these hypotheses, however, was supported by statistical testing, which led Kogut to conclude that there were no simple explanations for joint venture failure.

Planning, negotiating and managing joint ventures

According to Holton, 'the rather dismal history of international joint ventures could be improved' by more efficient planning, negotiation and management.[44] There is an extensive volume of literature covering the negotiation and implementation of joint venture agreements and this is reviewed in the present section, from both a theoretical and practical perspective (the 'do's and dont's' of joint ventures).

One of the most comprehensive analytical models of joint venture activity is that developed by Harrigan. The model, which is shown in Figures 6.3 and 6.4, covers all stages in the joint venture partnership from first contemplating co-operation to the eventual dissolution of the venture, including the cost and benefits of co-operating; the bargaining agreement; the viability of the venture; the relationships between the two parent companies, parent and child, and the child and its environment; and the evolution of the venture over time.

The starting point in the model is to determine the circumstances under which joint ventures will be formed and how they will be structured. According to Harrigan, firms should undertake a cost/benefit analysis at the outset before deciding on whether to enter into a joint venture. As previous sections have shown, firms derive a number of potential benefits from collaborating. There are, equally, costs associated with forming partnerships

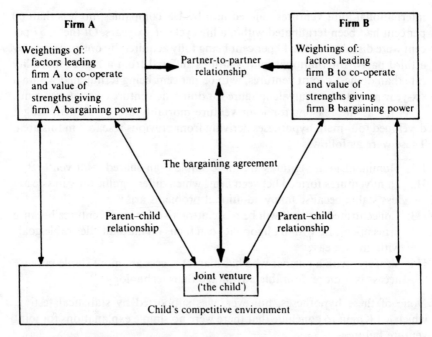

Figure 6.3 Partner-to-partner relationships creating a joint venture. Source: Harrigan, K.R. (1985), *Strategies for Joint Ventures*, Lexington Books, D. C. Heath and Co., Lexington, Mass., 50.

and a joint venture will be formed only if each firm believes that there is greater advantage in co-operating than there will be costs.

The negotiation of the bargaining agreement determines the structure of the joint venture, i.e. the child's domain of activities. Important components of the bargaining agreement include the determination of outputs (products, markets supplied, etc.); inputs (capital, materials, technology, human resources, etc.); control mechanisms (distribution of decisionmaking power, performance evaluation systems, etc.); and the duration and stability of the agreement. The form of the child (i.e. the bargaining agreement) is the net result of the bilateral bargaining power of its parents which in turn is determined by four factors: the resources contributed by the parent; the alternatives available for achieving their objectives; the need to co-operate; and barriers to co-operation (costs and other disadvantages). The greater the firm's resources and alternatives for achieving their objectives, the greater their bargaining power. On the other hand, bargaining power is reduced, the greater is the need to co-operate and the higher are the barriers to co-operation.

Finally, the model covers the dynamic aspect of joint ventures with a number of change stimuli precipitating either the renegotiation of the

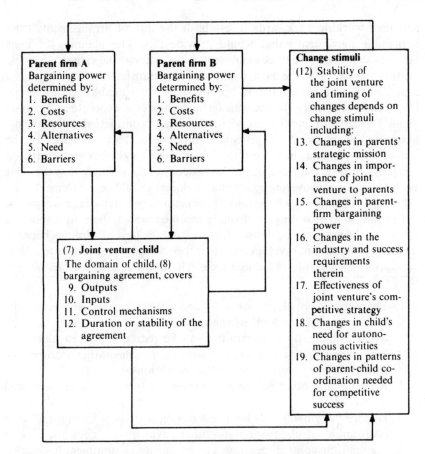

Figure 6.4 Model of joint venture activity. Source: Harrigan, K.R. (1985), *Strategies for Joint Ventures*, Lexington Books, D. C. Heath and Co., Lexington, Mass., 52.

bargaining agreement or an end to the agreement itself. Harrigan's model is then applied to a detailed analysis of the three relationships crucial to the success of joint ventures, namely, the relationships between the two parents, between parent and child, and between the child and its external environment.

Whereas Harrigan's model covers most aspects of the joint venture, Contractor's 'negotiations planning paradigm' is concerned mainly with the calculation of rates of return to the parent company from joint ventures with local partners in foreign (mainly developing-country) markets.[45] Rather than negotiating the joint venture agreement and then computing the extractable or repatriable cash flow (as is the practice in most companies), Contractor proposes a reverse procedure – targeting a particular compensation level and then working backwards to establish the mix of arrangements ('the bargaining agreement') that would provide this. The planning of joint ventures should involve three main steps. First, estimate the value to the joint venture partner and the host country of the transfer of technology and expertise. Second, determine an appropriate or reasonable rate of return from the host country for the transfer of technology, expertise and investment. Third, determine the mix of ownership and contractual arrangements best suited to achieve the target compensation level. This will determine the mix of repayments as between dividends, royalties and mark-ups on traded items. As regards the third stage, Contractor argues strongly that the joint venture agreement covering equity shareholdings should be supplemented by other agreements such as licensing or product supply/purchasing agreements.

In addition to providing an auxiliary income channel, there are important strategic advantages to be derived from mixing the flow of earnings between dividend repatriation, royalties and other forms of payment such as technical fees, profit margins on traded items, etc. These strategic advantages include the following:

1. The parent keeps all of the royalty and other payments, whereas profits are shared with the local partner.
2. Cyclical fluctuations in earnings can be reduced since royalties and other forms of payment are proportional to sales rather than profits, which are more sensitive to cyclical conditions.
3. Royalties and other payments are more easily audited and monitored than profits.
4. Dividend payments may be frozen during periods of foreign-exchange crisis and controls; royalty and other payments, by contrast, may be exempt from controls because of governments' commitment to contractual agreements and dependency on imported components, multinational exports, and technology transfers.
5. Finally, there may be important tax benefits in both home and host countries from mixing payments.

Practical recommendations regarding the 'do's and dont's' of formulating, implementing and managing joint ventures have been suggested by several authors.[46] Although there is some disagreement regarding points of detail, broad consensus exists on the various stages necessary for the establishment of successful joint ventures, and these are shown in Figure 6.5.

Joint venture objectives
A clear understanding of the objectives to be achieved by the joint venture is a necessary prerequisite for the implementation of successful partnerships. Is the joint venture expected to result in major competitive/strategic advantages (see classification of Harrigan reported earlier) or is the focus more narrow, e.g. access to restricted foreign markets? A specified time period for the

1. **Joint venture objectives**
   Establish strategic objectives of the joint venture and specify time period for achieving objectives

2. **Cost/benefit analysis**
   Evaluate advantages and disadvantages of joint venture compared with alternative strategies for achieving objectives (e.g. licensing) in terms of:
   • financial commitment
   • synergy
   • management commitment
   • risk reduction
   • control
   • long-run market penetration
   • other advantages/disadvantages

3. **Selecting partner(s)**
   • profile of desired features of candidates
   • identify/screening of candidates and draw up shortlist
   • initial contact/discussions
   • choice of partner

4. **Develop business plan**
   Achieve broad agreement on:
   • partner's inputs (commitments of finance; technology; management; etc.)
   • venture outputs (products and markets supplied; dividend and payout policy; etc.)
   • management style and decisionmaking processes (centralisation v. local autonomy; reporting relationships; etc.)
   • performance evaluation system (accounting and financial controls)
   • marketing policies and practices (marketing mix)
   • production and procurement policies
   • personnel policies
   • R&D policy

5. **Negotiation of joint venture agreement**
   Final agreement on business plan

6. **Contract writing**
   Incorporation of agreement in legally binding contract allowing for subsequent modifications to the agreement

7. **Performance evaluation**
   Establish control systems for measuring venture performance

Figure 6.5 Stages in planning, negotiating and managing joint ventures. Source: As reference 46.

achievement of objectives should be established in order to evaluate joint venture performance.

Cost/benefit analysis
Once objectives have been established, the costs and benefits of entering into a joint venture should be assessed, especially in relation to the alternatives

available for achieving the same objectives (licensing, etc.). Such analysis should be based on the criteria set out earlier, i.e. financial and management commitment; risk and control; synergy; long-run market penetration; etc.

Selecting partners

If it is accepted that a joint venture is the superior method of achieving the firm's objectives, the next stage is the selection of the venture partner. This would normally involve at least four separate stages as shown in Figure 6.5.

Harrigan recommends three criteria for the selection of appropriate joint venture partners.[47] First, the firm should consciously select its own partners rather than rely on requests from outsiders. Second, partners with previous experience of joint ventures should be chosen since there is a 'learning-curve' effect on co-operation. Experienced partners may be more flexible in negotiation than new ventures. Third, partners should be selected not simply in terms of their financial commitment. Rather, the choice of partner should be based on the complementarities which exist between the two enterprises in order to maximise potential synergies.

The business plan

According to most authors, the fourth stage in formulating successful joint ventures is the negotiation of the formal joint venture agreement. Holton, however, argues that the formalisation of the joint venture agreement should be postponed until the prospective partners have reached broad agreement on a business plan for the joint venture.[48] The premature involvement of lawyers in the writing of legal contracts has been identified by both Holton and Harrigan as a major reason why many joint venture proposals never go beyond the discussion stage. If the full implications of the potential joint venture have not been fully explored and agreed by the partners, this will become exposed during the formalisation of contracts. Although the legal aspects of contract agreements need to be left to lawyers, problems at this stage can be reduced if company executives have reached prior agreement on a business plan – which may be recorded in a memorandum of agreement or based on mutual trust and understanding. At a minimum, the business plan should provide agreement on the issues listed in Figure 6.5. As Holton argues, 'the business plan should not be viewed as a legal document, but rather as a discussion paper, or a series of discussion papers, in which every effort would be made to bring to the surface the expectations of the parties so that any inconsistencies in those expectations can be revealed and, if possible, resolved'.[49]

Negotiation of the agreement

Agreement on the broad business plan for the joint venture will be followed by negotiations between the partners on the precise details of the joint venture agreement, which will cover similar issues to the above. As Harrigan has shown, the eventual format of the agreement will be determined by the relative bargaining power of both prospective partners.

Contract writing
Once the agreement has been negotiated, it needs to be incorporated into a formally written and legally binding contract which should clearly specify the relationship between the two parents and between parent and child. In addition to covering the issues discussed previously, the formal contract should allow scope in at least three other areas. First, joint venture agreements should be designed not only as marriage contracts but also as divorce contracts specifying the conditions under which the venture can be dissolved. Second, contingency planning should be built into the business plan and the contract in order to take account of underperformance. Third, the contract should allow for changes in the business plan over time to account for unforeseen circumstances.

Performance evaluation
Finally, agreement should be reached between the two partners regarding an appropriate control system for measuring and evaluating venture performance, especially an advanced warning system to identify emerging difficulties.

The UNCTC[50] has developed a useful checklist as a guide to establishing effective joint ventures and this is shown in Appendix 6.1. It is suggested that the joint venture agreement should be comprehensive and cover all major aspects of the business, including the following:

1. The major goals of the partners.
2. Their contributions, responsibilities and obligations.
3. The equity share of each partner.
4. Means of financing the venture.
5. Products, customers and markets to be supplied.
6. The composition of the board of directors.
7. Procedures for selecting senior and middle management.
8. Provisions for technical training and management agreements which may be part of the joint venture.
9. Provisions for safeguarding patents, trade marks and technical secrets.
10. Duration of the agreement and ways of modifying it.
11. Management processes, including strategic and operational planning.
12. The control and information system.
13. Sources of supply for raw materials, intermediates and components.
14. Accounting standards.
15. Reporting requirements.
16. The audit and review of financial statements.
17. Means of settling disputes.

18. Policy regarding the declaration and distribution of dividends.
19. Procedures for dissolving the partnership and the distribution of assets.

Concluding comments on joint ventures

The discussion in this chapter has viewed joint ventures as a separate or alternative form of market entry and development from those considered in previous chapters. In many instances, this may not be the case. Joint venture contracts frequently include a series of related agreements covering the provision of associated services by one or more partner. These may include associated licensing agreements covering the transfer to the 'child' of technology, patents, know-how and trade marks and/or management contracts covering the transfer of managerial personnel and the training of local managers. The difficulties in negotiating an effective joint venture agreement, therefore, may be compounded by the need to establish associated licensing agreements or management contracts – and the problems these entail.

WHOLLY OWNED SUBSIDIARIES

The final stage in the implicit spectrum of international supply strategies examined in this book is direct investment in wholly owned foreign subsidiaries. As the international supply mode involving the greatest commitment of capital and managerial effort, the 100 per cent owned subsidiary involves a higher level of risk than the alternatives considered previously. On the other hand, wholly owned subsidiaries avoid the problems associated with negotiating contractual agreements (as in licensing, management contracts, etc.) and with shared decisionmaking (as in joint ventures). In addition, there may be important marketing benefits to be derived from establishing a greater presence in the foreign country.

Because of the high level of risk and the substantial commitment of capital and management, wholly owned subsidiaries are used most frequently by the larger international companies. The establishment of 100 per cent owned subsidiaries is, nevertheless, no longer the preserve of such companies and is increasingly being used by smaller firms, including those from developing countries.[51] The formation of a wholly owned subsidiary abroad is unlikely to be the first step in a small company's expansion overseas, as was indicated in Chapter 1. It will need to be considered as an option, however, at some stage in the internationalisation process. The comments in subsequent sections, therefore, although mainly applicable to medium-sized and larger companies, will also be of relevance to smaller firms and even to those in the early stages of internationalisation given the changed environmental circumstances of the 1980s.

Trends in foreign direct investment in wholly owned subsidiaries

Despite the recent growth in non-equity forms of international supply and in joint ventures, investment in wholly owned subsidiaries remains the most important international supply method – at least in terms of value of assets, if not in numbers. The last decade or so has seen a spreading of this supply method on a sectoral, size and nationality of ownership basis.[52] While the growth in foreign direct investment in wholly owned subsidiaries in the two decades following the end of the Second World War was accounted for mainly by large, US-based manufacturing MNEs, investment in services has increased significantly since then. Perhaps of more significance, there has been a very rapid increase in outward investment by non-US and smaller MNEs – mainly British, Continental European, Japanese and, increasingly, Third World MNEs. A significant proportion of this has taken the form of 'reverse investment' in the US itself, with the result that the US is now the largest single host country for inward direct investment, as well as remaining the largest source country. Table 6.3 shows the number of separate foreign direct investment transactions in the US between 1976 and 1986 as recorded by the US Department of Commerce.[53]

Several explanations have been offered for the rapid increase in inward investment activity in the USA in recent years[54] and these can be synthesised using Dunning's 'eclectic model' discussed in Chapter 1. According to the eclectic model, an increase in US inward investment would occur if both the following conditions applied:

1. There was an improvement in the ownership-specific advantages of non-US MNEs relative to US MNEs which allowed the former to compete more effectively in the US market.

Table 6.3 Number of foreign direct investment transactions in the USA, 1976–86: by source country

Source country	Number of transactions	Percentage of total
UK	1,572	17
Canada	1,557	17
Japan	1,480	16
West Germany	954	10
France	513	6
Netherlands	464	5
Switzerland	353	4
All others	2,383	26
Total	9,276	100

Source: US Department of Commerce, *Foreign Direct Investment in the United States*, International Trade Administration, Washington, various years.

2. The locational advantages of supplying the US market through direct investment improved relative to exporting to the US.

The US Department of Commerce has identified both ownership and location-specific factors as important determinants of the growth in inward investment as follows:[55]

1. A more widespread recognition among foreign MNEs of the size of the US market and a growing perception of the USA as a 'safe haven' of political stability in a turbulent world.
2 The emergence of large non-US MNEs with the ability to compete successfully in the US market.
3. Depreciation of the US dollar against a number of leading foreign currencies, reducing the foreign-currency cost of acquiring US companies, building new facilities, and expanding existing ones; dollar depreciation also increased the US dollar cost of exporting to the USA.
4. The narrowing of the gap in production costs between the USA and foreign locations, making investment in the USA more attractive compared with exporting.
5. Concern regarding possible US protectionist measures, which encouraged the establishment of subsidiaries in the USA to overcome trade barriers.
6. A relatively non-restrictive US policy towards inward direct investment, together with the active promotion of such investment by individual states, especially in the South.

It is interesting to note that whereas Japanese MNEs have entered the USA through the establishment of 'greenfield' subsidiaries, European firms have shown a higher propensity to acquire US companies. British companies, in particular, have made a very large number of US acquisitions in recent years, the performance of which has been disappointing in many cases.[56]

While the growth in foreign direct investment in America has attracted considerable attention recently, so too has the emergence of Third World MNEs such as Hyundai and Samsung of South Korea. Although most of the direct investments by such enterprises take the form of joint ventures in other developing countries, their investments in developed nations have been mainly in wholly owned subsidiaries. Such investments are limited, but are expected to increase significantly because of growing protectionist pressures.

Types of wholly owned subsidiaries

While wholly owned subsidiaries are characterised by complete ownership by the parent company, different types of subsidiaries exist and these may vary along several dimensions, including the following:

1. Nature of activity – as between sales/marketing, extraction, assembly and manufacture.

2. Orientation of the investment – market orientated; cost orientated and raw-material orientated.
3. Age of subsidiary – which may affect plant status.
4. Method of establishment – 'greenfield' or acquisition.
5. Subsidiary performance – and the measures used to assess subsidiary performance (cost centres v. profit centres).
6. Organisation and control – and centralisation/decentralisation of decision-making *vis-à-vis* production, marketing, R&D, etc.

Poynter and White[57] have developed a five-fold classification of wholly-owned subsidiaries according to the nature of the activity performed, the orientation of the subsidiary and its interrelationships with the parent company, and this is shown in Exhibit 6.5. Company size and the extent of internationalisation will be important determinants of the type of subsidiary established. For small companies and those in the early stages of internationalisation, their early foreign subsidiaries will be miniature replicas and/or marketing satellites. For larger MNEs and those adopting globally integrated and co-ordinated strategies, subsidiaries will tend to be rationalised manufacturers, product specialists or strategic independents.

EXHIBIT 6.5
TYPES OF WHOLLY OWNED SUBSIDIARY

Miniature replica	A business which produces and markets some of the parent's product lines or related product lines in the local country
Marketing satellite	Marketing subsidiaries which sell into the local trading area products which are manufactured centrally
Rationalised manufacturer	Where the subsidiary produces a particular set of component parts or products for a multi-country or global market
Product specialist	Where the subsidiary develops, produces and markets a limited product line for global markets
Strategic independence	Where the subsidiaries are permitted independence to develop lines of business for either a local, multi-country or global market

Source: Poynter, T.A. and White, R.E. (1984), 'The Strategies of Foreign Subsidiaries: Responses to Organisational Slack', *International Studies of Management and Organisations*, Winter

---

Advantages and disadvantages of wholly owned subsidiaries

As for the other international supply strategies examined previously, there are both costs and benefits arising from the establishment of wholly owned subsidiaries. The main advantages of this mode of market entry and development can be summarised under two broad categories, namely, the control dimension and the competitive dimension.

Control
Wholly owned subsidiaries allow for a greater degree of centralised control than any of the alternatives considered previously and this may provide a number of advantages to the investing firm, including control over quality standards; the internalisation of proprietary information; and the avoidance of problems associated with shared decisionmaking and the negotiation of contractual agreements. In the long run, the establishment of wholly owned subsidiaries may allow for the development of global strategies involving the co-ordination and integration of production and marketing in different countries.

Competitiveness
For a number of reasons, wholly owned subsidiaries may enhance the competitiveness of the investing company in foreign markets. Whereas exporting involves the transfer of products and licensing the transfer of technology, direct investment in wholly owned subsidiaries involves the transfer of a 'package of resources' (managerial, technical, marketing, financial and other skills). This may allow the company to exploit more fully its competitive advantages in the target market. Wholly owned subsidiaries may give rise to certain logistical advantages including the circumvention of tariff and non-tariff barriers and lower costs due to savings in transportation (as compared with exporting) and possible access to lower-cost factor inputs. Costs may also be reduced through the financial incentives made available to inward investors by many host-country governments.

Wholly owned subsidiaries may improve long-run penetration of foreign markets through the easier adaptation of products to local requirements; speedier and more reliable delivery; after-sales service; and closer contact with the market and customers.

The advantages of establishing wholly owned subsidiaries must be balanced against the disadvantages as compared with other forms of market entry and development. Wholly owned subsidiaries involve a greater financial and management commitment on the part of the investing firm. This may be a particular problem for smaller companies with limited capital and managerial resources. The higher resource commitment involved in establishing wholly owned subsidiaries increases the risks associated with this form of market entry and development. In particular, the issue of political risk becomes more important in the direct investment entry mode since wholly owned subsidiaries may be subject to close public scrutiny in many host countries. Finally, the establishment of wholly owned subsidiaries creates new management problems for the investing firm and these are considered in the next section.

Planning and managing wholly owned subsidiaries

The establishment of a new wholly owned subsidiary is one of the most important and risky decisions made by any firm. For small to medium-sized enterprises, in particular, the wholly owned subsidiary is a high-risk venture given the resource implications in terms of both capital and managerial time and effort. As with the alternative international supply modes discussed previously, establishing successful wholly owned subsidiaries requires effective decisions in a number of areas covering both the planning and operational management of the subsidiary (see Table 6.4).

Once the decision has been taken to set up a new wholly owned subsidiary (and this must be made by examining the alternatives available to the firm – see Chapter 7), the plant location decisionmaking process begins. This will normally involve at least four stages, moving from the choice of continent and country through to choice of site within a country and decisions regarding the size and timing of the investment.[58] A wide range of factors will influence the plant location decision, including the expected cost of the investment, the expected rate of return on the investment, the risk and uncertainty of the investment, and political and regulatory influences (see Figure 6.6). The above comments apply mainly to the establishment of new

Table 6.4 Decisionmaking checklist for establishing wholly owned foreign subsidiaries

Plant location	Choice of continent
	Choice of country
	Choice of site
	Size and timing of the investment
Entry method	Greenfield v. acquisition
Production/marketing decisions	Plant roles and inter-plant relationships
	Assembly v. manufacturing operation
	Products/markets supplied
	Subsidiary procurement policies
	Subsidiary R&D
Organisation and control	Subsidiary/parent company reporting relationships
	Locus of decisionmaking (centralised v. decentralised)
	Performance evaluation systems
Human resource management	Subsidiary staffing policies (home, host, third-country nationals)
	Expatriate policies
	Labour relations
Financial management	Financial planning and control
	Working capital management
	Capital expenditure management
	Corporate/subsidiary financial reporting responsibilities
	Repatriation
	Foreign-exchange risk management
	Transfer pricing
Political risk	Management of political risk

Cost variables
* Costs and availability of trained or trainable labour
* Capital costs as well as the cost of financing and/or the opportunity cost of the capital required
* The availability and costs of raw materials and services
* Transportation costs
* Productivity
* Home or host government policies
* Foreign-exchange considerations
* Impact of the new investment on costs of existing production

Variables influencing the expected return
* Market size and projected market growth
* Competitive considerations
* Foreign-exchange considerations
* Effects of the new investment on existing production

Variables influencing the riskiness of the investment
* Transparency and predictability of government policies
* Political and economic stability of the country
* The existence and reliability of safeguards incorporated in the contract with governments, as, for example, arbitration
* Flexibility for the company to divest or relocate its investment

Social and economic variables
* Investment climate
* Global politics
* Social responsibilities

Figure 6.6 Factors influencing the choice of plant location.

'greenfield' subsidiaries. Some attention should be given, however, to entry through acquisition. This may give speedier entry into the market, although 'greenfield' subsidiaries offer higher control. International acquisitions suffer from high failure rates and give rise to many problems.

Once the choice of plant location has been made and the entry mode decided, a whole series of decisions need to be made regarding the role and function of the subsidiary and its operational management and control as presented in Table 6.4. These include decisions regarding the production and marketing role of the subsidiary; parent company/subsidiary control and reporting relationships; staffing policies; financial management; and the management of political risk. Most of these issues also arise in the case of joint ventures discussed previously, e.g. determining the product/market role of the subsidiary; establishing control and decisionmaking procedures; and financial reporting. There are at least two areas, however, in which the management problems of wholly owned subsidiaries differ in magnitude from those of joint ventures, namely, staffing policies and political risk management.

As regards staffing policies, in a joint venture there may be some limited employment of parent-company nationals. Most senior management positions, however, will be staffed by local nationals, since the major contribution of the foreign partner is knowledge of the local market and business contacts. In wholly owned subsidiaries, on the other hand, the firm has a wider range of options regarding staffing, including the employment of home, host or third-country nationals. Each of these staffing policies has their own inherent advantages and disadvantages which have been discussed extensively in the literature.[59]

Regardless of the formal staffing policies adopted, most large multinational enterprises continue to employ a significant number of expatriates, with the evidence showing a very high failure rate among such employees.[60] Some of the major problems experienced by expatriates include the inability to adapt to a new working environment and culture and a loss of status or feeling of remoteness through working at the periphery. The main reason for expatriate failure, however, is family-related problems, especially the inability of the expatriate's spouse and children to adapt to a foreign culture. In order to reduce such problems, effective expatriate policies are required, covering recruitment, selection, pre-departure briefing, compensation and repatriation. While the number of expatriates employed in SMEs will be significantly lower, this is rising with the increasing involvement of such firms in international business. SMEs, too, will require to develop appropriate expatriate policies when establishing wholly owned subsidiaries abroad.

In addition to human resource management, the issue of political risk becomes vital in the case of wholly owned subsidiaries, which will be subject to closer and continuing public scrutiny by host-country governments, especially in developing countries, than the other market-servicing strategies discussed earlier. Political risk may be defined to exist when unanticipated discontinuities affecting corporate profitability and resulting from political changes occur in the business environment.[61] Such risk may be macro or micro in nature.[62] Macro risk exists when politically inspired environmental changes affect all foreign enterprises operating in the country (such as the 1979 Iranian revolution). Micro risk exists when environmental changes affect only selected companies or industries (such as expropriation of assets in the oil industry). A range of factors need to be considered in political risk assessment, including political stability, the foreign investment climate, attitudes of political parties to inward investment, restrictions on profit remittances, foreign exchange controls, taxation, expropriation, labour disruptions, and so on.

The effective management of political risk involves two important stages. First, the establishment of techniques and procedures for identifying and evaluating political risk. Second, the development of appropriate countervailing strategies to reduce risk. As regards the former, a number of techniques have been developed for identifying political risk. Some companies use sophisticated statistical models for estimating the probabilities of various political contingencies. Other, less quantitative techniques include the Delphi method, which solicits, collects, evaluates and tabulates the opinions of experts, and the 'old hands' approach whereby managers canvass the opinions of individuals possessing specific area or country expertise (including individuals both inside and outside the corporation). The use of outside consultants is becoming an increasingly important method of political risk assessment, especially in SMEs with limited internal resources for evaluating risk.

Once political risk and its likely impact on the firm have been identified, countervailing strategies for reducing such risk need to be considered. A range of options are available in this respect, including the threat of divestment, eliciting the support of home-country governments, legal defences, direct influence over host-country governments, establishing local allies, exploiting competition between host nations for internationally mobile investment projects, and so on. The success of such countervailing strategies depends on the relative bargaining power of host-country governments, on the one hand, and foreign firms on the other. Large, dominant multinationals may be in a strong bargaining position in negotiations with host-country governments and this may encourage the use of more direct forms of countervailing strategy (e.g. the threat to divest, direct political pressure). Smaller and non-dominant enterprises, on the other hand, may need to consider more indirect responses such as forming local allies and home-country government support.

FURTHER READING

1. Recent studies in joint venture activity, their advantages and disadvantages and guidelines for establishing successful joint ventures are discussed in United Nations Centre on Transnational Corporations (1987), *Arrangements Between Joint Venture Partners in Developing Countries, UNCTC Advisory Studies*, No. 2, Series B, UN, New York.
2. Theoretical analyses of joint ventures are to be found in Harrigan, K.R. (1985), *Strategies for Joint Ventures*, Lexington Books, D.C. Heath and Co., Lexington, Mass.; Harrigan, K.R. (1984), 'Joint Ventures and Global Strategies', *Columbia Journal of World Business*, Summer, 19(2); Contractor, F.J. (1984), 'Strategies for Structuring Joint Ventures: A Negotiations Planning Paradigm', *Columbia Journal of World Business*, Summer, 19(2); Beamish, P.W. and Banks, J.C. (1987), 'Equity Joint Ventures and the Theory of the Multinational Enterprise', *Journal of International Business Studies*, Summer, 18(2).
3. Practical recommendations regarding the planning, negotiation and implementation of joint ventures can be found in UNCTC, *Arrangements Between Joint Venture Partners*; Walmsley, J. (1982), *Handbook of International Joint Ventures*, Graham & Trotman, London; Holton, R.H. (1981), 'Making International Joint Ventures Work', in Otterbeck, L. (ed.), *The Management of Headquarter-*

Subsidiary Relationships in Multinational Corporations, Gower, Aldershot, 255–6; Killing, J.P. (1982), 'How to Make a Global Joint Venture Work', *Harvard Business Review,* May–June, 120–7.

4. A special issue of *Management International Review* entitled 'Co-operative Strategies in International Business' covers many of the topics discussed in this and in other chapters. See *Management International Review,* Vol. 28, 1988.

5. The growth of Third World MNEs, which has been mentioned on a few occasions in this chapter, is discussed in more detail in UNCTC, *Arrangements Between Joint Venture Partners;* Wells, L.T. (1983), *Third World Multinationals,* MIT Press, Cambridge, Mass.; Lall, S. (1983), *The New Multinationals: The Spread of Third World Enterprises,* John Wiley, New York.

6. The management problems involved in establishing wholly owned subsidiaries have been discussed only briefly in this chapter. For a more detailed discussion see Rugman, A.M., Lecraw, D.J. and Booth, L.D., (1985), *International Business: Firm and Environment,* McGraw-Hill, New York; Robock, S.H. and Simmonds, K. (1989), *International Business and Multinational Enterprises,* 4th Edition, Irwin, Homewood, Ill.; Globerman, S. (1986), *Fundamentals of International Business Management,* Prentice Hall, Inc., Englewood Cliffs, N.J.; Negandhi, A.R. (1987), *International Management,* Allyn & Bacon, Boston.

QUESTIONS FOR DISCUSSION

1. How would you distinguish equity joint ventures from non-equity, contractual forms of international collaboration? What factors have contributed to the growth and diversity of joint venture activity since the 1960s?

2. To what extent can joint ventures result in *competitive* and *strategic* advantages as opposed to simple cost reduction and resource sharing?

3. What advice would you give to a local enterprise in a developing country entering into a joint venture agreement with a developed-country MNE?

4. Is the establishment of wholly owned subsidiaries abroad an appropriate international market development mode for small and non-dominant MNEs?

5. What advice would you give to a company establishing its first wholly owned subsidiary in a foreign country?

NOTES AND REFERENCES

1. See Tung, R.L. (1981), 'Selection and Training of Personnel for Overseas Assignments', *Columbia Journal of World Business,* **16**(1), 68–78.

2. Friedman, W. and Kalmanoff, G., (1961), *Joint International Business Ventures,* Columbia University Press, New York and London, 6.

3. Walmsley, J. (1984), 'International Joint Ventures', paper presented at UK Academy of International Business Conference, Bradford, April, 4. Also see Walmsley, J. (1982), *Handbook of International Joint Ventures,* Graham & Trotman, London.

4. Sukijasovic, M. (1970), 'Foreign Investment in Yugoslavia', in Litvak, I.A. and Maule, C.J. (eds), *Foreign Investment: The Experience of Host Countries,* Praeger, London, quoted in Artisien, P. (1985), *Joint Ventures in Yugoslav Industry,* Gower, Aldershot.

5. Harrigan, K.R. (1984), 'Joint Ventures and Global Strategies', *Columbia Journal of World Business*, Summer, **19**(2), 7.
6. Tomlinson, J.W.C. (1970), *The Joint Venture Process in International Business: India and Pakistan*, MIT Press, Cambridge, Mass., 8; Beamish, P.W. and Banks, J.C. (1987), 'Equity Joint Ventures and the Theory of the Multinational Enterprise', *Journal of International Business Studies*, Summer, **18**(2), 1-16.
7. Harrigan, K.R. (1985), *Strategies for Joint Ventures*, Lexington Books, D.C. Heath & Co., Lexington, Mass., 5.
8. United Nations Centre on Transnational Corporations (1987), *Arrangements Between Joint Venture Partners in Developing Countries*, UNCTC Advisory Studies, No.2, Series B, UN, New York, 2.
9. Dunning, J.H. and Cantwell, J. (1982), 'Joint Ventures and Non-Equity Involvement by British Firms with Particular Reference to Developing Countries: An Exploratory Study', *University of Reading Discussion Papers in International Investment and Business Studies*, No.63.
10. Stopford, J.M. and Wells, L.T., Jr., (1972), *Managing the Multinational Enterprise*, Basic Books, New York.
11. Ibid.
12. Contractor, F.J. and Lorange, P. (1988), 'Competition vs. Cooperation: A Benefit/Cost Framework for Choosing Between Fully-Owned Investments and Cooperative Relationships', *Management International Review*, Special Issue, **28**, 5–18.
13. Kobrin, S.J. (1988), 'Trends in Ownership of American Manufacturing Subsidiaries in Developing Countries: An Inter-Industry Analysis', *Management International Review*, Special Issue, **28**, 73–84.
14. See UNCTC, *Arrangements Between Joint Venture Partners in Developing Countries*, 5, reporting Wells, L.T., (1983); *Third World Multinationals*, MIT Press, Cambridge, Mass., and Lall, S. (1983), *The New Multinationals: The Spread of Third World Enterprises*, John Wiley, New York.
15. See, for example, *The Banker*, November 1981, 197, which lists a total of twenty-nine joint venture banks in the City of London involving partners of different nationalities.
16. See, for example, Porter, M. (1986), *Competition in Global Industries*, Harvard Business School Press, Boston, Chapters 10 and 11; also, see references in Chapter 7.
17. Porter, *Competition in Global Industries*, 315.
18. This section is taken from UNCTC, *Arrangements Between Joint Venture Partners in Developing Countries*, 1–13.
19. See, for example, Holton, R.H. (1981), 'Making International Joint Ventures Work', in Otterbeck, L. (ed.), *The Management of Headquarter-Subsidiary Relationships in Multinational Corporations*, Gower, Aldershot, 255.
20. Connolly, S.G. (1984), 'Joint Ventures with Third World Multinationals: A New Form of Entry to International Markets', *Columbia Journal of World Business*, Summer, **19**(2), 18–22.
21. Contractor, F.J. (1984), 'Strategies for Structuring Joint Ventures: A Negotiations Planning Paradigm', *Columbia Journal of World Business*, Summer, **19**(2), 30.
22. Harrigan, *Strategies for Joint Ventures*, 29–36.
23. Beamish and Banks, 'Equity Joint Ventures and the Theory of the Multinational Enterprise'.
24. This section is derived from Walmsley, *Handbook of International Joint Ventures*; Harrigan, *Strategies for Joint Ventures*; Tomlinson, *The Joint Venture Process in*

International Business; UNCTC, *Arrangements Between Joint Venture Partners in Developing Countries*; Contractor and Lorange, 'Competition vs. Co-operation'; Holton, 'Making International Joint Ventures Work'; Connolly, 'Joint Ventures with Third World Multinationals'; and Beamish and Banks, 'Equity Joint Ventures and the Theory of the Multinational Enterprise'.

25. Harrigan, 'Joint Ventures and Global Strategies', 13.
26. Stopford and Wells, *Managing the Multinational Enterprise*.
27. Walmsley, 'International Joint Ventures', 4.
28. Ibid., 4.
29. Drucker, P. (1974), *Management: Tasks, Responsibilities, Promises*, Harper and Row, New York, 720.
30. Harrigan, *Strategies for Joint Ventures*, 29–36.
31. Connolly, 'Joint Ventures With Third World Multinationals'.
32. Beamish, P.W. (1985), 'The Characteristics of Joint Ventures in Developed and Developing Countries', *Columbia Journal of World Business*, Fall, **20**(3), 13–19.
33. Killing, J.P. (1982), 'How to Make a Global Joint Venture Work', *Harvard Business Review*, May–June, 120–7.
34. Janger, A.R. (1980), *Organisation of International Joint Ventures*, Conference Board, New York; Gullander, S.O. (1975), 'An Exploratory Study of Inter-Firm Co-operation of Swedish Firms', PhD Thesis, Columbia University; Tomlinson, *The Joint Venture Process in International Business*.
35. UNCTC, *Arrangements Between Joint Venture Partners in Developing Countries*.
36. Holton, 'Making International Joint Ventures Work', 255–68.
37. Killing, 'How to Make a Global Joint Venture Work'.
38. Tomlinson, *The Joint Venture Process in International Business*.
39. For a good summary see the special issue of *Management International Review*, **28**, 1988.
40. Killing, 'How to Make a Global Joint Venture Work'.
41. Janger, *Organisation of International Joint Ventures*.
42. Tomlinson, *The Joint Venture Process in International Business*.
43. Kogut, B. (1988) 'A Study of the Life Cycle of Joint Ventures', *Management International Review*, Special Issue 88, **28**, 39–52.
44. Holton, 'Making International Joint Ventures Work', 255.
45. Contractor, 'Strategies for Structuring Joint Ventures'.
46. See, for example, Walmsley, *Handbook of International Joint Ventures*; Harrigan, *Strategies for Joint Ventures*; UNCTC, *Arrangements Between Joint Venture Partners in Developing Countries*; Holton, 'Making International Joint Ventures Work'; Connolly, 'Joint Ventures with Third World Multinationals'; Contractor, 'Strategies for Structuring Joint Ventures'; Beamish and Banks, 'Equity Joint Ventures and the Theory of the Multinational Enterprise'.
47. Harrigan, *Strategies for Joint Ventures*, 355–6.
48. Holton, 'Making International Joint Ventures Work', 265.
49. Ibid., 265.
50. UNCTC, *Arrangements Between Joint Venture Partners in Developing Countries*, 30–2.
51. The growth of Third World MNEs is examined in Wells, *Third World Multinationals*; and Lall, *The New Multinationals*.
52. A discussion of trends in the growth and characteristics of foreign direct investment can be found in Hood, N. and Young, S. (1979), *The Economics of Multinational Enterprise*, Longman, London; United Nations Centre on Transnational Corporations (1985), *Transnational Corporations in World Development: Third Survey*, United Nations, New York; Dunning, J.H. (1983), 'Changes

in the Level and Structure of International Production: The Last One Hundred Years', in Casson, M. (ed.), *The Growth of International Business*, George Allen & Unwin, London; Stopford, J.M. and Dunning, J.H. (1983), *Multinationals: Company Performance and Global Trends*, Macmillan, London.

53. US Department of Commerce, *Foreign Direct Investment in the United States*, International Trade Administration, Washington, various years.

54. A number of studies have examined the growth of foreign direct investment in the USA: Ajami, R. and Ricks, D. (1981), 'Motives of Non-American Firms Investing in the US', *Journal of International Business Studies*, Winter, **12**(3), 25–34. Ajami, R. and Ricks, D. (1986), 'Foreign Direct Investment in the US: 1974–1984', *Journal of International Business Studies*, Fall, **18**(3), 149–54. Franko, L.G. (1976), *The European Multinationals*, Harper and Row, London. Franko, L.G. (1978), 'Multinationals: The End of US Dominance', *Harvard Business Review*, Nov–Dec, 93. Gray, H.P. (ed.), (1986), *Uncle Sam As Host*, JAI Press, Greenwich, Conn. Hood, N. (1986), 'Role and Structure of British Multinationals', in Macharzina, K. and Staehle, W.H. (eds), *European Approaches to International Management*, de Gruyter, Berlin, 79–92. Hood, N. and Young, S. (1980), 'Recent Patterns of Foreign Direct Investment by British Multinational Enterprises in the United States', *National Westminster Bank Quarterly Review*, May. US Department of Commerce (1984), *International Direct Investment: Global Trends and the US Role*, International Trade Administration, Washington.

55. US Department of Commerce, *International Direct Investment*.

56. Hamill, J. (1988), 'British Acquisitions in the US', *Strathclyde International Business Unit*, Working Paper No.88/2.

57. Poynter, T.A. and White, R.E. (1984), 'The Strategies of Foreign Subsidiaries: Responses to Organisational Slack', *International Studies of Management and Organisations*, Winter.

58. See, for example, Guisinger, S.E. and Associates (1985), *Investment Incentives and Performance Requirements: Patterns of International Trade, Production and Investment*, Praeger, New York; Organisation for Economic Cooperation and Development (1981), *Relationship of Incentives and Disincentives to International Investment Decisions*, USA-BIAC Committee on International Investment and Multinational Enterprise, OECD.

59. See, for example, Hamill, J. (1987), 'International Human Resource Management in British Multinationals', *Strathclyde International Business Unit*, Working Paper 87/1.

60. Ibid.

61. This definition of political risk is based on the views expressed by Thunell, L. (1977), *Political Risks in International Business*, Praeger, New York; Robock, S. and Simmonds, K. (1989), *International Business and Multinational Enterprises*, 4th edition, Irwin, Homewood, Ill.

62. A good summary of these two aspects of political risk management can be found in Globerman, S. (1986), *Fundamentals of International Business Management*, Prentice Hall, Inc., Englewood Cliffs, N.J., Chapter 5.

APPENDIX 6.1
OUTLINE OF MAJOR ASPECTS OF A JOINT VENTURE AGREEMENT

The following presents a comprehensive list of factors that could be included in joint venture agreements. It should be pointed out, however, that all of these aspects do not necessarily apply to every joint venture agreement.

1. Purpose and character of a joint venture:
   (a) major goals/strategy of foreign partner;
   (b) major goals/strategy of local partner;
   (c) products/industries/markets/customers served.

2. Contributions of each partner:
   (a) capital;
   (b) existing land, plant, warehouse, offices, other facilities;
   (c) manufacturing design, processes, technical know-how;
   (d) product know-how;
   (e) patents and trade marks;
   (f) managerial, production, marketing, financial, organisational and other expertise;
   (g) technical assistance and training;
   (h) management development;
   (i) local relationships with government, financial institutions, customers, suppliers, etc.

3. Responsibilities and obligations of each partner:
   (a) procurement and installation of machinery and equipment;
   (b) construction, modernisation of machinery and equipment;
   (c) production operations;
   (d) recruitment and training of workers and foremen;
   (e) quality control;
   (f) relationships with labour unions;
   (g) research and development;
   (h) general, financial, marketing, personnel and other management;
   (i) continuous training of personnel.

4. Equity ownership:
   (a) equity granted to foreign partner for manufacturing and product technology and industrial property rights;
   (b) equity granted to local partner for land, plants, warehouses, facilities, etc.;
   (c) ownership share of foreign partner;
   (d) ownership share of local partner.

5. Capital structure:
   (a) equity capital;
   (b) loan capital, national and foreign;
   (c) working capital;
   (d) provisions for raising future loan funds;
   (e) loan guarantees by partners;
   (f) future increase in equity capital;
   (g) transfers of shares of stock, including limitations.

6. Management:
   (a) appointment/composition/authority of the board of directors;
   (b) appointment and authority of executive officers;
   (c) expatriate managers, technicians and staff;
   (d) right of veto of appointment of officers and key decisions;
   (e) development of local managers, including time schedule;
   (f) organisation;
   (g) strategic and operational planning;
   (h) information system;
   (i) control procedures.

7. Supplementary agreements:
   (a) licensing and technology agreements;
   (b) management contracts;
   (c) technical service agreements;
   (d) allocation of foreign partner's corporate óverhead to affiliate.

8. Managerial policies:
   (a) declaration of dividends;
   (b) reinvestment of earnings;
   (c) source of supply of materials, intermediates and components, including price, quality, assurance of delivery;
   (d) major marketing programmes, including product lines, trade marks, brand names, distribution channels, promotion, pricing, service and expenditures;
   (e) export markets and commitments;
   (f) executive compensation and bonuses.

9. Accounting and financial statements:
   (a) accounting standards;
   (b) financial statements in currencies of host and foreign countries;
   (c) reporting requirements;
   (d) audit and review of financial statements.

10. Settlement of disputes:
    (a) board of directors and executive committee;
    (b) mediation;
    (c) arbitration.

11. Legal matters:
    (a) relevant local laws, regulations and policies;
    (b) governmental approvals required;
    (c) articles and by-laws of incorporation;
    (d) anti-trust considerations;
    (e) tax laws and considerations;
    (f) selection of legal counsel;
    (g) use of courts of host country.

7

CHOOSING THE MARKET ENTRY AND DEVELOPMENT STRATEGY

SUMMARY

1. The choice of foreign market entry and development strategy is a 'frontier issue' in international marketing, with the method of market servicing likely to have a major impact on a company's performance overseas and, indeed, on overall corporate performance. Choosing the most effective market supply strategy, however, is one of the most complex decisions facing the international firm. Choosing the most appropriate strategy will involve trade-offs between objectives. A firm may have multiple objectives in entering and developing a new foreign market (including non-profit objectives) and these must be included in any model of the entry strategy choice.

2. Three different approaches have been applied to the entry and development mode decision, namely, the *economic approach*; the *stages-of-development approach*; and the *business-strategy approach*.

3. The economic approach emphasises rational behaviour, with the costs and benefits of different entry and development modes being compared, to identify those options which maximise long-run profits. The degree of control available in different entry strategies is central to the economic approach since this determines both risk and the rate of return available. High-control entry modes increase return, but also risk. Low-control modes reduce resource commitment and thereby risk, but at the expense of return. Choosing the most efficient entry mode, therefore, involves rational trade-offs between control, resource commitment, risk and return.

4. The stages-of-development approach relates the entry mode decision to the internationalisation process. A shift towards entry and development strategies requiring greater resource (financial and managerial) commitment occurs over time with the increasing internationalisation of the firm.

5. Both of these approaches assume rational decisionmaking. The business strategy approach, on the other hand, emphasises the pragmatic nature of decisionmaking in most organisations which arises from uncertainty and the need for consensus.

6. The alternative international market supply model developed in this chapter recognises that firms may have multiple objectives in expanding abroad and that conflicts will exist between these objectives. The most appropriate strategy is the one which best results in the simultaneous achievement of multiple objectives, taking into account the relative costs and risks of alternative entry methods. A six-stage procedure for evaluating the relative attractiveness of different supply strategies is suggested.

7. Strategic alliances between global competitors, including small and non-dominant

firms operating in global industries, have become very popular in recent years. While there are a number of similarities between such alliances and the forms of international activity examined in previous chapters, there are also a number of important differences. This implies that new guidelines for planning and negotiating international strategic alliances need to be developed.

INTRODUCTION

Previous chapters of this book have examined in detail each of the foreign market entry and development strategies available to international firms, their advantages and disadvantages, and management implications regarding planning, negotiation and implementation. This final chapter synthesises the previous discussion by developing a foreign market entry and development model to assist managers in choosing the supply mode most appropriate for their company in a particular target market. The model builds on previous attempts at establishing entry and development mode selection criteria – some of which were briefly reviewed in Chapter 1.

Problems in choosing the foreign market entry and development strategy

It is very clear that the international supply strategy chosen can have a major impact on a company's performance in foreign markets, because of the costs, revenue, risk and control implications of the various alternatives (see Chapter 1). Choosing the most effective entry and development mode, however, is one of the most complex decisions facing the international firm. As should be obvious from the remarks in previous chapters, each of the alternative strategies has its own inherent advantages and disadvantages, with the choice of strategy being influenced by a range of often conflicting forces. The choice of strategy, therefore, will inevitably involve certain trade-offs between, for example, the extent of control available and the costs and riskiness of the alternative chosen. Entry and development modes giving the parent company a high degree of control tend to be more costly and risky than low-control modes. There may also be conflict between speed of entry into the market in the short run and long-term market penetration. While exporting will facilitate rapid entry, it may be less appropriate to long-term market development which may necessitate product development, local manufacture and after-sales service.

The complexity involved in choosing the most appropriate entry and development mode is compounded by the fact that the pros and cons of the different modes vary not only across the broad range of alternatives available but also within each mode as between, for instance, indirect and direct exporting; dominant v. shared joint ventures; etc. A further difficulty relates to the motivations underlying foreign market entry and development. Most of the existing international supply models assume conventional motivations such as cost-effective market penetration, which is usually measured in terms of the risk-adjusted rate of return on different entry modes. As stated in Chapter 1, however, the international market entry mode is only a means to an end, and firms may have multiple objectives in expanding abroad. While conventional marketing and profit objectives remain important, many of the international supply arrangements discussed involve wider strategic and competitive objectives. These must be included in any model aimed at establishing the most appropriate international market development strategy.

Choosing the most appropriate strategy ideally requires a systematic analysis of the alternatives. This is inherently difficult because of information deficiencies and the problems involved in evaluating uncertainty and risk. In addition, the most appropriate strategy for one product/target market will not necessarily be the best for another. Entry and development strategies need to be developed for each product/country market, which further compounds the information problem and the evaluation of uncertainty and risk. Finally, regardless of the preferred choice of strategy, the company must be pragmatic, since mode of entry will be affected by government policy in the target market.

APPROACHES TO THE CHOICE OF FOREIGN MARKET ENTRY/DEVELOPMENT MODE

Chapter 1 identified three broad approaches that have been used to establish the most appropriate foreign market entry and development mode: the economic approach; the stages-of-development approach; and the business-strategy approach. Before discussing the three approaches, it will be useful to summarise the use made of different international supply methods by sector and host country, and this is shown in Table 7.1. One important point to note is that the choice of method is more restricted than might have been assumed in previous chapters, with certain supply modes being more common in certain industries and host countries than in others. The factors influencing the sectoral and host-country distribution of entry modes are discussed later.

The economic approach

Economic approaches to business decisionmaking emphasise rational behaviour, with the costs and benefits of strategic alternatives being compared, to identify those options which maximise long-run profits.

Anderson and Gatignon have recently developed an economic approach (based on transaction cost analysis) to foreign market entry and development mode decisions, which aims at assisting managers to choose the mode which

Table 7.1 Sectoral and host-country patterns in internationalisation

	Exporting	Licensing	Franchising	Management contracts
Sector	All	Strong representation in chemicals, pharmaceuticals, health care and other processing industries, e.g. rubber and plastics. Also electronics	Soft drinks, fast foods, car rentals, hotels, personal and business services	Industrial (mining, oil exploration and refining, heavy engineering, sugar refining, etc.); public utilities (transportation, power, telecoms, medical care, port management); tourism, agriculture N.B. Management contracts are frequently found in association with other forms such as turnkey arrangements
Host country	All	All, with weighting towards developed countries	All, with weighting towards developed countries	Weighting towards developing countries
Influencing factors at host-country level	Small market size; restrictive investment policies; high production costs	Country regulations or political risk; transport or tariff barriers	As licensing	Mainly defensive reasons, as with licensing. Support equity investment or other contractual arrangements

	Turnkey contracts	Contract manufacturing/ international subcontracting	ICAs/contractual joint ventures	Equity joint ventures/ wholly owned subsidiaries
Sector	Heavy industry and basic materials including chemicals, energy plants, iron and steel, cement and glass, textiles, paper plants, etc.	Electronics and clothing principally, but now broadening out, e.g. auto components	Similar in many respects to management contracts and turnkey contracts esp. in projects with Eastern Bloc Within developed countries, wider industrial spread and perhaps more related to firm (non-dominant) than industry characteristics	R&D-intensive and advertising-intensive sectors principally, especially for wholly owned operations
Host country	Developing countries and Eastern Bloc	Export processing zones in developing countries, Eastern Bloc and PRC, Mediterranean Rim	Eastern Bloc and PRC (now encouragement of equity joint ventures) Growing activity in developed countries	Concentration within developed countries, esp. for wholly owned operations; joint ventures dominate in developing countries
Influencing factors at host-country level	Policy of indigenous industrial development. Adequate local human and technological capabilities	Low labour costs. EPZ incentives	State policies, focusing on need for modernisation and greater efficiency Strategic alliances among developed country firms	Market size and growth. Protectionism. Labour availability and cost. Service to customers

maximises long-run efficiency – measured in terms of the risk-adjusted rate of return on investment.[1] According to these authors, control is the single most important determinant of both risk and return. High-control modes of entry (e.g. wholly owned subsidiaries, dominant joint ventures) increase return, but also risk. Low-control modes (licensing and other contractual agreements) reduce resource commitment (and hence risk) but often at the expense of return. The foreign market entry mode decision, therefore, involves rational trade-offs whereby firms trade various levels of control for reductions in resource commitment, in the hope of reducing risk while increasing returns.

The basic framework for analysing the efficiency (risk-adjusted rate of return) of different entry modes is shown in Figure 7.1. The degree of control which the firm should attempt to retain in the choice of entry mode is influenced by four factors:

1. Transaction-specific assets: investments (physical and human) that are specialised to one or a few users or uses, including products and processes which are highly proprietary or unstructured and ill-understood; products which are highly customised to each user; and products in the introductory or growth stage of the life cycle.
2. External uncertainty: the unpredictability of the entrant's external environment, e.g. political instability, economic fluctuations, etc.
3. Internal uncertainty: the entrant's inability to determine its agents' performance, which is related to the entrant's international experience

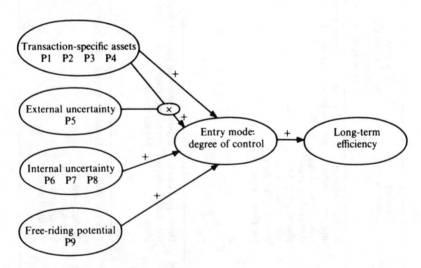

Figure 7.1 A transaction cost framework for analysing the efficiency of entry modes. Source: Anderson, E. and Gatignon, H. (1986), 'Modes of Foreign Entry: A Transaction Cost Analysis and Propositions', *Journal of International Business Studies*, **17**(3), Fall, 7.

and socio-cultural distance between the home- and host-country markets.

4. Free-riding potential: the agent's ability to receive benefits without bearing the associated costs, such as in the degradation of brand names.

As Figure 7.1 shows, the degree of control which should be aimed at is positively related to each of these four constructs. In other words, high-control entry modes should be chosen when the firm possesses transaction-specific assets; when external uncertainty is high; when it is difficult to control agents' performance; and when there is considerable opportunity for free-riding by agents. This leads Anderson and Gatignon to develop nine propositions regarding the choice of foreign market entry mode, as is shown in Figure 7.2.

A useful procedure for implementing an economic approach to the choice of foreign market entry and development mode has been developed by Jeannet and Hennessey and this is presented in Figure 7.3 and Table 7.2.[2]

Taking Figure 7.3 (and proceeding upwards), expected sales, costs and asset requirements should be calculated for each entry mode. These should

---

P1: Modes of entry offering greater control are more efficient for highly proprietary products or processes.

P2: Entry modes offering higher degrees of control are more efficient for unstructured poorly understood products and processes.

P3: Entry modes offering higher degrees of control are more efficient for products customised to the user.

P4: The more mature the product class, the less control firms should demand of a foreign business entry.

P5: The greater the combination of country risk (e.g. political instability, economic fluctuations) and transaction-specificity of assets (proprietary content, poorly understood products, customisation, product class, immaturity), the higher the appropriate degree of control.

P6: The entrant's degree of control of a foreign business entity should be positively related to the firm's consultative international experience.

P7: When socio-cultural distance is great:
   (a) low-control levels are more efficient than intermediate levels;
   (b) high-control levels are more efficient than intermediate levels;
   (c) high-control levels are more efficient only when there is a substantial advantage to doing business in the entrant's way.

P8: The larger the foreign business community in the host country, the lower the level of control an entrant should demand.

P9: Entry modes offering higher degrees of control are more efficient the higher the value of a brand name.

Figure 7.2 Propositions regarding the choice of foreign market entry mode: a transaction cost analysis. Source: Anderson, E. and Gatignon, H. (1986), 'Modes of Foreign Entry: A Transaction Cost Analysis and Propositions', *Journal of International Business Studies*, **17**(3), Fall, 7.

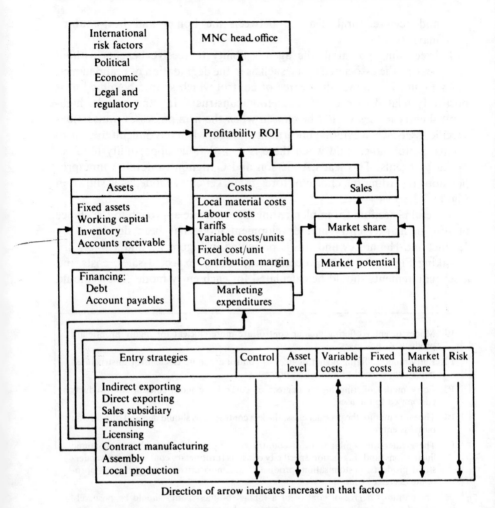

Direction of arrow indicates increase in that factor

Figure 7.3 Considerations for market entry decisions. Source: Jeannet, J.P. and Hennessey, H.D. (1988), *International Marketing Management: Strategies and Cases*, Houghton Mifflin Co., Boston, 297.

be evaluated over the planning horizon of the proposed venture (typically three to five years) and should also include an evaluation of the financial implications of the new venture on existing operations of the firm (see Table 7.2). This analysis will result in incremental financial data, incorporating the net overall benefit of the proposed venture (i.e. its profitability). This should then be subjected to sensitivity analysis, with different scenarios being developed to take into account international risk factors. Table 7.2 shows a typical financial analysis statement for this type of evaluation procedure,

Table 7.2 Financial analysis for entry strategy

Financial variables	Local values	Decreases elsewhere (due to new operation)	Incremental value
Assets			
Cash	New amount of assets needed to sustain chosen entry strategy in local market	Assets liquidated or no longer needed due to shift of operation	Net new assets required
Accounts receivable			
Inventory			
Equipment			
Buildings			
Land			
Liabilities			
Accounts payable	New amount of liabilities incurred due to entry strategy	Reduction or change in liabilities due to shift in operation	Net new liabilities incurred
Debt			
Net assets			Net asset requirement
Costs			
Unit variable costs (VC)	Amount of VC in newly selected operations	Diseconomies of scale due to volume loss by shifting production to new subsidiary	Net variable costs across all subsidiaries resulting from new entry mode
Material costs			
Labour costs			
Purchases			
Fixed and Semi-fixed Costs	Local fixed costs due to selected entry mode	Lost contribution if production shifted elsewhere	Net fixed burden of new entry mode
Supervision			
Marketing			
General administrative			
Expenses			
Total unit costs			Incremental total costs
Sales	Local sales of chosen entry mode	Lost sales in other units of the MNC subsidiary network	Net additional sales of entry strategy
Total sales			

Source: Jeannet, J.P. and Hennessey, H.D (1988), *International Marketing Management: Strategies and Cases*, Houghton Mifflin, Boston, 298–9.

with the incremental total cost of alternative entry modes being compared with the expected addition to net sales revenue in order to determine the relative profitability of alternatives (taking into account financial impact on new and existing businesses).

The stages-of-development approach

The stages-of-development approach to foreign market entry and development mode decisions is based on the incremental model of internationalisation as developed in Chapter 1. According to this model, internationalisation is an evolutionary process with firms gradually developing a greater commitment to foreign markets over time with increasing international experience, foreign sales, etc.

A stages-of-development approach to foreign market entry and development decisions has been developed by Brooke.[3] The model, presented in Figure 7.4, identifies the major options and sub-options available to firms at each stage in their international expansion. According to Brooke, decisions regarding foreign market entry modes are taken incrementally, with a shift to other entry modes occurring only when previous ones have proved inadequate. This may be because a particular entry mode has become unprofitable. Alternatively, an entry mode can become inadequate due to its own previous success, such as in the shift from exporting to more direct involvement in the market as sales volume increases.

Two of the economic models previously discussed in Chapter 1 namely, the product life cycle model of Vernon, and the Buckley and Casson model, are also relevant to the stages-of-development approach since both are concerned with the timing of a switch from one entry strategy to another.[4]

The business-strategy approach

Both the economic and the stages-of-development approaches assume rational decisionmaking. In the former, decisions regarding the choice of entry mode are based on calculation of the risk-adjusted rate of return on alternatives. In the latter, entry and development methods evolve rationally over time with increasing internationalisation of the firm.

The business-strategy approach differs from the previous two models by emphasising the pragmatic nature of decisionmaking in most organisations. Because of external uncertainty and the political nature of decisionmaking (involving consensus seeking), organisations may adopt a 'satisficing' or 'muddling through' rather than a 'rational-analytical' approach to decisionmaking (see Chapter 1). This may be particularly relevant in the context of international market-servicing decisions. Firms will have multiple objectives (including non-profit objectives) in expanding abroad and there will be conflicts between such objectives. In addition, the choice of market-servicing

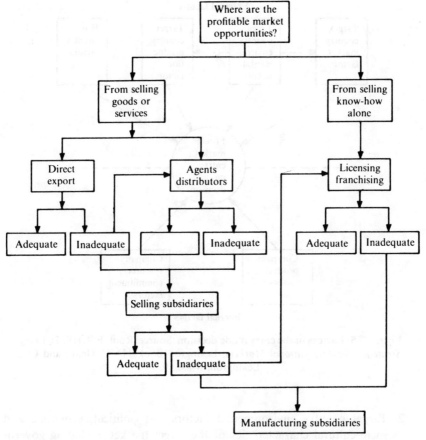

Figure 7.4 The foreign market entry mode decisionmaking process. Source: Brooke, M.Z. (1986), *International Management: A Review of Strategies and Operations*, Hutchinson, London, 40.

strategy will be influenced by a wide range of factors, both internal and external to the firm. This makes it extremely difficult to adopt a 'rational-analytical' approach because of uncertainty and the need to combine conflicting objectives. For small to medium-sized companies, applying a 'rational-analytical' approach is even more problematic due to limited resources.

The wide range of external and internal factors influencing the choice of market-servicing strategy have been listed by Root[5] (see Figure 7.5 and Table 7.3). The most important external factors include the following:

1. Target country market factors – market size and growth prospects; competitive structure; marketing infrastructure; etc.

External factors

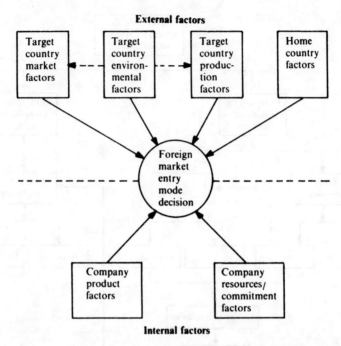

Internal factors

Figure 7.5 Factors in the entry mode decision. Source: Root, F.R. (1987), *Entry Strategies for International Markets*, Lexington Books, D. C. Heath and Co., Lexington, Mass., 9.

2. Target country environmental factors – the political, economic and socio-cultural characteristics of the target market, including government policies regarding inputs and inward direct investment; geographical distance; economic growth and performance; the country's external relations (including exchange-rate influences); cultural distance; and political risk.

3. Target country production factors – the availability, quality and costs of material inputs, labour and other factors of production together with the economic infrastructure (transportation, communications, port facilities, etc).

4. Home country factors – the market, production, competitive and environmental conditions of the home country which will influence the entry mode decision through their impact on firm size, competitiveness and reasons for expanding abroad.

The most important internal factors influencing the choice of foreign market entry mode are the following:

1. Company product factors – the extent of product differentiation; the

Table 7.3 External and internal factors influencing the entry mode decision

	Generally favours				
	Indirect and agent/ distributor exporting	Licensing	Branch/ subsidiary exporting	Equity investment/ production	Service contracts
External factors					
Foreign country					
Low sales potential	×	×			
High sales potential			×	×	
Atomistic competition	×		×		
Oligopolistic competition				×	
Poor marketing infrastructure			×		
Good marketing infrastructure	×				
Low production cost				×	
High production cost	×		×		
Restrictive import policies		×		×	×
Liberal import policies	×		×		
Restrictive investment policies	×	×	×		×
Liberal investment policies				×	
Small geographical distance	×		×		
Great geographical distance		×		×	×
Dynamic economy				×	
Stagnant economy	×	×			×
Restrictive exchange controls	×	×			×
Liberal exchange controls				×	
Exchange-rate depreciation				×	
Exchange-rate appreciation	×		×		
Small cultural distance			×	×	
Great cultural distance	×	×			×
Low political risk			×	×	
High political risk	×	×			×
Home country					
Large market				×	
Small market	×		×		
Atomistic competition	×		×		
Oligopolistic competition				×	
Low production cost	×		×		
High production cost		×		×	×

Table 7.3 (cont.)

| | Generally favours | | | | |
	Indirect and agent/ distributor exporting	Licensing	Branch/ subsidiary exporting	Equity investment/ production	Service contracts
Strong export promotion	×		×		
Restrictions on investment abroad	×	×			×
Internal factors					
Differentiated products	×		×		
Standard products				×	
Service intensive products			×	×	
Service products		×		×	×
Technology intensive products		×			
Low product adaptation	×				
High product adaptation		×	×	×	
Limited resources	×	×			
Substantial resources			×	×	
Low commitment	×	×			×
High commitment			×	×	

Source: Root, F.R. (1987), *Entry Strategies for International Markets*, Lexington Books, D.C. Heath and Co., Lexington, Mass., 16–17.

service content; technology intensity; and the ability to standardise products globally.

2. Company resource/commitment factors – management, capital and technology resources; production and marketing skills; and the company's overall commitment to international business.

The importance of these factors is that they allow managers to assess the relative attractiveness of different foreign market entry methods (see Table 7.3). Thus, exporting and licensing may be most appropriate for markets with low sales potential, with the establishment of marketing and/or production subsidiaries through direct investment being required in markets with high sales potential, and so on. For each of the external and internal factors, it is possible to identify appropriate and inappropriate market-servicing strategies.

While the figures identify the wide range of factors influencing the market-servicing strategy adopted, Root's model for choosing the 'right' entry mode is very much a 'rational-analytical' model. According to Root, the 'right' entry mode is that which maximises the profit contribution over the strategic planning period within the constraints imposed by the availability of company resources; risk; and non-profit objectives. A number of stages are involved in determining the most profitable mode of entry, as indicated in Figure 7.6. First, feasibility screening should be undertaken to reject those entry and development strategies which are not possible, given the

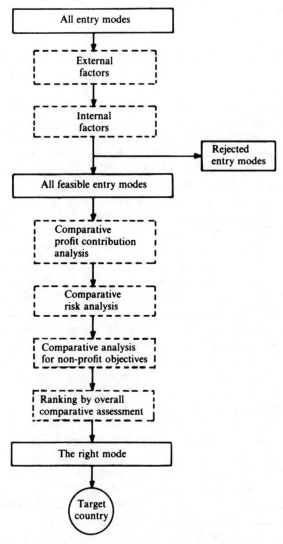

Figure 7.6 Deciding on the ideal market entry and development strategy. Source: Root, F.R. (1987), *Entry Strategies for International Markets*, Lexington Books, D. C. Heath and Co., Lexington, Mass., 164.

company's internal resources/commitment and the influence of external factors such as small market size, government restrictions, etc. Second, the estimated net profit contribution of all feasible entry methods should be compared – calculated on a net present value basis – in order to establish a rank ordering of feasible entry modes. Finally, an overall ranking of entry strategies should follow, with the net profit contribution of alternatives being adjusted to take into account political and market risk and the firm's non-profit objectives.

CHOOSING THE FOREIGN MARKET ENTRY AND DEVELOPMENT STRATEGY: AN ALTERNATIVE APPROACH

Although each of the above approaches provides useful guidelines regarding the choice of foreign market-servicing strategy, there are certain inadequacies apparent in the models. The stages-of-development approach provides a useful overview relating the entry mode decision to the level of the firm's internationalisation, which will prove helpful in identifying 'feasible' and 'unfeasible' modes of entry at different stages in the internationalisation process. However, the model implies a naive, or at best, a pragmatic approach to entry mode decisions with the same, or at least, the most feasible mode – rather than the 'right' mode – being adopted at each stage. Thus, while indirect exporting may be an 'adequate' mode of entry in the early stages of internationalisation, it may not be sufficient to fully exploit foreign market opportunities which may require, say, the establishment of selling subsidiaries. The stages-of-development approach also fails to take into account the fact that different foreign markets may require different entry strategies due to market size, government policy, degree of risk, and so forth.

The other two approaches place greater emphasis on the factors influencing the entry mode decision and the need to make such decisions specific to particular product/country markets. Their main disadvantage is their rather narrow view of a firm's objectives in entering and developing a new foreign market. While maximising long-term efficiency or the risk-adjusted rate of return on investment will be desirable objectives, firms are likely to have multiple, including non-profit, objectives in entering and developing new markets and these need to be incorporated into the entry mode decision. Furthermore, it may not be possible in many cases to estimate with any degree of accuracy the net return on different entry strategies due to uncertainty. This may be a particular problem for small to medium-sized companies lacking international experience and resources.

The alternative foreign market entry and development model described here recognises that firms often have multiple objectives in entering new foreign markets and that there will exist conflicts between these objectives, e.g. between short-term profitability and long-term market penetration. The most appropriate strategy is the one which best results in the simultaneous achievement of the company's multiple objectives, including profit and non-profit objectives. A six-stage procedure for evaluating the appropriateness of different strategies is suggested as shown in Figure 7.7.

The starting point in choosing the most appropriate entry and development mode is a clear statement of the main objectives to be achieved through entering the new foreign market – taking into account short- and long-run objectives; profit and non-profit objectives; and wider strategic objectives. While the nature of objectives will vary considerably between firms, the main objectives desired will normally be some combination of those presented in Table 7.4.

Given the likelihood of conflict between objectives, the second stage is to rank desired objectives in terms of relative importance. In assessing the relative importance of different objectives, the analysis presented in previous sections will prove useful since both internal (company-specific) and external (country-specific) factors will influence the ranking. For example, the retention of control may be the prime objective for companies with highly differentiated products, proprietary technology, etc., and this may override

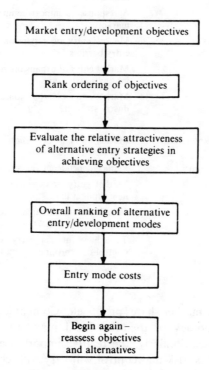

Figure 7.7 Procedure for choosing the most appropriate foreign market entry/development mode.

Table 7.4 Motivations underlying foreign market entry and development

Profit-oriented	
ROI	To achieve predetermined level of return on investment
Early cash recovery	In order to improve liquidity; will require immediate increase in sales
Cost reduction	Through access to lower material and factor costs; transport and communications costs; possible economies of scale through larger volume
Market-oriented	
Market stabilisation	Market entry or development with minimum disruption to avoid retaliation
Market skimming	Aimed at low sales volume in target markets, associated with market spreading
Market penetration	A more aggressive approach aimed at achieving a large market share
Competitive-oriented	
Build permanent market position	Market entry or expansion to defend or improve market share
Meet or follow competition	Market entry or expansion in response to competitor actions
Exchange of threat	A response to import competition in the domestic market
Prevent new competition	Market entry or expansion aimed at establishing entry barriers
Follow customers	Market entry or expansion in response to customers' internationalisation
Shaping competition	Market entry or expansion aimed at influencing industry structure
Strategic-oriented	
Technology (and other know-how) transfer	Market entry or expansion to gain access to know-how ('ear to the ground')
Geographical diversification	Reduce dependency on certain country markets
Product diversification	Market entry or expansion to gain access/develop new product lines
Leverage	To achieve additional leverage for key resources and investments (e.g. R&D)
Control	To achieve market entry while maintaining close control over proprietary know-how, etc.

concerns regarding market share, profits etc. Companies with standardised products and technology, on the other hand, may be more concerned with marketing objectives. Similarly, the relative importance attached to sales, market share, profits, risk and control will vary with characteristics of the target country's market and environment.

Once objectives have been ranked in order of importance, the firm needs to assess the relative attractiveness of alternative entry strategies in achieving these objectives. This could be assessed along the lines shown in Exhibit 7.1. Although only four alternative market-servicing methods are shown, the analysis could easily be extended to include additional modes, e.g. selling subsidiaries and dominant v. shared joint ventures. Once weighted scores have been assigned to each alternative, the fourth stage would then be to establish an overall ranking of the alternatives, i.e. the bottom line. This will show the relative attractiveness of different entry and development modes in simultaneously achieving the firm's multiple objectives. The relative attractiveness of the alternative supply strategies in achieving the firm's desired objectives then needs to be compared against the costs involved. A number of factors should be considered at this stage, including financial costs; management commitment; risks; reversibility; and the degree of control available. The final stage in the process is to begin again, since the nature of the firm's objectives and the attractiveness of alternative supply strategies in achieving these objectives will vary over time.

EXHIBIT 7.1
CHOOSING THE MARKET ENTRY AND DEVELOPMENT
STRATEGY – A HYPOTHETICAL EXAMPLE

Introduction
The following hypothetical example is based on a small, high-technology British company in advanced electronics considering entry into the US market. Initially, the company has identified four main objectives to be achieved through entering the US market and these have been ranked in terms of relative importance on a ten-point scale (where 10 = most important). The company's assessment of the relative attractiveness of four entry modes in achieving each short-run objective is shown (where 4 = most attractive). The overall weighted scores suggest that exporting will be the most appropriate supply strategy for achieving short-run objectives.

In the long run, the company is more concerned with establishing a permanent position in the US market which will provide leverage in terms of reducing unit R&D costs, while retaining control over its proprietary technology. This will require a switch from exporting to the establishment of a wholly owned manufacturing subsidiary in the US.

The switch from exporting in the short run to foreign direct investment in the long run is based on an assessment of alternative entry and development modes in simultaneously achieving the firm's multiple objectives. Clearly, however, this needs to be balanced against the costs and risks associated with different supply modes. The final section of the table shows that the company wishes to minimise both the costs and risks of market entry and development, as well as achieving its short- and long-run objectives. The rankings shown indicate that the company should continue with the export mode of market penetration since this best achieves market objectives consistent with the company's attitude towards costs and risk. Obviously, a different outcome would have emerged if the company had been less cost and risk averse.

Exhibit 7.1 continued

Market entry and development objectives	Weighting of objectives	Weighted attractiveness of alternative supply strategies											
		Exporting			Licensing			Joint venture			Wholly owned subsidiary (production)		
		Score		Weighted score	Score		Weighted score	Score		Weighted score	Score		Weighted score
Short run													
ROI	0.4	× 3	=	1.2	× 4	=	1.6	× 2	=	0.8	× 1	=	0.4
Early cash recovery	0.8	× 4	=	3.2	× 3	=	2.4	× 2	=	1.6	× 1	=	0.8
Market skimming	1.0	× 4	=	4.0	× 3	=	3.0	× 2	=	2.0	× 1	=	1.0
Control	1.0	× 3	=	3.0	× 1	=	1.0	× 2	=	2.0	× 4	=	4.0
Overall weighted ranking for short-run objectives				11.4			8.0			6.4			6.2
Long run													
Market penetration	0.9	× 1	=	0.9	× 2	=	1.8	× 3	=	2.7	× 4	=	3.6
Build market position	0.9	× 1	=	0.9	× 2	=	1.8	× 3	=	2.7	× 4	=	3.6
Prevent new competition	0.9	× 3	=	2.7	× 1	=	0.9	× 2	=	1.8	× 4	=	3.6

	Weight				
Leverage	09	09 × 3 = 27	09 × 1 = 09	09 × 2 = 18	09 × 4 = 36
Control	10	10 × 3 = 30	10 × 1 = 10	10 × 2 = 20	10 × 4 = 40
Overall weighted ranking for long-run objectives		102	64	110	188
Costs/risk					
Minimise financial costs	10	10 × 4 = 40	10 × 3 = 30	10 × 2 = 20	10 × 1 = 10
Minimise managerial commitment	10	10 × 4 = 40	10 × 3 = 30	10 × 2 = 20	10 × 1 = 10
Risk minimisation	10	10 × 4 = 40	10 × 3 = 30	10 × 2 = 20	10 × 1 = 10
Overall weighted ranking for cost/risk objectives		120	90	60	30
Total weighted ranking	280	336	234	234	234

The foreign market entry and development model described in this section offers a number of advantages over those discussed previously. The model recognises that firms may have multiple objectives in entering and developing foreign markets, with the choice of market-servicing strategy reflecting both short- and long-run, profit and non-profit objectives. Firms may have different attitudes towards the costs and risks associated with foreign market entry and development, and this is incorporated in the model through the weightings attached to such variables. Finally, the model is highly flexible, since it is the managers of the firm itself who will determine the number of entry modes to be compared, the firm's market objectives, and relative weightings.

STRATEGIC ALLIANCES

With the exception of direct exporting and the establishment of wholly owned subsidiaries, the various international market entry and development strategies examined in this book all involve (to varying degrees) corporate linkages between two or more business partners located in different countries. Although forms of international business activity such as licensing, management contracts and equity joint ventures are the focal point of the book, Chapter 1 also drew attention to an emerging form of cross-national collaboration, namely, strategic alliances – variously called strategic partnerships, corporate coalitions and competitive alliances. Such alliances have become very popular in recent years and are being increasingly used by global competitors, including small and non-dominant firms operating in global industries. Reports of new alliances being formed can be found in the business press almost on a daily basis, and some of the best known are shown in Exhibit 7.2.

This concluding section of the book examines whether strategic alliances represent a new and distinctive form of international market development activity. This involves a discussion of the motivations underlying and the management problems associated with strategic alliances as compared with the previous forms of international market servicing.

A 'Distinctive' form of international activity?

In a number of ways, strategic alliances are little different from the more conventional forms of international activity discussed to this point in the book. Jain, for example, defines strategic alliances as 'co-operation between two or more industrial corporations, belonging to different countries, whereby each partner seeks to add to its competencies by combining its resources with those of other partners'.[6] This definition would encompass most of the international market entry and development strategies examined

---

EXHIBIT 7.2.
EXAMPLES OF INTERNATIONAL STRATEGIC ALLIANCES

Partners	Products
General Motors; Toyota	Automobiles
British Leyland; Honda	Automobiles
American Motors; Renault	Automobiles
Chrysler; Mitsubishi	Automobiles
Ford; Toyo Kogyo	Automobiles
Alfa Romeo; Nissan; Fiat	Automobiles
ATT; Olivetti	Office equipment; computers
Amdahl; Fujitsu	Computers
ICL; Fujitsu	Computers
ATT; Philips	Telecommunications equipment
Honeywell; L.M. Ericsson	PBX system
General Motors; Fanuc	Robotics
AEG Telefunken; JVC; Thorn-EMI; Thomson	VCRs
General Electric; Matsushita	Electrical appliances
Corning Glass; Siemens	Optical cables
Hercules; Montedison	Polypropylene resin
United Technologies; Rolls-Royce	Aircraft engines

---

previously; as would Porter's view of international coalitions as 'formal, long-term alliances between firms that link aspects of their business but fall short of merger.'[7] Strategic alliances, and the other forms of international relationships, involve partners of different nationalities and this may give rise to conflicts and communications difficulties due to language barriers and differences in culture, management practices, etc. To a large extent, the motivations underlying the various types of international arrangements are similar, including market access; economies of scale; pooling of resources; technology transfer; etc. Finally, many of the problems associated with planning, negotiating and implementing previously discussed forms of international business activity also arise in the case of strategic alliances – especially the case of equity joint ventures discussed in Chapter 6.

Despite these similarities between conventional forms of international relationships and strategic alliances, the latter would be seen to be different from the former in a number of crucial respects.[8] Co-operation in conventional forms of market entry and development normally involves partners of unequal strengths and resources as, for example, in licensing or joint-venture agreements between developed-country MNEs and local firms in developing host countries. Strategic alliances, by contrast, involve collaboration between two or more partners – commonly both from industrialised countries – of comparable global strengths and resources, although this is not a necessary condition. In conventional forms of international relationships, there is little or no direct competition between partners. The partners to a strategic alliance, by contrast, will often be competing in the same product/geographical markets, as well as co-operating in various ways. In conventional relationships, there is an imbalance in partners' contributions. While the MNE contributes mainly capital, technology and management skills, the contributions of the local partner are mainly location-specific, including local market knowledge, business contacts, distribution channels, etc. In strategic alliances, the production, marketing and technology contributions of partners are still asymmetrical, but are more balanced.

The motivations underlying the formation of strategic alliances are different. Conventional relationships are motivated mainly by the need for market access and, in some cases, by economic factors such as economies of scale, pooling of resources, etc. These may be important in strategic alliances too, but the motivations underlying the latter are commonly more strategic and competitive in scope. Strategic alliances can have a major effect on shaping industry competition by influencing who firms compete with and the basis of competition. Co-operation may enhance competition by facilitating the entry of new firms into a particular product or geographic market; by affecting firms' cost structures; and by providing access to new sources of technology. In this respect, such partnerships may be a particularly important strategic option for non-dominant firms. Collusion may also be used to erect barriers to entry, thereby reducing competition.

The strategic and competitive implications of strategic alliances are, perhaps, the main distinguishing feature of such collaboration. According to Jain, strategic alliances can be distinguished from conventional international business relationships by the fact that the former are more often used as 'a strategic option or competitive weapon within mature economies to seek global power.'[9] Similarly, Porter argues that international coalitions are becoming 'more strategic, through linking major competitors together to compete worldwide... [While] more traditional coalitions were often tactical, involving tie-ups with local firms to gain market access or to transfer technology passively to regions where a firm did not want to compete directly.'[10]

Types and benefits of strategic alliances

Although the above characteristics are common to all strategic alliances, the form of collaboration and the strategic objectives underlying such co-operation may vary significantly. Six main types of strategic alliance coalitions have been identified:[11]

1. Technology development coalitions – co-operation aimed at reducing the costs and sharing the risks associated with technology development;

the pooling of R&D; and/or technology transfer from 'leaders' to 'followers'.

2. Operations and logistics coalitions – aimed at improving manu-facturing/production efficiency through scale and/or learning benefits; transferring manufacturing know-how; or exploiting country compara-tive advantage.

3. Marketing, sales and service coalitions – motivated by the need for market access.

4. Multiple-activity coalitions – co-operation which involves some combi-nation of the above.

5. Single-country and multi-country coalitions – which refer to the geogra-phical scope of the coalition.

6. x and y coalitions – which refer to the value activities undertaken by each partner (i.e. production, marketing, R&D, etc.). In x coalitions, value activities are divided (e.g. one partner manufactures, the other markets); in y coalitions, the partners share the performance of one or more activities.

Although there is a shortage of empirical evidence regarding the overall incidence of strategic alliances, it is generally accepted that this form of international business activity has become more common in recent years. A number of factors have contributed to this trend. The growing intensity of global competition in many industries has led to increased collaboration in order to achieve cost reductions through economies of scale. The increasing pace of technological change and the associated costs of technology devel-opment have encouraged collaboration in order to share costs and reduce risks. Greater technology complexity also encourages collaborations since few companies can control all elements of the technology mix internally. Collaboration allows concentration on a few critical internal R&D projects with other technology being sought externally. The need to reduce unit R&D costs by marketing more widely has encouraged collaboration in order to gain access to global markets and distribution systems. Finally, strategic alliances have been motivated by the need to overcome protectionism and other political pressures which have been influencing factors, for example, in the formation of alliances between Japanese and US automobile manufac-turers (see Exhibit 7.2).

From the above discussion it is now possible to list the potential benefits deriving from the formation of strategic alliances as identified in the litera-ture (see Table 7.5). It should be noted that these benefits also arise in other forms of international relationships. It is the global dimension of these benefits which distinguishes strategic alliances from conventional market agreements such as equity joint ventures. Thus, while both provide access to new markets, in the latter, this is mainly confined to the host-country market.

Table 7.5 Potential benefits of international strategic alliances

Economies of scale	Alliances to increase volume, thereby reducing large costs of R&D, capital investment, etc., required to remain globally competitive
Technology development	Cross-fertilisation and exchange of technology which allows specialisation
Risk reduction	Through sharing resources and reducing the costs of R&D
Shaping competition	Collusion to reduce competition; alternatively alliances may facilitate new firm entry or shape competition by affecting industry cost structure, technology, etc.
New market opportunities	Alliances to provide access to global markets and distribution systems
Neo-protectionism	Alliances to circumvent trade restrictions

Source: Derived from Porter, M. (ed.) (1986), *Competition in Global Industries*, Harvard Business School Press, Boston, Chapter 10; and Jain, S.C. (1987), 'Perspectives on International Strategic Alliances', *Advances in International Marketing*, Vol. 2, JAI Press, New York, 104–6.

Strategic alliances: the costs

As for the other forms of international market servicing discussed in previous chapters, the benefits from strategic alliances must be balanced against the associated costs.[12] Strategic alliances involve *mutual dependency* whereby each partner is dependent on the other's contributions and inputs. This could give rise to difficulties if one partner's contribution is insufficient. Most strategic alliances are established for long-term projects, the results of which are difficult to predict. Such *uncertainty about the outcome* makes it difficult to compare the value of strategic alliances against the alternatives available, such as 'going it alone'. Strategic alliances involve some degree of shared decisionmaking. Conflict over the *division of authority and decisionmaking power* may give rise to three problems: disagreements over objectives and plans; the need for compromised decisions which may be less than optimal; and a slowing down in the decisionmaking process. Finally, all major decisions regarding international strategic alliances are made by top management and this will be very costly in terms of *top management time and effort*.

In addition to the above costs, Jain identifies six major risks associated with international strategic alliances and these are presented in Table 7.6.

According to Porter, the costs associated with international coalitions fall into three broad categories:[13] co-ordination, erosion of competitive position, and creation of an adverse bargaining position. Co-ordination costs refer to the time and effort involved in managing divergent interests between coalition partners and attempting to integrate coalition activities into the broader global strategy of the MNE. The competitive costs of coalitions arise out of their potential for dissipating sources of competitive advantage and undermining industry structure. Either new competitors may be created or existing

Table 7.6. Risks associated with international strategic alliances

Imbalance in benefits	The risk that benefits deriving from the alliance will be unevenly distributed between partners causing conflict and a demotivation effect
Imbalance in commitment and motivation	The risk that partners' inputs may be unequal
Difficulty in arriving at an agreement	The risk that no agreement may be reached even after a considerable input of management time and effort in negotiation
Communication problems	The risk of misunderstandings as a result of language and cultural barriers
Conflict between partners	The risk of conflict and disagreements over major decisions, distribution of benefits, allocation of inputs, etc.
Retaliation from governments and competition	The risk of adverse reactions from governments and industry competition

Source: Jain, S.C. (1987), 'Perspectives on International Strategic Alliances', *Advances in International Marketing*, Vol. 2, JAI Press, New York, 110–11.

competitors may become more formidable through the transferring of expertise or the provision of market access. Such competitive costs will raise the co-ordination costs of managing coalitions since partners will often not trust each other's long-term motives. Finally, one of the partners to the coalition may find itself in an adverse bargaining position, if the other (due to its specialised or irreplaceable contribution) attempts to dominate the venture. This will create conflict with respect to the distribution of benefits associated with the coalition.

The costs of coalitions are likely to change over the life of the venture. Co-ordination costs may fall over time as partners gain experience in working with each other and trust is established. Similarly, competitive costs may fall if the coalition proves mutually profitable. On the other hand, co-ordination costs may rise if one or both partners' interests and goals shift; while competitive costs may also rise if one partner gains much of the expertise from the coalition and the contribution of the other falls.

The dynamics of competition between partners to a strategic alliance have been emphasised in a recent paper by Doz, Hamel and Prahalad.[14] According to these authors, the central issue in any strategic alliance is the evolving balance of power between partners and, in particular, the threat of strategic encroachment whereby one partner attempts to dominate the venture to achieve its own strategic or competitive objectives. A partner may enter an alliance with the strategic intent of global industry leadership. Under such circumstances, the strategic alliance is considered (by one partner) as a mere stepping-stone in the process of building, adding and layering sources of competitive advantage in the process of wresting advantage from the industry leaders. This will lead to an attempt to dominate the alliance and to exploit the other partner's technology, know-how, etc. According to Doz *et al.*, Japanese companies, in particular, have used a 'network' of strategic alliances to improve their global competitive position – often at the expense of the other partner's interests.

Many of the problems associated with strategic alliances exist, to varying degrees, in some conventional international relationships; for example, the problems of mutual dependency, decisionmaking and co-ordination, distribution of benefits, etc. Again, however, it is the global dimension of many of these difficulties which distinguish strategic alliances, such as strategic encroachment and the impact on global competitiveness.

The planning, negotiation and management of strategic alliances

One of the most important issues related to the growing importance of strategic alliances is whether the guidelines developed in previous chapters regarding the planning, negotiation and management of conventional international market entry and development modes are equally valid in the case of the former, or whether new guidelines need to be developed. Since there are certain similarities in the motives, benefits and costs associated with the different forms of international activity (including strategic alliances), it would seem that many of the guidelines developed earlier are still appropriate. Porter, for example, argues that identifying coalition partners is the single most important issue in establishing a successful coalition and that partners should be selected on the basis of their contribution to the coalition and the risks of forming linkages with them. Six criteria for choosing long-term coalition partners are recommended, as indicated in Figure 7.8.[15] According to Jain, there are four dominant characteristics of successful international strategic alliances: complementary needs of partners; complementary strengths; shared power; and balanced benefits.[16]

- Partners must possess the desired source of competitive advantage (scale, technology, market access or other contribution) that the coalition seeks
- Partners should have complementary or balanced resources in order that no one partner dominates
- Partners' international strategy should be compatible
- There should be a low risk of partners dissolving the coalition and competing independently
- The partner should possess pre-emptive value *vis-à-vis* rivals
- There should be organisational compatibility between partners

---

Figure 7.8 Criteria for choosing strategic alliance partners. Source: Derived from Porter, M. (ed.) (1986), *Competition in Global Industries*, Harvard Business School Press, Boston, 339–42.

The above guidelines are broadly similar to those developed in previous chapters (e.g. in the case of equity joint ventures). Doz, Hamel and Prahalad, on the other hand, argue that strategic alliances are different from conventional forms of international relationships.[17] Therefore, to adopt a similar management approach is not only inappropriate, but also dangerous given the threat of strategic encroachment. A number of guidelines for managing effective strategic alliances can be developed from the analysis presented by Doz et al. and these are shown in Exhibit 7.3.

EXHIBIT 7.3
GUIDELINES FOR PLANNING, NEGOTIATING AND
IMPLEMENTING INTERNATIONAL STRATEGIC ALLIANCES

Partnerships are a second-best solution and, therefore, should be entered into carefully and limited to situations where they are clearly needed.

Partnerships are strategic. Therefore, managers should be careful that seemingly sensible decisions that maximise results in the short run do not undermine their competitive positions.

Partnerships are dynamic with active management, in a clear strategic context, being as important as initial negotiations and contractual provisions. Active management is essential to prevent strategic encroachment.

Partnerships are different from more traditional joint ventures. Therefore, the experience gained in the latter is not easily transferred to the former.

Partnerships should be closely monitored by top management for signs of drift in unplanned directions.

Partners should constantly replenish their inventory of core skills which will increase the value of their contribution and, therefore, their bargaining power within the partnership.

Partners should regulate the flow of their contribution in order not to contribute too little (which may result in coalition failure) or too much (which may result in an imbalance in contributions).

The partner's organisation should be made more receptive to the venture in order to successfully assimilate and use the new knowledge obtained.

Source: Derived from Doz, Y., Hamel, G. and Prahalad, C.K. (1986), *Strategic Partnerships: Success or Surrender?: The Challenge of International Collaboration*, paper presented at Joint AIB-EIBA Meeting, London, 20–23 Nov., 18–24.

THE SINGLE EUROPEAN MARKET IN 1992 AND INTERNATIONAL BUSINESS ACTIVITY

The aim of the Single European Act, passed in 1986, is to create a European Community by 1992 where all barriers to the free movement of goods and services, people and capital have been removed. The vision of the Treaty of Rome which established the EC in 1958 was that of creating a single European economy, but progress was painfully slow subsequently – hence the 1992 initiative. Despite the abolition of intra-EC customs' duties, many other barriers to trade between member states have remained and indeed new ones have evolved to protect vested interests. These non-tariff barriers were of three main types: physical barriers, including customs' barriers and associated frontier controls; technical barriers, including different standards and product specifications in member states and preferential public procurement policies; and financial barriers relating to different rates of value added tax (VAT) levied by Community countries which necessitate costly customs' documentation and procedures. To give an illustration of the costs associated with customs' delays alone, it was estimated that customs' formalities at each border post take an average of 80 minutes per truck which when grossed up represents a cost of 5 to 10 per cent of the value of goods transported across frontiers.[18] These obstacles to free internal trade are of particular interest from the present perspective, although the Single Market programme is also designed to provide for free movement of labour and capital. To achieve these objectives will entail the passing of 300 pieces of legislation; it is doubtful if this can be done in time to create a 'Europe without frontiers' by 1992, and to that extent the date is symbolic only. Nevertheless, given the size of the European Community (320 million people), the Single Market programme is one of the major environmental changes in the world economy and thus has great relevance to the theme of this text.

Interest lies in the influence of Project 1992 on the forms of undertaking international business activity. To consider this, it is necessary to take into consideration not only the internal market programme itself, but also the external relations of the Community. Many aspects of the latter relating to trade and investment are subject to negotiation, and since a number of members of the EC have strong protectionist tendencies, fears of a 'Fortress Europe' (at its extreme, non-members being virtually excluded from selling into the market after 1992) have developed. In such circumstances, non-EC enterprises, especially firms in Japan and the Far East NICs, are seeking speedy entry into the Community through the establishment of wholly owned subsidiaries and other arrangements.

In regard to Community firms (and others established inside the EC), completion of the internal market should facilitate cross-border trade, enabling exporters to service their markets more efficiently from their home base. Similarly, companies with foreign direct investments in a number of

Community countries for market access reasons (to meet national standards, gain access to national procurement policies, etc.) should be able to centralise and rationalise their activities to exploit comparative advantage and/or economies of scale or scope.

Interestingly, however, the European Commission lays great store on industrial collaborative activity as a mechanism for exploiting the potential gains associated with 1992. To quote: 'As and when the internal market is developed further, enterprises... will become more and more involved in all manner of intra-Community operations, resulting in an ever-increasing number of links with associated enterprises ...'.[19] The basis of the argument is very much in accord with themes of this book and is therefore, worth repeating: 'The exchange of goods and services on an arms-length and *ad hoc* basis, i.e. "trade" in a text-book sense, between independent firms in two different countries is becoming the exception rather than the rule: Contractual relationships between links in the "chain of value added" are becoming an essential feature of the modern economy. Transborder links of this kind can involve one or all of the elements of the chain of value added, from basic research to R&D, organisational know-how, production or procurement of intermediate and final products, to marketing and other services.'[20] In support of their belief in the virtues of international collaboration, access to Community research and development support, through programmes like ESPRIT and BRITE, requires partnership activity between firms of different nationalities: 'EC-sponsored R&D programmes like BRITE..., way beyond their monetary significance, are a crucial focus for fusing cross-frontier innovation and business.'[21]

There is no question that all firms operating in the Community are having to face up to major changes in their operating environments. The most radical responses are taking place in industries where intra-EC trade is limited and the number of producers is quite large. In such national and fragmented sectors, including telecommunications' equipment, food processing and building products, very significant international restructuring via mergers and acquisitions, collaboration, etc. is taking place with the elimination of barriers and the opening up of public procurement to wider competitive bidding. In pharmaceuticals, harmonisation in drug pricing and formulation is expected to lead to the shut-down of a large number of drug formulation plants, with large-scale job losses. And both large and small enterprises are affected: the latter, many of which supply only local or national markets, will be faced with greater competition and will thus be forced to re-think their strategies, meaning product diversification and/or wider markets.

Because of definitional differences and difficulties in actually recording all the internal corporate agreements taking place, it is not easy to draw any firm conclusions concerning the relative importance of the different forms of international market entry and development within the EC, let alone their motives.[22] Trade between member states is continuing to expand rapidly, and the number of mergers and acquisitions has been increasing as has the incidence of joint ventures.[23] No data were available on other forms of collaboration on a time series basis; but Morris and Hergert identified 433 collaborative agreements involving EC firms linking up with other enterprises in the Community or with USA and Japanese companies over the years 1975 to 1986.[24] The links were compiled from announcements in *The Economist* and *Financial Times*, and indicated that almost two-fifths of these collaborative agreements involved joint development projects, with production only agreements and joint development alongside production, being next in importance. Reflecting the problems of data collection and methodology, however, other research on intra-Community activity has indicated that joint marketing has been the most important type of agreement, with market access as the major motive.[25] Where the various studies do seem to agree is in finding that collaboration between EC and non-EC partners is more important than agreements between Community members themselves. As non-EC companies seek access to the Community before 1992, an acceleration in such agreements would be expected, especially in mature and potentially over-capacity sectors of industry. Market access reasons for intra-Community collaboration will diminish with the completion of the Single Market, but small and weaker EC companies might be drawn into cross-border alliances for defensive reasons at a time when competition is bound to increase.

There is no question that 1992 will be a testing time for collaboration as a form of international business activity. Where Community firms (e.g. many West Germany enterprises) are confident of their competitive advantage, servicing of EC markets from central production points will be stimulated. Similarly, non-EC enterprises are likely to continue to invest in wholly-owned greenfield facilities (or majority-owned joint ventures) to protect their proprietary know-how and control their European strategies. Whether companies which are not in these situations can successfully compete through collaboration on a long-term basis remains to be seen.[26]

CONCLUSIONS AND IMPLICATIONS

This book has focused on a 'frontier' issue in international marketing, namely, the market-servicing strategies used by firms in entering and developing foreign markets. The emphasis of the book has been on the management aspects of planning and implementing various entry and development strategies, with the final chapter providing guidelines on how to choose the most effective servicing strategy.

It should, by now, be obvious that a wide range of factors (both internal and external to the firm) influence the entry and development mode choice. Changes in these factors over time will affect the relative appropriateness of alternative servicing modes and this is reflected in the evolutionary development of market supply strategies in many companies. While there may be merit in an incremental approach to foreign market entry and development decisions, firms need to adopt a pragmatic and flexible approach in order to fully exploit overseas market opportunities. Since the most appropriate strategy for one product/country market may not be the best for another, firms need to have the capability of operating a range of methods of foreign operations. The internationalisation of Japanese companies illustrates clearly the benefits of a pragmatic and flexible approach to entry and development mode decisions, with foreign markets being supplied through a combination of indirect and direct exporting, licensing, joint ventures, wholly owned subsidiaries, strategic alliances, and so on.

The need for a pragmatic and flexible attitude to foreign market entry and development decisions is reinforced by the rapidly changing nature of the international business environment of the late 1980s. While this makes forecasting difficult, it is possible to identify a number of 'international issues of the future' which will have major implications for the international manager's approach to foreign market servicing, especially in SMEs.

The increasing internationalisation of business, together with the growing intensity of global competition imply that many SMEs need to internationalise quickly. Speed of market entry and development, therefore, will become an important determinant of the choice of market-servicing strategy. The rapid increase in cross-border mergers and acquisitions (many of which have been made by SMEs) in recent years is one example, with companies attempting to rationalise and reposition themselves in international markets through buying market share. The concern with speed of entry, however, needs to be balanced against the associated costs and risks. The increased participation in international business of SMEs will lead to a growth in the use of foreign market entry and development modes involving the least cost and risk.

Rapid technology change, the increasing costs of technology development, shortening product life cycles, and so on, will have a major impact on market-servicing strategies. For many small and medium-sized high-technology companies, rapid internationalisation is necessary to amortise large R&D expenditures (in relative terms) and to fully exploit short-lived product advantages. Again, speed of market entry and development becomes crucial in choosing between alternative supply modes. While large multinational enterprises will continue to rely on internal R&D for generating new technology, SMEs will be required to adopt a range of strategies for accumulating and exploiting technology, including licensing, joint ventures, strategic alliances, etc. It is unlikely that smaller enterprises will remain competitive without a flexible approach towards technology development.

The international manager will also need to be aware of broad trends in the political and regulatory environment and the impact of these on foreign market-servicing strategies. While new market opportunities are being created through trade liberalisation in Eastern Europe and the People's Republic of China, flexible entry strategies will be required to exploit such opportunities, since government policies will continue to restrict choice. Appropriate and flexible entry strategies will be required to exploit the rapidly growing markets of the Pacific Rim countries; while in the US, the growing threat of protectionism remains an important issue in the choice of entry strategy. In Europe, smaller and medium-sized firms will be required to consider seriously pan-European collaboration (of various forms) to fully exploit the opportunities available in a single, unified common market. In many developing countries, there is evidence of a more liberal approach being adopted towards foreign imports and investment (e.g. export processing zones). This may create opportunities for foreign firms, as well as affecting methods of market servicing.

The above discussion is by no means exhaustive. For example, the current volatility of foreign exchange rates is, or maybe should be, for many companies a major determinant of market-servicing strategy. Sufficient has been said, however, to highlight the importance of pragmatism and flexibility in the choice of foreign market entry and development strategy.

FURTHER READING

1. An economic approach, based on transaction cost analysis, to choosing the most efficient foreign market entry strategy is developed in Anderson, E. and Gatignon, H. (1986), 'Modes of Foreign Entry: A Transaction Cost Analysis and Propositions', *Journal of International Business Studies*, **17**(3), Fall, 1–26.
   See also, Jeannet, J.P. and Hennessey, H.D. (1988), *International Marketing Management: Strategies and Cases*, Houghton Mifflin Company, Boston, especially 296–303.
2. A stages-of-development approach to foreign market entry is provided by Brooke, M.Z. (1986), *International Management: A Review of Strategies and Operations*, Hutchinson, London, 38–42.
3. The range of external and internal factors influencing the choice of foreign market entry strategy are discussed in Root, F.R. (1987), *Entry Strategies for International Markets*, Lexington Books, D. C. Heath and Co., Lexington, Mass., Chapter 1.
4. There is a growing literature on international strategic alliances. See, for example, Porter, M. (ed.) (1986), *Competition in Global Industries*, Harvard Business School Press, Boston, Chapter 10 and 11; Jain, S.C. (1987), 'Perspectives on International Strategic Alliances', *Advances in International Marketing*, Vol.2, JAI Press Inc., New York, 103–120; Doz, Y., Hamel, G. and Prahalad, C.K. (1986), *Strategic Partnerships: Success or Surrender?: The Challenge of Competitive Collaboration*, paper presented at Joint AIB-EIBA Meeting, London, 20–23 November.

QUESTIONS FOR DISCUSSION

1. Why is choosing the most appropriate entry and development strategy one of the most critical, but also one of the most difficult decisions for an international firm?

2. Using Table 7.3, identify the conditions which need to exist for (a) exporting and (b) foreign direct investment in production operations, to be the most appropriate market supply strategy.
3. Do you agree with the view that 'larger MNEs can adopt a "rational-analytical" approach to entry mode decisions, while a "satisficing" approach may be more appropriate for small firms'?
4. To what extent do strategic alliances represent a new form of activity and relationship in international business? What are the dangers involved in such collaboration?

NOTES AND REFERENCES

1. Anderson, E. and Gatignon, H. (1986), 'Modes of Foreign Entry: A Transaction Cost Analysis and Propositions', *Journal of International Business Studies*, 17(3), Fall, 1–26.
2. Jeannet, J.P. and Hennessey, H.D. (1988), *International Marketing Management: Strategies and Cases*, Houghton Mifflin Company, Boston, especially 296–303.
3. Brooke, M.Z. (1986), *International Management: A Review of Strategies and Operations*, Hutchinson, London, 38–42.
4. Vernon, R. (1966), 'International Investment and International Trade in the Product Cycle', *Quarterly Journal of Economics*, **80**, 190–207; Buckley, P.J. and Casson, M. (1985), *The Economic Theory of the Multinational Enterprise*, Macmillan, London, Chapter 5.
5. Root, F.R. (1987), *Entry Strategies for International Markets*, Lexington Books, D.C. Heath and Co., Lexington, Mass., Chapter 1.
6. Jain, S.C. (1987), 'Perspectives on International Strategic Alliances', *Advances in International Marketing*, 2, JAI Press Inc., New York, 103–20.
7. Porter, M. (ed.) (1986), *Competition in Global Industries*, Harvard Business School Press, Boston, Chapter 10, 315.
8. This section draws on Doz, Y., Hamel, G., and Prahalad, C.K. (1986), *Strategic Partnerships: Success or Surrender?: The Challenge of Competitive Collaboration*, paper presented at Joint AIB-EIBA Meeting, London, 20–23 November.
9. Jain, 'Perspectives on International Strategic Alliances', 104.
10. Porter, *Competition in Global Industries*, 315.
11. Ibid., 330–8.
12. Jain, 'Perspectives on International Strategic Alliances', 108–10.
13. Porter, *Competition in Global Industries*, 326–7.
14. Doz, Hamel and Prahalad, 'Strategic Partnerships: Success or Surrender?'
15. Porter, *Competition in Global Industries*, 339–42.
16. Jain, 'Perspectives on International Strategic Alliances', 115–16.
17. Doz, Hamel and Prahalad, 'Strategic Partnerships', 18–24.
18. 'Time to Cut Customs' Red Tape' (1984), *Europe*, No.5, May.
19. Commission of the European Communities (1985), *Completing the Internal Market: White Paper from the Commission to the European Council*, Luxembourg, 36.
20. Commission of the European Communities (1985), *Research on the 'Cost of Non-Europe': Obstacles to Transborder Business Activity*, 7, Brussels/Luxembourg.
21. Cecchini, P. et al (1985), *The European Challenge: 1992*, Wildwood House, Aldershot.
22. It is interesting that in the background research papers to the 1992 programme, the term 'transborder business activity' (TBA) is used as an umbrella term to describe all forms of non-trade relations between enterprises across market

frontiers, viz. 'TBA is defined as any relationship between two firms in different countries linked in a long-term contractual relationship and each of which carry out at least two functions with some autonomy from each other (e.g. selling, production, research). Only one of these functions need be the subject of a special contract. The link is often but not always accompanied by equity holdings'. A distinction is then made between two patterns of international industrial organisation: 'co-operative networking' and 'competitive expansion'; the distinction essentially relates to motivation, and thus parallels the distinction between the motives for strategic alliances and those for international market entry *per se* as used in this book. See Commission of the European Communities, *Research on the 'Cost of Non-Europe': Obstacles to Transborder Business Activity*, op.cit.

23. EC data shows the following pattern of mergers and acquisitions and joint ventures for the years 1983/84 to 1986/87:

	Mergers and joint ventures involving Community firms			
	National	Community	International	Total
Mergers (including acquisitions of majority holdings)				
1983/84	101	29	25	155
1984/85	146	44	18	208
1985/86	145	52	30	227
1986/87	211	75	17	303
Joint ventures				
1983/84	32	11	26	69
1984/85	40	15	27	82
1985/86	34	20	27	81
1986/87	29	16	45	90

Source: Commission of the European Communities (1988), *Seventeenth Report on Competition Policy*, Brussels/Luxembourg.

24. Morris, D. and Hergert, M.H. (1987), 'Trends in International Collaborative Agreements', *Columbia Journal of World Business*, Summer.
25. Commission of the European Communities, *Research on the 'Cost of Non-Europe': Obstacles to Transborder Business Activity*, op.cit.
26. This section draws substantially on Kay, N. M. (1989), *Corporate Strategies, Technological Change & 1992*, Working Paper Series, Standing Commission on the Scottish Economy, Fraser of Allander Institute, University of Strathclyde, April.

BIBLIOGRAPHY

Ajami, R. and Ricks, D. (1981), 'Motives of non-American firms investing in the US', *Journal of International Business Studies*, Winter, **12**(3), 25–34.

Ajami, R. and Ricks, D. (1986), 'Foreign direct investment in the US: 1974–1984', *Journal of International Business Studies*, Fall, **17**(3), 149–54.

Aliber, R.Z. (1970), 'A theory of direct foreign investment', in Kindleberger, C.P. (ed.), *The International Corporation*, MIT Press, Cambridge, Mass.

Anderson, E. and Gatignon, H. (1986), 'Modes of foreign entry: a transaction cost analysis and propositions', *Journal of International Business Studies*, **17**(3), 1–26.

Artisien, P.F.R. (1985), *Joint Ventures in Yugoslav Industry*, Gower, Aldershot.

Ashman, R.T. (1987), 'The way ahead for franchising and licensing', paper presented at the First European Franchising and Licensing Conference, Glasgow, 15–16 June.

Axelrod, I.L. (1987), 'Monitoring licenses, royalty payments', *Les Nouvelles*, **22**(1), 41–2.

Ayal, I. and Raban, J. (1987), 'Export management structure and successful high technology innovation', in Rosson, P.J. and Reid, S.D. (eds), *Managing Export Entry and Expansion*, Praeger, New York.

Baillie, I.C. (1987), 'Workshop on intellectual property (licensing aspects)', paper presented at the First European Licensing and Franchising Conference, Glasgow, Scotland, 15–16 June.

Banks, G. (1985), 'Constrained markets, "surplus" commodities and international barter', *Kyklos*, **38**(2), 249–67.

Barrett, N.J. and Wilkinson, I.F. (1985), 'Export stimulation: a segmentation study of Australian manufacturing firms', *European Journal of Marketing*, **19**(2), 53–72.

Beamish, P.W. (1985), 'The characteristics of joint ventures in developed and developing countries', *Columbia Journal of World Business*, Fall, **20**(3), 13–19.

Beamish, P.W. and Banks, J.C. (1987), 'Equity joint ventures and the theory of the multinational enterprise', *Journal of International Business Studies*, **18**(2), 1–16.

BETRO Trust Committee (1976), *Concentration on Key Markets*, 2nd edition, Royal Society of Arts, London.

Bilkey, W.J. (1978), 'An attempted integration of the literature on the export behaviour of firms', *Journal of International Business Studies*, **9**(1), 33–46.

Bilkey, W.J. (1982), 'Variables associated with export profitability', *Journal of International Business Studies*, **13**, Fall, 39–55.

Boddewyn, J.J., Halbrich, M.B. and Perry, A.C. (1986), 'Service multinationals: conceptualization, measurement and theory', *Journal of International Business Studies*, **17**(3), 41–57.

Bracher, R.N. (1984), 'If countertrade is inevitable make the best of it', *The Banker*, May, 69–71.

British Overseas Trade Board (1985), *Success in Japan*, BOTB, London.

British Overseas Trade Board (1986), *Exporting for the Smaller Firm*, BOTB, London.

British Overseas Trade Board (1987), *Into Active Exporting*, BOTB, London.

Brooke, M.Z. (1985), 'International management contracts: servicing foreign markets and selling expertise abroad', *Journal of General Management*, **11**(1), 4–15.

Brooke, M.Z. (1985), *Selling Management Services Contracts in International Business*, Holt, Rinehart and Winston, London.

Brooke, M.Z. (1986), *International Management: A Review of Strategies and Operations*, Hutchinson, London.

Brooke, M.Z. and Buckley, P.J. (1982–86), *Handbook of International Trade*, Kluwer, London.

Buckley, P.J. (1983), 'New forms of industrial co-operation: a survey of the literature with special reference to north–south technology transfer', *Aussenwirtschaft*, **38**(2), 195–222.

Buckley, P.J. and Casson, M. (1976), *The Future of the Multinational Enterprise*, Macmillan, London.

Buckley, P.J. and Casson, M. (1985), *The Economic Theory of the Multinational Enterprise*, Macmillan, London.

Buckley, P.J. and Casson, M. (1987), *A Theory of Co-operation in International Business*, University of Reading Discussion Papers in International Investment and Business Studies No.102, January.

Buckley, P.J. and Davies, H. (1981), 'Foreign licensing in overseas operations: theory and evidence from the UK', in Hawkins, R.G. and Prasad, A.J. (eds), *Technology Transfer and Economic Development*, JAI Press, Greenwich, Conn.

Buckley, P.J., Mirza, H. and Sparkes, J.R. (1987), 'Direct foreign investment in Japan as a means of market entry: the case of European firms', *Journal of Marketing Management*, **2**(3), 241–58.

Buckley, P.J., Newbould, G.D. and Thurwell, J. (1979), 'Going international – the foreign direct investment behaviour of smaller UK firms', in Mattsson, L.G. and Wiedersheim-Paul, F. (eds), *Recent Research on the Internationalisation of Business*, Almquist and Wicksell, Stockholm.

Bureau of Industry Economics (1984), *Australian Direct Investment Abroad*, Australian Government Publicity Service, Canberra.

Business International Corporation (1986), *A Guide to Corporate Survival and Growth. The New Thinking*, BIC, New York, June.

Calingaert, M. (1987), 'Policies for the future: the USA', paper presented at the First European Licensing and Franchising Conference, Glasgow, Scotland, 15–16 June.

Cannon, T. and Willis, M. (1985), *How to Buy and Sell Overseas*, Hutchinson, London.

Carstairs, R.T. and Welch, L.S. (1981), *A Study of Outward Foreign Licensing of Technology by Australian Companies*, Licensing Executives Society of Australia, Canberra.

Casson, M. (1982), 'Transaction costs and the theory of the multinational enterprise', in Rugman, A.M. (ed.), *New Theories of the Multinational Enterprise*, Croom Helm, London.

Casson, M. (ed.) (1986), *Multinationals and World Trade*, Allen & Unwin, London.

Cateora, P.R. (1987), *International Marketing*, 6th edition, Irwin, Homewood, Ill.

Cavusgil, S.T. (1980), 'On the internationalisation process of firms', *European Research*, **8**(6), 273–81.

Cavusgil, S.T. (1984), 'Differences among exporting firms based on their degree of internationalisation', *Journal of Business Research*, **18**, 195–208.

Cavusgil, S.T. (1985), 'Guidelines for export market research', *Business Horizons*, November–December, 27–33.

Cavusgil, S.T. (1987), 'Firm and management characteristics as discriminators of export marketing activity', *Journal of Business Research*, **15**, 221–35.

Cavusgil, S.T., Bilkey, W.J. and Tesar, G. (1979), 'A note on the export behaviour of firms: exporter profiles', *Journal of International Business Studies*, **10**(1), 91–7.

Cavusgil, S.T. and Godiwalla, Y.M. (1982), 'Decisionmaking for international marketing: a comparative review', *Management Decision*, **20**(4), 47–54.

Cavusgil, S.T. and Nevin, J.R. (1981), 'Internal determinants of export marketing behaviour: an empirical investigation', *Journal of Marketing Research*, **28**, February, 114–19.

Chaston, I. (1982), 'Regional marketing – an alternative USA market entry strategy for UK exporters', *Quarterly Review of Marketing*, Spring, 1–6.

Commission of the European Communities (1985), *Research on the 'Cost of Non-Europe': Obstacles to Transborder Business Activity*, **7**, Brussels/Luxembourg.

Connolly, S.G. (1984), 'Joint ventures with third world multinationals: a new form of entry to international markets', *Columbia Journal of World Business*, Summer, 18–22.

Construction Industry Research and Information Association (1983), *Management Contracting*, CIRIA, London.

Contractor, F.J. (1981), *International Technology Licensing: Compensation, Costs and Negotiation*, D.C. Heath and Co., Lexington, Mass.

Contractor, F.J. (1984), 'Strategies for structuring joint ventures: a negotiations planning paradigm', *Columbia Journal of World Business*, Summer, **19**(2), 30–9.

Contractor, F.J. (1985), *Licensing in International Strategy*, Quorum Books, Westpoint, Conn.

Contractor, F.J. and Lorange, P. (1988), 'Competition vs. Cooperation: a benefit/cost framework for choosing between fully-owned investments and cooperative relationships', *Management International Review*, **28**, Special Issue 88.

Contractor, F.J. and Sagafi-Nejad, T. (1981), 'International technology transfer: major issues and policy responses', *Journal of International Business Studies*, Fall, 113–35.

Cook, D. (1987), 'The Queen's award for export achievement. The first 21 years: an evaluation', in *Proceedings*, Marketing Education Group, Bradford.

Cooper, R.N. (1984), 'Why countertrade?', *Across the Board*, March, 36–41.

Crisp, J. (1984), 'Acorn pulls out of U.S. market', *Financial Times*, 6 December.

Cunningham, M.T. and Spigel, R.J. (1971), 'A study in successful exporting', *European Journal of Marketing*, **5**(1), 2–12.

Daniels, J.D., Krug, J. and Nigh, D. (1985), 'US joint ventures in China: motivation and management of political risk', *California Management Review*, **27**(4), 46–58.

Darling, J.R. (1985), 'Keys for success in exporting to the U.S. market', *European Journal of Marketing*, **19**(2), 17–30.

Davidson, W.H. (1982), *Global Strategic Management*, John Wiley, New York.

Davidson, W.H. (1987), 'Creating and managing joint ventures in China', *California Management Review*, **29**(4), 77–94.

Davidson, W.H. and McFetridge, D.G. (1985), 'Key characteristics in the choice of international technology transfer mode', *Journal of International Business Studies*, **16**(2), 5–21.

Department of Trade and Industry (1985), *Countertrade: Some Guidance for Exporters*, London, July.

Dicken, P. (1986), *Global Shift. Industrial Change in a Turbulent World*, Harper & Row, London.

Douglas, S.P. and Craig, C.S. (1983), *International Marketing Research*, Prentice Hall Inc., Englewood Cliffs, N.J.

Douglas, S.P., Craig, C.S. and Keegan, W.J. (1982), 'Approaches to assessing international marketing opportunities for small and medium-sized companies', *Columbia Journal of World Business*, 17(3), 26–32.

Doz, Y., Hamel, G. and Prahalad, C.K. (1986), *Strategic Partnerships: Success or Surrender?: The Challenge of Competitive Collaboration*, paper presented at Joint AIB-EIBA Meeting, London, 20–23 November.

Drauz, G. (1987), 'Policies for the future: the commission of the European Communities (EC)', paper presented at First European Licensing and Franchising Conference, Glasgow, Scotland, 15–16 June.

Drucker, P. (1974), *Management: Tasks, Responsibilities, Promises*, Harper & Row, New York.

Dunning, J.H. (1981), *International Production and the Multinational Enterprise*, Allen & Unwin, London.

Dunning, J.H. (1983), 'Changes in the level and structure of international production: the last one hundred years', in Casson, M. (ed.), *The Growth of International Business*, Allen & Unwin, London.

Dunning, J.H. and Cantwell, J. (1982), *Joint Ventures and Non-Equity Involvement by British Firms with Particular Reference to Developing Countries: An Exploratory Study*, University of Reading Discussion Papers in International Investment and Business Studies, No.63.

The Economist Intelligence Unit, *The World in 1988*, EIU, London.

Elison, R. (1975), *Management Contracts*, International Business Unit, UMIST, Manchester, mimeo.

Eretson Association Ltd. (1984), 'Counter-trade checklist', mimeo, London, 11 July.

Etele, A. (1985), 'Licensing and the pricing of technology', *Management Decision*, 23(3), 53–61.

Farhang, M. (1986), *Dimensions of Market Entry in the Middle East: Behaviour of Swedish Firms*, RP86/5, Institute of International Business, Stockholm School of Economics, May.

Financial Times Survey (1985), 'Countertrading', 6 February.

Financial Times Survey (1986), 'Guangdong', 22 September.

Financial Times (1987), 10 March.

Financial Times (1987), 'Technology transfer', 10 November.

Franko, L.G. (1976), *The European Multinationals*, Harper & Row, London.

Franko, L.G. (1978), 'Multinationals: the end of US dominance', *Harvard Business Review*, November–December.

Friedman, W. and Kalmanoff, G. (1961), *Joint International Business Ventures*, Columbia University Press, New York and London.

Gabriel, P.P. (1967), *The International Transfer of Corporate Skills*, Harvard University, Boston, Mass.

General Agreement on Tariffs and Trade (1987), *International Trade 86–87*, Geneva.

Gilligan, C. and Hird, M. (1986), *International Marketing*, Croom Helm, London.

Globerman, S. (1986), *Fundamentals of International Business Management*, Prentice Hall Inc., Englewood Cliffs, N.J.

Glueck, W.F. and Jauch, L.R. (1984), *Business Policy and Strategic Management*, 4th edition, McGraw-Hill, New York.

Goodnow, J.D. and Hanz, J.E. (1972), 'Environmental determinants of overseas market entry strategies', *Journal of International Business Studies*, Spring, 33–50.

Gray, H.P (1986), *Uncle Sam As Host*, JAI Press, Greenwich, Conn.

Guisinger, S.E. and Associates (1985), *Investment Incentives and Performance Requirements: Patterns of International Trade, Production and Investment*, Praeger, New York.

Gullander, S.O. (1975), *An Exploratory Study of Inter-Firm Cooperation of Swedish Firms*, PhD Thesis, Columbia University, New York.

Gullander, S.O. (1975), *An Exploratory Study of Inter-Firm Co-operation of Swedish Firms*, PhD Thesis, Columbia University, New York.

Hackett, D.W. (1976), 'The international expansion of US franchise systems: status and strategies', *Journal of International Business Studies*, Spring.

Hamill, J. (1987), 'International human resources management in British multinationals', *Strathclyde International Business Unit*, Working Paper No.87/1.

Hamill, J. (1988), 'British acquisitions in the US', *Strathclyde International Business Unit*, Working Paper No.88/2.

Hamilton, G. (ed.), *Red Multinationals or Red Herrings? The Activities of Enterprises from Socialist Countries in the West*, Frances Pinter, London.

Harrigan, K.R. (1984), 'Joint ventures and global strategies', *Columbia Journal of World Business*, Summer, 7–16.

Harrigan, K.R. (1985), *Strategies for Joint Ventures*, Lexington Books, D. C. Heath and Co., Lexington, Mass.

Heald, G. and Stodel, E. (1984), *The Market Research Society Newsletter*, June.

Hedlund, G. and Kverneland, A. (1984), *Are Establishment and Growth Patterns for Foreign Markets Changing? The Case of Swedish Investment in Japan*, Institute of International Business, Stockholm School of Economics.

Hein, C. (1988), *Multinational Enterprises and Employment in the Mauritian Export Processing Zone*, Working Paper No.52, Multinational Enterprises Programme, ILO, Geneva.

Hennart, J.F. (1982), *A Theory of Multinational Enterprise*, University of Michigan Press, Ann Arbor.

Hill, M.R. (1983), *East–West Trade, Industrial Cooperation and Technology Transfer*, Gower Press, Aldershot.

Hill, M.R. (1985), 'Western companies and trade and technology transfer with the East', in Schaffer, M.E. (ed.), *Technology Transfer and East–West Relations*, Croom Helm, London.

Hirsch, S. (1976), 'An international trade and investment theory of the firm', *Oxford Economic Papers*, **28**, 258–70.

Hogwood, B.W. and Gunn, L.A. (1984), *Policy Analysis for the Real World*, Oxford University Press.

Holton, R.H. (1981), 'Making international joint ventures work', in Otterbeck, L. (ed.), *The Management of Headquarter-Subsidiary Relationships in Multinational Corporations*, Gower, Aldershot.

Hood, N. (1986), 'Role and structure of British multinationals', in Macharzina, K. and Staehle, W.H. (eds), *European Approaches to International Management*, de Gruyter, Berlin, 79–92.

Hood, N. and Vahlne, J.-E. (1988), *Strategies in Global Competition*, Croom Helm, London.

Hood, N. and Young, S. (1979), *The Economics of Multinational Enterprise*, Longman, London.

Hood, N. and Young, S. (1980), 'Recent patterns of foreign direct investment by British multinational enterprises in the United States', *National Westminster Bank Quarterly Review*, May.

Hood, N. and Young, S. (1983), *Multinational Investment Strategies in the British Isles: A study of MNEs in the Assisted Areas and in the Republic of Ireland*, HMSO, London.

Hornell, E. and Vahlne, J.-E. (1982), *The Changing Structure of Swedish Multinational Companies*, Working Paper 1982/12, Centre for International Business Studies, University of Uppsala.

Horst, T.O. (1971), 'The theory of the multinational firm – optimal behaviour under different tax and tariff rates', *Journal of Political Economy*, **79**(5), 1059–72.

Hurley, D. (1987), 'National limits to technology transfer', *Les Nouvelles*, **22**(2), 52–5.

Ivanov, I.D. (1987), 'Joint ventures in the Soviet Union', *The CTC Reporter*, **23**, 48–51.

Jain, S.C. (1987), 'Perspectives on international strategic alliances', in *Advances in International Marketing*, 2, JAI Press, Inc., New York.

Janger, A.R. (1980), *Organisation of International Joint Ventures*, Conference Board, New York.

Jankovic, P. (1984), 'Compensation trading', Alcon (Compensation Trading) Ltd, mimeo.

Johansson, J.K. and Nonaka, J.K. (1987), 'Market research the Japanese way', *Harvard Business Review*, May–June, 16–22.

Jeannet, J.P. and Hennessey, H.D. (1988), *International Marketing Management: Strategies and Cases*, Houghton Mifflin Company, Boston.

Johanson, J. and Wiedersheim-Paul, F. (1975), 'The internationalisation of the firm: four Swedish cases', *Journal of Management Studies*, **12**(3), 305-22.

Johnson, G. and Scholes, K. (1984), *Exploring Corporate Strategy*, Prentice Hall, Hemel Hempstead.

Jones, S.F. (1984), *North/South Countertrade*, Special Report No.174, The Economist Intelligence Unit, London.

Kacker, M.P. (1985), *Transatlantic Trends in Retailing: Takeovers and Flow of Know-how*, Quorum Books, New York.

Killing, J.P. (1982), 'How to make a global joint venture work', *Harvard Business Review*, May–June, 120–7.

Kobrin, S.J. (1979), 'Political risk: a review and reconsideration', *Journal of International Business Studies*, **10**(1), Spring/Summer, 67–80.

Kobrin, S.J. (1988), 'Trends in ownership of American manufacturing subsidiaries in developing countries: an inter-industry analysis', *Management International Review*, **28**, Special Issue 88.

Kobrin, S.J., Basek, J., Blank, S. and La Palombara, J. (1980), 'The assessment and evaluation of noneconomic environments by American firms: a preliminary report', *Journal of International Business Studies*, **11**(1), Spring/Summer, 32–4

Kogut, B. (1986), 'On designing contracts to guarantee enforceability: theory and evidence from East–West trade', *Journal of International Business Studies*, **17**(1), 47–61.

Kogut, B. (1988) 'A study of the life cycle of joint ventures', *Management International Review*, **28**, Special Issue 88, 39–52.

Lall, S. (1983), *The New Multinationals: The Spread of Third World Enterprises*, John Wiley, New York.

Larimo, J. (1985), 'The foreign direct investment behaviour of Finnish companies', paper presented at the 11th European International Business Association conference, Glasgow, 15–17 December.

Lebkowski, M. and Monkiewicz, J. (1986), *Equity Co-operation Ventures Domiciled in the Socialist Countries. Trends and Patterns*, World Economy Research Institute Working Paper No.8, Central School of Planning and Statistics, Warsaw, Poland, December.

Lessem, R. (1987), *The Global Business*, Prentice Hall, Hemel Hempstead.

Lindblom, C.E. (1979), 'Still muddling. Not yet through', *Public Administration Review*, **39**, 517–26.

Lowe, J. and Crawford, N. (1984), *Innovation and Technology Transfer for the Growing Firm*, Pergamon Press, Oxford.

Luostarinen, R. (1979), *The Internationalisation of the Firm*, Acta Academic Oeconomicae Helsingiensis, Helsinki.

McFarlane, G. (1978), 'Scots Queen's award winners don't excel', *Marketing*, April, 27–32.

McMillan, C.H. (1981), 'Trends in East–West industrial co-operation', *Journal of International Business Studies*, **12**(2), 53–67.

McMillan, C.H. (1987), *Multinationals from the Second World*, Macmillan, London.

Millman, A.F. (1983), 'Licensing technology', *Management Decision*, **21**(3), 3–16.

Mills, D. (1985), 'Big is beautiful in countertrade', *Euromoney*, January.

Modiano, P. and Ni-Chionna, O. (1986), 'Breaking into the big time', *Management Today*, November, 82–4.

Morrow, A. (1985), 'British consulting engineering: where will it be in 1990?', *Multinational Business*, **3**, 18–22.

National Economic Development Office (1987), *Corporate Venturing. A Strategy for Innovation and Growth*, NEDO, London.

Nicholas, S.J. (1986), *Multinationals, Transaction Costs and Choice of Institutional Form*, University of Reading Discussion Papers in International Investment and Business Studies, 97, September.

Nunes, T. (1986), 'Licensing and the small business', *Les Nouvelles*, **22**(1), 41–2.

Ohlin, B., Hesselborn, P.O. and Wiskman, P.M. (eds) (1977), *The International Allocation of Economic Activity*, Macmillan, London.

Oman, C. (1984), *New Forms of International Investment in Developing Countries*, OECD, Paris.

Organisation for Economic Cooperation and Development, (1981), *Relationship of Incentives and Disincentives to International Investment Decisions*, USA-BIAC Committee on International Investment and Multinational Enterprise, OECD, Paris.

Organisation for Economic Cooperation and Development (1987), *International Technology Licensing: Survey Results*, OECD, Paris.

Ostrach, M.S. (1985), 'Biotechnology licensing issues', *Les Nouvelles*, **20**(3), 101–4.

Paliwoda, S.J. (1981), *Joint East–West Marketing and Production Ventures*, Gower, Aldershot.

Paliwoda, S.J. (1986), *International Marketing*, Heinemann, London.

Parkes, A.J.A. (1987), *Trade Marks, Patents and Copyright*, Irish Export Board, Dublin.

Piercy, N. (1982), *Export Strategy: Markets and Competition*, George Allen & Unwin, London.

Porter, M.E. (ed.) (1986), *Competition in Global Industries*, Harvard Business School Press, Boston, Mass.

Porter, M.E. and Fuller, M.B. (1987), 'Coalitions and global strategy', in Porter, M.E. (ed.), *Competition in Global Industries*, Harvard Business School Press, Boston, Mass.

Poynter, T.A. and White, R.E. (1984), 'The strategies of foreign subsidiaries: responses to organisational slack', *International Studies of Management and Organisations*, Winter.

Reid, S.D. (1987), 'Export strategies, structure and performance: an empirical study of small Italian manufacturing firms', in Rosson, P.J. and Reid, S.D. (eds), *Managing Export Entry and Expansion*, Praeger, New York.

Roberts, E.B. (1982), 'Is licensing an effective alternative?', *Research Management*, **25**(5), 20–4.

Robles, F. and Hozier, G.C., Jr. (1986), 'Understanding foreign trade zones', *International Marketing Review*, **3**(2), 44–54.

Robock, S. and Simmonds, K. (1983), *International Business and Multinational Enterprises*, Irwin, Homewood, Ill.

Root, F.R. (1987), *Entry Strategies for International Markets*, Lexington Books, D.C. Heath and Co., Lexington, Mass.

Rosenblum, J.E. (1985), 'Licensing second-source suppliers', *Les Nouvelles*, **20**(2), 93–4.

Rugman, A.M. (1985), 'Internalisation is still a general theory of foreign direct investment', *Weltwirtschaftliches Archiv*, September.

Ryan, W.T. and Bonham-Yeaman, D. (1982), 'International patent cooperation', *Columbia Journal of World Business*, **17**(4), 63–6.

Sapir, A. (1986), 'Trade in investment-related technological services', *World Development*, **14**(5), 605–22.

Scottish Development Agency (1986), *The Marketing of Scottish Architects Worldwide*, SDA, Glasgow.

Seringhaus, F.H.R. (1987), 'Export promotion: the role and impact of Government service', *Irish Marketing Review*, **2**, 106–16.

Shaojie, C. (1987), 'Effect of PRC's open-door policy', *Les Nouvelles*, **22**(2), 75–8.

Sharma, D.D. (1983), *Swedish Firms and Management Contracts*, Department of Business Administration, University of Uppsala.

Silvia, W.F. (1985), 'Case against licensing', *Les Nouvelles*, **20**(1), 20–2.

Simon, H.A. (1960), *The New Science of Management Decision*, Prentice Hall Inc., Englewood Cliffs, N.J.

Simpson, C.L. and Kujawa, D. (1974), 'The export decision process: an empirical inquiry', *Journal of International Business Studies*, **5**, Spring, 107–17.

Smith, A. (1776, Glasgow edition, 1976), *An Inquiry into the Nature and Causes of the Wealth of Nations*, Book IV, Chapter III.

Snowden, P.N. (1987), 'International equity investment in less developed countries' stockmarkets: the replacement for bank lending?', *National Westminster Bank Quarterly Review*, February.

Solovykh, D.A. and Voinov, I.L. (1986), 'Licensing into/out of USSR', *Les Nouvelles*, **21**(4), 169–71.

Stern, L.W. and El-Ansary, A. (1982), *Marketing Channels*, Prentice Hall Inc., Englewood Cliffs, N.J.

Stopford, J.M. and Dunning J.H. (1983), *Multinationals: Company Performance and Global Trends*, Macmillan, London.

Stopford, J.M. and Wells, L.T., Jr., (1972), *Managing the Multinational Enterprise*, Basic Books, New York.

Sukijasovic, M. (1970), 'Foreign investment in Yugoslavia', in Litvak, I.A. and Maule, C.J. (eds), *Foreign Investment: The Experience of Host Countries*, Praeger, New York and London.

Tansuhaj, P.S. and Gentry, J.W. (1987), 'Firm differences in perceptions of facilitating role of foreign trade zones in global marketing and logistics', *Journal of International Business Studies*, **18**(1), 19–33.

Teece, D.J. (1977), 'Technology transfer by multinational firms: the resource cost of transferring technological know-how', *Economic Journal*, **87**(346), 242–61.

Teece, D.J. (1983), 'Multinational enterprise, internal governance and market power considerations', *The American Economic Review*, **75**(2), 233–8.

Telesio, P. (1977), 'Foreign licensing policy in multinational enterprise', DBA dissertation, Harvard University.

Telesio, P. (1984), 'Foreign licensing in multinational enterprises' in Stobaugh R. and Wells L.T., Jr (eds), *Technology Crossing Borders*, Harvard Business School Press, Boston, Mass.

The Small Businesses Research Trust Survey (1987), in *Into Active Exporting*, BOTB, London.

Thunell, L. (1977), *Political Risks in International Business*, Praeger, New York.

Tomlinson, J.W.C. (1970), *The Joint Venture Process in International Business: India and Pakistan*, MIT Press, Cambridge, Mass.

Tsurumi, Y. (1980), *Technology Transfer and Foreign Trade. The Case of Japan, 1950–1966*, Arno Press, New York.

Tung, R.L. (1981), 'Selection and training of personnel for overseas assignments', *Columbia Journal of World Business*, 16(1), 68–78.

Turnbull, P.W. (1987), 'A challenge to the stages theory of the internationalisation process', in Rosson, P.J. and Reid, S.D. (eds), *Managing Export Entry & Expansion*, Praeger, New York.

Turnbull, P.W. and Valla, J.P. (1986), *Strategies for International Industrial Marketing*, Croom Helm, London.

United Nations Centre on Transnational Corporations (1980), *Transnational Corporations in International Tourism*, UNCTC, New York.

United Nations Centre on Transnational Corporations (1982), *Management Contracts in Developing Countries: An Analysis of Their Substantive Provisions*, UNCTC, New York.

United Nations Centre on Transnational Corporations (1983), *Features and Issues in Turnkey Contracts in Developing Countries: A Technical Paper*, UNCTC, New York.

United Nations Centre on Transnational Corporations (1983), *Transnational Corporations in World Development: Third Survey*, UNCTC, New York.

United Nations Centre on Transnational Corporations (1987), *Arrangements Between Joint Venture Partners in Developing Countries*, UNCTC, New York.

United Nations Centre on Transnational Corporations (1988), *Transnational Corporations in World Development: Trends and Prospects*, UNCTC, New York.

University of Manchester in association with Licensing Executives Society (UK and Ireland) (1986), *Recent Developments in International Patenting*, Papers CP 86/1, University of Manchester.

US Department of Commerce, *Foreign Direct Investment in the United States*, International Trade Administration, Washington, various years.

US Department of Commerce (1984), *International Direct Investment: Global Trends and the US Role*, International Trade Administration, Washington.

Vahlne, J.-E. and Wiedershiem-Paul, F. (1977), *Psychic Distance–An Inhibiting Factor in International Trade*, Working Paper 1977/2, Centre for International Business Studies, University of Uppsala.

Vernon, R. (1966), 'International investment and international trade in the product cycle', *Quarterly Journal of Economics*, 80, 190-207.

Verzariu, P. (1980), *Countertrade Practices in East Europe, The Soviet Union and China*, US Department of Commerce, Washington D.C., April.

Walmsley, J. (1982), *Handbook of International Joint Ventures*, Graham & Trotman, London.

Walmsley, J. (1984), 'International joint ventures', paper presented at UK Academy of International Business Conference, Bradford, April.

Walter, B.J. and Etzel, M.J. (1973), 'The internationalization of the US franchise system: progress and procedures', *Journal of Marketing*, 37, April, 38–46.

Wells, L.T. (1983), *Third World Multinationals*, MIT Press, Cambridge, Mass.

Welt, L.G.B. (1983), 'Straight cash for goods? No longer a sure bet!', *American Import/Export Management*, October.

Welt, L.G.B. (1984), 'Why Latin America is wary of barter', *Euromoney*, January, 132–4.

Wiedersheim-Paul, F., Olson H.C. and Welch, L.S. (1978), 'Pre-export activity: the first step in internationalisation', *Journal of International Business Studies*, **9**, Spring/Summer, 47–58.

Wilczynski, J. (1976), *The Multinationals and East–West Relations*, Macmillan, London.

Wind, Y. and Perlmutter, H. (1977), 'On the identification of frontier issues in international marketing', *Columbia Journal of World Business*, **12**, 131–9.

World Bank (1988), *World Development Report 1987*, International Bank for Reconstruction and Development, New York.

Wright, R.W. (1981), 'Evolving international business arrangements', in Dhawan, K.C., Etemad, H. and Wright, R.W. (eds), *International Business: A Canadian Perspective*, Addison-Wesley, Don Mills, Ontario.

Young, S. (1987), 'Business strategy and the internationalisation of business', *Managerial and Decision Economics*, **8**(1), 31–40.

Young S., Hood, N. and Hamill, J. (1988), *Foreign Multinationals and the British Economy*, Croom Helm, London, Chapter 2.

INDEX